# The Stream of Music

## RICHARD ANTHONY LEONARD

NEW AND REVISED EDITION
WITH SIXTEEN ILLUSTRATIONS

Dolphin Books
Doubleday & Company, Inc.
Garden City, New York

To Charles G. Norris

*Originally published in 1943 by*
*Doubleday & Company, Inc.*
*Dolphin Books edition: 1962*
*Library of Congress Catalog Card Number 62–14692*
*Copyright © 1943, 1962 by Richard Anthony Leonard*
*Printed in the United States of America*

# PREFACE TO THE REVISED EDITION

Almost two decades have passed since this book was originally written, and the demand for a new edition presents the author with the happy opportunity to revise some of his estimates, to correct errors, and (he hopes) to improve the book in general. Some of the original material has been condensed or left out, so that much new material might be added. For example, the final chapter offers an entirely new and up-to-date survey of the contemporary musical scene. The scope of the book was originally limited so that only the greatest composers and those responsible for the most significant forward movements in music were chosen. In this new edition a number of other important men and their music are included for discussion, with the hope that the book will be a more rounded exposition of its subject.

The purpose of the book remains, of course, the same: to trace the development of the art of music during the past three hundred years. My method has been to use as a basis the lives and personalities of the composers who made this music. The particular period (roughly 1650 to the present) is a fairly obvious choice: it represents the most resplendent age in the entire history of music, the age that produced a high percentage of the important works which are performed today and in which public interest is centered.

I should say again that one of my primary aims has been to simplify and to restrict. The main stream of music, so to speak, is kept always in the foreground. The men whose work forms its main tributaries are discussed in detail; the lesser men are sometimes ignored. I have simplified otherwise, too. Music is a complex art, with innumerable problems of a highly technical nature that must be understood if a composer's work is to be appreciated. These technical aspects cannot be ignored; they must be met head on. I have therefore discussed many of them freely and sometimes at length; at the same time I have tried to avoid the minutiae, the blueprint details that interest only the professional musician.

"Nature will have its course," said Cervantes; "every production must resemble its author . . ." Conversely, if we are to find the meaning of any piece of music, the reasons for its particular form and style, we must look to the artist himself. That is why, in discussing these composers, I have tried to describe them both as men and artists—to sketch their lives and personalities, their historical backgrounds, the important events (both inward and outward) that shaped their thoughts and so governed their creative impulses.

It is again a pleasure to record here my indebtedness and my thanks to an old friend, Eric Hodgins, who read part of my original manuscript in its early stages, and who gave me advice (both editorial and musical) that was of very great benefit to the entire book. In the preparation of the new chapters, especially that on Handel, the editorial comments of Herbert Weinstock have been invaluable. I am also indebted to Mrs. Emma Reifenberg, for her kindness in permitting me to reproduce the portrait of Bach. The reproduction of the Chopin daguerreotype was made with the kind permission of the late Courtlandt Palmer.

To my wife, again, a special measure of thanks, for encouragement, patience, and understanding, that never seems to run out.

R. A. L.

Larchmont, New York
January 1961

# CONTENTS

*All music is what awakes from you when you are reminded
   by the instruments,*
*It is not the violins and the cornets, it is not the oboe nor
   the beating drums, nor the score of the baritone singer
   singing his sweet romanza, nor that of the men's
   chorus, nor that of the women's chorus,*
*It is nearer and farther than they.*

WALT WHITMAN

*The Stream of Music*

# Introduction

I

Anything deeper than a superficial understanding of music today must come from knowledge of the people who have dominated it so long. The first requisite therefore is a backward glance into the recesses of German history—to the middle of the seventeenth century, when a thin stream of music began to flow from that perpetually disturbing land that lies between the Alps and the plains of Denmark. The stream grew into a torrent, fed all through the eighteenth and nineteenth centuries by one man of genius after another, until it became one of the most fabulously productive movements in the history of any art.

This supreme development of the music art has a curious and in all probability an immensely significant place in history. It lies almost precisely between two gigantic wars—between the close of the Thirty Years' War in 1648 and the outbreak of World War I in 1914. That period marks the rise and fall, not alone of the art that remains the finest creation of the German people in their entire history, but also of the nation itself. The hideous state of Germany under Adolf Hitler, the ruination of its moral character, the pollution of its entire intellectual life, was not a sudden act of self-destruction climaxing the misfortunes of a few decades. The causes extend back at least three centuries, to a conflict that threatened for a time to exterminate the peoples of central Europe.

The Thirty Years' War was the last and worst of all

the religious wars that Europe suffered with the coming of the Reformation. It broke out in Bohemia in 1618, when a Holy Roman Emperor tried to suppress the Protestants. It spread slowly over central Europe, gathering in intensity and fury. After Catholic and Protestant Germans had mauled each other horribly, the war took on political significance, in which all the greater powers of Europe gradually became embroiled. The Holy Roman Empire of the Hapsburgs was supported by Catholic Spain; against them in support of the Protestants of Germany were finally ranged Sweden, Denmark, England, and France.

As the war dragged on, with first one side and then the other gaining the upper hand, the population of Germany was slowly clawed to death. The first negotiations for a general peace were begun in 1642, after a quarter of a century of conflict; but the problems of settlement were so involved that six years went by before the end came. The Peace of Westphalia, signed on October 24, 1648, is one of the jutting promontories of history. It put an end for many years to wholesale religious persecution; it broke the power of Spain and the Holy Roman Empire, establishing France as the dominant state of Europe; it ended the power of the medieval Church of Rome as a possible unifying force in Christian Europe.

The Thirty Years' War left the Germanic states in indescribable chaos. At least a quarter and possibly a half of their population had been killed. Towns and villages by the hundreds were wiped out of existence by the plundering armies of both factions. Ruinous taxes and war levies drained away the wealth of the people until industry and agriculture both were paralyzed. Thousands of men, women, and children, facing starvation, became followers in the wakes of the armies. Some records of the misery and horror of the times even mention the practice of cannibalism.

Modern historians have sometimes questioned these frightful accounts of the Thirty Years' War, maintaining that the German historians of the nineteenth century themselves exaggerated the facts in their efforts to excuse the backward state of their nation in the years following the Peace of Westphalia. But there is no denying that the German Protestant states paid a terrible price for their religious freedom and their release from the domination of the Holy Roman Empire. For years they lay numb and beaten. They were disorganized—a mass of more than three hundred political entities, ranging from states the size of Bavaria to single free cities. Each had its own sovereign, its own coinage and taxation, its jealously guarded boundary lines. The people of these petty, quarreling, disunited states remained poor for generations. The soil of Germany has always been the least productive of Europe, with few of the natural resources enjoyed by France, Britain, or Russia. The Germans also lost out in the colonization and development of the New World. Lacking the strength and the enterprise of the nations to the West, they shared in none of the wealth that flowed into England, France, Spain, and the Netherlands from the Americas and the Indies.

Meanwhile, even during the blackest years of the war, the rest of Europe was surging forward with a new impulse that has marked the seventeenth century as one of the most remarkable in history. That century was in fact the placenta in which was nourished the present modern world. It was an age of great scientific, industrial, social, artistic, and philosophical advances—the age of Galileo, Bacon, and Descartes, of Spinoza, Newton, Harvey, Milton, Bunyan, Locke, Rembrandt, Racine, Torricelli, Velásquez. Men's ideas and social habits were undergoing a profound change. The new scientific method, based on reason and experiment, had opened the doors to modern chemistry, medicine, biology, and metallurgy. In the course of a few generations the man of Europe was given a new conception of himself and of the world and universe in which he lived. The Americas and the Indies were sending him a steady stream of new foods to eat, beverages to drink, materials to process. In England were being hatched the first ideas of a new political freedom. Barely three months after the Peace of Westphalia, Charles I was beheaded by his own subjects. From that moment the divine right of kings would begin to give ground to the rights of man; monarchy would slowly dissolve before a rising modern democracy.

The reader who surveys the broad panorama of that tremendous century can hardly fail to observe how small a part the Germanic states contributed to its progress. The centers of the new intellectual energy were England, the Netherlands, and France, with Spain and Italy slowly receding from the flood tide of their high Renaissance. It required more than two hundred years for the Germans to recover from the exhaustion and impoverishment caused by the Thirty Years' War. They were not even politically united until 1871—the last of the great peoples of Europe to achieve a national unity. One of the most sinister effects of the long ordeal was the sense of inferiority that gradually became rooted in the German mentality. At first this was manifested by a wholesale importation of ideas from foreign sources. In the century after the Peace of Westphalia the shining sun of Europe was France, and in no country was French culture copied more assiduously than in Germany. German writers loaded their works with French phrases; every German prince aped in his Teutonic way the court of Louis XIV; many of them disdained their own language and spoke only French. The North Germans also turned for culture and enlightenment to the Netherlands. It was typical of the times that Frederick William, the Great Elector of Brandenburg, was sent as a boy of fifteen to Leyden for an education. In the south, Italy was still a center of the cultural world, and from that source came many of the German ideas on art and music.

II

The seventeenth century was the era of baroque art. It was the age dominated in painting by the Netherlands— the Flemish school of Rubens, the Breughel family, and Van Dyck; the Dutch school of Hals, Ruysdael, and Rembrandt. Portraiture, landscape, and genre painting all reached a new climax. But the spirit of the baroque was nowhere manifested more fully than in music.

Practically every phase of the art of music as it developed in seventeenth-century Europe is indicative of the spirit epitomized by the term "baroque": it was ornamental in the extreme, opulent, extravagant, fantastic, complex in design and bold in imagination, richly expressive and at times rhapsodically free. While this baroque style was growing and exfoliating, another and more fundamental change in the art was also taking place. For centuries music had been under the domination of the Church. With the coming of the seventeenth century composers began to search for new avenues of expression. They were tired of the age-old formulas for church music based on choral polyphony; like the navigators and the scientists of their day, they wanted to explore and to invent. Before them, like the vast untouched continent of the Americas, lay the field of secular music; and into this they proceeded with bold steps.

One of the most important of the new developments was the rise of the keyboard instruments—the various claviers and the organ. At the beginning of the seventeenth century these instruments were still in a comparatively primitive state; at its end they were a dependable and resourceful musical means, with a splendid literature awaiting their command. The same was true of other individual instruments—especially the members of the viol family.

By far the most spectacular development in secular music was the invention of the opera, which took place in Italy shortly before 1600. The rise of this new form of entertainment is remindful of the strange crazes that seized the populations of Europe at various times during the Middle Ages. Opera spread through Italy like wildfire, until there was hardly a city or town that did not support a number of operatic theaters (either public or in private homes), while a small army of composers was kept busy turning out operatic scores with the speed of commercial artisans. Soon Italian opera became so conventionalized that its whole point and purpose was to show off a new and splendid vocal art. Here again was a clear manifestation of the spirit of the baroque, for the more ornamental, florid, extravagant, and difficult the aria, the more wildly the singer would be acclaimed by the audience. Opera singers achieved a point of fame and public adulation reserved in other ages for gladiators and motion-picture stars. The *castrati*, or male sopranos, created by a revolting practice of mutilation when they were boys, were the most popular performers of all. The schools of singing that grew up at the time in Italy remain unsurpassed in thoroughness and excellence.

Within a century Italian opera had swamped the music of the rest of Europe. Its domination was so complete that to this day the nomenclature and terminology of music are still basically Italian.

Not all the energies of the Italian composers were concentrated on the opera. There was still a vigorous school of church composers whose art was based on the old traditions. Here too the spirit both of the baroque and of bold invention asserted itself. Girolamo Frescobaldi (1583–1644), the organist at St. Peter's in Rome, was the most celebrated instrumentalist of his time. He drew audiences of thirty thousand people. His style was typical of the era—a mastery of the older polyphonic forms, of fugue, and chorale variation, plus an inventive genius for rich and varied harmony, brilliant improvisation and rhapsodic personal expression. The Catholic Mass itself, once the vessel of Palestrina's rarefied polyphony, took on the new musical vestments of baroque ornamentation and color. At the height of the period of the so-called "colossal baroque" the choir of singers was joined by orchestras of viols, trombones, trumpets, cornets, and organs—a concordance of timbres and a range of dynamics that must have awed the worshipers of that day with its gorgeousness.

It was inevitable that the influence of Italian music should invade the German states of the seventeenth century, when even the more vigorous nations like France and England succumbed completely, especially to the fascination of Italian opera. The Catholic Germans of the south and the Austrians welcomed the invasion. Vienna became a center of Italian opera, dominated by Italian composers and singers down to the time of Mozart. Protestant Germany, however, remained an island of resistance, one of the few places in Europe where the new Italian entertainment affected but did not overwhelm the native product. This fact was one of great importance to the future history of music, for from this stubborn assertion of individuality in a comparatively limited locality grew the most magnificent musical structure in history.

No historian has ever explained why, after the misery and wreckage of the Thirty Years' War, German music alone should have remained alive, when practically every other cultural activity lay paralyzed. German painting, by contrast, almost disappeared throughout the seventeenth century and for half of the eighteenth, and literature did not fare much better. Possibly the reason lies in the connection between music and the two religions over which the frightful war had been fought. In the Catholic Church music had been for centuries the handmaiden of ceremony; the same was true in the Lutheran Protestant Church, whose old hymns and chorales, many of them coming from the Reformer himself, were an indispensable part of every church service. Thus in Germany, after three decades of a wasting conflict, the institution of music in the churches was one of the few solaces left for a weary and dejected people.

The first genius who could be said to herald the coming importance of German music was Heinrich Schütz. Born in Saxony in 1585, exactly one hundred years before Johann Sebastian Bach, Schütz began his musical career like many of the most famous—as a choirboy. He became an organist of repute, and then court conductor at Dresden. He made several visits to Italy for purposes of study, and he escaped some of the worst times of the Thirty Years' War by living in Copenhagen. Schütz became the most influential composer of German church music of the midseventeenth century. His historical importance lay in the fact that he imported from Italy musical ideas which impressed him profoundly. He infused the severe old German forms with a new and more dramatic style, and hence a deeper expressiveness.

Before Schütz died (in 1672) the beginnings of a strong

new musical art were already evident in Germany. Its center of gravity was a school of church organists who operated chiefly in the Lutheran churches. In modern times the names of these men have become dimmed under the shadow of their descendant, Johann Sebastian Bach, but in the latter years of the seventeenth century they had already carved out an art that surpassed the best that Italy was then producing. In their seriousness of purpose, their mastery of a complex technique, in the depth of their emotional responses, these men made the other music of their time seem thin and even frivolous.

One of the first of the fraternity was Franz Tunder (1614–67), who was born and died in the ancient Hanseatic town of Lübeck, on the North Sea. As a young man he had studied with Frescobaldi at Rome, returning to his native city to become organist at the old Church of St. Mary's. Tunder set about imitating the magnificent choral and instrumental choirs he had heard in Italy, training a group of violin, viola, and wind instrument players to perform with the organ and the choir.

Tunder was succeeded by the most famous of all pre-Bach organ composers, Dietrich Buxtehude (1637–1707). This fiery young Scandinavian took over the post at St. Mary's when, according to the custom, he married Tunder's daughter. (This curious convention made at least one pivotal change in the course of music history. Years later, when it became Buxtehude's turn to retire, one of the candidates to succeed him was eighteen-year-old George Frideric Handel, who declined after he had met Buxtehude's twenty-eight-year-old daughter. Handel turned away from an organ career, becoming instead the master of oratorio and of opera in the Italian style in the early eighteenth century.) Buxtehude set a new standard of organ virtuosity. He also enlarged the scope of Tunder's instrumental group to establish the *Abendmusiken* (evening musicals), which were in effect concerts held in the church. They became musical events of the first order, to which other organists made pilgrimages from all parts of Germany. Buxtehude had a profound influence upon Bach. He was a rugged individualist who dared to play and compose brilliantly and with more freedom and invention than any of his fellows.

Other contemporaries of Buxtehude were Johann Pachelbel (1653–1706), who held various posts both in the north and south of Germany; and Jan Adam Reinken, the organist of St. Catherine's at Hamburg, who was born in 1623 and lived to be ninety-nine. These men were outstanding in their fraternity, but there were many others —the German churches were in fact full of musicians of exceptional skill.

It is interesting to note how this northern phase of the musical art combined two elements which would seem on their face to be irreconcilable—the ancient hymn tunes of the Lutheran Church and the wildly luxuriant baroque style. The hymns and the chorales which had come down from the time of Luther himself were fine old tunes, symmetrical and plain, deeply devotional but simple enough to be sung by the congregation. After the sermon itself they were the most important feature of every Lutheran church service. Naturally they were the bones and sinews of every organist's equipment. Just as the baroque architects took the simplest blocks and reared them into buildings of great amplitude and fantastically complex ornamentation, so these organists used their hymn tunes as a point of departure for all sorts of elaborate, highly decorative musical forms.

Most of the baroque forms were based on the variation principle: the chorale prelude, the passacaglia, the chaconne, and the supreme example of all—the fugue—were all a proliferation of many decorative ideas from a single basic theme. The toccata was a showpiece, a swirling mass of figuration to show off the player's digital skill; while the fantasia was a challenge both to the composer's imagination and the organist's artistry at registration.

The organs themselves were typical products of the baroque era, with their several manuals and pedals, their scores of stops, their endless multiplication of sounds and timbres. The greatest of these seventeenth-century instruments (Buxtehude's at Lübeck had fifty-four stops) were nothing less than mechanical and aesthetic triumphs, as they were also mirrors of the bold imagination of the players.

Circumstance as well as tradition helped to form the character of these North German organists and to produce their art, so pregnant for all music of the future. The mastery of organ playing and composition was a lifework of enormous difficulty; a post in a large church demanded a man of talent and training, to say nothing of intellect. With his responsibility went dignity, and a matchless inspiraton. From his organ gallery he might look down the nave of some ancient Gothic structure, with its soaring piers and arches, its incredibly high mullioned windows; ranged in the galleries along the sides were his choir and perhaps the instrumentalists; under his hands and feet was an organ whose ringing voice could fill the vast church. All this apparatus of visual and musical beauty was at his command, and in the service that celebrated the glory of God he was second only to the minister or priest. It would have been a man of small soul indeed who did not respond to such a stimulus.

The time and all circumstances were ripe, therefore, for the production of genius; and as the seventeenth century drew to a close he appeared in the person of a young organist from Thuringia. He was one of the Bach family, the most famous clan of musicians in all Germany.

# Bach
## 1685—1750

I

The mighty fortress of the art of music, Johann Sebastian Bach, still stands like a challenge to the modern world.

There is no longer any question of appreciation; the present age is ravenous for Bach's music. His works rival even Beethoven's as the most exhaustively studied and the most avidly played. As yet there is no sign of pause in the steadily widening scope of its popularity, or its enormous prestige. It is Bach the man who still escapes us. It is the personality of the artist, paled out by the passage of time, that has left unanswerable questions.

Bach's case is one of the rarest in art. In spite of his genius his work was not appreciated during his lifetime, for the reason that all music in that era was undergoing a deep-rooted change. During the years of his maturest productivity Bach had already become old-fashioned. When he died, what fame he had fell like a stone dropped into water. For the greater part of a century his works were forgotten, and some of them were lost. Only when a new generation of romantic composers, headed by Mendelssohn and Schumann, discovered old Sebastian Bach was it realized what a treasure trove lay under the years of neglect. The music was slowly exhumed in all its splendor, like an Angkor Vat of a vanished age; but in those years of darkness something was lost—the essential personality of Bach the man.

One of the chief difficulties in the way of approach to this composer is the lack of human documents touching upon his personal life. The biographers reached Bach too late. Philipp Spitta, the German musicologist, began publication of his definitive work on the composer in 1873. He was followed by some of the best modern authorities —Parry, Schweitzer, and Terry—all of whom advanced notably the present-day appreciation of Bach's art. But in their efforts to reach the soul of the man they have all had to thumb through the same dry, meager body of anecdote which is all that remains of firsthand evidence. Only a handful of Bach's letters survives, and they are all of a business nature, pertaining to his career as organist and church cantor. There are no personal letters written by him to any member of his large family or even to any close personal friend. There are various descriptions by contemporaries of Bach the organist, but none of Bach the man. The main outlines of the composer's life are known, but there are long stretches of years in which absolutely nothing is left, aside from the name of the town in which he lived, a few details of the job he was filling, and the birth dates of his children.

The music itself only serves to increase one's sense of bewilderment. Its vastness, its detailed perfection through a range of size that extends from miniatures to veritable temples of sound, its fathomless emotional depth—the more these are studied, the farther they seem to move beyond the capabilities of a single artist. The greatness of the spirit that emerges fails utterly to square up with the historical portrait of the modest Thuringian organ virtuoso who preferred his family of children to fame, who lived most of his days in feudal quietude, and who explained his life's accomplishment by saying simply, "I worked hard."

## II

Halfway between the Elbe and the Rhine and about one hundred miles southwest of Leipzig rises an ancient landmark—the Wartburg. From this castle in the heart of the Thuringian Forest has come a rich historical endowment for both music and religion. It was the seat of the art-loving landgraves of Thuringia, and in the twelfth and thirteenth centuries the German poets congregated there for their song contests. Walther von der Vogelweide, Wolfram von Eschenbach and other medieval minstrels visited the Wartburg and joined in the tourneys of song—scenes re-created by Richard Wagner in his opera *Tannhäuser*. There, too, the mighty struggle for religious liberty had its rise, for in the Wartburg Martin Luther took refuge after the Diet of Worms. In 1521 he worked at his translation of the Bible, and to this day personal relics of the Reformer are preserved in the castle.

A few miles to the north of the Wartburg lies the village of Eisenach. There, on the twenty-first of March 1685, Johann Sebastian Bach was born. From the very soil of his native country were drawn the two profoundest impulses of the future composer's life—music and a deep and abiding faith in the religion of his fathers.

The Bachs were the outstanding musical family of history. They were also the most prolific. For four generations before Johann Sebastian they had been organists, cantors, and town musicians in large numbers. In the early eighteenth century there were as many as thirty organists in Germany, all named Bach. Johann Sebastian himself had eleven sons and nine daughters by his two wives, and several of the sons became the most noted composers of their time.

Bach's father, Johann Ambrosius Bach, was a town musician, a highly respected performer on the violin and the viola. When Johann Sebastian was ten years old both his father and mother had died, so the care and education of the young orphan were entrusted to his older brother, Johann Christoph, who was twenty-four years old and already a musician of considerable attainments. He was a church organist and in his youth had had the rare advantage of study with Johann Pachelbel.

Johann Sebastian lived with his brother for five years. During that time Johann Christoph taught him to play the harpsichord. The boy's unusual interest in music is indicated in one of the most frequently repeated anecdotes. The older brother had a valuable manuscript copy of works by Buxtehude, Pachelbel, Froberger, Böhm, and other noted organ composers. The manuscript was kept in a locked bookcase, and for some reason Johann Sebastian was not permitted to see it. He was so eager to study it, however, that he got it out secretly at night and set about copying it. As he could not use a candle, he could work only on moonlight nights. After six months he had made a complete copy, but then his brother discovered what he was about and took the copy away from him.

At the age of fifteen Bach was sent to a convent school at Lüneburg, where he was a soprano in the choir until his voice broke. The organist at one of the churches in the town was Georg Böhm, a master of the art and a pupil of Jan Adam Reinken. Young Bach was so inspired by Böhm's prowess at the organ that he several times walked thirty miles from Lüneburg to Hamburg to hear the aged Reinken himself at first hand. He also walked sixty miles to Celle, where a celebrated *Kapelle* (or small orchestra) at the ducal court performed French music.

Bach thus had the advantage of first-rate teaching that stemmed from direct contact with the royal line of North German organists, the ablest musicians of his age. It is also evident that the serious youngster himself, greedy for music and willing to travel miles to hear it, was his own best teacher. Self-improvement was a passion that remained with him throughout his life. He never missed an opportunity to hear other noted musicians. He found keen enjoyment in the study of contemporary music, not only German but also French and Italian; and because in those days printed music was scarce he did a vast amount of copying of other men's scores. Once he said candidly that his favorite method of stimulating himself to composition or improvisation was to begin by playing a favorite work of some other composer.

In 1703, when he was eighteen, Bach was already so proficient in his art that he was able to win the post of church organist in the town of Arnstadt, where he had at

his disposal a fine organ of twenty-six stops. Toward the
end of his second year there he applied for a month's
leave of absence. He proposed to make the longest of all
his pilgrimages, a journey of two hundred miles northward
to Lübeck, to hear the great Dietrich Buxtehude. What
specifically attracted him was one of Buxtehude's festivals
of religious music, the *Abendmusiken*. Here occurs one of
the most exasperating of all the gaps in our knowledge of
Bach's personal life. Nothing is known of this journey,
which undoubtedly had to be made on foot and in the
dead of winter; nothing is known of his experience at
Lübeck. It is not certain whether he even met Buxtehude,
whose work had such an influence on his own later style.
He most certainly heard the Northern master play, for he
stretched his leave of absence from one month to four.

Shortly after his return to Arnstadt, Bach was called
upon the carpet to explain to the Consistorium the reasons for his prolonged absence. The minutes of that meeting are perserved, giving one of the few detailed accounts
of an episode in the composer's life. The council asked him
why he had left his post in the first place, and why he had
so long overstayed his leave. Bach's answers were stubbornly evasive, so the council pressed another matter. It
was said that his work since his return had taken on an
alarming aspect; his accompaniments of the hymns now
included such "surprising variations" and "irrelevant ornaments" that the melody was obliterated and the congregation left in a state of confusion. Moreover, they accused
him of neglecting to train his choir, and of allowing his
young singers to leave the organ loft during the sermon to
visit a beerhouse. They threatened to dismiss him if he did
not mend his ways.

It is clear that the experience of hearing Buxtehude had
set the young man's imagination afire. His hands and feet
were running away with him at the organ; and his pen,
busy in imitation of his hero, was consuming every moment he could spare from his duties. But he did not mend
his ways. Already Arnstadt was getting too small for him.

Some months later Bach was again accused of neglecting choir practice, and of admitting a strange lady to the

choir. He resigned, to become organist at the Church of
St. Blasius in Mülhausen. His salary there was eighty-five
gulden a year (about forty dollars) plus allowances of corn,
firewood, and fish. Thrown in for good measure was the use
of a wagon to convey his household goods from Arnstadt.

During his stay of one year at Mülhausen, Bach married
his cousin, Maria Barbara, who is believed to have been
the strange lady of the choir. Then in 1708 he had a stroke
of good fortune. He received an appointment to the court
of the Duke of Saxe-Weimar, as organist and chamber
musician. Weimar was not strange to him, for as a young
man of eighteen, just before he went to Arnstadt, he had
spent several months there as a violinist in the court orchestra. His return signalized the beginning of the first
great period of his creative life.

III

Weimar, the capital of the Grand Duchy of Saxe-Weimar, was to be glorified in a later age as "the German
Athens," a seat of literature and music made illustrious by
the names of Goethe, Schiller, and Liszt. When Bach went
there in 1708 it was poor, provincial, and in all probability
very dull. The reigning sovereign was Duke Wilhelm
Ernst, a solitary man of abstemious if not wholly forbidding tastes. Personal frustrations had darkened his life, for
he was estranged from his wife and his brother; but he
found compensation in a lifelong devotion to religion. He
loved theological discussions and was absorbed in the problems of the church and the clergy. The duke's sole secular
passion seems to have been numismatics. The regimen of
court life was severe; everyone went to bed at nine o'clock
in the summer and eight in the winter.

The record of Bach's personal life during his nine years
at Weimar is an almost complete blank. It is known that
as organist he performed on a small organ of twenty-five
stops in the ducal chapel. He also played the harpsichord
and the violin in the chamber orchestra. In 1714 he was
made concertmaster of the orchestra. During these years
at Weimar seven children were born to Maria Barbara,

four of whom survived. Very little else is known of Bach in this period, except that he developed from a young man of talent to one of superlative genius. At Weimar he produced some of his most brilliant organ works and he extended his powers as organist and clavier player to a point of virtuosity that had never been equaled.

In view of the interest in Bach today it is surprising that most of his organ works still remain *terra incognita* to the average music lover. Actually they comprise but a small part of his gigantic output, yet modern organists are probably right in contending that they are his most personal works, the most intimate voicing of his feelings and aspirations. Certainly the most casual hearing of many of these pieces is all that is necessary to disprove the notion that Bach was a kind of musical machine who turned out notes to mathematical formulas. Refuted too is the impression (unhappily perpetuated by many a frontispiece) that he was a man without humor, warmth, or the blood of life.

Consider such pieces as the "Jig" Fugue in G major, the Little Fugue in G minor, and the Prelude and Fugue in D major. If ever youthful exuberance and high spirits were captured in music it is surely in such essays as these. The Prelude and Fugue in D major especially is famous as an organist's showpiece—a whirling shower of notes, a hexentanz in the major mode, in which the usually ponderous organ moves with the speed and lightness of a fiddle.

The Toccata and Fugue in D minor is another virtuoso work, in a contrasting mood. Somber, ominous, almost elemental in its gravity, but vitally dramatic, it presents all the aspects of modern "program" music. Vast forces of nature seem to be at work. Scale passages rushing up and down the manuals at headlong speed alternate with chords of earth-shaking power, until the listener's mind is inevitably filled with pictures of the sea, the avalanche, and the thunderstorm. Anyone who thinks of Bach in terms of the dry or the academic need only hear the opening dozen bars or so of this work as a corrective.

Another showpiece of Bach's Weimar period is the Toccata in F. The word "toccata," based on the Italian word meaning "to touch," originally meant a free, fantasialike movement in which the fingers were given a thorough workout in rapidly moving scales and elaborate passage work—in short, a speed exercise. The Toccata in F is an example of Bach's ability to take such an uninspired, utilitarian form and build from it a monument of tonal splendor. A long movement of tremendous vigor and immense mural-like sweep, it taxes the powers of the greatest performers. It is also one of the best examples of Bach's powers of development, of taking a few basic musical ideas and expanding them prodigiously.

There was a special purpose behind the composition of these bravura pieces of Bach's Weimar period. His reputation as an organist began to spread, and he seems to have made tours almost every year to neighboring towns and to courts, giving recitals and trying out new organs. For such occasions he had to develop a repertoire that would show off his organ technique. From all contemporary accounts it was an astonishing skill: "His fist was gigantic; he could stretch a twelfth with his left hand and perform running passages between with the three inner fingers." His finger dexterity was so smooth and effortless that "his hand was never weary and lasted out through a whole day's organ playing". . . while "with his two feet he could perform on the pedals passages which would be enough to provoke many a skilled clavier player with five fingers." The organs of Bach's time, it must be remembered, often had actions so stiff that they would cripple the hands of most modern organists, used to effortless electrical actions.

Bach once gave a recital at Cassel before the heir apparent who later became King Frederick of Sweden. It is believed that he performed his Toccata in C, which has a brilliant pedal solo. The stupefied prince snatched from his finger a ring set with precious stones and presented it to Bach on the spot. Someone else who was present remarked that Bach's feet "flew over the pedal board as if they had wings; and the ponderous and ominous tones fell upon the ear of the hearer like thunder."

Another story of Bach's prowess concerns his encounter

with J. L. Marchand, a celebrated French musician. Marchand was extremely proud of his reputation as a clavier player and improviser. He was the idol of Versailles, and in 1717 when he visited Dresden he created a sensation at the court there. Bach happened to visit Dresden at the same time and some of his admirers conceived the idea of a contest between the two. Marchand and Bach agreed to meet, but when Bach arrived on the day of the joust and declared himself ready it was found that Marchand had left town that morning. It was believed that the Frenchman had availed himself secretly of an opportunity to hear Bach at practice, and that what he heard had dismayed him.

From all accounts it would seem that no one ever approached Bach at the art of improvisation. Certainly no one of his time was better qualified to appraise his skill than the patriarch of all the North German organists—Jan Adam Reinken. In 1720, when he and Bach met in Hamburg for the last time, Reinken was ninety-seven years old, and his experience had extended back through the long era of the baroque in music. After listening to Bach extemporize for half an hour on the theme of the chorale, *An Wasserflüssen Babylon* [*By the Flowing Waters of Babylon*], Reinken embraced him and declared, "I thought that this art was dead, but I see it still lives in you." When asked by distinguished visitors for an exhibition of his skill, Bach could extemporize on a single theme for over an hour. First he would use the theme as the basis for a prelude and fugue; then he would combine and interweave it with some familiar chorale melody; finally he would use it as the subject of a fugue for full organ, often combining the original theme with other themes derived from it.

IV

Toward the end of Bach's term at Weimar a decided change became apparent in his organ music. He had passed the years of his youth, and his interest in brilliance and show began to decline. As his art matured, his ideas became more serious and contemplative. He produced a series of organ works which he himself never surpassed, in their union of technical mastery and inspirational depth. Among them are the Passacaglia in C minor, now widely known through various transcriptions for orchestra; the Prelude and Fugue in A minor, one of Franz Liszt's most successful piano transcriptions; the Fantasia and Fugue in G minor, probably Bach's most celebrated organ work; and the Dorian Toccata and Fugue in D minor.

The passacaglia is an old form derived, somewhere in the dimmed-out past, from a Spanish dance. It is one of the theme-and-variation species, in which a short tune in the bass is repeated over and over again, while the variation material is reared above it. The form is a twin brother to the chaconne, and the lack of a clear distinction between the two has almost turned the wits of modern program annotators. Bach went for a model for his Passacaglia to Buxtehude, who had written a number of works in the form. Bach's eight-measure theme—simple, slow-moving and gravely expressive—is first stated alone, softly, in the pedals. Around it Bach constructs twenty variations, with the theme itself generally in the bass but sometimes in the treble or the middle voices. The music seems to grow, to rise, to expand in all directions; until at the end of the twentieth variation it bursts into a double fugue. Here the first four measures of the theme are joined by a new subject and developed at length. Again there is the feeling of enormous expansion, of a gradual irresistible movement toward some far-off goal.

The Fantasia and Fugue in G minor synthesize many of the ripest elements of Bach's art in organ composition. They also illustrate the extent to which he summed up, expanded, and perfected polyphonic music itself and the entire baroque style. His Fantasia is the last word in a form that had long been a favorite with the North German organists. It is baroque to the core—a rambling, rhapsodically conceived structure, marked with heavy chordal masses, pedal points and slow-moving step passages in the bass, ornamented above with recitativelike arabesques. Two features of this great essay especially impress the listener today—the modernity of its dramatic style and its harmonic daring.

The fugue as a form is indissolubly linked with Bach's name because of his peculiar and unrivaled mastery of it. He did not, of course, invent the fugue. It was an old and even hackneyed form and an especial favorite with the German organists who provided him with his early models. It is another typical baroque framework, an arbitrary and highly artificial set of rules for the development of an elaborate movement from a single basic theme. It makes special demands on both the composer and the listener. The composer faces the problem of manipulating these complicated rules and of creating from them a genuine art work, instead of an abstruse intellectual exercise. The listener has to be sufficiently aware of (and in sympathy with) the composer's purely mechanical problems to be able to appreciate the aesthetic triumph of their ultimate solution.

The appreciation of fugal music suffers today from the fact that it is the product of a vanished age of polyphony. Moreover, many musicians, including some of the most eminent, do not know how to perform it. They do not understand that coexisting with design in this music is texture, which must be clarified and differentiated with the utmost care; and that it must be animated by a rhythm which impels every instant of its life. Too often the performances of Bach's fugues are caricatured into a jumbled mass of sound which the public is right to reject. By contrast, there are few more satisfying aesthetic experiences than a performance of these same works by competent hands.

As for fugal construction, Bach's mastery was unique; he was able to manipulate these intricate pieces to suit his very moods. There are Bach fugues that are gay and sparkling, irresistible as dance tunes; others are somber, deliberate, filled with pathos and heartbreak. Some are frankly showpieces to spotlight the performer's skill; others are exalted proclamations of man's noblest thoughts.

The various Weimar fugues illustrate Bach's growing mastery over mood and technique. The G minor Fugue is a triumph of sheer mechanical and melodic splendor. Its flawless form recalls the beauty of pure mathematics; its spontaneous movement is like the grace of some exquisitely made machine. Wholly contrasting in mood is the Dorian Fugue in D minor, a work suffused with melancholy, dignified, devoid of display. Harvey Grace, foremost of the English writers on Bach's organ music, points out the basic difference between Bach's procedure with the fugue and that of his predecessors. Even able composers like Buxtehude were seldom careful enough with the theme itself; they ran to repeated notes and zigzag intervals that would impress themselves on the mind of the listener chiefly because of their eccentricity. Bach soon learned that a fugue could never rise above its theme, and thereafter he molded and perfected his basic tunes with extreme care. That was one of the secrets of his command of mood in his fugues, of his ability to rear a structure like the Dorian Fugue, in which the mechanics of the form are made to serve an emotion of the most poignant sort.

V

Sometime in the year 1717 Bach had a quarrel with Duke Wilhelm Ernst and decided to leave Weimar. The exact nature of the dispute is not known, but Bach may have been irked because the post of Kapellmeister in the duke's orchestra was not offered to him when it became vacant the year before. It may have been an honor that he strongly desired, for when he resigned from the duke's service he announced his intention of becoming Kapellmeister to Prince Leopold of Anhalt-Cöthen. There is also a possibility that the composer left Weimar to better himself financially. At Cöthen he was offered a salary of about six hundred dollars a year, which was almost four times the amount for which he began at Weimar.

Whatever the cause, the results of the resignation from Weimar were startling. The Duke put Bach under arrest and detained him at his palace. If more were known of this episode, interesting light might be thrown upon the composer's personal life at Weimar. What seems to be indicated is a clash of temperament. Bach was a very stubborn man. Again and again in the course of his career he ran into trouble by his refusal to budge when he thought his rights were being infringed upon. In this case his obstinacy and independence seem to have angered the Duke, for he was detained a whole month before he was permitted to go. Fortunately, this period of his disgrace was turned to good purpose. The composer occupied his time by compiling his *Orgelbüchlein* [*Little Organ Book*], a collection of chorale preludes.

The chorale prelude was a form that Bach seemed to love above all others, for he turned to it again and again in the course of his long career—from the time when he was a mere boy at Lüneburg first trying his hand at composition, to the last days of his life at Leipzig. It was an old form, and one that Bach made singularly his own; not because it gave him (like the fugue) a vehicle for his technical skill, but rather because it provided an outlet for his deeply emotional, poetic, and religious nature.

The chorale prelude was an integral part of the Lutheran church ritual. At a certain point in the service, just before the congregation was to sing the particular hymn of the day, the organist would deliver a short musical interlude to lead up to the old song. To avoid the monotony of simply playing a verse of the hymn itself as an introduction, the practice grew for the organist to "preludize"; that is, to compose or improvise a short piece based on the hymn, but adorned with elaborate polyphony so the tune itself was not too obviously exposed. Naturally Bach would excel at a form such as this; but there was another aspect of the chorale prelude that attracted him powerfully. This was the opportunity that it afforded him to paint in music the ideas expressed by the hymn's words. Bach's whole nature—his deep-rooted faith in his religion, his humanity and tenderness, his love of the poetic and the dramatic—every spiritual part of him responded to the sentiments of these beautiful old sacred songs.

Despite the importance of these chorale preludes in the general scheme of Bach's art and the clues they revealed to his procedures, they were for years the most neglected and the least understood of all his works. In the nineteenth century, when Bach's music began to be exhumed, the chorale preludes still in existence were published at first without the words to the hymns. The hymn tunes themselves had in some cases been forgotten, or were often so deeply embedded in Bach's variation material that they could not be traced. Thus these pieces often seemed like so many enigmas, mere mathematical exercises whose true point and purpose remained a mystery.

It was only after modern musicologists had unearthed and studied the words of the hymn tunes that these chorale preludes came into their own. It was then that scholars like Schweitzer were able to discover that they were the very antithesis of what Bach's music was so long believed to stand for—the purely formal, the impersonal, and the abstract. Instead they are pictorial and descriptive to a remarkable degree, and they throw a revealing light upon Bach's methods of composition and his entire aesthetic approach to music.

In these pieces Bach paints scenes, portrays emotions and moods, depicts the most elusive shades of meaning expressed by the words, actually anticipating the idea behind the modern song style of Schubert, Schumann, Mussorgsky, and Wolf. For this purpose Bach gradually evolved an extensive set of musical symbols—small expressive figures and themes which became his means of expressing such ideas as grief, gladness, adoration, sighing, weeping, etc. "Some are directional," writes Professor Terry, "denoting ascent or descent, height or depth, width, distance, and so forth. The act of hastening or running, and, conversely, the idea of rest or fatigue, are indicated by appropriate symbolic formulas. The moods, again, are distinguished by themes diatonic or chromatic to express joy or sorrow. The thought of laughter, of tumult, of terror, and the forces of nature, the winds, waves, clouds, and thunder have their indicative symbols, which do not vary. Bach was one of the tenderest and most emotional of men, with the eye of a painter and the soul of a poet. But the fact is only fully revealed to those who take pains to translate him."

There are close to one hundred and fifty chorale preludes by Bach in existence. During his lifetime he made several collections, of which the *Little Organ Book* containing forty-six was the first. This group of pieces was described by Bach himself as a collection "wherein the Beginner may learn to perform Chorals of every kind and also acquire Skill in the Use of the Pedal"—in short, they were intended as a means of instruction. Nevertheless, that purpose actually turns out to be secondary. These pieces have a special quality of intimacy and confidence, as if the composer were opening both his soul and the inmost treasures of his art to the aspiring young student of the organ, or to anyone else who would listen to his message with sympathy and understanding. They encompass an astonishing range of emotional intensity and of mood, with a measure of personal expressiveness unsuspected of the composer who wrote the fugal abstractions, the preludes, toccatas, and fantasias for the same instrument.

Of the chorale preludes in general Ernest Newman wrote with justification that "they are the key to the very heart of Bach," and that "if everything else of his were lost, from them we could reconstruct him in all his pathos and almost all his grandeur."

## VI

Bach's departure from Weimar occurred late in 1717. He had been there nine years, a period of astonishing artistic growth and productivity. Now he was entering upon a new career, one which would require musical composition of a wholly different order. At Weimar, as organist and choirmaster, his works were almost entirely concerned with the organ and the church service; at Cöthen he was the leader of the prince's small orchestra of eighteen players, and as such would be required to produce quantities of chamber music. Moreover, the church at Cöthen was Reformed, which meant that the stanchly Lutheran Bach was completely cut off from all the church music which he loved so well and which had been his life study. The Reformed churches of Germany were members of the Calvinist branch of Protestantism, abhorring music as part and parcel of the Roman ritualism.

The real mystery of Bach's move to Cöthen is his relinquishing of his career as virtuoso organist. In the new post he had no adequate organ at his disposal, only a tiny instrument in the grim little Calvinist chapel, no organ at all for a player of Bach's caliber. This meant that he deliberately gave up his organ career, even though at the time he was famous all over Germany as a virtuoso of the first rank.

During his five years at Cöthen the composer's output was almost exclusively instrumental—a flood of music that included the Brandenburg Concertos, a group of orchestral suites, the violin and clavier concertos, sonatas for various instruments, and a large collection of works for the keyboard, including the English and French Suites, the Little Preludes and Inventions, the Chromatic Fantasia and Fugue, and Part I of *The Well-tempered Clavier*. These works contain some of the most magnificent music in existence; many of them are sovereign examples of their particular type. Yet most of them were composed as part of Bach's job, which was to provide musical entertainment for the prince. Practically all of Bach's vast output falls in this same category, i.e. its basic purpose was utilitarian. It was created as part of the artist's job in life, his means of staying alive. It was not conceived primarily as a "work of art," detached from the business of life. That type of music is a modern conception, and the production of it on a large scale begins with Beethoven.

The apparent ease with which Bach turned from religious to secular music for totally different instruments indicates his method of work. Only an artist who enjoyed an easy balance between his inspiration and his technical resources could have operated as Bach did. He was the opposite of the artist whose nervous system is raked by the effort of creation, whose work echoes the birth pangs of his creative ideas, and whose life and temperament and personality are colored and warped and made eccentric by the agony of the inner struggle. With Bach composition was an intellectual struggle, not a nervous one. Geared to his musical talent were a stupendous technical equipment and a boundless imagination. Thus gifted, he had no need for soul-shattering effort.

Prince Leopold of Anhalt-Cöthen was an agreeable and sympathetic patron. He was only twenty-four years old when Bach entered his service; but he had traveled extensively, was well educated, had cultivated tastes in the arts, and was passionately fond of music. His affection for Bach and his respect for the composer's art seem to have been marked. He paid a liberal salary, and several times he asked Bach to accompany him on his travels. He also stood as godfather to the composer's seventh child, a condescension not frequently encountered among eighteenth-century princes.

Two of the journeys were important events in Bach's life. These were trips to Carlsbad, where the prince went to take the waters. It was the custom of the time for wealthy noblemen (imitating, of course, the court of Versailles) to take with them on their travels the more gifted artists or musicians attached to their courts, as an indication of their own tastes and predilections. Prince Leopold was accompanied by Bach and a quintet of string players from his orchestra. He also took along a harpsichord, with several servants to look after it.

The first journey was made in 1718, the second in 1720. On one of these occasions Bach was fortunate in meeting a famous Prussian prince—Christian Ludwig, Margrave of Brandenburg, the youngest son of the Great Elector. The Margrave was a man of extravagant tastes happily combined with great wealth. He loved music, and it was his pleasure to collect for his library manuscripts of concertos by the noted composers of that day. He probably heard Bach perform at one of Prince Leopold's musical soirees, for he gave the composer a commission. The result was six concertos, now known as the Brandenburg Concertos, which Bach completed in 1721 and sent to the Margrave in Berlin.

The fate of the Brandenburg Concertos after they were

received in Berlin is important because it indicates how Bach's music was regarded during his lifetime. The Margrave could not have remotely guessed that these six pieces were to be the avenue to immortality for himself and his whole proud line. It appears that they were never performed for him at all. He did not even have them included in the catalogue of his library, which recorded the names of numerous other contemporary composers. After his death in 1734, the Margrave's library was sold. Various concertos by composers then famous but now dead beyond all hope of resurrection were carefully identified; but Bach's manuscripts were disposed of unnamed, in a job lot, and at a price so low as to indicate that they were practically worthless. They might have been lost forever had they not happened to come into the possession of one of Bach's pupils—J. P. Kirnberger, a noted composer, conductor, and theorist. This man in turn passed them on to one of his own pupils, Princess Amalie, a sister of Frederick the Great. From her they went to the Royal Library in Berlin.

"The eighteenth-century concerto," wrote Lawrence Gilman, "was a very different bird from the thing known to the nineteenth and twentieth centuries by the same name —which is essentially . . . a showpiece for a soloist, with more or less unwelcome interruptions by the orchestra." In Bach's time there were several types of concertos. Most popular were the *concerto grosso* ("grand concerto") in which a small group of solo instruments was featured against the background of a large group of instruments; and the *solo concerto*, in which a single instrument was featured. The large group consisted of strings alone or sometimes strings and wind instruments. The conductor, sitting at a harpsichord, helped to fill out the harmonies of the large group. The essential characteristic of concerto music was therefore the use of beautiful and effective contrasts between the delicate solo playing of the small group and the bold, sweeping declamations of the large.

The concerto form was of Italian origin, a product of the magnificent age of string playing that developed in that country in the years of the late baroque. At the time when

Bach's immediate forerunners in North Germany were exploring and developing the organ, the Italians were concentrating on the violin. The precise place in history of the master of all violin makers, Antonio Stradivari (1644?–1737), is a milestone that marks both the production of the finest instruments of their kind and a school of violin virtuosi who played them. For these and their kindred instruments a splendid new musical literature gradually evolved; forms like the sonata, the trio sonata, and the concerto began to take shape.

The peculiar form of the concerto has caused historians to believe that it grew up in the homes of the nobility who, like Bach's employers, were wealthy enough to maintain private orchestras. A few expert players performed the more difficult parts of the small group. The larger group of players had much less difficult music to perform because they were largely made up of servants who regularly performed menial duties in the house and could double with fair skill on some instrument.

Among the Italian composers of the late baroque, Giuseppe Torelli (o. 1650–1708) and Arcangelo Corelli (1653–1713) were the first to weld the concerto into an established form; but it was Antonio Vivaldi (1675?–1743) to whom Bach went for his immediate models. Of all the foreign music that Bach studied during his lifetime none seems to have influenced him more or brought him more pleasure than that of his Italian contemporary. While still at Weimar Bach had become acquainted with Vivaldi's concertos. He transcribed at least two of them for organ, and later in his life he transformed a number of others for harpsichord. These works were clearly in his mind when he started on the Brandenburg Concertos, his first original works in instrumental music on what might be called a symphonic scale.

In general, Bach took from Vivaldi the three-movement form of the concerto, which included a brilliant, bustling first movement, a more lyrical slow movement, and a rushing finale. In details of workmanship Bach far surpassed his Italian models. He manipulated his instrumental groups with boldness and variety. He grouped them, contrasted them, featured them, all in a manner brilliantly effective and largely untried before his time. He also made exorbitant demands upon the players. The hacks or the servants of his day could hardly have attempted these concertos, which can be played even today only by experts. The polyphonic writing in these works ranks among the best that Bach himself ever accomplished. Stringed instruments are eminently suited to the linear weaving of melodic lines, and Bach took every advantage of his opportunity. The interplay of various voices on contrasting tonal planes is masterly. His slow movements, too, are far beyond those of his predecessors, in depth of feeling and the poetic richness of his ideas.

Every one of the Brandenburg Concertos calls for a different combination of instruments, as if the composer meant deliberately to show his patron what he could do with various groupings. While a few of the instruments that Bach used are now obsolete, and others have changed so that for modern performances certain adjustments have to be made, the works are fixtures in the repertoire of every symphony orchestra. Aside from their intrinsic beauty, they are interesting as the nearest approach that Bach made toward music for the modern symphonic orchestra.

Bach wrote no other concertos in the Brandenburg style, possibly because the happy occasion of a commission never again offered itself. He did, however, write a number of works for solo instruments and strings, and they happen to present a particularly uncomfortable bed of thorns for musicologists. Of these concertos three are for violin, including the famous double concerto in D minor for two violins—a work beloved by generations of virtuosi. Then there are eight concertos for solo clavier, three for two claviers, two for three claviers, and one for four claviers —all of course with strings accompanying. But two of the clavier concertos are *duplicates* of the violin concertos; another is identical with the Brandenburg Concerto No. 4; one of the concertos for two claviers is identical with the double concerto for two violins, and the concerto for four claviers is actually a transcription of a concerto for four

violins by Vivaldi. Moreover, another of the concertos for
two claviers is believed to be identical with a lost concerto
for violin and oboe; while some modern Bach scholars
believe that several other of the clavier concertos are also
identical with other lost violin concertos.

The conclusions to be drawn from this knotty puzzle
are more obvious than the solution of the puzzle itself.
It is clear that Bach, an incorrigible transcriber both of his
own and other men's music, did not consider his own
works inviolate or irrevocably cast in the particular medium in which he first put them. Throughout his life he
did not hesitate, when the press of work or lack of time
demanded, to take an old score and put it into a new form,
"achieving the most astonishing translations from one medium to another, transcribing concerto movements into
great choruses, and, conversely, turning arias into slow
movements of concertos." This point needs to be stressed
at the present time, when the spread of public interest in
Bach's music has produced an enormous number of transcriptions for all sorts of modern instruments and combinations—from the symphonic orchestra to the harmonica.
For some musicians transcriptions by anyone other than
the composer himself are damned per se on the ground
that the composer alone is aware of the proper medium for
his ideas. Certain modern Bach transcriptions have come
in for the severest criticisms of all, when as a matter of fact
if any music actually lends itself to transcription it is
Bach's. He composed at a time when highly specialized
music writing fitted for specific instruments was only beginning to be realized. Schweitzer remarked, "At bottom
he conceived everything for an ideal instrument: one that
had all the possibilities of polyphonic playing possessed by
the keyed instruments, and all of the bowed instruments'
capacities for phrasing. This is how he came to write
polyphonically for even a single instrument of the string
family."

It would seem that the only criterion to be applied to a
transcription of Bach's or any other music is whether or
not it possesses interest and beauty in its new medium,
regardless of what the composer might have thought of

that medium. Each transcription must be judged separately, and on its own merits as a piece of music. In Bach's case the purists' stand against transcriptions is particularly shaky, not only because of the composer's own practices but also because most of the instruments for which he actually did write are completely changed today. He would be astounded by our vast modern organs; our pianos are totally different instruments from his own claviers, and even the violin has changed, for in Bach's time it was still played with a loose bow and had a flat bridge which permitted the sounding of unbroken chords and even polyphony. It is one of the glories of Bach's music that it has kept pace with the development of modern instruments; and that no matter how intricate or how vast some of them have become, or how different in tone color from what he might have been able to conceive, they are still far from outgrowing the possible range of his art.

VII

On his return from the second Carlsbad journey in 1720, Bach had a shocking experience. He came home to find that his wife had died during his absence and was already buried. According to one version of the story, he had actually entered his own house before his tragic loss was made known to him. His life during the next year must have been a very sad one, with four motherless children, one of them only five years old. It was during this time that the composer worked at the Brandenburg Concertos and at the compilation of another and even more famous masterpiece—Part I of *The Well-tempered Clavier*.

The title, *The Well-tempered Clavier*, was chosen by Bach with special intent. It proclaimed his championship of a new theory which was agitating the musicians of his day, and which concerned the method of tuning keyed instruments. The old method of tuning (the "mean tone" or "unequal temperament" method) was based on a theoretical acoustical correctness. Its difference from the new "equal temperament" can be indicated most simply on any modern piano. In our present keyed instruments, tones like C sharp and D flat are identical. According to acoustical fact, however, they are two entirely different tones, the C sharp being slightly higher in pitch than the D flat. The old method of tuning recognized this strict scientific fact, to the extent that on the old keyed instruments the key of C major was tuned "true," and the other tones forced to conform to it. This meant that the player could perform only in a few keys closely related to C major. The more remote keys would sound badly out of tune. A composer could not modulate freely from one key to another, but had to restrict himself in any given composition to a few preferred keys. If an instrument were built that would provide all the various keys with their scientifically correct scales, a fingerboard with fifty-three digitals to the octave would be required.

It is true that the old tuning produced a depth of sonority that musicans were loath to lose; nevertheless it began to be recognized that clinging to it was stultifying a new and growing keyboard art. The champions of equal temperament proposed a system of tuning in which the slight differences in pitch between such tones as C sharp and D flat would be disregarded. Instead, these tones would be combined into single notes. Thus the keyboard could be divided into twelve equal half steps to the octave, and the scale of every key, instead of just a few, would then be approximately in tune. The "acoustical falsehood" thus created was well-nigh imperceptible, but the resulting convenience and freedom gained for the composer and the performer were incalculable.

Equal temperament was thus a compromise, a practical solution to a difficult physical problem. It is noteworthy that Bach, with his interest in harmonic freedom, saw the value of the new system and became one of its strongest proponents. *The Well-tempered* [i.e. equal-tempered] *Clavier*, with its prelude and fugue in each of the twenty-four keys, major and minor, all capable of being performed on the same keyboard, *provided the instrument was tuned in equal temperament*, was an irrefutable argument in favor of the new method.

As for the precise instrument for which these pieces were intended, it is probable that Bach meant them for any of the keyed instruments; but it is certain that he himself preferred to play them upon the clavichord. This instrument is not to be confused with the clavicembalo (or harpsichord), which was large enough to resemble the modern wing-shaped grand piano, and which often had two manuals with a set of pedals controlling its tone quality. The clavichord had no pedals, but was merely a small box about five octaves long, which could be placed upon a small table and was light enough to be carried easily. Under the fingers of a master like Bach it was capable of producing sounds of exquisite quality and gradation. It was said to possess a soul and the ability to "reflect every shade of the player's feelings as a faithful mirror," or to "quiver just like a voice swayed by emotion." Bach loved the clavichord, preferring it to the clavicembalo, whose tone he thought coarse and unsympathetic. In this collection of preludes and fugues he very likely exhausted the possibilities of the smaller instrument.

Aside from the controversial purpose of *The Well-tempered Clavier*, the collection was also intended for the instruction of Bach's children and his pupils. This pedagogical phase had a curious effect upon the fortunes of the great work. At first it helped to keep the music alive. During the century or so after the composer's death, when the rest of his music lay in oblivion, *The Well-tempered Clavier* was known and used by many German piano teachers. Even well into the present century, however, it was still studied and played only in private, and generally for its instructional purpose. Thus the great emotional and aesthetic basis of these pieces was largely ignored.

Except for his organ works, *The Well-tempered Clavier* affords the best instrumental access to Bach's art. In these short pieces are synthesized his command of polyphony, of melodic and rhythmic invention, his perfectly knit style, even something of the noble span of his emotional range. Some of the preludes are little masterpieces of baroque scrollwork, purling arabesques in which the fingers must run and leap at breathless speed; others, e.g., the C sharp minor and the B minor, are examples of the purest polyphony, the joining of several lines of melody into one superbly proportioned whole. The opening Prelude in C major is of a baffling and mystic serenity; the preludes in F major and G major are gay and exuberant; still others are suffused with melancholy, while the E flat minor is an elegy in tone and one of the most sorrowful works in music.

For his fugues in this collection Bach scaled down the form to miniature size without damage to its essential beauty and effectiveness. These pieces range from the little two-voiced example in E minor, in which two strands of melody go chasing and dodging each other up and down the keyboard at lightning speed, to the lordly B flat minor in five voices—a slow-moving and closely woven essay of great majesty and depth of feeling. Certain fugues, like that in G major, radiate health and high spirits; others like the F sharp minor are poignantly expressive, the mechanical outlines of the fugue form being lost in the shadows of a deep despondency. The G minor Fugue, only thirty-four measures long, is a masterpiece of concision; while the last, in B minor, is an extended movement that resembles some of the composer's lengthy works for the organ.

Today the preludes and fugues of *The Well-tempered Clavier* are more than a part of every pianist's technical background. They have entered the concert repertoire, where they belong. More than two centuries have passed since Bach composed them, and in that time the instrument for which they were intended has passed through a metamorphosis so profound that Bach himself would doubtless be amazed at the sound of his pieces on a modern grand piano. In time to come the piano too may change and develop even more radically; but it does not seem likely that *The Well-tempered Clavier* itself will become obsolete. While there are keyboard instruments in the world it is likely to remain a living source of beauty.

In 1721, the year after the death of Maria Barbara, Bach married again. His second wife was Anna Magdalena Wülcken, the daughter of a court trumpeter. She was twenty-one years old at the time of their marriage and Bach was thirty-six. The personality of Maria Barbara has been utterly lost in the shrouding silences of history, but something is known indirectly of Anna Magdalena. All evidence points to the fact that her union with Bach was an unusually happy one. Between 1723 and 1742 she bore the composer thirteen children. She was very musical, having been a court singer at Cöthen before her marriage. She was also able to play the clavier, and Bach took obvious pleasure in encouraging her musical talents. He wrote two collections of little pieces for her instruction, one of which is called *The Little Clavier Book of Anna Magdalena Bach*.

Anna Magdalena helped Bach greatly by relieving him of much of the drudgery of copying music. Many of his cantatas are in her hand, as are works of other composers which he wanted to study. She once copied out a large part of a Passion by Handel. In spite of the paucity of the evidence relating to her, Anna Magdalena passes into history as one of those wives of great men who were helpmates in every sense; she was her husband's devoted companion and assistant, the source of inspiration for some of his most charmingly intimate works.

Among the music that seems to have been composed for Anna Magdalena is a group of little clavier pieces known as the French Suites. The name became attached to them probably because Bach was imitating the French style of writing of that period, a style made popular by Marchand and Couperin. The French composers made their suites out of short pieces which were based on dances—the gavotte, the minuet, the passepied, the bourrée, the gigue, etc. The differences in tempo, rhythm, and mood of these dances gave the composer an opportunity to create a sheaf of pieces of considerable variety.

Bach wrote a number of suites for clavier. There are six of the French Suites, and six so-called English Suites (the reason for this name is not known), all of which were written at Cöthen. Years later at Leipzig he completed six more kindred works which were titled partitas. Paul Henry Láng writes, "It is a sheer wonder to see the grave

Lutheran cantor, the epitome of German baroque massiveness, clad in the impeccable silk stockings, lace-trimmed jacket and powdered wig of the French rococo, and moving about in this circle with the assuredness of the very masters whose style he attempted to imitate."

Bach's suites all contain six or seven short movements, each of them beginning with an allemande or prelude and ending with a gigue. No more graceful or charming pieces are to be found in German music. Bach's workmanship is like that of a fine line drawing or an etching, for many of the movements are in two-voiced counterpoint—the two delicate lines of melody without any other support whatever performing the entire function of providing melodic interest, harmonic structure, and rhythmic animation.

Not all of these pieces are imitations of French elegance. Bach could not resist intensifying and broadening every musical form that he touched. Certain of the sarabandes become not merely stately dances but poignant slow movements, and there are some fugal movements of considerable length and complexity. This is even more marked in the later groups of partitas, some of which begin with elaborate and majestic overtures and often depart far in mood and texture from the rococo. The sixth and last partita, in E minor, has burst the boundaries of the simple little French forms to become an extended work, serious in mood and spacious in design. Here is the later eighteenth-century sonata in embryo.

## VIII

Shortly after his second marriage, a rift began to appear in the placid relations of Bach and his patron. The Prince also married and his bride caused a decided change in the order of things at Cöthen. She was a light-minded and flighty young person, described as caring only for "balls and fireworks." Her appreciation of music was adolescent. In the playing of her husband's Kapelle, and particularly in the weighty music of its director, she had no interest whatever. Bach termed her an "*amusa*" and, realizing that the Prince's interests were diverted from his music, he began to look about for another post. For a long time the urge seems to have been strong in him to get back into church music, to a post that would put a choir and an organ once again at his disposal. In 1723 he got what he wanted.

In Leipzig there was a famous school for boys, St. Thomas's, a venerable institution that had been founded in the thirteenth century. Bach heard that the cantorship was vacant, so he applied for the post. The duties of the cantor included teaching singing and Latin to some fifty boys between the ages of fourteen and twenty-one, and acting as music director of the two churches with which the school was connected—St. Thomas's and St. Nicholas's. It was the latter phase of the cantor's duties that attracted Bach, for it meant that he had to provide an elaborate program of music in one of the two churches every Sunday and on certain feast days.

Early in 1723, Bach underwent the trials for the appointment, and on Good Friday of that year he conducted his hastily composed *St. John Passion* in St. Thomas's Church, as proof of his ability. A few months later he was formally appointed. The leave-taking from Cöthen was under unforeseen and tragic circumstances. Nine days before Bach and his family departed the *amusa* died. Two years later the Prince married again; but in 1728, five years after Bach left his service, he too was dead. Bach's affection for the young nobleman who had treated him so kindly is shown by his journey to Cöthen to attend the Prince's funeral and to provide music for the memorial service.

The Leipzig post was Bach's last. He remained there for twenty-seven years, until his death in 1750. He went to Leipzig in his thirty-eighth year, an artist with almost two decades of very great accomplishment behind him. All this, however, was only the prelude to what was to come. The music of the Leipzig period is difficult to appraise because in physical bulk alone it is gigantic. Bach was a busy man much of the time, occupied with the routine tasks of his cantorship; yet during these years he composed the *St. Matthew Passion* and the colossal Mass in B minor, which are his greatest works; the Magnificat, six motets, a series of organ pieces that crown his entire accomplishment for that instrument, more superlative works for the clavier, and a vast series of church cantatas. Not only is this music enormous in physical bulk, but also some of it is on a scale of architectonic design that is mountainous and inspired beyond any music composed before its time or since.

Viewing these accomplishments, it is hard to believe that the cantorship of St. Thomas's was a sorry disappointment to the composer. The existing record of his office is a long recital of misunderstanding and petty bickering, quarrels with associates who tried to cheat him out of his perquisites, with church authorities who treated him like a hack, and with narrow-minded rectors who had no sympathy with his music and no realization of his stature as an artist. When Bach went there in 1723, he found that the school was badly run down, in the hands of an old rector who was tottering and senile. The boys were an undisciplined gang of young ruffians, morally weakened by having to beg in the streets of Leipzig for donations to the school, and often ill and miserable from undernourishment and neglect. Their musical education was poor and their voices were wretched. Moreover, the older singers and instrumentalists who were hired from the town to fill out the choir and the orchestra were also inadequate. When Bach complained about these conditions, he only got himself on bad terms with the rector and the town council.

With the death of the old rector in 1729, a new one named Gesner was appointed, and for the next five years improvement and order reigned at St. Thomas's. But Gesner was followed in 1734 by one Johann August Ernesti, a hardheaded bigot who became one of Bach's worst persecutors. He hated music, disparaged its importance even in front of the boys, and did his best to humiliate the cantor. Bach was something of a match for him. Always proud when his dignity was affronted and pugnacious when the rights of his office were at stake, the composer stood by his guns to the bitter end. One of his worst encounters with Ernesti began when the boys of the choir, unruly because Bach was a poor disciplinarian, behaved in a scandalous manner during a wedding. This led to a quarrel between Bach and Ernesti over the right to appoint a prefect. The battle lasted for two years, during which time both cantor and rector bombarded the council with petitions, charges, and countercharges. It did not end until Bach at last petitioned the King of Saxony. His Majesty resolved the matter by a compromise, with Bach on the long end of the stick.

Bach and his family lived in one of the wings of the school building itself. When they first went to St. Thomas's, the ancient structure was overcrowded and badly in need of repair. It housed the family of the rector, the schoolrooms and dormitories of the boys, and the family of the cantor. The crowded and unsanitary conditions are blamed by Professor Terry for the depressing record of mortality among Bach's children during his early years in Leipzig. Of the first eight children born to Anna Magdalena only two survived, one of whom was an imbecile. The other six children died at ages ranging from one day to five years. After Bach had been there eight years, the building was enlarged and renovated. Of the five Bach children born thereafter four were healthy and survived their father many years. Among them was Johann Christian (1735–1782), one of the most illustrious of the sons. Through his successes as a composer in London he became known as the "English" Bach.

In the gloomy, congested quarters of the cantor one room was reserved for his study. It was small and narrow, lighted by a single window. A thin whitewashed partition separated it from one of the classrooms, and from it could be heard the sound of a near-by mill wheel. This was Bach's workroom for many years.

The most important of Bach's duties as cantor was the composition of music for the church services. The regular Sunday service was a mixture of worship, preaching, and music of appalling length. It began at seven in the morning and lasted until nearly noon. Some slight relief was afforded the boys in the choir: if the church got so cold that they could no longer endure it, they were marched back to the school to listen to a sermon. The only respite for adult worshipers occurred about midway in the eighteen-part service, when (on alternate Sundays) the choir would perform a cantata accompanied by organ and orchestra. The cantata was an elaborate collection of solos, recitatives, duets, and choruses, with occasional orchestral interludes. It lasted about half an hour.

The cantata as a musical form occupied Bach's attention over a space of forty years. He wrote his first cantata in 1704 when he was the boy organist at Arnstadt, and his last in Leipzig in 1744. The sum total is believed to be two hundred and ninety-five cantatas, of which the great majority belong to the Leipzig period. There, in the space of about twenty years, he composed about two hundred and sixty-five cantatas, an average of one a month. About two thirds of these works are extant.

The cantata was in reality a sacred concert that had gradually grown up in the Lutheran service. It was customary for the cantata to be linked with the particular Gospel of the day; in fact it was a kind of musical exposition of the Gospel text. For the words of some of his early cantatas at Weimar, Bach went directly to the Bible, piecing together various verses to suit his purpose. Thereafter he began using librettos prepared by various religious writers and in common use throughout Germany. These librettos provided the composer with a ready-made framework for his music. There were rhymed stanzas, portions of blank verse, excerpts taken directly from the Bible text, and generally as a conclusion a stanza from one of the old Lutheran hymns—all bearing directly on the day's Gospel.

Bach's treatment of the words of his cantatas was identical with his procedure in his organ chorale preludes. He sought always to make his music express as vividly as possible the ideas conveyed by the words. He painted pictures, imitated sounds, portrayed emotions, often with complete realism. The musical symbols that he used were the same as those he evolved for the chorale preludes, a tonal language that anticipated the speech of many of the nineteenth-century song composers.

In a number of his last cantatas Bach dispensed with librettos entirely and evolved the so-called "chorale cantatas." Just as the organ chorale preludes are a polyphonic expansion of the simple old hymns, so the chorale cantatas are an even more elaborate and extended glorification of these same sacred songs. Using both the words and music of some chorale as his basic thematic idea, Bach constructed recitatives, ariosos, duets, choruses—weaving a spreading polyphonic fabric out of a single slender thread. Only at the end of the cantata was the basic hymn tune heard in its original form, when the choir, proclaiming it simply, but with Bach's incomparable harmonization, was probably joined by the congregation.

Even though his immense collection of cantatas comprises by far the greater bulk of Bach's entire output, it remains the least known of all his work. The reason lies partly in the fact that the cantata as part of church worship is long since obsolete. It had passed from the liturgy of many churches even during Bach's lifetime. In modern times few countries have had musical organizations with the training and the traditional background necessary for adequate performances of Bach's cantatas. These works require soloists of exceptional talent and intelligence, first-rate instrumentalists, and choruses equipped to sing in a musical style of great difficulty—in short, a group as perfectly trained and organized as a modern symphony orchestra.

IX

On the afternoon of Good Friday, 1729, the congregation of St. Thomas's assembled according to an ancient custom to hear a presentation of the Passion of our Lord in musical form. In this particular year the biblical account was to be that contained in the Gospel according to St. Matthew. Bach was ready with a newly composed work, and around him in the organ loft he had assembled an exceptionally large group of singers and instrumentalists.

In addition to his regular chorus there was a second chorus made up of singers who did not usually perform at the church; organists were ready at both organs; and there were two orchestras, the usual group being augmented by players from the town, the school, and a local university. This impressive band of performers must have indicated to the congregation that the cantor had prepared something of an exceptional order.

One of Bach's pupils who was present at this first performance of the *St. Matthew Passion* recorded that the members of the congregation were confused by what they heard, and left unappreciative. "Some high officials and well-born ladies in one of the galleries began to sing the first chorale with great devotion from their books. But as the theatrical music proceeded, they were thrown into the greatest wonderment, saying to each other, 'What does it all mean?' while one old lady, a widow, exclaimed, 'God help us! 'Tis surely an opera-comedy!'" It is doubtful that the cantor himself, retiring to his home in the Lenten twilight after his strenuous labors, had full realization of the magnitude of his accomplishment.

Representations of the Passion of Jesus Christ, both musical and dramatic, are as old as the Church itself. Medieval mystery plays, oratorios, and musical Passions all stemmed from the same impulse—a desire to illustrate and act out the stories of the Bible so they could be made clear and vivid to the masses who no longer understood the Latin tongue of the Catholic service. The Passion as a musical form had begun in the early centuries of the Church as a simple dramatic recitation. Through the Middle Ages it had been joined to music, with the parts of the Evangelist, the Saviour, and the Disciples intoned in plainsong instead of merely recited. With the gradual enrichment of the art of music, the Passion evolved into an elaborate and extended form employing soloists, chorus, and instrumentalists.

The exact number of Passions that Bach wrote is in doubt, despite exhaustive research by Bach experts. Only two are extant—the *St. John Passion*, which he composed hurriedly for his examination as cantor, and the *St. Mat-*

*thew*. It is known that he composed a *St. Mark Passion*, which is lost. There is a strong possibility that he composed a fourth, also lost. However, it is certain that of all these works it was the *St. Matthew* which received his most mature inspiration, that it was the most elaborately conceived and the most carefully wrought. Thus we are fortunate in having Bach's masterpiece in the Passion form, the greatest work of its kind in existence.

The literary framework of the *St. Matthew Passion* indicates the process of evolution that must have gone on through the centuries that preceded it. Composers obviously had grown tired of repetitions of the same words from the Gospels describing the Passion; they sought to vary and to enrich the scenario itself. Bach's work indicates how this was done. The main burden of the story is taken directly from the Bible—from Chapters xxvi and xxvii of Matthew. These biblical verses are set to music by Bach in the form of recitatives, with the words of the Evangelist sung by a tenor and those of Jesus by a bass. Interspersed between these verses are short poems from the pen of Picander, a religious writer of the period. Bach set these in the form of arias and choruses with orchestral accompaniment; and in essence they are a sympathetic commentary, like that of the chorus in the Greek drama, upon the biblical story as it unfolds. Finally, several of the old Lutheran chorales are also set between the recitatives and arias. These were sung by the chorus, joined probably by the congregation.

The framework of a Passion was thus a piece of literary joining which required considerable skill. The man who made Bach's libretto was one Christian Friedrich Henrici, who wrote under the pen name of Picander. He was a post-office official and tax collector. On the side he amused himself by writing satirical verse, some of it scandalously vulgar. Quite incongruously he turned to religious poetry, writing one of the most popular sets of cantata texts. Bach knew Picander well, and most of his Leipzig cantatas are based on this writer's words.

Like the church cantata, the Passion was a dying form when Bach produced his masterpiece. It did not disappear from the liturgy of the churches as rapidly as the cantata, but it was definitely on the way out. In reality Bach said the last word on it, for in the entire history of religious music there is nothing to compare with his portrayal of the Passion of Jesus Christ. This work stands at the end of a long evolution of devotional music; it is modern in complexity and scope, but its mystical ecstasy, its emotional fervor, its passionate absorption in the divine epic of the Christian faith—all this is medieval in spirit. That spirit was soon to vanish from music, just as a century before Bach's time it had begun to disappear from the art of painting.

For Bach the Passion of Jesus Christ was no mere religious allegory; it was a drama of reality, and its poignancy touched the deepest chords of his nature and his lifelong faith. In the *St. Matthew Passion* he is first of all a tonal dramatist, striving to bring to life with all the power and vividness at his command the personal portrait as well as the epic tragedy of the Man of Sorrows. He took full advantage of the tragic and dramatic side of the story; in fact it is astonishing how nearly operatic in the modern sense many of his devices are. But the focal point of the entire work remains always the portrait of the Saviour. Through the long and complex score—the swirling masses of choral polyphony; the arias with their incredible richness of texture, and their adorning obbligatos of violin, oboe, and flute; the devotional chorales, strewn through the score (in Terry's phrase) "like jewels of price"— through all this gorgeousness, it is nevertheless the music accompanying the words of Jesus that achieves the inspirational apex of the entire score. By the simplest means Bach attains his ends. When the Evangelist relates his story, it is fairly simple recitative, accompanied by sparse chords from the orchestra. When the voice of Jesus is heard, it is always to the accompaniment of soft string passages. No more moving music has ever been written for the human voice. The brooding sadness, the infinite compassion of the Saviour are limned in these vocal lines; while around Him, in the superb harmonies of the strings, glows the nimbus of divinity. In this portrait Bach is like a

Rembrandt of the tonal art. He had seen in his own heart the piercing vision of the Man he was portraying; he had enveloped his subject with his own boundless sympathy.

The *St. Matthew Passion* had a few performances in the Leipzig churches while Bach was still alive, but it seems to have made no special impression. After the composer's death it lay silent and forgotten for more than three quarters of a century. On Good Friday, 1829, exactly a century after its *première*, Mendelssohn revived it with a performance in Berlin. With that event began the resurrection of Bach's music for the modern world.

Great as it is, the *St. Matthew Passion* does not stand alone in Bach's catalogue. One other work, the Mass in B minor, must be ranked with it as a summation of the composer's art.

In July 1733, Bach's oldest son, Wilhelm Friedemann, was installed as organist in a church in Dresden, and his father went along as his sponsor. While there Bach took the opportunity to ask a favor of his sovereign, Frederick Augustus II, Elector of Saxony. He wanted an appointment as court composer, an honor that was finally conferred three years later. To pay homage he sent Augustus the manuscript of the Kyrie and Gloria of a Mass in B minor, together with a letter in which the composer referred to the work as a "trifling example of my skill in Musique."

Sometime during the next few years (no one knows exactly how or when), the composer added to the Mass by constructing a Credo, Sanctus, and Agnus Dei. Much controversial ink has been shed on the question of how Bach, a stanch Lutheran, came to write a Roman Catholic Mass. Terry's explanation seems to be the most logical. The original Kyrie and Gloria, he points out, were in reality part of the Lutheran church service. When Bach expanded the work with a Credo, Sanctus, and Agnus Dei, he did not create a purely Roman Catholic Mass. For one thing the work is far too long for a church service, and it departs in a number of instances from the strict letter and order of the Roman liturgy. Terry believes that "the Mass is neither Roman nor Lutheran in intention and outlook, but the expression of a catholic Christianity. . . . Bach's genius was Teutonic in its inclination to complete a design" . . . and "in the compulsion to express himself in an art form which he had studied deeply."

The final Mass is gigantic in size. It consists of twenty-four movements for chorus, orchestra, and five solo voices. Fifteen of the movements are for chorus, with six solos and three duets. A complete performance requires almost three hours. The work was not entirely original; the composer borrowed and adapted about one third of the movements from his other works—chiefly from his church cantatas. Bach appears to have worked at the Mass over a period of five years, and the adaptations of the old sections as well as the composition of the new were done with extreme care, so that the vast architectonic scheme could be satisfying in every detail.

The Mass in B minor contrasts strongly with the *St. Matthew Passion*. The latter work is far more personal, both in style and approach. It relates a biblical story, first translated into the German language and then into illuminating and deeply expressive music. The Mass in B minor has, of course, no story to tell. It expounds in music the tenets of a great faith. Its text is in general the Ordinary of the Roman Mass. Bach takes those Latin words, phrase by phrase, and builds them into lengthy movements. The result is a series of stupendous murals, each affirming a phase of the beliefs that are the foundation stones of Christianity. In his *St. Matthew Passion* Bach had worked with the deeply human perceptions of a Rembrandt, and at times the mystical insight of a Leonardo; in the Mass in B minor he is a Michelangelo, the painter of colossal frescoes. His vision sweeps across vast distances, spanning heaven and earth.

The main burden of this structure is carried by the choruses. The arias and duets between them, though bearing the thread of literary continuity, are in reality moments of respite from the weight and impact of the choral masses. It is true that some of them fall below the inspirational level of the greatest arias in the *St. Matthew Passion*, perhaps because the words of the liturgy are often dogmatic abstractions which almost defy musical setting. The best of them is the pathetic Agnus Dei for contralto.

The choruses dwarf everything else by comparison. All but one are in five vocal parts, with the orchestra adding a contrapuntal web of its own. The dimensions of the Mass, its exalted mood, the majesty of its subject, are all set in the first four measures of the Kyrie eleison that open the work. There follows a long and stunning exposition, developed fugally, the vocal lines interweaving and overlapping in a bewildering pattern of sound as they proclaim again and again a powerful basic theme. The inspirational level is high, but Bach maintains and even surpasses it in the fourteen choral movements that follow. Some are exultations of the most brilliant sort, like the Gloria in excelsis Deo, or the dazzling fugue Cum sancto spiritu. Others are solid, broadly developed affirmations of dogmatic faith—for example, the Credo which is based on a theme intoned in the church for more than fifteen hundred years. Still others are poignant and sorrowful—like the second Kyrie eleison, the Qui tollis and the Et incarnatus—movements that are saturated with pathos and tenderness.

The Crucifixus stands alone in the entire range of musical expression. Bach's portrayal of the tragedy of Calvary exemplifies the enigma in which his art remains eternally wrapped, defying analysis and dissection. For this supreme moment in the history of mankind the composer had first to decide upon a musical form commensurate with the idea. He chose a passacaglia. A desolate falling theme in the bass, four measures long, is repeated, note for note, thirteen times, while above it the chorus intones its grief-stricken vision of the dying Saviour. Thus the basic structure of this music, which is unplumbed in emotional depth, is found to be a problem in pure musical mathematics.

In the nineteenth movement, the Confiteor, there is an adagio of twenty-six measures, to the words "Et expecto resurrectionem mortuorum." Here Bach paints the prophecy of the great Resurrection. All contrapuntal movement suddenly slows down; the music evolves through a long series of harmonic progressions that are a hundred years ahead of the composer's time in their daring modernity. The dead rise from their tombs for the Last Judgment.

The climax of the entire Mass (and of the composer's whole creative effort) is reached with the Sanctus. In a six-part chorus the scene of paradise and the Almighty unfolds. "Holy, holy, holy, Lord God of Hosts. Heaven and earth are full of Thy glory." We behold the adoration of the heavenly hosts, with the higher voices of the chorus simulating the antiphony of the seraphim and the quiring angels, while the basses intone a vast theme that strides in octaves—gigantic pillars of tone upon which the nave of heaven rests. The movement is one great rolling thunder of music that seems to echo to the last boundaries of a limitless creation.

x

When Bach finished the Mass in B minor he was close to fifty years old and entering the last phase of his life. He never again attempted anything of such dimensions, and the swift current of his production began to abate somewhat. However, there was not the slightest sign of a flagging inspiration. He maintained his standard to the last days of his life.

After years of not composing for the organ, he returned to that instrument, making several collections of his chorale preludes for publication. A number of these were based on the Lutheran Catechism hymns. They contain some of his weightiest music and are massive specimens of his mature organ style. Two works especially tower above the rest—*Aus tiefer Noth* [*In Deepest Need*], a gloomy and ascetic monument in six-part harmony with double pedal; and the incredible *Kyrie, Gott heiliger Geist* [*Kyrie, Thou Spirit Divine*]. Bach himself never surpassed the latter work either in the development of a mountainous structure of tone from a few notes or in the building of dramatic climax.

In this last period of his life the composer also returned to the clavier. His most notable work was the second part of *The Well-tempered Clavier*, which appeared in 1744. This second set of twenty-four preludes and fugues is one of those rare species of the arts—a sequel that actually surpasses the original.

The so-called Goldberg Variations, published in 1743, were written to order. The Russian envoy to the Dresden court was a certain Count Kayserling who was tortured by chronic insomnia. He hired a clavicenist named Goldberg, a young pupil of Bach's, to play for him at night when he could not sleep. He also commissioned Bach to compose something that would soothe his nerves during the long wakeful hours. The fee was a generous one—a snuffbox containing one hundred louis d'or. Bach responded with a set of thirty variations, a work of such amplitude and quality that the count certainly got his money's worth.

Goldberg must have been a performer of unusual ability, for these Variations bristle with technical difficulties. Until recently they were seldom performed in public because they were originally written for harpsichord with two keyboards, which permitted the hands to cross each other in a manner impossible on the modern piano keyboard. Modern editors have found ways to surmount these difficulties and today the Variations are frequently played.

The main theme that Bach used for his thirty-room structure is a charming Aria in G major, ornate with grace notes. The variations grow out of this central stem in a bewildering variety of melodic and rhythmic ideas. However, they are far from being simply variations. Digging under the surface of this luxuriantly blooming plant, one finds the real roots of the composer's ideas. The piece is actually a kind of passacaglia. A bass line of thirty-two notes governs it. It is not strictly adhered to, but nevertheless it forms the basis of all growth. Even that is not the end of the technical design. At every third variation a canon is introduced, that is, a strict imitation in another voice of the particular theme of the movement. There are nine of these canonic movements in all, beginning with the unison and ending with the ninth. Moreover, there are movements in the form of a fughetta, a French overture, and a quodlibet, the last being an ancient form in which the theme is combined contrapuntally with folk tunes. In this case Bach used two popular German songs.

From this elaborate structural framework it would be easy to infer that in the Goldberg Variations the old cantor was chiefly bent on showing off his technical wizardry, like a pedagogue compiling a dry textbook of mathematical problems and their solutions. The Variations could in fact be used as an instructional work for the use of ornamentation, variation, passacaglia, and canon. If that were their main virtue they would be dead these many years, instead of holding their place among the most beautiful works in keyboard literature. They prove again the paradoxical fact of Bach's creative processes—that mathematical problems were far from shackling his imagination; that actually they stimulated the flow of his ideas, with the result that many of his works that are most rigidly bound in technical fetters are the most poetic, emotional, and humanly expressive of all.

Sometime during the last decade of his life Bach rounded off his organ works in the prelude-and-fugue style with four famous specimens—the preludes and fugues in E flat major, C major, E minor (the "Wedge" Fugue), and B minor. All are big works, representing the accumulated thought and the technical mastery of the composer's lifetime at his favorite instrument. The B minor Prelude and Fugue is probably the ripest of all. Its key, it is worth noting, was obviously a favorite of Bach's; he used it for many of his finest works. The E flat Fugue, popularly known as the "St. Anne" Fugue, is most frequently played. Speaking of this piece, and of the final entry of the main theme in the pedals—a thrilling, roaring declamation—Harvey Grace quotes an old English musician who said that it sounded "as if it ought to be fired off with cannon!"

In the spring of 1747, when Bach had reached the age of sixty-two, he enjoyed a unique personal triumph on the occasion of his visit to the young King of Prussia, later to be known as Frederick the Great. This is one of the few episodes in the composer's life that is documented in some detail.

Bach went to Potsdam to see his son, Karl Philipp

Emanuel, who was harpsichordist in Frederick's court orchestra. The King, who later became the arch-Prussian war lord, was passionately fond of music. He had studied the flute from childhood (to the disgust of his tyrannical father, Frederick William I), and he tried seriously to become a composer. The story is told that one evening Frederick stood, flute in hand, before his orchestra, ready to play a concerto. The list of visitors to the court was handed to him. Suddenly he exclaimed, "Gentlemen, old Bach is here!" The composer was quickly summoned from his son's house. He had no time to change from his traveling clothes, a detail that embarrassed him in the presence of the King.

Frederick gave over the flute concerto and led the old man through his palace, showing him the new Silberman claviers with hammer actions—forerunners of the modern piano. Bach asked the King for a fugue subject upon which he might extemporize, and Frederick wrote one out for him. Bach's improvisation astonished the King, but the composer still held something in reserve. The next day he returned to the palace, and this time on a subject of his own he improvised a six-part fugue. Several times Frederick cried out in amazement, "There is only one Bach!"

A few months later the composer repaid the King with a graceful tribute. He sent Frederick *The Musical Offering*, in which he used the King's theme as a subject of two fugues and a number of canons, adding for good measure a trio for flute, violin, and clavier.

The journey to Potsdam was Bach's last. He was an old man now, and the body that had borne such a heavy burden of labor for so many years began at last to fail. Even so, he was not ready to stop. He set to work upon *Die Kunst der Fuge* [*The Art of Fugue*], a study that would demonstrate with finality his mastery of the old form. The resulting work is one of the most unusual in music; it is a puzzle that remains unsolved because the composer died before its completion, leaving doubt about certain of his purposes.

One phase of the work is perfectly clear. By taking a single theme and treating it in a great variety of ways, developing it through all the devices known to fugal and canonic procedure, from the simplest to the most astonishingly intricate, Bach intended to expose, as it were, the mechanism of his art as a writer of fugue. However, when the work was published, there was nothing to indicate for what instrument or instruments it might be intended. It was long believed, therefore, that *The Art of Fugue* was not intended to be played at all, but was instead a tremendous abstraction, aimed chiefly to instruct and to inform. Even Schweitzer found no aesthetic purpose in the work. He wrote, "It introduces us to a still and serious world, deserted and rigid, without color, without light, without motion; it does not gladden, does not distract; yet we cannot break away from it."

Various modern editors have sought to prove that the piece is much more than cold theory. Some of them have scored it for instruments, and worked out completions of the final fugue, left unfinished by Bach. One of the best proofs that *The Art of Fugue* is suited to actual performance and is music in its fullest sense was an arrangement for chamber orchestra made in 1927 by Wolfgang Gräser, a young Swiss genius of music (and of mathematics, physics, and Oriental languages), who killed himself in 1928 at the age of twenty-two. Convincing as his arrangement is, Gräser's is clearly not the last word on the subject, and *The Art of Fugue* is likely to fascinate and mystify students of music and Bach arrangers in particular for generations to come.

XI

Bach did not complete *The Art of Fugue* because his eyesight began to fail. He was finally persuaded to consult an English oculist, Chevalier John Taylor, who was then visiting and practicing in Germany. Early in 1750, Taylor performed an operation of some kind on Bach's eyes. The operation failed, and Bach emerged totally blind. The excruciating pain of the ordeal and the long confinement that followed broke down the composer's physical strength. For weeks Bach lay in his bed, a broken man. During the year preceding the operation he had turned for the last time to his beloved chorale preludes, and in moments when his eyes would permit, was copying and revising eighteen of them for the engraver. Contained in this collection are some of his finest examples in the form, among them the exquisite *Schmücke dich* [*Deck Thyself, My Soul, with Gladness*]. Almost a century later, Robert Schumann heard this work performed by Mendelssohn, to whom he afterwards wrote, saying that around the old chorale hymn "hung winding wreaths of golden leaves, and such blissfulness was breathed from within it, that you yourself avowed that if life was bereft of all hope and faith, this one chorale would renew them for you. I was silent and went away dazed into God's acre, feeling acutely pained that I could lay no flower on his urn."

The last of the collection, *Wenn wir in höchsten Nöthen sein* [*When We Are in Deepest Need*], remained unfinished during the last days when the blind composer lay waiting for death. Making his final effort, he dictated to his son-in-law the completion of this work, changing its title to that of another hymn on the same tune, *Vor deinen Thron tret' ich allhier* [*Before Thy Throne I Come*].

Ten days later, on the twenty-eighth day of July 1750, Bach died. He was buried in the ancient graveyard of St. John's Church in Leipzig.

## XII

Neglect of Bach's music began almost with the instant of his death. Public interest in it was so small that when Karl Philipp Emanuel published *The Art of Fugue* only a handful of copies were purchased, and he finally sold the plates for the value of the metal. The oldest son, Wilhelm Friedemann (who later became an alcoholic), cared so little for his father's work that he lost a number of the manuscripts of the cantatas that had been willed to him. The sons did not even care for their stepmother. Anna Magdalena died ten years later in poverty. Gradually the manuscripts and published works of the father dropped from sight; soon the place of his grave was forgotten. During the next seventy-five years the name "Bach" meant not Johann Sebastian but Karl Philipp Emanuel.

It would be wrong to assume that the age that neglected Bach's music must be accused of a lack of aesthetic perception. Bach belonged to the baroque era, and he arrived on the scene in time to sum up its style in music. Long before he had finished, the baroque had begun to fade. The younger composers found they could no longer express themselves in the formulas that a century of usage had worked dry. They wanted no more of fugues and chorale preludes, of toccatas, passacaglias, and chaconnes. They were as sick of them as churchgoers were of cantatas and Passions.

In France the baroque age had passed into the rococo, impelled by the enormous personal force of Louis XIV. Art, music, and architecture all reflected the spirit of a new age that was to rule Europe. The baroque had been ornamental and florid, with its lush, decorative exterior covering a platform of massive strength. It had aimed to impress, to glorify, to move deeply. The rococo was also decorative; but it was delicate, refined, poetic, with an elegant charm that was essentially shallow. Its purpose was to entertain, to beguile.

The German composers could not help but be impressed by these changes, but their own version of the rococo was a much more sober product than the French. Theirs was chiefly a rationalizing process, and part of it took the form of simplification. New ideas and procedures had to be sought and explored. Polyphony, which had ruled musical thought for a thousand years, began to crumble. Bach himself had exhausted the possibilities of contrapuntal science; no one could match his purely mathematical skill. The New Music with which his sons were experimenting would be based instead on homophony, a musical pattern built upon a single line of melody instead of several. The great new form that arose was the sonata; soon the symphonic orchestra and the string quartet would appear. For the next century the best creative minds would be engaged in the development and exploitation of these new concepts of form and medium. Opera would flourish as never before, while music for the church would rapidly decline.

In this evolution Bach's music had nothing to offer. It belonged to a vanished past whose ideas and methods the newer composers were trying to avoid and to forget. Moreover, only a small portion of it had been published in the composer's lifetime, so that it could influence little even those whose predilections might be toward the music of the past.

Almost a century had to pass before the wheel would turn full circle. When composers like Chopin, Mendelssohn, Schumann, and Liszt, all romantic emotionalists, discovered Bach and the emotion that lay under his technique, they regarded him with amazement and adoration. Schumann declared that music owed him a debt as great as religion owed to its founder; for Wagner he was "the most stupendous miracle in all music." With Mendelssohn's revival of the *St. Matthew Passion* in 1829 the Bach resurrection began, and all through the rest of the nineteenth century the work of discovery and compilation and editing went on. It was not until 1894, after long search, that the composer's bones were found and identified in St. John's graveyard. By that time he needed no epitaph but his name.

The history of mankind has recorded no greater achievement than his, in the entire realm of human endeavor that is called art.

# Handel
## 1685—1759

I

If the baroque era in music had produced but one creative artist of the stature of Bach, history might well record that the entire age had richly justified itself. But, incredibly, Bach did not stand alone. The same age and the same country produced a second composer of gigantic stature and achievement—George Frideric Handel.

The two men could hardly have been more different— in personality and temperament, in their careers, and in their private lives. Bach was the introspective, mystic-minded servant of the church, the devoted family man who lived most of his life in seclusion, and whose art was dedicated chiefly to the adornment of the church liturgy. His public was the congregation.

Handel was a man of the world who left his name and art emblazoned on the pages of eighteenth-century English history. He never married. His life was the theater. He was composer, virtuoso, impresario, and businessman, and he made and lost fortunes trying to please the opera public of London. At least twice he was near bankruptcy, and twice he went on to triumphant solvency. All his life he was a storm center—of backstage bickering among prima donnas and castrati, of the machinations of rival composers and managers, and of court intrigue that extended even up to personal vendettas between members of England's royal family. Stubbornly, resolutely, Handel took it all in his giant stride, as with torrents of energy he poured forth a stream of more than forty operas, twenty oratorios, and hundreds of shorter pieces—a lifework almost equal in bulk to the combined efforts of Bach and Beethoven. When he died, the English nation tendered its thanks with a tomb in Westminster Abbey.

Handel was born in Halle, Germany, in 1685, the son of a barber-surgeon. As a child he learned to play the organ, harpsichord, violin, and oboe, and he had excellent instruction in composition. His dour, strait-laced father wanted him to study the law, but instead he became organist at a church in Halle and quickly developed into a virtuoso. In 1703 young Handel went to Hamburg, where he played in the second violin section of an opera orchestra. Two years later he composed an opera, *Almira*, which was an instant success. But Hamburg could not hold him long, because Italy, the golden land of opera, was beckoning.

During the years from 1706 to 1710 Handel was a pilgrim in Florence, Rome, Naples, and Venice, where he was fascinated by Italian opera, oratorio, cantata, and chamber music. The tall, handsome young Saxon was bursting with creative energy and virtuosity. His prodigious skill at the organ and harpsichord gained him entree to the most exclusive society and the most sumptuous palaces. He composed an opera, *Rodrigo*, which was produced in Florence in 1707. Two years later his *Agrippina* was an immense success, but now Italy could not hold him. In 1710 he went to London, and for the rest of his life England became his home, artistically and spiritually.

Writes Paul Henry Láng: "He acquired his means of expression, his forms, and his technique from German, Italian, and French traditions, but the climate which ripened this equipment into a great, free art was that of English civilization and culture."

Handel went to London at a time when there was a void in English music. Fifteen years before, Henry Purcell had died. At the end of his brief life span (1659–95) Purcell had left England a rich legacy of anthems, songs, cantatas, odes, instrumental works, and incidental music for the stage, all crowned by his operatic masterpiece, *Dido and Aeneas*. He was one of a royal line of English composers that had extended back to Tudor days. But he was the last of that line.

We cannot trace here the magnificent flowering of English music, which, in the fifteenth and sixteenth centuries, had matched the finest music of Italy and the Netherlands. We can but mention names like Thomas Tallis (c. 1505–85), called the father of English church music, and a great master of the contrapuntal art; his pupil, William Byrd (1543–1623), who excelled in so many fields—church music, the madrigal, early keyboard music—that he has been called by Paul Henry Láng "after Shakespeare, the most imposing figure of the English Renaissance"; Byrd's pupil, Thomas Morley (1557–1602), composer of instrumental music, and eminent madrigalist; Thomas Weelkes (c. 1575–1623) and John Wilbye (1574–1638), both composers of exquisite madrigals; John Dowland (1562–1626), one of the first composers of solo songs with lute accompaniment; Orlando Gibbons (1583–1625), organist at Westminster Abbey, a gifted madrigalist, and a pioneer in chamber music; John Bull (c. 1562–1628), a keyboard virtuoso who composed brilliantly for organ and virginals; and John Blow (1649–1708), versatile composer, organist at Westminster Abbey, and teacher of Purcell.

With Purcell's death at the end of the seventeenth century, it seemed that the glorious tree of English music had withered and died. Now the aristocracy of London wanted only Italian opera, and so, on February 24, 1711, George Frideric Handel gave them his *Rinaldo*. He had composed it in a fortnight. It was a masterpiece, and a resounding success, and from that moment the composer's life and the history of English music were pointed toward a new destiny.

II

Opera as a recognizable art form had begun in Florence, just after the year 1600, when a small group of scholars

and amateur musicians tried to re-create the ancient Greek
mode of presenting tragic drama—that is, as speech with
musical accompaniment. In the earliest of these Florentine
efforts the singers declaimed the story of the drama in
musical tones, to a background of instrumental music that
followed their vocal inflections. This was the birth of the
dramatic "recitative" upon which the entire conception of
opera rests.

The first opera composer of genius was Claudio Monteverdi (1567–1643), who brought to the new art form an
already-distinguished artistry in sacred music and the
madrigal. His *Orfeo* (1607) is often termed the first great
opera in history. Musicologists find in this work, and in
Monteverdi's later operas, so many seeds of future procedure that they marvel at his prescience, his bold in-
ventiveness, and his command of emotional resource.

From nebulous beginnings the two main elements of
opera slowly took shape—the arias and the recitatives. The
arias were the songs, the set pieces that formed the main
body of the work, and they were accompanied by the
entire orchestra. The recitatives were the connecting links
between the arias, in which the singers acted out the
drama, singing their dialogue in notes that imitated
roughly the cadences of the speaking voice, to a light
accompaniment of chords on a clavier. Thus the early
opera composers, faced with the problem of wedding music
and drama, compromised by not wedding them at all.
In the recitatives they let the story of the drama and the
action unfold while the music practically stopped; in the
arias the dramatic action slowed down to zero while the
composer elaborated his purely musical ideas.

By the time Handel came upon the London scene, Italian opera had swept Europe in a craze of popularity, but
it had also become hopelessly stereotyped. The plots had
to be drawn from ancient historical or classic mythological
sources; the arias had to follow certain fixed rules, and
they had to be distributed among the singers in a fixed
order. The singers, in fact, now ruled the lyric theater. It
was the golden age of the vocal art, especially of the great
castrati who carried the classical Italian *bel canto* style to

a peak of perfection never since approached. What the public came to hear was singing, the more spectacular the better. As a result, what the average opera composer produced was merely a collection of from twenty to thirty arias and duets loosely strung together by means of a libretto (often in execrable verse) that ignored even the pretense of true dramatic action, but was designed chiefly to provide a vocal springboard for the singers.

Handel did not quarrel with these conventions; he used them to the hilt. Year after year, in opera after opera, he poured forth arias by the hundred—a flood of vocal melody of incredible richness, variety, dramatic intensity, and emotional range. Almost equal in melodic beauty were his recitatives, while his command of sheer theatrical effect was unsurpassed in his time.

Only a man of gigantic stature, stamina, and will power could have lived through a career like Handel's in London. It was a battle fought on three levels—musical, financial, and social—with the ebb and flow of fortune carrying him back and forth between triumph and defeat. After the first production of *Rinaldo* the composer became famous overnight, and the idol of London. In 1713 he produced *Teseo*, another success; but the manager absconded with the proceeds. In 1717 Handel became composer in residence at Canons, the estate of the enormously wealthy war profiteer who later became Duke of Chandos; but working under the patronage system did not please the Saxon composer. In 1719 he was back in London as head of the newly formed Royal Academy of Music, producing Italian opera under the aegis of King George I, who, as Elector of Hanover, had already been Handel's sovereign and friend. At first the venture was a success, and during the next six years Handel created some of his finest operas—*Radamisto*, *Floridante*, *Ottone*, *Giulio Cesare*, *Tamerlano*, and *Rodelinda*.

With the accession of George II, in 1727, the composer and his operas became a political issue, the center of a poisonous family quarrel between the new King and his son, Frederick, Prince of Wales. Because the King, and Queen Caroline, warmly admired Handel's music, the

Prince did everything in his power to defame and destroy it. The battle lines were drawn with the King, the Whigs, and the Handelians on one side, ranged against the Prince of Wales, the Tories, the Jacobites, and a rival Italian opera composer, Giovanni Battista Buononcini, on the other.

In 1728 Handel's fortunes received a catastrophic blow from an unexpected quarter—the production of John Gay's *The Beggar's Opera*. This earthy, tuneful satire not only ridiculed opera but also stole the business away from the Italian opera company. Later, as Handel tried to stave off ruin, the Prince of Wales set up a rival troupe headed by another Italian composer, Niccolò Porpora, with a brilliant company of singers that included Farinelli, the most fabulous castrato of the age.

For several years the glittering contest went on, with Handel grinding out opera after opera, often taking no more than a few weeks for the composition of an entire work. His enemies, adding personal insult to financial injury, campaigned against him in the press with caricatures that make present-day political cartoons seem like flattering portraits. He had become in fact a huge figure of a man, grossly fat, a gluttonous eater and drinker with a cyclonic temper. But even a Handel had his limits of endurance. In 1734 he appeared (writes his biographer, Newman Flower) "partly demented, a wild, hunted figure, throwing reason to the winds." By 1737 the London public had grown so tired of Italian opera that both companies failed and closed their doors. Handel collapsed and suffered a stroke of paralysis. Only a public benefit concert saved him from being thrown into a debtor's prison.

The stricken man went to Aix-la-Chapelle, and there, happily, his health was restored. He returned to London with a new idea in mind. He would try to find a market for his genius in the field of English language oratorio, in which he had already had several successes. In 1733 an Oxford University audience had hailed his oratorios, *Esther, Deborah,* and *Athalia.* (On this occasion the hot-tempered composer disdained the offer of a doctorate of music as not worth the required fee of £100.) In 1736

London had similarly acclaimed his magnificent *Alexander's Feast*, after the poem by Dryden. In 1738, in a space of four months, Handel accomplished a prodigious feat—the creation of *Saul* and *Israel in Egypt*, two of his greatest oratorios. In spite of their grandeur both works failed at their first London performances. So did Handel's last opera, *Deidamia*, produced in 1741. Late that summer, immersed in gloom and despair, the composer began work on another oratorio. In a space of only twenty-three days he created *Messiah*.

It was not London, but Dublin, that heard the birth of this masterpiece. Handel was called to Ireland late in 1741, and for the next nine months he was lionized and his works hailed by immense audiences. The first singing of *Messiah* occurred in Dublin, on April 13, 1742. London did not hear it until almost a year later, on March 23, 1743.

Handel had meanwhile returned to England and resumed the battle. One magnificent oratorio after another now poured from his pen—*Samson* in 1742, *Semele* and *Joseph* in 1743, *Belshazzar* in 1744. Nevertheless, a financial crisis again closed his theater, and again Handel was plunged heavily into debt. Then the tide turned for the last time. The stunning impact of the Handel oratorios began to impress the London audiences. In 1747 *Judas Maccabaeus* was a success. In a tremendous burst of creative fervor Handel composed *Alexander Balus* and *Joshua* in hardly more than two months (1747), and in a similar frenzy, *Solomon* and *Susanna* (1748). But as he struggled to finish *Jephtha* (1751), a new and implacable enemy assailed him. He began to go blind. Chevalier Taylor, the surgeon whose operation had ruined Bach's failing eyes, performed similarly on Handel's, and with the same results.

In the spring of 1759, when he was seventy-four years old and almost completely sightless, Handel conducted performances of ten of his massive oratorios, and with no sign of failing strength. As he conducted the aria, "Total Eclipse," from *Samson*, many of his hearers were moved to tears. *Messiah*, performed on April 6, was his farewell. A week later, during the night of Good Friday, April 13, and Saturday the fourteenth, he died.

## III

Handel's legacy to the art of music is difficult to appraise in the present age. His operas offer the prime problem, because the entire enormous bulk of this music was dragged down almost into oblivion with the decline of all *opera seria* in the late eighteenth century. The appearance of the comic counterpart, *opera buffa*, had practically killed the vogue of the older form all over Europe. The castrati, that anomalous breed, disappeared forever from the lyric stage, and without them many of Handel's operas could never be re-created in true musical focus. Thus these works were neglected for almost two hundred years, with only concert performances of isolated arias keeping alive the memory of the buried treasure. Shortly after World War I, in Germany, a brief period of revival unearthed for a time some twenty of the Handel operas; but the problems of singing, instrumentation, and stylistic convention still present formidable problems for modern opera companies.

With Handel's instrumental music—the dozens of concertos, sonatas, suites, etc.—the problem is one of inequality. Some of these pieces would hardly have survived without their composer's illustrious name, for they often had to be tossed off in great haste. Many, however, remain brilliantly alive, e.g. the finer organ and orchestral concertos, the *Royal Fireworks Music* (composed in 1749 for a public celebration of the Peace of Aix-la-Chapelle), and the incomparable *Water Music*. This last, an orchestral suite, is made up of pieces believed to have been composed for two "river concerts," that were arranged, in 1715 and 1717, for the pleasure of George I. A contemporary account of the second occasion noted that the monarch went out on the Thames on his royal barge, followed by another craft that floated some fifty musicians—players of "trumpets, hunting horns, oboes, bassoons, German flutes, French flutes à bec, violins, and basses . . ." Today, after nearly two hundred and fifty years, we still partake of the delight of the King, who ordered the glorious music twice repeated, both before and after a sumptuous supper at Chelsea.

With Handel's oratorios we enter a world of monumental vocal epics upon which this composer's fame has rested, and always will rest, securely. The Handelian sacred oratorio is a hybrid in which are blended the drama of the theater and the devotional fervor of the church. It is in reality a form of stage play, without costumes, scenery, or action, but with all the composer's masterful command of dramatic vocal writing—arias, recitatives, and above all, choruses.

In the Handel oratorio the chorus rises to a place of majesty comparable to its original significance in the Greek drama, and upon it the composer flung every last resource of his boundless skill. Writes Paul Henry Láng: "The stupendous polyphonic structure of the massive choirs alternating with powerful homophonous passages, double, triple, and quadruple fugues, the revived apsidal choirs of the old Venetians, occasional *a capella* passages written with a sure hand, majestic motets, inexorable *ostinati*, grandiose vocal *ciaccone*, chorale fantasias, simple choral declamations or choral recitatives, crisp dance songs, and burlesque passages in madrigal style, all find their place, summarizing with a well-nigh incredible richness and pomp the achievements of the baroque. Italian, German, and French sources are discernible in this ocean of music, but the wondrous beauty of choral setting goes back directly to the great English traditions of choral music, disclosing an intimate knowledge of the anthem and the Service, with Purcell standing there as revered godfather."

With the last of Handel's masterpieces the baroque age came to its towering end, and for generations English musicians would stand awed by this majestic display.

# Haydn
## 1732—1809

### I

In the year 1740, when Johann Sebastian Bach was wrestling with the difficulties that beset the cantor of a school full of rowdy boys, there was a certain eight-year-old peasant lad whom he would have delighted to add to his choir. At that time the boy was just entering the choir of St. Stephen's Cathedral in Vienna, and Bach died, of course, without ever hearing the remotest whisper of his name—Franz Joseph Haydn, the man whose destiny it was to crystallize the New Music, which displaced and for almost a century completely obliterated Bach's; the man under whose hands the noblest of musical media, the symphonic orchestra, was to be established and modeled and projected into the future; the man who was to give similar form and spirit and impetus to the string quartet.

He was born in the village of Rohrau, in Lower Austria, sometime during the night of March 31 and the morning of April Fools' Day, 1732, five weeks after the birth of George Washington. His father was a wheelwright, his mother a cook in the household of a nobleman in the vicinity. Joseph was the second of twelve children. It was a poor and crowded home in all probability, for when Joseph was only five years old his family gave him away. A schoolmaster relative noticed him one day imitating the gestures of a fiddler on a make-believe instrument and offered to take his musical education in charge. The child never again lived with his father and mother. During the next two years, at a country school, he learned to play the harpsichord and the violin, and to sing in the choir at Mass. It was hard schooling; Haydn said in after life that "there was more flogging than food."

When he was eight, opportunity arrived for the little boy working his way up in the world. It came in the person of the Kapellmeister of the great St. Stephen's Cathedral in Vienna, who was searching for boys for his choir. He engaged Master Haydn and took him to Vienna.

At St. Stephen's, Haydn's life was similar to that of Bach's youngsters at St. Thomas's. In exchange for their work in the choir the boys were boarded, lodged, and taught the elements of catechism, Latin, and singing. They also learned, at the hard workbench of experience, that churches supported by municipalities were generally pinched for funds, and that economizing meant short rations and hunger for the boys. To gain a little extra money for an occasional square meal, they were permitted to sing in street serenades, at banquets, and in the homes of the wealthy and noble, where they often filled the double role of choirist and scullery helper. Thus Haydn's first hearing of chamber and orchestral music, upon which he was to exert so profound an influence, was probably gained (as one of his biographers has remarked) "while he was running with an armful of plates from the kitchen to the dining room, in the mansion of some great nobleman."

In spite of his talent, Haydn received no special treatment at St. Stephen's. Once the Kapellmeister proposed that he be emasculated to preserve his excellent soprano voice, but his father refused permission. He admitted in his old age that he had never had a real master in music. He studied the harpsichord and violin along with the rest of the boys, but his first childish attempts at composition were laughed at rather than encouraged.

When Haydn was seventeen years old, he found out what eighteenth-century churches had in store for choirboys after their voices broke. Because he was no longer of any use, he was put out abruptly onto the streets of

Vienna. His wardrobe consisted of three shirts and an old coat; he had no money, no voice with which to sing for a living, and not enough skill on a musical instrument to play for one. Starvation was staring him straight in the face. He slept that night in the open air; and then a friend who was a church singer and almost as poverty-bitten as himself took him in to share a wretched lodging in a garret.

That was the lowest point in Joseph Haydn's life. From then on he was to rise in the world, slowly but steadily, until he became one of the most illustrious men of his time. Meanwhile, he did not waste time arguing with his own fate. Calmly, uncomplainingly he went through life, one of the most industrious, orderly, and good-natured of men. He had health, serenity of soul, and the inward driving force of genius. For him these were the ingredients of happiness.

In one other respect he was fortunate, for in any other city except Vienna he would very likely have starved. For several centuries the Austrian capital had been a catch basin for all the good-natured, easy-living peoples of the south—the Bohemians, Hungarians, Magyars, Moravians, Croats, Czechs, Bavarians—those who were at least slightly more interested in good food, beautiful houses, and generally pleasant surroundings than they were in commerce or war. With good food and good wine there must inevitably be song, and while making their city a distinguished center of gastronomy and civic beauty they also proceeded to fill it with splendid music. Every café had its singer or small orchestra, every palace its Kapelle. No person of wealth or rank would think of giving a dinner party without calling in a group of singers or choirboys. As a result the streets swarmed with serenaders who sang and played and danced for the delight of the Viennese. And that is how Joseph Haydn scratched for his living for ten years. He joined the serenaders in the streets; he fiddled for dances; he gave music lessons to children—anything to stay out of the potter's field.

All the while he was also struggling for a chance to learn musical composition. By a lucky chance he came to know Niccolò Porpora, who had written fifty-three operas and had been a rival of Handel in the opera-mad town of London. He was most famous as a teacher of singing, at which art he very likely had no peer. He kept one of his pupils, the male soprano Caffarelli, working at a single page of vocal exercises for six years, then turned him out to become one of the greatest singers of the age, the idol of London and Italy. When Haydn came to know him, Porpora was old, disillusioned, and near the end of his career; he was dirty and miserly, with a vile temper and a vocabulary made up of verbal sewage. Haydn became his accompanist and valet. In return, Porpora corrected the young man's exercises in composition. It was while accompanying Porpora's pupils on the harpsichord that Haydn probably learned most—listening to the filthy old tyrant expound the secrets of the vocal art, absorbing the priceless doctrine that melody is the soul of music, and that unless melody is properly projected, music remains earth-bound.

## II

When he was twenty-seven, the tide of Haydn's life suddenly turned. He became composer and director of music in the household of a certain Count von Morzin. It was an attractive post, with a salary of two hundred florins a year, residence in summer at a lovely castle in Bohemia, and a small orchestra of a dozen players at his disposal, for whom he wrote divertimenti and his first symphonies.

Haydn had arrived. Never again was he to feel the screws of economic necessity; so he celebrated his good fortune by marrying. He made an odd match. One of the men who had befriended him in Vienna was a wigmaker named Keller. Haydn gave music lessons to Keller's two daughters, and he fell in love with the younger one. But when he found that she had no intention of marrying and wanted instead to become a nun, he became engaged (with the father's urging) to the elder sister, who was three years his senior. Haydn married Anna Maria Keller in 1760. She turned out to be one of the most notorious shrews in history, bore him no children, spent his money extravagantly, and had no inkling of the fact that her husband was a genius. She used his music manuscripts for curlpapers and as underlays when she baked cakes. Haydn reacted to her just as any man of an amiable and uncombative nature would. He put up with her for forty years, until her death in 1800.

After two years with Count von Morzin, Haydn captured one of the most brilliant musical posts in all Europe. He became Vice-Kapellmeister in the service of the great Esterhazy family, whose wealth, prestige, and noble history place them almost on a par with reigning monarchs. They owned vast estates in Hungary, comprising immense tracts of land, hundreds of towns and villages, and a score of castles. It was to the ancestral castle of Eisenstadt, thirty miles from Vienna, that Prince Paul Anton Esterhazy took Haydn in 1761. A year later the prince died and was succeeded by his brother, Nicolaus "the Magnificent."

The Esterhazy income was so enormous that Nicolaus could not possibly spend it all—even after he had indulged himself in the usual fantastic luxuries of the time, including a wardrobe of uniforms studded with diamonds. There was not even a costly war going on; so Nicolaus decided to build himself another palace, even though he already had twenty or more. In the eighteenth century, when an enormously wealthy prince set about building a new palace, there could be only one model in his mind—Versailles. The French kings and all their fabulous doings had a fatal fascination for the nobility and royalty of the rest of Europe; and so when Prince Nicolaus planned his new palace a few miles from Eisenstadt his idea was to outdo if possible *le roi soleil*. Esterhaz (as it was called) was completed in 1766, and it was a masterpiece of architectural splendor, sumptuous appointments, and unnecessary expense. It contained more than a hundred rooms, all filled with art treasures, priceless tapestries, beautiful furniture, and books. Acres of land around the palace were given over to lawns, fountains, and flower gardens, to hermitages, grottoes, temples, hothouses, and deer parks. There were also two separate theaters. One was an opera house large enough to seat four hundred spectators; the other was a

marionette theater completely equipped with large mario-
nettes, elaborate manipulating devices, and scenery.

In the midst of this dream palace of artificial splendor
Haydn lived and worked for the next quarter of a century.
His position there needs explaining at the outset. He had
no social standing whatever; he was merely one of the
servants. He ranked as an "upper servant," it is true, but
between him and, say, one of the guests of the Esterhazys
there was a fathomless gulf. This was the common and
accepted lot of most musicians of the time. They remained
on a level with cooks, valets, and flunkies until Beethoven
(aided by the spirit of the French Revolution) demanded
and got the social distinction that he knew he deserved.

Haydn's job, moreover, was far from a sinecure. A palace
like Esterhaz was like a great modern hotel in that it
required a corps of trained men to run it. The various
chiefs in charge of the food, the wine, the gardens, the
servants, the prince's clothing, the musical entertainment,
all had to be men with executive ability in addition to
their special talents. The duties of the Kapellmeister (to
which position Haydn was promoted in 1766) were particularly arduous. He had full charge of the orchestra,
which meant that he had to see they they behaved themselves and that they all appeared neatly dressed in the
prince's livery. He had to look after the music and the
musical instruments; and twice a day he had to wait upon
His Serene Highness in an antechamber to receive orders
for the day. He presided over the orchestra rehearsals,
directing all performances at the palace and in the opera
house and marionette theater. For all these functions he
had to write large quantities of music.

The catalogue of Haydn's works produced for the Esterhazys is enormous—some sixty symphonies, forty string
quartets, five masses, eleven operas, incidental music to a
number of marionette plays, several dozen piano sonatas,
and no less than one hundred and seventy-five compositions featuring an instrument called the baryton. This
was one of the viol family, about the size of a cello; it
had six gut strings that were fingered, and beneath them
six wire strings that vibrated in sympathy. Prince Nicolaus

was passionately addicted to playing this instrument and fancied himself a virtuoso on it, hence Haydn's enormous number of baryton works. Haydn even learned to play this instrument, hoping thereby to please his employer. Instead the result was a chilling disapproval; Nicolaus made it plain that he preferred no rivalry. Practically all of Haydn's baryton works were lost in two fires that destroyed parts of Esterhaz, in 1768 and 1776.

### III

Working away year after year at Esterhaz, calmly and placidly, but with immense energy and thoroughness, Haydn produced some of the most beautifully wrought music in existence. He also proved himself one of the most original creative artists of his time, a composer whose inventions were to affect all music and musicians for the next two hundred years. Haydn himself said, "My prince was always satisfied with my work. Not only had I the encouragement of his constant approval, but being at the head of an orchestra entirely under my orders, I was able to make experiments and try effects. Cut off from the rest of the world, I had nothing to worry about, and I was compelled to be original."

His greatest work was done in connection with the symphony orchestra, of which he has always been known as the father. The extreme beginnings of the modern orchestra can be traced to the early seventeenth century, when groups of instruments were used to accompany the first Italian operas. Monteverdi used in 1608 an orchestra of thirty-six pieces to accompany one of his operas. From him, along with other remarkable effects (including the pizzicato and the tremolo for the bow), came the idea of a body of strings as a foundation for the orchestra. By the time of Bach and Handel this idea was well established, as indicated by the development of the concerto grosso.

One of the most difficult problems of instrumentation in the early eighteenth century was that of selection. A composer was faced with a variety of instruments of every description, some remarkably articulate and musically pleasing, others hopelessly archaic and unreliable. For example, there was the family of viols and their various progeny. They comprised at least a dozen different instruments of various sizes, shapes, ranges, and tone quality, including the violin, the violino piccolo (a small violin tuned a fifth higher), the viola, the viola pomposa (with five strings), the viola d'amore (which had two sets of seven strings, one set fingered, the other set vibrating in sympathy), the baryton (already described), the viola da gamba (a small cello with five or six strings), the violoncello, and the bass viol. There was also an important group of plucked strings—the lute, the theorbo (a large bass lute), and the inevitable harpsichord. The wind instruments were fewer in number; but their problems arose chiefly from the fact that most of them were extremely limited in their technical resources, and often they were so poorly constructed that even in the most carefully trained orchestras they were expected to sound out of tune.

By the middle of the eighteenth century, when Haydn began to write his first symphonies, the string group had been considerably weeded out in most orchestral groups. Violins, violas, cellos, and basses had demonstrated their fitness and superior resourcefulness and now formed a fairly permanent body of string tone. Of the plucked strings, only the harpsichord remained. Composers were trying to find a combination of woodwind and brass tone to match their excellent string tone, but the solution still eluded them. One famous Kapelle of the year 1740 had forty-three instruments, of which eight were trumpets and five trombones—more than Wagner used a century and a quarter later in his gigantic orchestra for *The Ring of the Nibelung*. An opera orchestra of 1754, of about the same size, had five oboes and five bassoons.

It remained for Haydn to establish a workable combination, and the matrix from which all symphonic music was henceforth to be built. Shortly after he came to Eisenstadt his Kapelle consisted of five violins, one cello, one double bass, one flute, one oboe, two bassoons, and two horns. As the years went by and his ideas on orchestration gradually developed, the Kapelle was enlarged. When he had reached the height of his career, on the occasion of his first visit to London in 1791, he was writing for an orchestra of from thirty-five to forty players, comprising sixteen violins, four violas, three cellos, four double basses, two flutes, two oboes, two bassoons, two horns, two trumpets, and two tympani. Later, following the lead of Mozart, he added two clarinets to his woodwind section.

It is noteworthy that, of all the instruments that Haydn ignored in his symphonic writing, all except one have become obsolete and have never succeeded in re-entering the orchestra. The exception was the trombone, which, curiously enough, Haydn used in his operas but refused admission to his symphonies. (Mozart did exactly the same thing; and it remained for Beethoven to establish this instrument in the symphonic brass section.) The only instrument that Haydn used which has since dropped out of the orchestra was the harpsichord. But even with Haydn the harpsichord survived in the ensemble more as a conventional appendage than as a necessity. It had long been the custom for the leader of an orchestral group (often the composer) to conduct from the harpsichord. His part generally consisted of a kind of musical shorthand known as "figured bass," which provided him with the proper chords to be struck as the music progressed, and by which he could establish the rhythm and tempo, and generally keep the orchestra playing together. In Haydn's later years, however, ensemble playing had improved to such an extent that the harpsichord as a rhythmic policeman was no longer needed, and it quietly disappeared from the scene.

In his treatment of orchestral forces Haydn also set standards that composers follow to this day. For years he studied the tonal qualities and resources of the various instruments, something that very few of his predecessors understood. They usually treated all instruments in much the same way, giving them the same work to do, in spite of the fact that some were best fitted to play long, sustained notes, while others were valuable for their agility. Bach, for example, often wrote for the trumpet as if it had the dexterity of a violin—passages so florid and so completely outside the native possibilities of the instrument that even the most gifted modern trumpeters attempt them only at the risk of apoplexy. Haydn learned to give each instrument the work it was best fitted to do. To the horns he assigned the long, sustained notes that form a foundation of chords under the rest of the orchestra. Occasionally he also gave them small melodic passages, delightful contrasts to the string and woodwind tone, but always made up of notes easily within the compass of the instrument. Trumpets, too, he used to sustain and build up the general volume of orchestral tone, but he saved their brilliant high notes to add dramatic touches to the climaxes.

It was in his handling of the woodwinds that the master of Esterhaz performed his most remarkable instrumental feats. First of all, he built up the choir in size and power until it could really balance the strings. This meant that he could drop the strings entirely for a number of measures at a time and give the entire burden of work to the woodwinds, thus affording a fine contrast and giving the ear of the listener a rest from the continual string tone. It also meant that he could color and modify the string tone in soft passages by adding a woodwind or two to the various string parts. And of course there was his exquisite use of the woodwinds in solo passages, where they sang the melody as only woodwinds can. These and countless other devices Haydn worked out during his years of toiling at Esterhaz, until the symphonic orchestra had become an instrument of marvelous variety, flexibility, and resourcefulness; capable of a magnificent range of tonal color and volume, from the exquisite to the grand, full of subtlety and surprise, articulate to a degree undreamed of by any composer before his time.

IV

While this splendid early growth of the symphonic orchestra was going on under his hand, Joseph Haydn was also contributing to an even more profound metamorphosis that was affecting the entire art of music. This was the gradual conquest of the polyphonic style of composition by the New Music, or homophonic style. Not nearly enough has been written about this evolution to make it understood today other than by music specialists. The average listener realizes, even without technical knowledge of music, that early eighteenth-century composers like Bach and Handel wrote their music in a style that sounds to us rather archaic; and that the next generation, Haydn and Mozart, and their contemporaries, were writing in a style that was totally different and much more modern. The change that had taken place in that short span of years was nothing less than a revolution.

For centuries, most serious music except opera had been polyphonic, i.e., made up of two or more strands developed from the same melody and woven, by simultaneous presentation, into a harmonious rope of sound, with no one strand of necessity more important or dominating than another. This art of polyphony finally reached a stage where further progress seemed impossible. An overwhelming urge began to impel composers toward a simplification of musical style. Accelerating the movement was the rise in popularity of the keyboard instruments in the late seventeenth and early eighteenth centuries—the clavichord and the harpsichord—instruments which, by their very nature, demanded a simpler type of music. It was a comparatively easy matter for a choir of voices or an orchestra to perform polyphonic music and to keep the various threads of counterpoint clearly defined and easily audible; but to a single performer on a keyboard instrument the problem of handling more than a few polyphonic strands becomes insoluble—as anyone can prove for himself by playing on a piano some of the five-voiced fugues in J. S. Bach's *Well-tempered Clavier*.

The simplification that slowly took place assumed the form of homophony. Instead of a number of strands, all coexisting, all developed from the same musical germ, one of the melodic strands took the lead to the exclusion of the rest. The others were condensed and contracted into chords, which supported the chief melody at intervals, like piers under a long bridge. One of the great advantages of this idea lay with the listener, who could obviously follow much more easily the progress of a single melody, carefully featured and framed as it were, than that of a group of melodies all sounding much alike because of their derivation from the same thematic idea.

The homophonic type of music finally burgeoned into widespread use with the rise of Italian opera, which was built upon the idea of a single dominating melody supported by a simple accompaniment of chords. The older composers of the early eighteenth century still clung to their polyphonic style, resisting change; but the New Music spread like wildfire among the younger composers who were beginning their careers as J. S. Bach was ending his. Chief among them were several of Bach's sons. It was Karl Philipp Emanuel Bach in particular who laid one of the cornerstones of music history by his work in connection with the supreme structural design in the homophonic style—the sonata form. Joseph Haydn, following the lead of Emanuel Bach, helped to set music firmly and irrevocably in the homophonic pattern that has endured to this day. Coming as he did from Austria, which was steeped in Italian traditions, Haydn understood the newer ideas of melody; but he also had the Germanic concepts of rounded craftsmanship. The style that he evolved in his maturity combined the open melodic freedom of homophony and a modified counterpoint derived from the old age of polyphony.

Like every other great composer, Haydn was first of all a melodist. He said himself that "it is the air which is the charm of music, and it is that which is most difficult to produce. The invention of a fine melody is the work of genius"—a remark that ought to be painted in red on the walls of every music school in existence. For the inspiration of much of his melodic material Haydn went to an unusual source for his time: the folk tunes that came to him from the farmers and villagers around Esterhaz and from his own peasant ancestry. These simple songs saturate the whole body of his instrumental work. But even they do not explain the clarity and the spontaneity of his melodic style. It used to be the habit to speak of Haydn's melodies as if they were artlessly simple, lacking in subtlety; but only the blatantly ignorant make that mistake today. To examine closely some of his melodic ideas that seem most obvious is to discover that they are not simple at all, but that they have been subjected to the most scrupulous turning and polishing and perfecting. He never set down a note that he did not ponder over.

With the growth of orchestras and the improvement of the various claviers, composers had long been groping toward some large, well-organized musical form that would be commensurate in scope and dignity with their splendid new media. There were already in use a number of forms that embraced more than a single movement—e.g., the suite, the divertimento, the cassation, the concerto grosso, and the sonata. Most of these were loosely conceived structures, the details of organization and the exact number of movements often varying with individual composers. It was Karl Philipp Emanuel Bach who finally established the sonata as the leading multiple form, with a series of brilliant essays written for the clavier. At about the same time a kindred structure had grown up which was in reality a sonata for orchestra, and this had taken the name symphony.

There is no need to trace here the precise details of K. P. E. Bach's contribution to these developments. Suffice to say that what he started Haydn expanded, strengthened, perfected. Haydn was chiefly responsible for the peculiar thematic organization of the first movement of the sonata. In the old polyphonic music most of the forms had been based on the development of a single theme and its variants. The first movement of the new sonata provided an important innovation: it was built on two themes. Moreover, these themes were contrasting and separately presented. The first was rapid, brilliant, declamatory; while the second was quieter, more lyrical, less bold. The presentation and development of the two themes was carried on according to a definite set of rules, but with enough leeway to afford scope for the composer's imagination. What the sonata form really provided was a new element of contrast—a richness of variety in melody, mood, rhythm, and key—which had been lacking in the single-movement forms of the past. It was one of the best ideas in pure form that music has so far produced.

Haydn loved the sonata form and he spent the better part of fifty years experimenting with it, until he had produced more than a hundred symphonies, almost as many string quartets, and a host of small chamber and clavier pieces based on it. The symphonies and the quartets were the works which made him famous all over Europe, and which were to set the standards and permeate the thought of composers for the next half century.

V

It is not an easy matter to evaluate Haydn's music today, especially to the satisfaction of many listeners who are willing to admit the historical importance of the man and his accomplishments, but who are nevertheless disquieted by a failure to be greatly moved by the music itself. Many people today are bored by Haydn's music, and they are likely to attach insincerity to the motives of others who claim to love it.

The truth is that we are not living in the best age for the appreciation of an art of Haydn's type. The modern world of the arts has just passed through a century and a half of the most intense and variegated romanticism, followed by several decades of a violent realism. In the broad cyclical movement through which all the arts continually pass we are now probably at a point exactly opposite the age of formal, elegant classicism to which Haydn belonged. One of the distinguishing features of the arts on our side of the circumference is the complete freedom which the artist is allowed in expressing his emotions. We have in fact become accustomed to emotional orgies—in music, painting, literature, and even sculpture. Haydn's age was one of emotional restraint; the fashion in music was for abstractions, for classic designs with only moderately sensuous, emotional, or pictorial qualities. This type of beauty (of which Haydn was one of the supreme masters in music) does in itself call forth emotion in the sympathetic listener. True, it is a pure and rarefied emotion, too thin and subtle for many in this age; but for those who do find it, it is a lifelong fascination and delight. Musicians themselves are fortunate in this respect. The most ardent admirers of the Haydn type of music are generally those gifted enough to be able to play it. For them there are few deeper joys in music than the closeup view of this beautifully refined art in all its subtle ramifications.

The real lover of Haydn's music is always careful to take it for exactly what it is—a product brimming with melodic freshness and charm, exquisite in design, perfect in craftsmanship, and definitely one-sided. It is one-sided not alone in style but also in mood. The composer's good nature was bound to permeate his work, and his music has always been famous for its joyousness. He was an optimist by nature and habit, and that fact is perfectly evident in the vast majority of his works. A revealing clue to the composer's own attitude is found in his sixteen Masses. Although Haydn was an ardent Catholic, he was not a man to whom religion meant the very heart of life, as it did to Bach; his cheery nature and his optimism were proof against morbid thoughts of hell-fire and damnation. Consequently his Masses have (for some) a disturbing secular quality that can only be described as lively. Mendelssohn said that one of them was "scandalously merry." Another ends in a presto in six-eight time—a movement so animated that it might easily set a congregation to dancing out of the church. Haydn knew perfectly well that many of the devout were shocked by the lack of religious solemnity in these works, but he said, "I cannot write them otherwise. When I think of God my heart is so full of joy that the notes gush forth as from a fountain. Since God has given me a joyful heart, he will forgive me for having served him joyfully."

VI

As the years slipped quietly by at Esterhaz, Haydn's fame slowly spread. Publishers in Germany, France, England, and the Netherlands sought his works, and often pirated them when they could not obtain them honestly. Kings, queens, and archdukes gave the composer their praise and patronage; other noble persons who visited the palace left him snuffboxes, rings, and gold pieces as mementos of their favor. But Haydn, genial, modest, and unaffected, went about his work year after year with methodical regularity. He seldom varied his daily routine—to rise with the dawn, dress himself carefully, and then sit down to his task of writing music. Every evening he appeared before his Kapelle, dapper and immaculate, in the pale blue-and-silver livery of the prince. He was far from being a handsome man. His body was too heavy for his short, spindly legs; his face was large, and marred by a jutting lower jaw with teeth that protruded through the lips; his nose was prominent, and made ugly by a polypus; pockmarks covered his face.

Haydn's life was a lonely one because there was not much entertainment for those at Esterhaz whose business it was to entertain. For relaxation he loved to hunt and fish in the forests and marshes that surrounded the palace; otherwise he could find little to do but work. Each year he longed for the few winter months when he could return to Vienna and enjoy the convivial life, the excellent food, and the companionships that were denied him in the servants' quarters at Esterhaz.

Haydn's admiration for beautiful women led him into one particularly incongruous romance. In 1779 a young singer named Luigia Polzelli and her husband, a violinist, were engaged at Esterhaz. They stayed for a year and a half, during which time Haydn, then forty-seven, fell in love with Luigia, who was nineteen. One tie of sympathy between them was the fact that each was married to an uncongenial spouse; another, in the case of the lady, was undoubtedly the sums of money that Haydn regularly sent her on request for a number of years after she left the palace. When ten years had elapsed the husband, with seeming co-operation, died; and Haydn was moved to remark in his letter of condolence to the widow: "Perhaps that moment may yet arrive which we have so often desired, when two pairs of eyes will be closed. Here is one pair shut! But what of the other? May it be as God wills!" The second pair were slow in shutting. Eleven more years went by before Anna Maria Haydn finally died, and by that time the composer was sixty-eight. Luigia then got him to sign a legal document in which he promised to marry her in case he should consider marrying again and to leave her an annual income on his death. The first part of the promise was soon revoked by Luigia herself, when she married an Italian singer; the second part was faithfully carried out, with Haydn's characteristic lack of resentment, when he bequeathed her an annuity in his will.

One of the happiest associations in Haydn's life was the friendship which grew up between him and Mozart. The occasion of their first meeting is not known; but it was sometime in 1781 or 1782, during one of Haydn's winter visits to Vienna. Mozart was twenty-five, Haydn close to fifty. The younger man was traveled and experienced far beyond his years; from childhood he had known public adulation. He was witty, charming, ebullient, though at intervals morbidly despondent—and he was divinely gifted in music. Haydn was drawn to him instantly in spite of the disparity in their years, lives, and natures; the bond of affection between them was based on sincere admiration. Mozart said that Haydn was "the first man who taught me how to write quartets"; and Haydn told Mozart's father, "I declare to God, as a man of honor, that your son is the greatest composer of whom I have ever heard." Throughout the remainder of their lives the work of each was profoundly influenced by the other. It was not a rivalry in any sense, but a mutual stimulation that spurred them to do their best work.

## VII

In the year 1790 the magnificent and beloved Prince Nicolaus died; and his heir, having no taste for music, dismissed the Kapelle. For the first time in twenty-eight years Haydn was out of a job. He went back to Vienna and settled himself down with the idea of spending the rest of his days in leisurely enjoyment of the charming city and his friends. Hardly had he arrived when a man came to see him, saying, "I am Salomon, of London. I have come to fetch you." To the astonished composer the man proposed a trip to London for a series of concerts. Haydn was to compose an opera, for which he would be paid three hundred pounds; for six new symphonies he was to get five hundred pounds, and for some twenty other compositions, two hundred pounds. He was guaranteed a further two hundred pounds from a benefit concert.

The composer, bewildered by the boldness of the scheme, at first had qualms. But Salomon was not to be talked down. This remarkable man was the forerunner of the modern impresario. He had been an accomplished violinist, quartet player, and Kapellmeister before he established a reputation in London as an organizer of subscription concerts. He was that rare combination, a cultured musician and able financial manager. When he heard of the death of Prince Nicolaus, he sped to Vienna, for he knew the magic in the name of Joseph Haydn; and above all he knew the peculiarly fortuitous circumstances that presented themselves in London at that time. The city typified the country in general, which was producing no important native music of its own; yet there was an urgent demand for music of every kind, especially the best. Fifty years before, Handel had become a national hero by supplying London with magnificent operas and oratorios. Salomon knew that the time was ripe for the appearance of another great musical personality.

Haydn arrived in London on New Year's Day, 1791, and was accorded not merely a triumph, but a whole series of triumphs. Musical associations fell over one another trying to honor him by playing his works and giving him medals; ambassadors and other noble persons called on him in droves; he was invited to St. James's Palace and received by the Prince of Wales, afterward George IV. ("He is the handsomest man on God's earth," wrote Haydn. "He has an extraordinary love for music and a great deal of feeling, but very little money.") Invitations to dinners and banquets poured in upon him until he had no time to compose or to rest, and he had to limit his acceptances to those from persons of title.

The first of Salomon's concerts took place in March. It was a splendid success, with the composer, who presided at the harpsichord, receiving ovation after ovation. The subsequent concerts of the series enjoyed similar success, and all through the rest of the year the public enthusiasm for Haydn showed no signs of abating. He went to Oxford and received a degree, after which he recorded in his diary, "I had to pay one and a half guineas for the bell peals at Oxforth [sic] when I received the doctor's degree, and half a guinea for the gown." He was a guest at a gargantuan public banquet and ball given by the Lord Mayor of London and attended by twelve hundred persons; but the composer was bewildered and oppressed by the uproar, the continual shouting of toasts, the intense heat, and the bad music for the dancing. Besides various members of the royal family and the nobility, he met many other celebrities of the time, including Sir Joshua Reynolds; Bartolozzi, the famous engraver; Herschel, the great astronomer; innumerable musicians, and various hostesses noted for their dinners and salons. The beautiful ladies especially enchanted him. There was a certain Mrs. Schroeter who fell desperately in love with him, and in the early months of 1792 an affair developed between them. Haydn said later, "She was lovely and amiable, and I should in all likelihood have married her if I had been single."

During all this activity Haydn was obliged to find time to compose the various works that he had pledged to Salomon. Meanwhile, a rival management tried to cash in on the Haydn success. They brought to London Ignaz Pleyel, a young and inconsequential composer and former pupil of Haydn's, and they set him up as a counterattraction. All through the spring of 1792 the rival concerts contended for the public favor. It was all in the spirit of clean sport; both composers paid courteous visits to each other's concerts. But Haydn had to work like a galley slave to complete his music. "My eyes have suffered," he wrote, "and I have written many a time all through the night. . . . I am tired out, exhausted with so much toil, and I long for rest with all my heart."

In June 1792 he was at last able to start for home, worn out by the activity of a decade crowded into a year and a half. He returned to Vienna, bought a house with some of his London profits, and settled down to rest. He was saddened by the loss of his friend Mozart, who had died during his absence; but just at this time another young genius of music came into his life when the twenty-one-year-old Ludwig van Beethoven became his pupil. Unfortunately there was no repetition of the Mozart association. Haydn was an indifferent teacher; and Beethoven, impatient and headstrong, his imagination already filled with grandiose ideas, considered the older man stodgy and behind the times. The lessons did not last long. After a period of rest, Haydn again listened to the persuasive voice of Salomon, who wanted another series of London concerts and six more symphonies. So, early in 1794, the composer arrived in London for a second visit of eighteen months.

The triumphs of the first visit were repeated except that the frenzied excitement had calmed down somewhat, and Haydn was able to conserve his strength and enjoy a more reasonable regimen of work and entertainment. The twelve Salomon concerts were again tremendously successful, and so were the six new symphonies. The composer was officially invited to make a permanent home in England. The ultimate honor descended upon him when he was presented to King George III, at a concert at York House. The King remarked, "You have written a great deal, Dr. Haydn." "Yes, sire," the composer replied, "more than is good for me." The visit came to an end in August 1795, when Haydn returned to Vienna with another twelve hundred pounds, a further assurance that he could end his days in peace and security. He also brought home with him the usual collection of odd gifts which the public (for reasons not entirely clear) insist upon sending to celebrities—whether musicians, statesmen, or cinema stars. Among Haydn's specimens were a valuable talking parrot and half a dozen pairs of stockings embroidered with the notes of some of his best-known musical themes.

The most astonishing thing of all about Haydn's two London visits is the fact that, in spite of the quantity of music he had to produce and the strenuous conditions under which he had to produce it, his work during this period is the finest of his entire career. The twelve Salomon symphonies continue to this day to be the most representative and the most frequently performed of all his instrumental works. Most popular are the "Clock" Symphony, the "Surprise" Symphony, the "Military" Symphony, and the Symphony "With the Drum Roll"; but every one of the twelve is exemplary of Haydn's genius at its summit, larger in scope than anything he had done before, overflowing with his best melodies, controlled and shaped at every point by his maturest technical mastery.

Haydn wrote about a hundred symphonies (a hundred and four is the exact figure set by expert Haydn editors). Of these only about twenty are played with any degree of frequency today. Many of the rest are never played at all, for the reason that they have never been published. They lie in European archives and in the hands of private individuals. They have been slow in reaching modern performance because they often require the most careful editing by musicologists, to correct mistakes caused by the haphazard publishing methods of the eighteenth century, and in many cases to establish their authenticity. Thus we actually know today only a fraction of Haydn's immense volume of orchestral work. It may seem that we are therefore judging him on the basis of very incomplete data, and that knowledge of what lies hidden in the unpublished works might alter completely our estimates of him as a composer. This is unlikely. As the unknown works have gradually appeared in publication they have invariably substantiated rather than challenged the views long held about Haydn—about his craftsmanship, his remarkable inventive powers, his genius for finding new

ways of performing his routine tasks, his steady growth
as an artist.

Haydn was thus one of those artists whose genius ripens
slowly, for the Salomon symphonies were written after he
had reached the age of fifty-eight. And after them he was
to crown his life's work with his two oratorios, *The Creation* and *The Seasons*, both written when he was in his
late sixties. These however were composed under great
difficulty; the spirit of the old man was willing and eager,
but the flesh was weak. After the completion of *The Seasons* in 1801, Haydn was exhausted and finished. The few
remaining years of his life were spent in Vienna, his
strength gradually declining, his mind dimming; but full
of honors and at peace.

The French biographer Michel Brenet gives an affecting
portrait of Haydn in his last years. "Strangers admitted
to greet him found him seated in a big armchair, carefully
dressed in the old style, in an embroidered vest and a
coat of fine brown cloth, with breeches of black silk, white
stockings, buckled shoes, a frilled shirt, a white cravat,
and a long wig curled, powdered, and reaching to within
an inch of his eyebrows; on his finger, the ring from the
King of Prussia; and near him, on a table, his hat, stick
and gloves. . . . When he was in a good mood, he would
get his secretary or valet to bring in the relics of his career
which he took pleasure in displaying to his visitors. . . .
He grew animated when talking, ransacked his memories,
and delighted to tell the innocuous jests of his youth. . . .
At other times, his natural gaiety suddenly abandoned
him; he grieved over the uselessness of old age, and over
the loss of his memory; sometimes he wept."

In May 1809 the French army under Napoleon captured Vienna. Haydn was shocked and depressed by his
country's downfall; he was startled further one day by the
appearance at his house of a French officer. This man sat
at his piano and played one of the airs from *The Creation*,
so Haydn embraced him. A few weeks later the composer
died in his sleep.

There was a postlude—both curious and macabre—the
details of which were recorded by Olin Downes in the

New York *Times.* Haydn was buried in a churchyard in Vienna, but in 1820 his remains were exhumed by Prince Esterhazy so they could be transferred to a church in Eisenstadt. It was discovered that the skull was missing. Two days after Haydn's funeral two Viennese officials had secretly opened the grave and carried off the composer's head, their purpose being to study the theories of Dr. Gall, the founder of phrenology. When their act was discovered, they confessed and promised to return the skull to Prince Esterhazy. Instead, one of them sent him a skull from another body. This second deception was not revealed until the other thieving official died and bequeathed the true skull to the museum of the Viennese Friends of Music. There it remained for years on display with other Haydn relics despite the bitter demands and lawsuits of the Esterhazy family, who had built a magnificent mausoleum for the composer's remains but refused to inter them without the correct skull. Thus the matter rested for many years, until after World War I, when Austria and Hungary were split apart and the Esterhazy family, stanch Hungarians, left Eisenstadt, which was now in Austria, and in disgust removed themselves and their possessions to Budapest. Finally, in 1938, after the German conquest of Austria, the friendship of Hungary became a matter of prime importance to the Nazi government. By official act the skull was taken from the Viennese Friends of Music and given to Prince Esterhazy, thus bringing the head and body of Haydn together again at last.

# Mozart
## 1756—91

### I

The word "prodigy" is altogether inadequate to describe the childhood genius of Wolfgang Amadeus Mozart. At the age of three he began to pick out chords on a clavier. At four he received his first music lessons and at five he began to compose. He wrote violin sonatas at the age of seven and his first symphonies at eight. By that time he was famous in half a dozen European capitals for his astonishing virtuosity on the clavier, violin, and organ. He could play the most difficult music at sight; he could improvise for half an hour on a given theme; and he could write out perfectly music that he had heard played but once. Some aspects of his genius recall those juvenile wizards who defeat a score of their elders at simultaneous games of chess, or the young men who perform mental mathematical computations of astronomical size; except that Mozart's skill went beyond even those miracles. Such mental feats are essentially static and sterile; while Mozart, before he had reached the age of ten, had transmuted his talents into incredibly profuse powers of creation.

Mozart paid a heavy price for his gifts, for his personal life after his fabulous childhood was a tragic failure. He died at the age of thirty-five, leaving behind him a body of work staggering in size and of a quality that placed him next to Bach and Beethoven. Had he lived another twenty-five years there is no imagining the channels into which he might have turned the course of music's stream.

Mozart owed an immense debt, for both good and evil, to his father. Leopold Mozart was a violinist, composer, and teacher of unusual ability. He had studied theology, logic, and law at the University of Salzburg in southern Austria; but his natural interests led him to music, and he eventually became Vice-Kapellmeister and court composer to the Prince-Archbishop of Salzburg. He married Anna Pertl, a native of that town. She was an unusually pretty girl, with none of Leopold's mental attainments, but good-natured and full of gaiety. It was from her that her illustrious son inherited several of his most conspicuous traits—his high spirits and his love of nonsensical fun. The latter trait broke out in his letters, which are spattered with obscenity so coarse that his shocked biographers, all through the pious nineteenth century, were kept busy at the process of bowdlerizing, excising, and generally dry-cleaning his correspondence. Leopold had little humor; he was an austere, sarcastic man, shrewd and calculating. He knew music thoroughly; and in 1756, the year of Wolfgang's birth in Salzburg, he published a book on violin playing which became known all over Europe and which remained a standard method for more than half a century.

Leopold first discovered extraordinary talent in his daughter Maria Anna (called "Nannerl"), who was five years older than Wolfgang. It was while the father was giving music lessons to the daughter that Wolfgang, a mere baby, began to take noticeable delight in the sounds of music. When he was four the father began to teach him too. Within a year he was trying to compose little minuets; and then at last the father realized the extent of the stewardship that had been placed in his hands. The rest of Wolfgang's boyhood was devoted to one thing—music— to the systematic, rigidly enforced training of the greatest artistic talent the world has ever witnessed in a child. Leopold sacrificed the rest of his life and his own career to the task. For twenty years the precious son was hardly ever out of his sight.

In 1762, when Nannerl was eleven and Wolfgang six, the father took them to Munich to play before the Elector of Bavaria, Maximilian Joseph III. Later they went to Vienna where the youngsters performed for the Empress Maria Theresa and her family. On this occasion the affectionate little Wolfgang jumped up on the Empress's lap, put his arms around her neck, and kissed her. The Empress was genuinely touched; she had borne sixteen children herself. After that the Mozart children played repeatedly for the royal family, and they even became familiar with the Empress's children. Once Wolfgang slipped and fell on a polished floor in the palace and one of Maria Theresa's daughters, who was but two months older than he, helped him to his feet. Wolfgang thanked her and said, "When I grow up I shall marry you." The little archduchess was later married, not to a common musician but to a dauphin, with whom she met an infamous death. Her name was Marie Antoinette.

After the success of Vienna, the four members of the Mozart family embarked on a tour that lasted more than three years—through southern Germany and the Rhineland to the Netherlands, France, England, and Switzerland. Everywhere the children were a sensation. They gave a concert in Frankfort for which Leopold Mozart wrote a public notice advertising their wares: "The little girl, who is in her twelfth year, will play the most difficult compositions of the greatest masters; the boy, who is not yet seven, will perform on the clavicin or harpsichord; he will also play a concerto for the violin, and will accompany symphonies on the clavier, the manual or keyboard being covered with a cloth, with as much facility as if he could see the keys; he will instantly name all notes played at a distance, whether singly or in chords, on the clavier, or any other instrument, glass bell, or clock. He will finally, both on the harpsichord and the organ, improvise as long as may be desired and in any key. . . ." It happened that that Frankfort concert impressed itself with vividness upon the mind of a dreamy-eyed boy of sixteen, Johann Wolfgang von Goethe, who was present with his father. Sixty-seven years later the old poet-philosopher remarked to

Eckermann, his Boswell, "I still remember quite clearly the little fellow with his wig and sword."

They went on to Paris, where they presently received the call for which Leopold had been praying—to Versailles. Leopold was a prodigious letter writer (a habit that his son inherited) and he left a detailed picture of that incredible scene, especially New Year's Day, 1764, when Louis XV and the royal family dined in state, with a large gathering of distinguished persons watching them. The Mozarts stood in the crowd when the royal family entered, and "as they passed us they spoke to our Wolfgang and we then followed them to the table. . . . My Wolfgang was graciously privileged to stand beside the Queen the whole time, to talk constantly to her, entertain her and kiss her hands repeatedly, besides partaking of the dishes which she handed him from the table."

Though the Queen treated him with the same kindness that she would a pet spaniel, Wolfgang was less fortunate with Madame la Marquise de Pompadour. When he played for her in her apartments, which were "like a paradise, looking out upon the gardens," she stood him upon a small table that she might talk to him and look him over. He bent forward to kiss her, but she turned away from him coldly. "Who is this who does not want to kiss me?" he cried. "My Empress kissed me!"

In the spring of 1764 the Mozarts went on to London, where they remained for more than a year, appearing a number of times before the young King George III and Queen Charlotte. The royal couple were charmingly courteous, but Leopold was disappointed by the fee. It was only twenty-four guineas for each appearance, but at least it was paid immediately on their leaving the King's apartment. The Mozart children gave public concerts too, for which Leopold hired an orchestra. The music played was all composed by Wolfgang, and it included his first few symphonies, one of which he wrote in a house in Chelsea. After London, they went on a tour through Holland, then back to Paris, to Switzerland (where they just missed meeting Voltaire), and finally by way of Munich back to Salzburg.

## II

From certain aspects the grand tour had been a triumph, not only for Wolfgang but also for Leopold. It is impossible not to admire the courage and resourcefulness with which the father faced the task of transporting a family of four around eighteenth-century Europe and the adroitness with which he won the attention of the people whose attention meant most. He had a knack for getting introductions to the nobility, to high churchmen, to ambassadors, and even to royalty. That was all part of the game of patronage, and Leopold played it for all it was worth. He had to, because the public concert, a fairly modern invention, was just beginning to exist.

Even if the childhood tours of Wolfgang Mozart were not important in music history for the effect they had on the artist's maturity, they would still be noteworthy as a record of the workings of the patronage system. Leopold's letters bring to light facts long forgotten about that system, which made lackeys and panderers of serious musicians. In Mozart's time it was on its way out; another generation and it would be swept away, along with other eighteenth-century social, economic, and political refuse. But Mozart came in for some of the worst of it. Thousands of musicians in his day had no economic security whatever, for the reason that they had no way of reaching a large enough public. Lacking public concerts and royalty systems, they became the parasites of the Church and the aristocracy. A few of them like Haydn fell into comfortable berths; but for the great majority life was a struggle even more degrading than that of young Samuel Johnson trying to get a foothold in literary London. Many of them traveled around Europe in their efforts to keep alive, and they were treated not much better than gypsies.

When Leopold Mozart took his children to play in some great house or palace he never knew exactly what the fee would be, whether money or a gift of some sort. If it turned out to be money (for which he always secretly prayed), the sum might be generous or miserly, depending on the whim of the giver; and often he and his family had to wait around in some obscure town for several weeks while a slow-paying prince or archbishop finally got around to settling up. The gifts that they collected were remarkable, both for their value and their absurdity. There were rings, watches, coats, cloaks, laces, ribbons, armlets, and fichus; there were gold and silver boxes, and traveling writing cases, and there were snuffboxes by the score. Wolfgang got several swords, and Nannerl received "an uncommonly beautiful, heavy toothpick case of solid gold." As a result of this absurd custom Leopold had a hard time making expenses, even when the catch of gulden or louis d'or was good. Traveling expenses were often enormous, and wherever they went they had to keep up appearances.

Even worse than the moral effects of these years of polite barnstorming were the physical effects on a frail child like Wolfgang. In the eighteenth century a traveler in Europe had to contend with roads that were wretched, inns that were foul, food that was better left uneaten. One of Leopold's letters from Italy mentions the "preserved veal accompanied by a most fearful stinking smell," and wine that could not be drunk because it was a laxative. Wherever they went they were haunted by the fear of epidemics, especially of smallpox. In Holland, Nannerl became ill and was at the point of death for days. Then Wolfgang got the same fever, "an illness," wrote the father, "which in four weeks has made him so wretched that he is not only absolutely unrecognizable, but has nothing left but his tender skin on his little bones."

The modern parent who is conscious of a child's need for proper diet, hygienic surroundings, and, above all, regular periods of mental and physical rest, can only read of the ten most formative years of Wolfgang Mozart's childhood with mingled feelings of pity for the child and contempt for his father. Along with superb musical tutelage, the father gave the son a frail, spindly, and probably rachitic body, a nervous system that soon broke down under the shock and strain of life, and in some respects a character whose weaknesses were to hasten his death.

Shortly after the three-year tour, when Wolfgang had

hardly recovered from a severe case of smallpox, his father had him writing an opera, a little work called *La Finta Semplice*. Leopold could not pull enough wires to get it produced in Vienna, but he did get a commission for a second opera from the famous and wealthy Dr. Anton Mesmer, whose mesmerism later became the fashionable quackery of the day. *Bastien und Bastienne* was privately produced at the doctor's house, and in some ways is an astonishing work. Naturally its operatic conceptions are infantile; it is hardly more than a small packet of the most obvious musical clichés. Even so it shows the mental discipline of which Wolfgang was already capable as a child of twelve—a sustained effort easily comparable to the writing of a short novel.

The next year, when Wolfgang was approaching fourteen, the father and son set out for Italy—the last and by far the most formidable citadel of the music world which was left for the boy to conquer. At Rome young Mozart performed one of his most celebrated feats. During Holy Week he heard a performance in the Sistine Chapel of the famous "Miserere" by Allegri, a work that the papal choir guarded jealously, permitting no copies to be made. After a single hearing, Wolfgang went back to his lodgings and wrote out the whole score from memory. At Bologna he was elected a member of the Accademia Filharmonica after he had finished in half an hour a test in contrapuntal writing which often took the most learned musicians more than three hours. In Milan he completed an opera, *Mitridate, Rè di Ponto*, which was performed under his direction a few weeks before his fifteenth birthday. It was such a success that it received twenty performances.

During the next four years, in the course of three separate visits, young Mozart was received at the great houses and villas of Italy's aristocracy, the proudest in Europe; he was present at the country's most resplendent operatic performances; he met a number of the most famous musicians of the time, including Niccolò Piccinni, who was Gluck's operatic rival; he was decorated by the Pope. He met many noted castrati, and also the great Padre Martini, whose reputation as a teacher, music theorist, and historian was world-wide. Martini gave young Mozart lessons and corrected his exercises in counterpoint. The effect on the young man of these associations, and of the entire musical scene of Italy, was nothing less than profound. At his most impressionable age he was steeped in Italian music, the finest elements of whose style, idiom, and essential beauty were later to reappear, distilled through his own Teutonic genius, in the creations of his maturity.

At the age of twenty-one young Mozart not only had composed a vast quantity of music—operas, symphonies, string quartets, church music, concertos, and piano works —but also was a virtuoso on three instruments. No musician of his time could match his record or his potentialities. What he needed now was an appointment to some court, where he would be relieved of the business of making a living—just such a post as Haydn enjoyed at Esterhaz. No one realized this more clearly than Leopold. All through the son's childhood the father's correspondence is peppered with his apprehensions of what Wolfgang's future might be, after the boy could no longer cash in on his youth. As it turned out, the father's fears were completely justified. The appointment never arrived. Mozart's talents brought him little money and no security. His personal life descended into disorder, and finally into desperate poverty. The father stood by helplessly through it all, but was spared by his own death from witnessing the final degradation. Utterly inexplicable is the fact that the music, the fruit of those brief and hectic years, is one of the richest testaments of beauty in existence. It is completely unstained by the misfortunes of the man who created it.

III

Leopold Mozart's own appointment as composer to the Prince-Archbishop of Salzburg had been something of a sinecure. He was permitted to leave his post for long periods of time to make the various tours. But in 1777, when Wolfgang was twenty-one years old, a new Archbishop decided that he was not getting his money's worth from the

Mozarts. When Leopold asked permission to leave for another tour (and secretly to search for an appointment for his son), the Archbishop refused point-blank to let the father go. This left Leopold in a dilemma; although Wolfgang was of age, his father did not trust him to make his way alone in the world. The father finally decided that the young man's mother should accompany him on the tour. The day they left Salzburg, Leopold lay on his bed for hours, a soul-stricken man. The fabulous son who had hardly been out of his sight for a day, and whose triumphs he had always shared, had now left him for two years; and although he did not know it, he was never to see his wife again.

The young man and his mother had gotten no farther than the town of Mannheim when they met up with trouble—in the person of an indigent musician named Fridolin Weber. This man had a wife who was shifty, unscrupulous, and addicted to drink; and he had four young daughters. One of them, the seventeen-year-old Aloysia, had a lovely soprano voice. Wolfgang fell madly in love with her and began making extravagant plans for transporting the entire family to Italy, where fame and fortune would await Aloysia. When Leopold heard of this, he nearly died of disappointment and exasperation. He crushed his son's notions under a volley of angry letters, warning him of the end of a genius who did not keep his head—"captured by some petticoat, bedded on straw, and penned-in with an attic-full of starving children. . . . Off with you to Paris, and that soon! Find your place among great people. *Aut Caesar aut nihil.*"

Young Mozart gave in, and he and his mother went on to Paris. There another disappointment awaited him. At that time the music public of the city was churned up over the Gluck-Piccinni feud, in which the champions of the two operatic composers were engaging each other with all the acrimony, heat, furore, and buffoonery of a political campaign. No one had much interest in Mozart. Instead of the darling boy of eight in his satin coat and powdered wig and sword, performing his effortless miracles, Paris now saw merely an undersized young man with a small body, spindly legs, an oversized head with a mass of fine-textured hair and gray lackluster eyes—and with nothing whatever in his appearance to advertise his genius. The only appointment offered him was that of organist at Versailles, but the pay was so small that he could not afford to accept it. In the midst of these discouragements his mother died. He was alone now for the first time in his life, far away from home and without friends, so he left Paris and turned back toward Salzburg.

It is fortunate that the voluminous correspondence which passed between Mozart and his father during this period is preserved, for it is an eye-filling revelation of the minds and characters of the two men. Young Mozart had undergone a profound change. As a child he had been studious and even solemn; but with manhood he became high-spirited, mercurial, impulsive. He loved fun and nonsense of all sorts; he wanted to dance and play billiards, and in congenial company he was generally the life of the party. Like the typical middle-class Salzburgers from whom he sprang, he thought nothing of expressing his ideas in terms of the coarsest functional humor. To a young lady cousin whom he called "Die Bäsle," he wrote the choicest of the obscenities that stunned his early biographers.

Leopold was deeply disturbed by this change in his son's character. He realized that Wolfgang was utterly lacking in a sense of the practical, and that he couldn't hold on to money. Leopold wrote him constantly, advising him, begging him to give heed; and often the irresponsible young man simple glossed over his father's agonized beseeching or did not reply at all.

After the failure of the Paris venture and the collapse of his hopes for marrying Aloysia, young Mozart returned to Salzburg; and to his father's immense relief settled down to a dreary job in the Archbishop's service. The next two years were torture. He hated the dull town of Salzburg. He loathed the Archbishop (Hieronymus von Colloredo), and the prelate disliked him. The only bright spot in Mozart's life at this time was the composition of the opera *Idomeneo*, when he was twenty-five. The work was written at the invitation of the Elector of Bavaria, for a carnival at

Munich. It is Mozart's first opera of enduring quality. More than that, it is a work of seriousness and gravity; it has an emotional depth only hinted at in his music up to that time.

*Idomeneo* was composed under difficulties that would defeat any modern composer. The libretto was based on a turgid Greek tragedy, and it was supplied by Archbishop Hieronymus' chaplain, one Abbé Varesco, who knew as much about dramatic values as an eight-year-old acolyte would know of the canon law. The singer entrusted with the title role was sixty-six years old, several others in the cast were also on the shady side of their prime, and the male soprano had never before set foot on a stage. Mozart did what every composer in those days was expected to do; he accommodated his music to the singers, trying where he could to cover up their defects. *Idomeneo* is seldom heard today, although there have recently been two modernized versions, one by Richard Strauss and another by Ermanno Wolf-Ferrari.

The immediate result of the first production of this opera, in 1781, was a final break between Mozart and the Archbishop. At a meeting of the two in Vienna the holy man forgot his dignity and called Mozart "scoundrel, knave, and scurvy fellow"; and later one of his courtiers kicked Mozart bodily out of his rooms. Hieronymus has been excoriated by Mozart's biographers for this episode and his failure to understand that he was dealing with a great genius instead of merely a trying young man with an inflated ego.

Mozart was terribly humiliated. He refused to return to Salzburg at all, but decided to remain in Vienna. Thus he removed himself at long last from the domination of his father. In Salzburg, Leopold had to cling to his own precarious post with the Archbishop, with only his spinster daughter Nannerl near him for comfort. Meanwhile, the Weber family, who had a fascination for young Mozart of nothing less than evil-eye intensity, were also living in Vienna, and it was not long before Wolfgang went to live with them. Presently gossip reached the ears of Leopold concerning his son and Constanze, the eighteen-year-old sister of Aloysia. The true story of this romance remains obscure, but the prime mover was undoubtedly the girl's mother. Her schemes succeeded in August 1782, when Wolfgang and her daughter were married.

The story of the marriage is a pitiful one. The poor girl was far too weak in both character and physical stamina to act as the prop that Mozart's own unstable nature so badly needed. She was coquettish, feather-headed, and helpless, hardly more than a child, with no more sense than her husband of how to order their home, their finances, or their lives. From house to house they moved as their fortunes rose or fell, accompanied generally by a servant—one more slovenly than the next. In nine years Constanze bore six children, but only two survived infancy.

## IV

The steadily mounting flame of Mozart's musical genius had flared up brilliantly with *Idomeneo*; it blazed anew with another opera produced at the time of his marriage to Constanze—*Die Entführung aus dem Serail* [*The Elopement from the Harem*]. This work owed its existence to the fact that the National Theater in Vienna, under the aegis of Emperor Joseph II, wanted to cultivate a truly German type of opera in competition with the foreign works that then filled its repertoire. The libretto of *Die Entführung* was therefore in German, and the piece was an admitted attempt to translate the popular Italian *opera buffa* form into a thoroughly Germanic work. The Turkish setting of the story was chosen merely to cash in on the public's interest in the Orient—its color, romance, and mystery, and particularly the intriguing matter of its harems. Mozart tinctured his music lightly with what then passed for the "Turkish style," a style that he had used so charmingly in the last movement of his Piano Sonata in A major (K. 331).

When *Die Entführung* was first performed in Vienna, in July 1782, it was an immediate success, and Mozart personally received much acclaim—although very little money. The piece is often called the first real German opera, and there is no doubt that it provided the roots for the great tree of German operetta which flourishes to this day. It is also the first work of Mozart's in which he begins to reveal his incomparable gift for operatic comedy.

Another Mozart work of the same vintage is the "Haffner" Symphony, in D major (K. 385). Haffner was a wealthy merchant of Salzburg, for whom Mozart had previously written a charming serenade (in the same key) to celebrate the marriage of a daughter. Now this family requested an entire symphony. Mozart demurred when his father first wrote him of the commission, for he was busy arranging *Die Entführung* for wind instruments—a hack job but a difficult one. ("If I don't," he wrote, "someone else will anticipate me and secure the profits.") Nevertheless he undertook the symphony and turned it out in two weeks. It remains today one of the masterpieces of Mozart's instrumental work, and it would be an astute critic who could find the slightest sign of haste in its exquisite workmanship. Mozart himself made an interesting and revealing comment upon it. Six months after he composed it, his father returned the manuscript to him, and he wrote in reply, "My new 'Haffner' Symphony has positively amazed me, for I had forgotten every single note of it. It must surely produce a good effect."

Shortly after his marriage, Mozart began work on the famous set of six string quartets that he published three years later with a dedication to Haydn. These were by no means the first of his works in this form. His earliest string quartet had been composed when he was fourteen years old, during one of the Italian journeys. This was followed by a number of other juvenile efforts, and then he dropped the form for almost ten years. Sometime during the winter of 1781–82 occurred his first meeting with Haydn, in Vienna, and the beginning of their friendship. Haydn had just brought out his group of Russian Quartets. He too had hardly touched the form for ten years, and these new works were a fresh approach, more carefully wrought than any he had done before. Like a flint striking fire, Mozart's imagination was set off by the master of Esterhaz. For the next few years he studied the older man's work assiduously.

In many respects the string quartet is the most difficult of all musical media, for both the composer and the listener. The very size of the playing group—a pair of violins, a viola, and a cello—indicates at once the process of reduction, of distillation, with which the composer is faced. From every side the pitfalls of monotony ring him in: the four weak-voiced instruments collectively cannot approach the dynamic scope of even a single piano, and the range of their tonal coloring is even more limited. The symphonic orchestra, by contrast, has a way of hiding structural and even melodic defects; it can beguile the ear by the sheer opulence of its tone coloring. Not so the string quartet. Composing for it resembles the writing of a sonnet, in which the poet must declaim his ideas, however lofty, within the confines of a handful of lines. Every phrase, every word must be weighed with precision instruments, and then fitted into the whole pattern so that no joint exists to hamper the flow of thought. In the same way, every note uttered by the four instruments of a string quartet must be alive and glowing with beauty. There can be no padding. The composer's ideas are exposed without mercy; his workmanship is viewed through a glass and at close range.

It was one of Mozart's major triumphs that he could turn out, before he was thirty years old, six of the finest examples of the form in existence. Even though as a person he was earthy as a young peasant, Mozart was yet the most fastidious of musicians, and the string quartet gave him a perfect mirror for the natural elegance and purity of his style. It also gave him an opportunity to exercise his mastery of polyphony. During his boyhood in Italy he had studied hard the science of counterpoint, until he had gained a remarkable facility in applying such old devices as fugue, canon, inversion, and pedal point.

The finest of the six "Haydn" Quartets is probably the second, in D minor (K. 421). It is remarkable for several reasons. It is in a minor key, which Mozart usually avoided; it is suffused with an intense melancholy, a mood that was just beginning to find its way into the work of this man whose nature it was to seek the sunlight; and its poignant

Andante movement indicates a crisis in his personal life. It was written during one of his most desperate hours—in the early morning of June 17, 1783, while Constanze was in the next room giving birth to their first child.

Mozart himself never surpassed his "Haydn" Quartets, although he produced several superb works in the form of quintets (the fifth instrument being a second viola). The most famous of these is the great Quintet in G minor (K. 516), which is another of the infrequent confessions by the composer of an inner wellspring of black despair. Four of its five movements are expressions of gloom and heartbreak. Another great quintet is that in E flat major (K. 614), written in the spring of 1791, when death was awaiting him but a few months ahead.

The concerto is another form upon which Mozart left unfading marks. He wrote a long list of concertos for various instruments, including piano, violin, clarinet, horn, and flute; but the richest are those for piano. They were an indirect means of making money at a time when he was usually hard up. Because he lacked an appointment, Mozart had but two sources of income—music lessons and subscription concerts. The former were drudgery for him, but for the latter he created some of his best-known piano sonatas and his magnificent piano concertos.

Subscription concerts were part of the patronage system. Occasionally they were open to the public; more often they were held in the private homes of socially prominent persons, with the composer himself soliciting the financial assistance of his wealthy friends. Mozart gave many of these concerts during the brilliant social seasons in Vienna, and he drew the cream of the nobility for his audiences. The programs were nothing less than appalling —for both length and richness—often including two whole symphonies, a concerto, several arias by assisting vocal artists, a group of short piano pieces, and a session of improvising. Mozart was kept busy providing himself with new works for these concerts. This accounts for the fact that in his last ten years he wrote no less than seventeen piano concertos, along with hundreds of other compositions.

In the face of such prodigious industry it might sound like insanity to say that Mozart was a procrastinator, but at times he was. Often he put off composition until the last moment; then in a burst of activity he would perform miracles of speed. In one respect his creative processes were unique. During moments of seeming idleness or even distraction he would block out whole movements in his mind, often completing them mentally down to the last note. Then at some future time he would sit down and put what he had composed on paper. On one occasion he composed a sonata for violin and piano (K. 454) for a concert with a noted lady violinist. He delayed so long that he had time to write out only her violin part; he performed the piano part from memory and without having written it down. The feat was discovered by Emperor Joseph II, who noticed from the audience that Mozart was playing from a blank piece of music paper.

What Mozart accomplished with the concerto as a form was hardly more remarkable than what he avoided. The first requirement for a good one is simply good taste. Lacking that, it becomes the instrumental equivalent of many an old Italian operatic aria—a scaffold from which musical gymnasts may perform high dives. Concertos in general did not degenerate to this stage until the middle of the nineteenth century. Mozart's concertos would naturally be elegant and in good taste; but more than that he gave them dignity of design by building them on the solid framework of the symphonic form—with the first movement in the sonata form, a slower second movement in the style of a contemplative aria, and a fleet closing movement in the rondo, sonata, or variation form. Moreover, his orchestra does not merely accompany; it carries on jointly with the solo instrument the burden of real symphonic development. Practically all the Mozart piano concertos are first-rate Mozart, which means they must be included in any gallery of the finest music produced in the late eighteenth century.

V

Long before Mozart's time Italian opera had reached a morbid stage of degeneration. Conventions had grown around it like barnacles, until many composers, shutting their eyes to the preposterously stilted librettos of the day, could do little more than pander to the public demand for spectacular singing. The reformer who finally arose to attack the clutter of conventions was Gluck. That doughty, hardheaded and hot-tempered German fought for twenty-five years to achieve a more logical balance between the musical and dramatic elements of opera. In 1767, when he produced his *Alceste* in Paris (where some of his best battles were fought), he published a famous pronunciamento, in which he insisted that the music should follow, interpret, and enhance the story of the drama, not hamper and interrupt it; that there should be no vocal or orchestral display merely for the sake of ornament; and "there is no academic rule," he stated bluntly, "which I have not willingly sacrificed to dramatic effect."

Mozart was wild about opera. From the days of his boyhood in Italy no other musical form attracted him so strongly. With *Idomeneo* and *Die Entführung* he had begun to feel his powers, but for a long time he was frustrated, largely by conditions at the Viennese court. There, as in most music centers where opera was performed, the order of things was held in the grip of the Italian singers. Powerful cabalists in their own behalf, they looked upon the opera as their property, and they tried their best to strangle the attempts of native composers to gain a hearing. Mozart was one of their victims; until there came into his life, in 1783, a man of remarkable talents and background—the brilliant, eccentric, half-mountebank, half-genius, Lorenzo Da Ponte. This was the man who provided Mozart with the librettos for three of his four operatic masterpieces—*The Marriage of Figaro, Don Giovanni,* and *Così fan' tutte.* Together they made a team for the creation of operatic comedy which has never been surpassed in the history of the lyric stage.

Da Ponte was born in an Italian ghetto, in 1749, of Jewish parents. He subsequently embraced Catholicism and even studied for the priesthood. But a natural predilection toward women, those of a wide range of ages and a generously broad standard of attractiveness, soon weakened his piety, and he embarked on a career of amorous adventure only surpassed in that morally lawless age by his friend, Giovanni Jacopo Casanova de Seingalt. Besides a naturally charming manner, Da Ponte was aided by his striking appearance. His frame was tall and commanding, dressed in clothes of exaggerated elegance; his face was dark, his head long and narrow, with a jutting jaw and sunken, cadaverous cheeks; his eyes were deep-set, black and piercing; while between them was a great beaklike nose that bespoke the man's intellectual strength. He had in fact a considerable mastery of classic literature and for a time was professor of rhetoric at Treviso University. Gradually he acquired a reputation as a poet and librettist, and when Mozart first met him he had just been appointed opera poet to Joseph II. Sometime after Mozart's death, having made himself *persona non grata* in Europe, he turned up in New York. There he gave private lessons in Italian, and later became a farmer, distiller, and operator of a grocery store. In his old age he was the first professor of Italian at Columbia College. He died in New York in 1838, in his ninetieth year.

Da Ponte was not by any means a great poet, but he was a clever librettist. Moreover, he had a genuine appreciation of Mozart's genius, something that was generally lacking in Vienna. At his suggestion the two decided to write an opera together, gambling on Da Ponte's influence with the Emperor to get it performed. Mozart's choice for a story was the vivacious comedy, *The Marriage of Figaro*, by the French dramatist Beaumarchais. (Beaumarchais wrote a trilogy of Figaro comedies, of which *The Marriage of Figaro* was the second, and *La Mère coupable* the third. The first was *The Barber of Seville*, which had already been set to music by Giovanni Paisiello, and would be used again, a generation later, by Rossini.) *The Marriage of Figaro* was at first under a ban. Louis XVI would not permit its performance in France because it was a mixture of dangerous political satire and libertinism so unrestrained as to be a possible menace to public morals. Naturally this aroused the public interest in the piece to fever heat. In order to get the permission of Joseph II for his and Mozart's operatic version, Da Ponte had to convince the monarch that he had excised from the story all its politically subversive elements.

Be that as it may, the story is undeniably funny. Figaro, the central character, had been a barber in Seville, and is now a valet in the service of a Spanish count. This nobleman finds his chief diversion in the pursuit of women, among them the daughter of his gardener and the charming Susanna, fiancée of Figaro. His wife, the lovely and melancholy countess who still loves him, plots with Figaro and Susanna to expose her husband's infidelities. The ensuing situations revolve around the age-old comedy device, beloved by librettists from the earliest *opera buffa* to W. S. Gilbert—that of mistaken identities, with everyone at one time or another suspecting everyone else. Among the subsidiary characters are a young page, callow, silly, and adept at getting himself into compromising situations; and a formidable middle-aged duenna (a type also beloved by Gilbert) who tries to trap Figaro into marriage, but finally turns out to be his mother.

The whirl of amusing (if not too refined) nonsense that Da Ponte concocted was transfigured by Mozart into the finest Italian comic opera that had yet been created. Mozart wrote the score in six weeks, and on its first performance, on May 1, 1786, it was received by the Viennese audience with frenzied acclaim. So many of the numbers had to be repeated that the performance ran to twice its actual length, and at later performances the Emperor had to forbid encores.

*The Marriage of Figaro* is a prime example of what can happen when a form, beaten into a lifeless pulp by years of hard usage, is taken in hand by a great genius. In outline this opera is simply the standard mixture of arias and ensembles, punctuated by recitatives; but where it differs from its contemporary Italian models is first in workmanship—which is as finely drawn as a string quartet—and second in the quality of Mozart's melodies. They are so vital and charming and abundant that from beginning to end the opera never loses a champagnelike exuberance. Moreover, each melody contributes something to the character who sings it. This was one of Mozart's chief technical contributions to the development of opera. Before his time most operatic characters were mere paper dolls, types whom the audience could recognize by their costumes and their particular places in the plot. Mozart was one of the first composers to attempt genuine character delineation in his operatic music, and he had to do it without the aid of the leitmotiv idea, which was not widely developed. By this device Wagner, its most famous exploiter, was able to fasten a single descriptive theme upon an idea and follow it throughout an entire opera.

## VI

It is almost unbelievable that after its brilliant opening *The Marriage of Figaro* ended its first season in Vienna a failure. Only nine performances were given in six months, and the work was finally withdrawn. Royalties being then unknown, Mozart's only income from the opera was a small lump sum (about four hundred dollars) paid for the first performance. His financial affairs were getting steadily worse, so for a time he thought of going to England. There he might have enjoyed a measure of the good fortune that awaited Haydn a few years later; but the project fell through when he and Constanze realized that they would have to take their two small children with them. They first approached Mozart's father with the suggestion that he care for the children in their absence, but Leopold turned them down with disdain. He was now an embittered old man, still unreconciled to his son's marriage and way of life, still brooding over the ruination of his golden boy. He died the next spring. No record is left of his personal correspondence with his son during the last years, for after Wolfgang's death Constanze destroyed every letter that Leopold had written them after the day of their marriage.

Instead of going to England the young couple went to Prague. Mozart had heard to his amazement that *The Marriage of Figaro* had been produced there with tumultuous success. He found that the whole town was in fact mad about his opera. "Here," he wrote, "they talk nothing but *Figaro*; scrape, blow, sing, and whistle nothing but *Figaro*; no opera draws but *Figaro*, always *Figaro*." He went to a performance, was recognized by the audience, and for the first time since his boyhood received a public ovation that did justice to his genius. He received not a cent from any of these performances, but he did leave Prague with a commission for a new opera, to be produced there the following autumn.

Naturally he turned to Da Ponte for another libretto; and naturally too, after their success with the amours of the Spanish count in *The Marriage of Figaro*, they hit upon the familiar legend of the archlibertine, Don Juan. Lorenzo was busy at the time, preparing librettos for two other composers; so he had to parcel out his time, giving his "mornings to Martini, afternoons to Salieri, and evenings to Mozart." For two months (at least, according to his own account) he worked twelve hours continuously every day. On his table were a bottle of wine, a box of snuff, and an inkwell; at the touch of a bell there came (again, according to his own account) a beautiful girl of sixteen who lived in the house. She brought him food, coffee, and inspiration. "I should have preferred to love her only as a daughter, but alas!"

Mozart meanwhile came down with a serious illness, which sounds as if it might have been typhoid fever. The summer went by, and little of the opera had taken shape. So in August the Mozarts and Da Ponte went on to Prague to finish their task. By a humorous chance they met up there with Da Ponte's old friend and hero, Casanova himself. The one-time great lover had reached the black ashes of life. He was old, penniless, and envenomed; his voracious appetite for amours had vanished, and there remained only his ability to write about them. He was a librarian now, in the castle of Count Waldstein, working on his celebrated memoirs. No one could be better suited to give advice and counsel, as Da Ponte spun out his story of Don Juan, than this living prototype; and so legend has it that Casanova took a hand in the creation of Mozart's operatic masterpiece, *Don Giovanni*.

The *première* of *Don Giovanni* took place on October 29, 1787, a date that has become a landmark in the history of opera. Prague received the work with a hurricane of applause; Mozart, who conducted, was cheered like a national hero. On thousands of occasions since then the verdict of that audience has been sustained, for *Don Giovanni* is one of the oldest works in the repertoires of the world's opera houses. After more than a hundred and fifty years its vitality shows no signs of abating. *Don Giovanni* has been crowned with the encomiums of the greatest musicians and critics. Often it has been termed the most nearly perfect of all operas. Part of the credit must go to Da Ponte. His play is written with style, finish, and wit; it is filled with good situations, dramatic surprises, and a variety of interesting characters. In short, it is first of all a good show.

The notorious Don is portrayed in all his suave licentiousness. He has seduced women by the hundreds. His servant, Leporello, lists their number as 2065, including women from Italy, Germany, France, Turkey, and Spain; women from every station in life, from princesses to rustics; women of all types, ages, and degrees of pulchritude. In the opera Don Giovanni tries to despoil the virtuous Donna Anna, and when her father, the Commendatore of Seville, comes to her aid, kills the old man in a duel. He then tries to seduce a peasant girl, Zerlina, luring her into his home by giving an elaborate party. In this scene the orchestra plays music for three dances simultaneously, a waltz, a contredanse, and the famous minuet. Later, while hiding in a graveyard from still another amorous adventure, the Don receives a solemn warning from the voice of the dead Commendatore's statue. With blasphemous insolence he invites the statue to supper. It is a rash gesture, for in the final scene, while Don Giovanni is dining, the stony specter enters and invites him to supper. A pit opens and Don Giovanni is dragged down to hell by a chorus of demons.

Mozart took wonderful advantage of the highly dramatic moments in this opera—the duel scene in the opening act, the appearances of the statue, and the final damnation of the Don. His work is therefore a blend of the lyricism of his finest Italian operatic style, and the most effective dramatic music written up to that time.

Mozart and Da Ponte had one more collaboration. In 1789, *Figaro* was revived in Vienna with such success that Joseph II commissioned them to write *Così fan' tutte* [*They All Do It*]. It was produced in January 1790. The story, partly suggested by the Emperor himself, concerns two young Neapolitan noblemen who are engaged to two young ladies. A cynical bachelor friend of the young men doubts the constancy of the two ladies (and of all women, for that matter), so he lays a wager that they can be won away from their respective sweethearts. The two young men pretend to be called away to war, but return on the very same day disguised as Albanian noblemen. In short order each one woos the other's fiancée and gains her consent to marriage. Then the "Albanians" disappear and the original lovers return, to charge the ladies with their perfidy. All is soon forgiven and the opera ends happily.

*Così fan' tutte* fell far short of the success enjoyed by its two predecessors. It gradually came to be known as one of Mozart's few failures. Da Ponte's libretto was often blamed—either as a piffling piece of nonsense or as a downright affront to the moral sensibilities of all good Victorians. Modern revivals, however, have put the work in a very different light. The story is no more preposterous than that of many another comic opera, and Da Ponte's handling of it is exceedingly clever. Moreover, Mozart wrote for it a beautiful score, as charming and satirical as the little puffball of a plot demands.

## VII

After the productions of *The Marriage of Figaro* and *Don Giovanni*, Mozart's personal life entered a slow spiral of dissolution. Aside from his financial troubles, which grew desperate, there began a definite moral weakening. The free and easy life of Prague, the association with Da Ponte, a loosening of the ties that bound him to Constanze—all served to accelerate the decline. He drank a great deal and there were rumors of affairs with various singers in his operas. His health began to show signs of a serious breakdown; in certain portraits of him made at the time there is evidence in the sallow face, the haggard, protruding eyes. His frail little body was rebelling against his reckless habits, the alternating periods of dissipation and cruel overwork.

After the *première* of *Don Giovanni*, Emperor Joseph II in a burst of tardy generosity made Mozart court composer, a post left vacant by the death of Gluck; but at the same time the salary was reduced from two thousand florins a year to eight hundred. If the salary was a source of damage to Mozart's pride, the work required of him was even worse—nothing but inconsequential pieces of dance music for the court balls. Meanwhile Constanze's health had broken down from continual pregnancies and childbearing. She was obliged to spend many months at a near-by health resort, another drain on their resources. Mozart began to borrow money. Having joined the Masonic order, he turned to a fellow Mason, a man named Michael Puchberg, who was a well-to-do merchant and amateur musician. Puchberg's generosity in answering Mozart's numerous calls for financial help is the one ray of light in the gathering pall of misfortune that settled about the last years of the composer. During the summer of 1788, in the midst of these distractions and a sudden despondency caused by the death of a six-month-old daughter, Mozart began writing a symphony. He ended by writing three—and by achieving a feat of technical and inspirational speed that was without parallel even for him.

He began sometime in June, and by the tenth of August had composed the E flat Symphony (K. 543), the G minor Symphony (K. 550), and the C major Symphony, the "Jupiter" (K. 551). Any one of the twelve movements might well have demanded the time he took to compose the entire group, yet he flung them from his pen with breathless speed. Perhaps his haste presaged the shortness of the time left him. These three symphonies—quite possibly the finest produced before Beethoven—were his last.

Mozart's experience with the symphonic form was similar to that with the string quartet. He had written more than thirty symphonies before he reached the age of eighteen; but they are slight and immature works for the most part, composed chiefly to show off his precocity. When he came of age he turned to the form much less frequently. When he did it was to produce such splendid examples as the "Haffner" Symphony, the "Linz" Symphony and the "Prague" Symphony. Obviously, as a mature composer he began to sense the enormous possibilities of the symphonic form and the problems awaiting the artist who attempted their expansion. Here was no half-random collection of movements bound together loosely as a serenade or a cassation; rather it was a union of several complex designs, each a separate entity and yet subtly affecting the others, all joined to make a large architectonic unit.

The realization of these factors was clearly upon him as he wrote his last trio of great symphonies. Each has a separate mood, an individual hue, belonging to itself alone. Thus the E flat Symphony, after a slow, lordly introduction, streams with lovely melodies—warm, sunlit, and tranquil. The composer seems completely possessed by his youthful, carefree spirits. The G minor Symphony is suffused with melancholy. This was the brooding, dark strain in Mozart's music which startled his contemporaries, and which was one of the beginnings of romantic emotion finding its way into the classic forms. The G minor is the most often played of all Mozart's symphonies. It is also the most beloved, because it contains so much of its composer's profuse art at its ripest, and perhaps because in its gentle melancholy it reminds the listener of the fate of its maker

—like Keats and Shelley, Raphael and Schubert, to be divinely gifted, and to die young. As for the C major Symphony (called the "Jupiter" by no one knows whom, or precisely why), its last movement is a famous salient in symphonic history. The movement is roughly in the sonata form, but of a type that no one ever attempted before or since. The composer uses five separate themes and develops them fugally, spinning them into elaborate counterpoint, or singly in canon, and winding up with a coda in which all five themes sing together. The result is a triumph of polyphony worthy of J. S. Bach.

As for the symphonic form as a whole, Mozart's contribution to its growth was typical of what he did in every other form that he touched. He did not invent: he enriched. The larger outlines of the symphony he passed on to Beethoven much as Haydn had passed them on to him. He added a depth of personal emotion that Haydn's music did not have; otherwise most of his improvements were internal, and lay chiefly in the field of orchestration. He increased the size of the orchestra to gain a greater range of dynamics and thus a richer expressiveness. His handling of the woodwinds was superb. Besides adding the clarinet to the choir, he gave all the woodwinds a more important voice in the instrumental discourse. His sense of their tonal values was extremely subtle, permitting him to achieve effects of a delicate beauty that remain unsurpassed. After Haydn had studied Mozart's last symphonies he remarked that only then had he really understood the proper use of wind instruments, and he lamented that he was then too old to make use of what he had learned.

VIII

In July 1789, Mozart wrote to Michael Puchberg, "Great God! I would not wish my worst enemy to be in my present position. And if you, most beloved friend and brother, forsake me, we are altogether lost, *both my unfortunate and blameless self* and my poor sick wife and child." Puchberg responded again and again to these frantic calls, but it was no use. The money disappeared, no one knows quite how; the debts piled up. During the following winter there were times when the Mozarts did not have enough firewood to keep their lodgings warm. In desperation the composer began to turn out potboilers—innumerable sets of popular dances for Viennese parties and balls, and even a group of pieces for chiming clocks and music boxes. By the beginning of 1791 he was on the verge of collapse, and his output of serious music for the entire previous year had dwindled to almost nothing. Then there was a sudden awakening of inspiration and strength. He wrote the great E flat major Quintet (K. 614), and he began work on *The Magic Flute*.

The genesis of this opera was a vague train of notions in the mind of a man named Emanuel Schikaneder, who was actor-singer-manager of a third-rate theatrical company then performing at a cheap playhouse just outside of Vienna. Schikaneder was a coarse, vulgar man; but he was a shrewd purveyor to the public taste. His troupe played everything from comic operas to garbled versions of Shakespeare's plays. At the moment he wanted something that he termed a "magic opera," a kind of romantic fairy tale which would be a vehicle for spectacular stage effects then craved by the public. He approached Mozart, whom he knew casually, and the composer accepted the idea with avidity.

Schikaneder proposed to write the libretto himself, so according to his habit he stole an idea from a collection of Oriental fairy tales. As the work progressed, the two men found that a rival company had beaten them to the same story; so they switched the motivations of their characters, making the good ones evil and the evil ones good. Then, because both collaborators were Freemasons, they got the further idea of making the opera symbolic of certain rites and mysteries of their order. Due to this odd agglomeration of ideas the libretto of *The Magic Flute* is a ragbag of confusion, from which it is now impossible to extract meaning or logic.

The story is laid in ancient Egypt, and involves the search by a young Japanese prince for the lovely Pamina, daughter of the evil Queen of the Night. Pamina is held prisoner by Sarastro, a high priest of Isis. Tamino is aided in his quest by a flute which has magic powers. He is accompanied by a bird-man, Papageno, who has a set of magic bells. Sarastro is revealed as a man of such noble ideals and character that Tamino tries to become his disciple. But the priests of Isis decree that he must pass through a series of ordeals before he may possess Pamina. After various vicissitudes, and with the aid of the flute, the lovers are united.

Even though this libretto contained no vestige of sense (at least to those outside the Masonic order), it did have a kind of vaudevillian variety; and of this Mozart took full advantage. He wrote arias of solemn and mellifluous beauty for Sarastro, and magnificent choruses for the priests—music that reflects the Masonic background of the story. For Papageno, a clownish part played at the *première* by Schikaneder himself, he wrote comic songs in his best *Figaro* manner. To the malignant Queen of the Night he gave music that is pure Italian coloratura, full of vocal stunt flying and including a terrifying high F. Thus *The Magic Flute* is like a sheaf of samples of Mozart's skill in half a dozen different musical moods, each one representative of his art at its ripest and most opulently beautiful.

During the early work on the opera, Constanze, again pregnant, went to Baden; so to keep a close eye on the composer Schikaneder installed him in a small summer house (hardly more than a shack) near the theater. There the masterpiece took shape, Mozart pausing only for occasional drinking bouts with Schikaneder and his troupe. One day in July there was an interruption. A gaunt, cadaverous-looking man dressed in somber gray appeared at Mozart's lodgings and presented him with an anonymous letter. It was a commission to write a requiem, with the composer naming his own price. There was one condition: he must promise never to attempt to discover the name of the person who had commissioned the work. Mozart accepted, asking fifty ducats for the score; and then he began to be tortured by morbid speculation. His overworked mind conceived the idea that the gray stranger who would not reveal his name was actually the Devil commissioning him to write his own death music.

He had hardly begun before there was another interruption. The new Emperor, Leopold II, was to be crowned King of Bohemia at Prague early in September 1791, and Mozart was asked to compose an opera for the occasion. The subject was to be *La Clemenza di Tito* [*The Clemency of Titus*], a tedious Italian tragedy. In great haste, Mozart and his wife set out for Prague. Realizing that he could not possibly complete the opera in the short time left, he took with him a favorite pupil, Franz Süssmayr, to help him with the recitatives and the orchestration. During the journey they worked in the carriage and at night at the inns. At Prague the entire piece was completed, rehearsed, and produced in the incredibly short space of eighteen days—a nerve-shattering ordeal that broke the composer's spirit. At its *première Titus* was a complete failure, and Mozart wept. He must have realized that even his genius had its limits of endurance, and that at last he had driven it too far.

The terrible effort of *Titus* killed Mozart. He returned to Vienna in a state of mental and physical exhaustion. But rest was denied him, for he had to put the finishing touches to *The Magic Flute*; and after its *première* on September 30, 1791, the task of the Requiem still faced him. Desperately he wanted to complete that work, and heroically he tried—in spite of horrible attacks of sickness during which his hands and feet swelled and his body stiffened. There were times when the effort of work was torture, but he would keep on until he fainted. Always the thought of the gray stranger haunted him like a specter.

He did not finish the Requiem. By the end of November he was bedridden, but still he tried to go on, discussing the work constantly with Süssmayr, calling in groups of friends to sing the parts for him. One Sunday afternoon as they were grouped around his bed he gave them the parts of the Lacrimosa. They had sung but a few bars when he broke down, and they had to stop. He died in the early hours of the following morning, December 5, 1791, within a few weeks of his thirty-sixth birthday.

Constanze had practically no money, so he had to be given a pauper's funeral. At the last minute the few friends who went to attend the burial were driven away by a violent rainstorm. His body was placed with a dozen others in an unmarked grave, whose location the gravediggers could not remember when Constanze sought it out later. It remains unknown to this day.

IX

The Requiem, which was born in a caul of mystery, was destined never to be entirely freed of doubt. The circumstances of the gray stranger were a comparatively simple matter: the man was merely the steward of a certain Count Franz von Walsegg, a wealthy music amateur whose secret habit it was to commission works from well-known composers and then have them privately performed as his own. The Requiem was ordered for a memorial service for his dead wife, and it was so performed in 1793, with the Count himself conducting and posing as its composer. But the Mass was actually only half, or even less than half, Mozart. We know that he completed the first two of the twelve parts (including the Requiem, Kyrie, and Dies Irae), that he had left the next six parts in an unfinished state, and that his manuscript broke off entirely at the ninth bar of the Lacrimosa. After his death Constanze gave the work to Süssmayr to finish. He had followed the Mass from its inception, had talked about it again and again with Mozart; so he filled out the unfinished portions, constructed others from Mozart's sketches, and added whole new sections of his own. Not only was Süssmayr's imitation of his master's musical idiom deceptively good, but the final manuscript that he made and presented to Count von Walsegg was amazingly like Mozart's handwriting.

The result of this double deception and forgery is that no one knows how much of the Requiem is Mozart's and how much is Süssmayr's. The wonder is that the work contains what it does of Mozart's true greatness. His opening pages are superb, poignantly harmonized yet archaic in spirit, the ancient Church's expression of exalted grief. He rises to tremendous heights in the Dies Irae, painting the vision of the Last Judgment in a smoking, flaming prophecy. But thereafter inspiration falters; the commonplace ideas appear; only occasionally (as in the wonderful Confutatis) does the music match the text.

In a sense the Requiem emphasizes the tragedy of Mozart's own life, both as man and artist. His death was a destruction of genius even more grievous than the death of Schubert. Because he left such an enormous amount of music in so many forms, one is likely to forget that it represents possibly half of what he might have accomplished. Beethoven had almost forty years of creative life after he had passed his boyhood, and Bach had almost fifty. Mozart had less than twenty. Moreover, the finest of Mozart's music is so perfect in design, exquisite in taste, undying in melodic vitality, that it is difficult to imagine how he might have progressed beyond it.

The difficulty is increased by contradictions that seem to exist between the man and his art. Bach's music is a paradoxical union of mathematics and emotion; similarly, Mozart's joins emotion with the most austere and formal classicism. His operas are a blend of joyous, ribald human comedy with music of flawless style and rectitude. His greater symphonies, concertos, and string quartets are the finest flowering of instrumental classicism in its golden age; yet they were created by a man who has been called the least intellectual of great musicians, who cared little for literature or the kindred arts, who lived a disordered and at times dissipated life that often seemed to belie serious artistic purpose.

These contradictions are in part responsible for a portrait of Mozart that has endured too long—as a kind of high-speed musical machine, operated with infallible skill, but not geared to man's deeper inspirational impulses; an artist whose polished perfection of design and execution arouses admiration but never touches the heart. There are hundreds of pages of Mozart's earlier music which give credence to that view. But almost the whole of his mature output refutes it utterly. Such works as the Quintet in G minor, the Quartet in D minor, the last three symphonies, the piano Fantasia in C minor and the opening sections of the Requiem could never have been written by a man whose only concern was facility or surface brilliance, and whose art did not impinge upon his soul. In their great moments these works touch the human spirit as no music had done for fifty years before Mozart's time, not since Bach had written his last chorale preludes.

# Beethoven
## 1770—1827

### I

In the history of all the arts it would be difficult to find a counterpart for the idolatry that the world of his time and of a century after him reserved for Beethoven. During his lifetime he was acclaimed the foremost composer of his age; at his death all Vienna mourned, and twenty thousand people watched his funeral procession; he became the universal genius of music, and his work became the standard by which every note of music written after him had ultimately to be judged. There have been periods in the past when Beethoven's music seemed destined for a decline, the inevitable result of overpraise and overplaying; but as yet the recessions have never proceeded very far.

Beethoven's greatest music is so immense in scope and so revolutionary in spirit that it is natural to expect that the man who created it must himself have been of heroic stature, and that his life must have been a supreme adventure in the tragedy of human existence. Beethoven *was* one of mankind's great heroes, but not at all in the sense in which his early biographers tried to picture him. Outwardly, his life was anything but heroic. It was prosaic and unadventurous, almost dull. His boyhood was spent in the small Rhenish town of Bonn, where he was born in 1770; thereafter he lived the rest of his fifty-seven years in Vienna, with only a few brief excursions to other Austrian and German towns. He never left the boundaries of the Germanic countries. He never married; and though he came to know casually some of the other illustrious men of his age like Goethe, the close friendships that he made were for the most part uninteresting. He had many love affairs, but they followed one another with such regularity and were allowed to cool with such rapidity that there clings to them now a faint air of the ludicrous. The conclusion is inevitable that Beethoven's outward life was one of those (not uncommon among men of the arts) which are entirely subordinated to some inner spiritual existence. It was merely an adjunct to a great drama which was playing itself out in his intellect, and which manifests itself to us with overpowering effect in his works.

Beethoven's family was Flemish in origin; they came from the neighborhood of Louvain. There had been a few painters, sculptors, and singers in his ancestry, and there had also been several dealers in wine. The composer's paternal grandfather was a wine merchant, and also a court singer to the Elector of Bonn. He seems to have been a man of character and stability; but his wife became a dipsomaniac and ended her days in an asylum. Their son, Johann Beethoven, the composer's father, was also a drunkard. He followed his father's example to the extent of becoming a court singer, and in 1767 he married the young widow of a valet. This woman, who was to give the world one of its great geniuses, was the daughter of a cook. She accepted her life with the dissipated Johann uncomplainingly, struggling with fortitude against poverty, too frequent childbirths, and ill-health. She was a sweet-tempered and patient woman who did what she could to make the lives of her children decent, but it was said that no one ever saw her smile.

The second child of the couple was Ludwig, born on December 16, 1770. His boyhood was the nightmare to be expected for a child unfortunate enough to be born into a poverty-stricken family, ruled by a sot of a father. When he was five, Johann set the boy to work studying music, starting with the violin. Several other teachers (all of them incompetent) gave him lessons on the organ and clavier. Johann drove the boy unmercifully. In his mind was the vagrant hope that his son might turn out to be a second Wolfgang Mozart. In 1778, at Cologne, he actually displayed the lad in a public recital on the clavier, advertising his age as six years. The boy was eight, and the father's deception was responsible for Beethoven's own mistaken belief that he was born in 1772, an error he did not discover until he was middle-aged. The prodigy scheme fell flat, so Ludwig settled down to the life of an ordinary schoolboy at Bonn. When he was nine he was lucky enough to get his first music instructor of genuine ability, a man who owned a manuscript copy of J. S. Bach's *Well-tempered Clavier*. That immortal work, as yet unpublished and known only to a few musicians, remained Beethoven's Bible to the end of his life.

In spite of his failure to emulate Mozart, the boy Beethoven did have remarkable talent. By the time he was twelve he was a competent organist; at thirteen he had published three piano sonatas and a group of variations, and the next year he got an official appointment as assistant to the court organist. When he was sixteen, he was taken to Vienna, where he astonished Mozart with his ability at improvising. "Watch that chap," exclaimed Mozart. "Someday he is going to make a noise in the world."

By the time he was seventeen, young Beethoven had begun to be noticed by certain aristocratic families in Bonn, in particular the Breunings. Mme. von Breuning, a woman of culture and breeding, took a keen interest in the gauche young man. She became his second mother and her house became his second home, a place where he met many persons of high social standing. Under Mme. von Breuning's guidance he gained his first contacts with literature and the other arts. At that time he also met the nobleman who was to be his first patron, the profligate young Count Waldstein, who had recently moved to Bonn from the dark castle of Dux in Bohemia, where Casanova toiled at his *Memoirs*. Waldstein's financial help, bestowed with great tact, was repaid in later years with the dedication of the piano sonata that bears his name. Meanwhile Beethoven secured a place as violist in a theater orchestra, a position he held for four years. Then, in 1792, Joseph Haydn passed through Bonn, on his way home after his first visit to England. He urged the young Rhinelander to come to Vienna and study with him. Waldstein concurred in the plan, arranged for Beethoven a long leave of absence with pay from the Elector, and sent him on his way with a message that was both an inspiration and a prophecy: "Receive the spirit of Mozart from the hands of Haydn."

## II

The composer was then twenty-two, and he was a strange figure of a man. He was squat in appearance, being barely five feet four in height; but he was stockily built. His head was massive, with a shock of rumpled black-brown hair, and a complexion so brown and swarthy that people called him "the Spaniard." His cheeks were marked by smallpox, his teeth protruded, and he spoke with a comical Rhenish accent. But any smiles that the sight of this uncouth, unkempt young provincial might at first provoke were likely to be checked, for from the burning eyes came a morose and belligerent stare. He moved at first into an attic, but did not remain there long. Letters from Waldstein got him into the salons of the best Viennese society; thereafter he needed only to seat himself at a clavier, and the rest was easy.

His forte was improvising. He could take a theme, any theme whatever, and extemporize upon it by the hour. From the instrument there poured an amazing stream of musical ideas—tempestuous bursts of tone contrasted with sudden and delicate pianissimos, headlong speed alternating with lyric tenderness. This was something new in music, something unheard of in an age devoted to the rococo and the elegant; the aristocracy of Vienna was fascinated. Young Beethoven found patrons eager to subsidize him, but when he accepted their favors it was with a far different attitude from that of most musicians before him.

Within two years he was living in the house of Prince Lichnowsky as one of the family.

The lessons in composition that Beethoven took from Haydn did not turn out very well. The older man was in fact an indifferent teacher, and Beethoven finally began going secretly to another tutor to get his exercises in counterpoint corrected properly. This deception continued for a year, until Haydn departed for his second visit to London; and then Beethoven went to one of the best teachers in Vienna, Johann Albrechtsberger, who was noted for his skill at ramming the essentials of counterpoint and theory into aspiring pupils. He was a rigid dogmatist, but the young man who was to be music's great iconoclast went to him three times a week for two years, deliberately subjecting himself to a discipline he hated. There must have been painful scenes between the old professor and his headstrong pupil, for Albrechtsberger once said that Beethoven never learned anything and that he would never write anything worth while.

Beethoven's first works of any consequence are three trios, for piano, violin, and cello, which appeared as Opus 1 in 1795, when he was twenty-five. Published through the subscriptions of more than one hundred persons, including some of the most distinguished members of Viennese society, the trios made a fine first impression. To modern ears they are very close to the idiom of Mozart and Haydn, but the musicians of his time had the feeling that something out of the ordinary was going on in them. Haydn was so disturbed by the third trio, in C minor, that he advised Beethoven not to publish it.

The next year Beethoven published his Opus 2, and this time he passed a milestone of immense significance. The opus consists of three piano sonatas, the first of the company of thirty-two works which Beethoven left in this form, and which go hand in hand with his symphonies, his concertos, and his string quartets as his most enduring contributions to the art of music. Compared with the huge specimens that he produced in his maturer years, these first three sonatas now seem small in size and restricted in emotional content. The best way to discover their historical importance, however, is to play first some of Mozart's piano sonatas, enjoying to the full their elegance, their exuberance, and their fluent lyricism—and then to turn to these first three by Beethoven. Instantly the impression gained is one of expansion, of bigness. A creator with a large hand and a bold imagination is at work; he is stretching not only the scope of the music, but the resources of the instrument as well.

First of all, he increases the number of movements of his sonatas to four. (Mozart and Haydn had written four movements for their symphonies but generally wrote but three for their sonatas.) At the same time, Beethoven charges his music with more dramatic drive. His chords are bigger and heavier, he makes copious use of fortissimos and sforzandos, he spreads the hands farther apart on the keyboard to widen the tonal palette, and he frequently underlines his themes, making them burly and masculine, by declaiming them in the low bass register. In the slow movement of the second sonata we come upon something like a revolution. The old type of slow movement stemmed from the operatic aria; it copied a lyric style suited to the human voice. But, lacking the warmth of the voice, many eighteenth-century slow movements sound shallow and repetitious. They were in fact meant to be more ornamental than emotional. The slow movement of Beethoven's second sonata is marked Largo appassionato, and it is the forerunner of a type of which Beethoven became a consummate master—movements of infinite pathos, solemnity, and mystery.

In the succeeding movement of the same sonata there is another revolution. The minuet movement had become a problem for composers. Haydn once remarked frankly that he wished someone would write a new minuet. In this sonata Beethoven dropped the old dance form for a scherzo, a substitution that he later made standard not only for sonatas, but also for symphonies. It was a stroke of genius; for it provided something that the sonata (and the symphony), with its growing seriousness of purpose, badly needed—the contrast of humor. The very word "scherzo" connoted a piece of musical whimsey—a joke.

The scherzo of Beethoven's second sonata is delicate and light as a fairy piece; that in the succeeding third sonata is bolder and more rollicking, giving a hint of the bursts of roaring Beethovian laughter that would later be heard in his greater symphonies.

III

Early in 1798, when he was twenty-seven years old, Beethoven made the shocking discovery that he was growing deaf. The precise reasons for this personal calamity remain unknown, even though biographers, researchers, and medical men by the hundreds have sifted every possible shred of fact and hearsay in the composer's life. It is fairly certain that Beethoven had contracted syphilis, and to this misfortune was for a long time attributed not only his deafness but also every other failing of his body, mind, and character. However, modern doctors are agreed that this disease definitely did not affect his hearing. Whatever the causes, the results were a disaster that threatened for a time to unhinge the young man's mind.

At first he tried to hide his tragedy from the world, avoiding the society of other people. He became morose and irascible from the continual whistling, humming, and roaring in his ears. For a time he even contemplated suicide. In 1802, in the little village of Heiligenstadt where he spent the summer, he gave vent to his feelings in a written record of the horrors through which he was passing. This is the famous *Heiligenstadt Testament*, which he addressed to his two brothers. Unfortunately, it is such a wallowing in self-pity that it almost destroys a modern reader's sympathy. In essence the composer states that only his art has stayed his hand from self-destruction. "O, it seemed to me impossible to quit the world until I had produced all I felt it in me to produce; and so I reprieved this wretched life."

Although Beethoven's deafness in part ruined his life, the fact remains that it immeasurably enriched the art of music. First of all, it shut him off from the career of piano virtuoso and forced him to turn the full stream of his intellectual energies inward—toward composition. Then it put a wall of solitude around him, leaving his mind undisturbed to wrestle with some of the hardest problems that ever faced an artist. The first effects are clearly noticeable in the catalogue of his published works. With the year 1798 he began composition in earnest, and thereafter the works came thick and fast. This is the so-called "first period" of his creative development, when his music is still based largely upon the styles of Haydn and Mozart, with occasional and startling leaps into the altitudes of the later style that was so peculiarly his own. Further effects of his mental state are also noticeable in the deepening emotional character of his music.

The temptation to explain the emotional content of works of art by events affecting the lives of the artist at the time of creation is dangerous in the case of Beethoven, who often turned out music of unclouded serenity while at the bottom of some dreadful mental abyss—and vice versa. The tranquil Second Symphony was composed in 1802, the period during which he wrote the *Heiligenstadt Testament*. Nevertheless, among his works in the closing years of the eighteenth century, there are a few unmistakable hints of the tragedy that was desolating his personal life. One is the slow movement of the Sonata Opus 10, No. 3—the Largo e mesto, which is like a revelation of the inmost reflections of a sorrowing mind. Another is the Sonata Opus 13, which followed, the *Pathétique*.

In spite of the mauling and battering that it has taken at the hands of several generations of piano students and of concert pianists more richly endowed with technique than with intellect, this famous work still ranks high in the literature of piano music. The debt it owes to Mozart's piano masterpiece, the C minor Fantasia, is incontestable: the opening Grave and the following agitated Allegro present not only the pattern but also much of the spirit of the older work. But these facts do not detract one whit from the stature of the *Pathétique* Sonata. Its Grave sets the stage for some tragic drama, and in the Allegro the struggle begins. The whole tempestuous movement recalls the composer's own words in a letter to a friend concerning his

deafness: "I will seize fate by the throat. . . ." Seize fate
he did, and the piano strains from the fury of the attack.
Here Beethoven was sounding another new note in music,
driving the piano to dramatic, passionate utterance never
attempted before his time.

## IV

Beethoven waited until he was thirty-one years old before he published his First Symphony. At that age Mozart
had written more than forty symphonies; but Beethoven,
besides being a slow and meticulous workman, was naturally cautious when he approached any form for the first
time. The symphonic form was one that especially attracted and at the same time somewhat awed him. Not
only did he delay writing his First until rather late, but he
wrote in his entire life only nine symphonies—remarkably
few from the viewpoint of his contemporaries. However, a
glance at these works will reveal the real reasons for their
comparatively small number.

The first two symphonies are in many ways similar to
the first three piano sonatas. Basically they are patterned
on eighteenth-century models, but with internal evidence
that their composer was trying to expand, intensify, and
vary a style that had become hackneyed. They are full of
charming melodies, their workmanship is as deft and easy
as that of the elder Haydn, and their ideas flow with the
spontaneity of Mozart's—even though we know that spontaneity in Beethoven's music was a mask, miraculously
covering the most labored of creative methods. The Minuet of the First Symphony is a little gem, one of the most
engaging movements in the two works. The last movement
is equally good; it shows what a genius can do with artlessly
simple creative ideas. The best thing in the Second Symphony is an exceptionally beautiful Larghetto.

There is special interest in the opening measures of the
First Symphony because of the pother they caused when
first performed in public. It was the custom of the time
for composers to begin their symphonies with a few loud
chords, as a polite signal to the audience to cease their

chattering and pay attention to what was coming. These notes were invariably the tonic (or basic) chord of the particular key in which the work was written. Beethoven's First Symphony, though in C major, opened with a chord that led momentarily to the key of F. This piece of audacity jolted the critics so badly that they attacked the composer as a dangerous iconoclast.

Beethoven's Third Symphony is the great *Eroica*, in E flat. It dates from 1804. Viewed from almost any angle, it must be rated one of the most important creations in the entire range of art. The *Eroica* ended the reign of eighteenth-century music. It pushed the works of Haydn, Mozart, and their contemporaries into a past that would have a steadily lessening effect upon the music of the future. It ended the convention of strict, impersonal classicism; and it began the new era of a boldly expressed emotionalism, which led directly into the romantic movement itself. With the *Eroica* Beethoven also brought about a fundamental change in the symphonic form itself. He rebuilt it entirely from the eighteenth-century framework and gave it the stature by which we recognize it today—the noblest, most commanding of all musical forms. At the same time he expanded enormously the possibilities of the symphonic orchestra to meet emotional demands hitherto untried.

Thus the *Eroica* is a division point in music, from which the entire art begins to move in a new direction. This fact is obvious to anyone who listens to a performance of Beethoven's Second Symphony followed by one of the *Eroica*.

The title *Eroica* (or *Heroic*) was given to the symphony by Beethoven himself. The composer, like so many intellectual young men of his time, believed in the new ideal of liberty and the equality of man. He greatly admired Napoleon Bonaparte as the deliverer of the French and the possible emancipator of all mankind. His *Eroica* Symphony was to be a hymn of praise for his hero—who soon afterward let the composer down in the worst possible way by proclaiming himself emperor. When Beethoven heard the news he was so angry that he scratched out the name "Bonaparte" from the title page of his symphony. Seventeen years later, when Napoleon I died at St. Helena, Beethoven remarked, "I have already composed appropriate music for that catastrophe," referring to the second movement of the *Eroica*, the Funeral March.

The first thing that impressed the early hearers of the *Eroica* (and still impresses us today) was its physical size. It is nearly twice as long as the average symphony by Haydn or Mozart, with every one of its four movements laid out on a huge scale. In the first movement the composer completely rebuilt the sonata form. To fulfill his grandiose ideas he had first to discard a lot of old restrictions, the chief of which concerned the middle or development section, in which the two chief themes of the exposition are "worked out." In this section Beethoven added entirely new episodes not based on themes previously announced in the exposition—a grievous piece of audacity to the purists, but one that gave the effect of adding height and breadth to his movement. Then in his recapitulation he restated the themes of his exposition according to the rules, but altered them for variety and amplification. Finally, he stretched out his coda to unprecedented lengths. Instead of a brief tailpiece that summed things up quickly and gracefully, he constructed a closing section that is almost like another development. The result was a structure that must have frightened its first hearers in the year 1805, in the Theater-an-der-Wien. No single movement so gigantic had been conceived since the opening Kyrie of Bach's Mass in B minor.

Stunning though it is, the first movement does not by any means dominate the entire symphony, for it is followed by another movement that is in every aesthetic respect its equal. Having already outraged the tories, Beethoven gave them still more to talk about by making his slow movement a funeral march. In size it is another Titan; in emotional force it actually surpasses the first movement. The apex of the movement is a huge central section that begins with one of the oldest of technical devices, the fugato (i.e., a fugal treatment of a theme without formal restrictions). The progress of the theme through the various choirs of the orchestra lifts the entire movement to an elevation lofty beyond description.

Obviously the conventional minuet was too puny a form to follow in the company of two such giants, so Beethoven made his third movement a scherzo—the first time this form had appeared in a symphony. This is also the first appearance of the true Beethoven scherzo—that apotheosis of cosmic laughter which roars and rollicks and dances until it seems to set the world to shaking. It is his most original contribution to music, an echo of the strange inner reservoir of bacchic humor which was stored up in his soul and which counterbalanced his heavy burden of sorrow.

v

Beethoven's creative processes, besides being among the most powerful ever to develop in a human brain, were also among the most curious. By a rare piece of good fortune a picture of their inner workings has come down to us—in the form of his sketch books. Some forty of these are preserved, covering practically the whole of his creative life. In these books Beethoven recorded the hundreds of musical ideas that were the life germs of his works. Here the great themes that are now part of the world's language were born, but it was seldom that one of them came to life full grown. He had to work over them, with endless and agonizing labor in order to shape them into the final form in which we meet them in his scores. At times he made as many as twenty different versions of an idea or theme before it finally suited him. Sometimes after twenty different tries he went back and chose the first. Schumann remarked that "Beethoven finds his motives lying about in the street, but—he fashions them into cosmic utterances."

Beethoven's creative methods were unusual in another respect. There is strong evidence that, instead of beginning with the small bricks of his musical ideas and building them up into imposing structures, he worked in the opposite direction. He seems to have conceived first the building in all its magnificence and then tried to fashion the

thematic stones that would have the necessary strength
and adaptability for the construction process. As Ernest
Newman expressed it: "We have the conviction that his
mind did not proceed from the particular to the whole,
but began, in some curious way, with the whole and then
worked back to the particular. . . . The long and painful
search for themes was simply an effort, not to find workable atoms out of which he could construct a musical edifice according to the conventions of the symphonic form,
but to reduce an already existing nebula, in which that
edifice was implicit, to the atom, and then, by the orderly
arrangement of these atoms, to make the implicit explicit."

The difficulties of creating music according to such a
method must have been tremendous; but Beethoven was
fortunate in that he possessed, along with a sovereign imagination in the field of formal design, a genius for thematic development. He could make his musical materials
*seem* to expand with the utmost naturalness and freedom,
when actually he was manipulating them to fit closely a
preconceived design of considerable rigidity. That is why
he was able to succeed so brilliantly in the dramatic style
of utterance that characterizes his bigger symphonies, overtures, concertos, and piano sonatas. In these works Beethoven spoke as no composer had ever spoken before him.
Fundamentally he was borrowing abstract designs from
the spoken drama and adapting them for the first time to
music. The long-drawn-out crescendos, rising from whis-
pers to furious climaxes; the ringing declamations that
are like battle cries, and the sudden silences that are as
crushing as death—these were all effects for which he had
practically no precedents in music, and he had to work
them out with the utmost care. To this day they retain
their elements of suspense and surprise, despite countless
repetitions and imitations. He achieved them because he
took the pains to suit his materials to an idea, not an idea
to his materials.

The price that Beethoven paid for his methods of work
was one that might be expected. When he succeeded he
succeeded magnificently, but when he failed his failure
was complete and hopeless. No other first-rate composer

left a body of work so glaringly unequal in merit, with so much that is downright bad. It was obviously impossible for him to turn out his best music to order. If he had had to compose as Haydn and Bach did, as part of the daily routine of making a living, he would have ended up in the footnotes of music history. He needed time to compose. Some of his greater works lay germinating in his mind for years, and often he had half a dozen of them in various stages of construction at the same time. If he was hurried, or if he began to lose interest in a particular work, it was likely to be botched. Practically all of the large number of potboilers that he turned out for a quick fee from the publishers are unworthy.

Few men verified more fully the popular notion that to be a great artist one must be fantastically eccentric. His temper was volcanic. In a restaurant he once threw a dish of lungs and gravy into the face of a waiter. Nor was his wrath confined to his social inferiors; it was poured just as liberally over his most generous patrons. At a rehearsal of his opera *Fidelio* he flew into a rage because a bassoon player was absent. When Prince Lobkowitz tried to placate him he nearly had an apoplectic fit. On his way home he burst into the prince's palace and roared out to the horrified servants, "Lobkowitz is a donkey! Lobkowitz is a donkey!"

In matters of personal hygiene he never advanced far beyond the Neanderthal stage. His table manners were so disgusting that people avoided sitting near him in restaurants. At home he would spit freely, as the spirit moved him; on more fortunate occasions he took advantage of an open window, but at times of momentary confusion caused by intense preoccupation he might spit into a mirror. His lodgings were a slum of disarray, with clothes, books, broken furniture, and portions of uneaten meals lying about. His pianos were piled high with assorted manuscripts and papers; their cases and even their insides were spattered with ink. One of them lay on the floor, without legs. This baffling phenomenon was once explained by a biographer with the surmise that Beethoven must have liked to work while lying prone on the floor. Another suggests that because he moved so often it became too troublesome to have the legs continually taken off and put back on when the instrument was carried up and down stairs. He seldom remained more than a year in any house, and there were times when he moved so frequently that he was paying rent to several landlords at once. He must have been something less than the ideal tenant. As his deafness increased, he often roared and shouted and sang at the top of his voice when he composed; but he was acutely resentful of any disturbances that might emanate from the apartments of his neighbors. A passionate lover of nature and the open spaces, he refused to shut out the air and sunlight from his rooms with such crude devices as curtains and shutters. As a result, persons in the neighborhood were often startled by the sight of a formidable, bearlike man shaving at an open window, attired in a night shirt (or even less); he in turn would be annoyed and somewhat mystified that the boys in the streets should be shouting ribald remarks at him.

## VI

Whole volumes have been devoted to the many peculiar aspects of Beethoven's love life. A man of strong sexual impulses and immense vitality, he was passionately attracted to women. He was wildly in love with a number of them at various times, but he once admitted that his longest love affair lasted seven months. As soon as his ardor cooled, the lady would disappear from his life, and another whom he thought just as desirable would take her place. He seems to have had no difficulty in making his conquests. There was something of the fascination of ugliness about him. Remarkable (even significant) is the fact that many of the women whom Beethoven loved were from the highest strata of Viennese aristocracy. They ran to a type—cultured, often physically beautiful, and with a kind of frail gentleness. Several of these ladies were so highborn that marriage with a commoner like Beethoven was obviously impossible. There is a strong suspicion that he dramatized to himself the pangs of his frustration.

The most famous mystery in music concerns the identity of Beethoven's "Immortal Beloved." After the composer's death there was found in a secret drawer of his cashbox a wildly effusive love letter, the only one he is known to have written. The year is missing from the date, and the name of the woman to whom it was addressed is not given. The composer simply calls her his "Immortal Beloved." To this day no one knows for certain who she was, although specialists in Beethoviana have ransacked the archives of Europe for clues and their own brains for theories. Among the candidates suggested for the honor are two sisters named Brunswick; their cousin Julietta, to whom the composer dedicated his *Moonlight* Sonata; a fifteen-year-old girl named Teresa Malfatti over whom he made a fool of himself when he was forty; Bettina Brentano, the poetess and friend of Goethe—and a score of others. Every biographer seems to have his own favorite; but one of the shrewdest guesses is that of the American musicologist, Oscar G. Sonneck, who believed that the letter was written at a time when Beethoven must have been in love with two women at once. One was a lady named Amalie Sebald; the other was the mysterious unknown.

The real mystery in Beethoven's love life concerns not any particular woman, but rather his conduct toward all of them. A favorite solution of the biographers is that he was searching, Don Juan-like, for an ideal woman whose discovery eluded him to the end of his days. Others (more prosaically minded) believe that because he had contracted syphilis he realized that marriage with any woman would have been dishonorable if not disastrous. But the causes are probably deeper, and psychological. The implication is fairly plain that Beethoven had a subconscious antipathy to marriage. He knew instinctively that a wife (and the possibility of children) would mean giving hostages to his art, that they would be impediments indeed to his great enterprises. Few men have ever had a greater need for solitude than Beethoven, and few have subjected themselves more slavishly to the sacrifices of their work. That is why his actual life story reads like a series of relatively unimportant events; it is only when we study his music that an entirely new and vast existence opens up. This is the world of Beethoven the artist, one that impinges but occasionally upon that of Beethoven the man. In this existence no woman had any place whatever.

VII

The year 1804 (Beethoven's thirty-fourth) was a great one in the composer's life. It marked the beginning of a period that lasted about five years, during which he produced a whole series of famous masterpieces. His two greatest piano concertos, his violin concerto, two of his best overtures, the *Waldstein* and *Appassionata* sonatas for the piano, the Rasoumovsky and *Harp* quartets, the *Eroica* and the Fifth symphonies—all are products of this refulgent period.

Beethoven wrote five concertos for his favorite instrument (not counting two youthful indiscretions now ignored), and the last two must be ranked among his most successful works. These are the Fourth, in G major, and the Fifth (the *Emperor*), in E flat major. The *Emperor* dates from 1809, when the French were besieging and later occupying Vienna. At one time Beethoven had to flee to the cellar of his brother's house, not because warfare had as yet reached that enlightened stage which includes bombing noncombatants, but because the noise of the cannon distracted him so that he could not compose.

The *Emperor* Concerto is a work of regal splendor. For a hundred years it fascinated piano and orchestral composers who used it as their model—its dazzling passage work, its roar and clang of battle as piano and orchestra meet in jousts of strength and speed, the contrast of its affecting slow movement. It became the sire of a whole stable of battle horses upon which several generations of virtuoso pianists have pranced to glory. One can hardly blame them, for a piano concerto of this type can be one of the most exhilarating experiences for the listener, while for a performer it must provide satisfactions akin to a Roman triumph.

The Fourth Concerto, in G major, was written oddly

enough during a previous occupation of Vienna by the French, in 1805 and 1806. It is one of the rare treasures of instrumental music. It has often been called the feminine counterpart of its masculine successor. In a sense the two works epitomize the two hemispheres that later made up the romantic movement—that upheaval in the arts during the nineteenth century for which Beethoven among the musicians generated the original pressure. Both works depart from the rigid forms, from the coldly classic dogmatism of the eighteenth century; both strike out into the new domain of a free and outspoken individualism. In the *Emperor* the heroic element predominates, presaging romanticism at its most vigorous and brilliantly colorful. In the G major Concerto it is the poetry of romanticism that begins to unfold—the sentiment, the personal emotion that eighteenth-century classicists had held in restraint.

There is no more richly poetic work in music than this G major Concerto, yet its special beauty lies equally in its utter lack of pretentiousness. The tenor of the entire work is made clear in the opening measures. Instead of the usual florid orchestral opening, which served to give the solo instrument a later imposing "entrance," the piano itself begins—alone—stating its theme with the utmost simplicity and ingenuousness. In the whole length of the work thereafter there is not an extravagance or an overstatement. Rather, we seem to be listening to an intimate conversation between the piano and the orchestra. In the slow movement the dialogue suddenly becomes serious, and here Beethoven unfolds a matchless page. The form is like a series of musical questions and answers in which the voice of the orchestra has grown agitated, overbearing, savage, while that of the piano tries pleadingly to make itself heard. Ultimately the quiet voice gains the ascendency and the stormy emotions subside.

Beethoven's Violin Concerto, in D major, is the composer's only essay in this form. Once again he employed his most characteristic procedure—that of taking an existing form and magnifying it to heroic proportions. In this case the procedure was far more difficult than with the piano concertos. The violin is not only one of the smallest of musical instruments; it is shallow in dynamic range, and with an even more limited range of tonal coloring. Yet it is pitted against the tremendous resources of the symphonic orchestra. The composer must use all the ingenuity he can summon to avoid having the solo instrument crushed by the sheer weight of the orchestral forces, or conversely of favoring it to the extent of having the accompanying body sound emasculated. Beethoven solved the problem, and in so doing produced the first modern violin concerto and the model for most of the works in this form since his time.

Beethoven's work is noteworthy for the scope he gives to the best capabilities of the violin—its agility and its wonderfully moving emotional voice. The first and last movements are a virtuoso's stamping ground; while in the slow movement there is a soaring and singing of violin tone that is rich in the extreme, and yet never cloys. Few works by Beethoven are more completely in the vein of tranquillity than this concerto. No cloud of his dark despairs, no hint even of his moodiness, ever appears in its bright sky.

VIII

It is one of the curiosities of music that the most dramatic of instrumental composers should have had only indifferent success when he turned to opera. Beethoven wrote but one opera, *Fidelio,* and it caused him some of his most acute disappointments. The instigator of this work was Emanuel Schikaneder, the impresario who sired Mozart's *The Magic Flute* (and who later died insane). In 1803, when Schikaneder commissioned Beethoven to write an opera, the composer pondered for a long time over a choice of subjects. He considered among others Romeo and Juliet, Alexander the Great, Macbeth, Ulysses, Bacchus, the Ruins of Babylon, and the Founding of Pennsylvania. He finally chose a libretto adapted from the French—*Leonore, or Conjugal Love*—one of the few important opera librettos to be based on this praiseworthy but comparatively unexciting subject. The story concerns the efforts of Leonore to free her husband Florestan from a dungeon in a Spanish castle, where he is held a political prisoner. She disguises herself as a boy and enters the service of the jailer. Virtue and conjugal devotion are rewarded when, at the moment of Florestan's execution, an off-stage trumpet announces the arrival of the Minister of State, who frees the prisoner.

The piece was first produced in November 1805, and it failed. To say that the time was not ripe is to put it mildly. Napoleon's troops had just captured Vienna, the aristocracy and wealth of the city had fled, and the audience was made up chiefly of French soldiers. Soon afterward a group of Beethoven's friends met with him at Prince Lichnowsky's palace and pleaded with him for hours to make cuts and alterations in his score. At first he defended his brain child desperately, but finally he consented to make the changes. In 1806 there was a revival of the reduced (and apparently much improved) version; but still it was not right. Finally, in 1814, Beethoven made a further complete revision after the libretto too had been altered, and this time the opera was a success, with its future life assured.

*Fidelio* has been described as one of those perplexing works by a great master—one which some persons cherish, but which opera companies try studiously to avoid. Its performances today are infrequent, but they prove that the opera is far from Beethoven at his best. He was clearly out of his element in the opera house; he had no sympathy with its people and its conventions. Moreover, words hampered rather than inspired him—a fact also apparent in his songs. In spite of his marvelous dramatic sense in abstract music, he had no theatrical sense, no instinct such as Mozart had for the feel of stage situations. The best thing in *Fidelio* is one of the four overtures that he composed at various times for the opera—the one known as *Leonore No. 3*. In this work he established a new form in music.

Previously the opera overture had usually been a simple curtain raiser—either a short prelude to establish the mood of the piece to come or a loosely strung together collection of melodies to be heard later. In *Leonore No. 3*, Beethoven created an overture that was a kind of miniature of the opera itself. It established the mood, gave a concise outline of the rise and fall of the dramatic action, and a clue to the ultimate resolution of the emotional crisis. It was a brilliant idea, and the composer carried it out brilliantly and forcefully. *Leonore No. 3* established the overture as a form artistically complete in itself. It also paved the way for an entirely new musical form—the tone poem, i.e., the symphonic exposition of a purely literary idea. This latter form was not developed by Beethoven himself, but by Franz Liszt, and it became one of the most characteristic essays of a long line of nineteenth-century romanticists.

Beethoven produced two other great overtures, one that was part of his incidental music to Goethe's *Egmont*, the other to that for Collin's drama, *Coriolanus*. Both are masterly projections in tone of the dramas they synthesize. In certain respects it is *Coriolanus* that is the most typical of all the Beethoven overtures. Added to its lofty pathos is a Baconian compactness that intensifies the tremendous driving force of the composer's ideas. Nothing could be more characteristic (and more a justification) of Beethoven's creative procedure than his handling of the motive that opens this overture—the two chords proclaimed forte by the orchestra, one long, the other snapped off short like the crack of a whip. It would be hard to imagine a less simple or a less promising musical idea, and yet Beethoven expands it into such a thunderhead of malignant power that it dominates the entire work.

To the effulgent period between 1804 and 1809 belong two of Beethoven's most famous piano sonatas—Opus 53 in C major, known as the *Waldstein*, and Opus 57 in F minor, the *Appassionata*. The former is a memento of Beethoven's passion for Nature and all her works. He composed it in 1804 during a sojourn at Döbling, in the midst of the idyllic countryside to the north of Vienna. It is one of those rarest birds in music—a virtuoso piece in the poetic vein. The first movement is especially beloved, for not even Beethoven, the archpriest of Nature, ever captured more of her serenity in music. The *Appassionata* is another emotional torrent, more powerful even than the *Pathétique* Sonata, for here the composer's grip on his materials has the assurance of mature mastery. The first movement, with its opening of mystery and foreboding, its sinister four-note motive (which Beethoven later immortalized in his Fifth Symphony), and then its wild and savage outburst of revolt, gives us *Sturm und Drang* in essence.

## IX

Beethoven wrote sixteen string quartets, and there are good reasons for the often expressed opinion that they represent his art at its summit. His first six quartets were grouped as his Opus 18, published in 1801. During his great "second period" he wrote five more, including three magnificent ones dedicated to Count Rasoumovsky, one of his patrons. Then he dropped the form until the close of his life, when he produced the five last quartets that were his valedictory to music. These works are not as well known as the symphonies or the piano sonatas, and by their very nature they are much less spectacular. But in them Beethoven maintained his highest level of inspiration and workmanship. To study them is to follow the progress of his art through all its stages, and to encounter only the choicest examples of each stage.

The six quartets in Opus 18 belong to the period of the First and Second symphonies, when the composer was still imitating Haydn and Mozart. What they lack in depth of feeling they make up in the deftness of the workmanship, the skill with which the young composer handled his delicate polyphonic strands. With the three Rasoumovsky Quartets, published in 1808 as Opus 59, he bridged a gap almost as wide as that between the Second Symphony and the *Eroica*. As a compliment to the Russian count to whom they are dedicated, Beethoven was supposed to have woven a Russian theme into the melodic fabric of each of these works; but that fact now retains only an academic interest. The listener today is fascinated by the surpassing skill and richness of these quartets. It is hard to believe that the pedants of Beethoven's time were disturbed by them. More than one thought that the composer was playing jokes on his public. A certain violinist who was also a quartet composer said to him, "Surely you do not consider these works to be music?" Beethoven replied, "Oh, they are not for you but for a later age." The Rasoumovsky Quartets are indeed a forecast of the last period of the composer's life, when his art had taken another sharp turn. This was noticeable especially in their increasing interest in pure polyphony—as for example in the closing movement of the third Rasoumovsky Quartet, in C major, which is a tremendous and dazzling fugue. At the end of his career the homophonic style obviously began to become too thin and pallid for him; he began to pack his music so densely and heavily, crowding it to the brim with such detail, that he inevitably had to return to the older polyphonic forms for his models.

x

After he finished the *Eroica* Symphony, Beethoven had begun work on a symphony in C minor, the one now known as the Fifth. He laid it aside and composed, in the summer of 1806, the symphony in B flat that was later published as his Fourth. No one knows why he dropped the Fifth as he did, but from its character it is easy to surmise that he had trouble with it. The Fourth must have been a far easier creative task. It is a straightforward work, bearing little resemblance to the tremendous symphonies on either side. Schumann, in a famous remark, likened it to "a slender Greek maiden between two Norse giants."

The Fifth Symphony, in C minor, is the best known and most popular of all Beethoven's works, in addition to being the most popular symphony ever written by any composer. This remarkable drawing power, as might be expected, has almost led to the ruination of the work itself. Conductors looking for an easy triumph have played it until, to many concertgoers, it must seem worn down like an old stone. When doubts arise about its ultimate value, however, one need only remain away from the Fifth

Symphony for a few years, and then listen to it again with an interest that has been allowed to freshen.

For sheer dramatic excitement it is one of the most effective pieces of music in existence. Every one of its four movements is superb; the last has the special merit of being the rousing finale for which Beethoven had long been groping. The entire work is so concisely stated and so judiciously balanced that there is hardly a superfluous note anywhere. Beethoven is here the complete master of his materials, and every one of his effects comes off with stunning power. A thousand commentators have let go their flights of fancy in describing the Fifth Symphony, for the music seems to be telling some tale of heroic adventure, both glorious and hair-raising. Remarking on the famous opening theme of the first movement, the four notes that have sounded their way to immortality, Beethoven himself said, "Thus Fate knocks at the door." Beyond that he gave no hint whatever of any further program for the work.

The first movement is notable for its immense vigor, which is projected almost without respite and at breakneck pace. The music races like an engine, roaring and bellowing and threatening. The Scherzo is one of Beethoven's greatest, as it is also one of his strangest. "That dream of terror which we technically call a scherzo," is Professor Tovey's phrase for its macabre atmosphere, for the measured tread of the *something* that comes toward us out of the darkness, and for its sudden roars of sardonic laughter. By a master stroke Beethoven did not end this Scherzo at all, but ran it straight into his closing movement. The music moves through deep and tortuous subterranean passages, almost perishing from lack of breath, at last to burst forth into the blazing light of the finale. A superb effect, and one that has never grown stale. With Beethoven it was more than mere effect. It served to lace together the entire last half of his symphony; it gave cohesion to the work as a whole. By this device (and by actually restating part of the Scherzo in the last movement) he anticipated the modern conception of the symphony—as a closely integrated unit, instead of a loose-leaf collection of separate ideas.

Beethoven's Sixth Symphony (the *Pastoral*), written in 1808, is unique in that it presents a definite program, thus anticipating romanticism in symphonic music by several decades. Beethoven himself described the movements in his score as follows: "I. Awakening of happy feelings on arriving in the country. II. By the brook. III. Merry gathering of country folk. IV. Thunderstorm. V. Shepherd's song. Happy and thankful feelings after the storm." The composer also remarked that his was an "expression of feelings rather than painting," i.e., that he was giving an *impression* of nature rather than an imitation. Actually the symphony is a mixture of both procedures.

Beethoven's love of nature was an uplifting passion, the noblest attribute of his strange character. It was inevitable that this feeling should find its way, somehow, into his large-scale music. The *Pastoral* Symphony is remindful of the exquisite peace that descends upon a man who leaves behind an oppressive city and reaches the haven of a quiet wood. The Scherzo, in the style of a country dance, with its folklike tunes and its rustic dance rhythms, is magnificent throughout. As for the Thunderstorm, it was the first thing of its kind in music, and it remains the best. Beethoven is completely pictorial here, with the patter of the rain, the crashes of thunder and the general atmosphere of suspense and terror.

## XI

When Beethoven reached his fortieth year the gushing stream of his creative inspiration began to run dry. He entered upon a period of almost a decade which was so barren as to constitute a mystery. No one knows for certain why the torrent dropped down to a thin stream, but the speculations have been various. Some biographers think that because he had achieved a certain financial independence he began to take things easy. His fame had spread to such an extent that publishers all over Germany, and even England, were bidding for his music.

Beethoven's personal life at this time was certainly far from satisfactory. His deafness was now almost complete; ultimately his conversations had to be carried on in writing. A number of the *Conversation Books,* the tablets that recorded his social intercourse, are preserved—pathetic yet valuable witnesses to a great human tragedy. His career as a piano virtuoso was of course ruined. Spohr, who heard him rehearse in 1814 for a performance of the B flat Piano Trio, Opus 97, related that "there was scarcely anything left of the virtuosity of the artist which had formerly been so greatly admired. In *forte* passages the poor deaf man pounded on the keys till the strings jangled, and in *piano* he played so softly that whole groups of tones were omitted." That was Beethoven's last public appearance as a pianist. He suffered spells of deep melancholy, his irascibility and his outbursts of temper increased, and he developed a persecution complex. In 1812, when Goethe met him for the first time, the poet noted that "unfortunately he is an utterly untamed personality (not altogether in the wrong in holding the world to be detestable) but who does not make it any more enjoyable either for himself or others by his attitude. He is to be excused, on the other hand, and much to be pitied."

Biographers no longer try to hide the fact that one of the weaknesses of Beethoven's character was plain dishonesty. He considered publishers fair game, cheating them right and left, until one of them in London warned his colleagues, "For God's sake, don't buy anything of Beethoven." He even bilked the Royal Philharmonic Society of London. When they commissioned him to compose something especially for them he sent three old and inferior scores—the *King Stephen, Ruins of Athens,* and *Name Day* overtures. For his greatest sacred work, the *Missa Solemnis,* he reserved his most flagrantly dishonest dealings of all—a long and involved series of shady negotiations with half a dozen publishers who were bidding for the rights to the score.

One of the meanest chapters in the composer's life concerns his treatment of his two sisters-in-law. His brother Johann had been entangled in an affair with a young lady of uncertain morality. It was none of brother Ludwig's business, yet the composer suddenly became righteously indignant and demanded that Johann and his paramour separate at once. When Johann refused, Ludwig went to the church and civil authorities, and a police order was issued giving the woman notice to get out of town. Johann then proceeded to marry her, thus making an honest woman of the lady and a fool of his brother.

Equally unfortunate was Beethoven's treatment of the widow of his brother Carl, who died in 1815. Carl's will stipulated that the guardianship of his nine-year-old son should be shared by his widow and his famous brother. It was a foolish idea, for Carl knew very well that these two disliked each other. There was a further stipulation in the will that the boy was definitely to remain in the custody of his mother. In spite of his brother's dying wish, the composer immediately tried to get young Carl away from his mother, and there ensued a long series of family wrangles that were as sordid as they were stupid. Beethoven took his case to the courts, and for years the affair dragged on—a minor *Jarndyce and Jarndyce* that drained the composer's fortunes and ruined what was left of his temper. He finally got full legal custody of young Carl, but it was a Pyrrhic victory. Even though Beethoven loved the boy with the maudlin devotion of a lonely bachelor, he was the worst possible kind of guardian; the mere presence of the boy in a household as chaotic as Beethoven's was scandalous to begin with. In 1819 young Carl ran away and went back to his mother. Again the uncle went to the courts, and the unwilling nephew was returned. As he grew to manhood Carl turned out to be a weakling. He became an increasing trial to his uncle until finally, when he reached the age of twenty, he tried to kill himself. At his trial he declared publicly that his uncle had driven him to the desperate act by constantly tormenting him about his conduct.

Few portraits of great men are less flattering than that of Beethoven in these middle years of his life—wrangling with the unfortunates who were his relatives, venting his spleen on his best friends, letting his affairs descend into disorder while he sat in the gloom of his terrible solitudes, his art almost at a standstill; forgetting the principles of common honesty and, at times, decency, surrendering the finer attributes of his character to the misanthropic and the mean. It is well to remember that, as Goethe said, he was to be excused and much to be pitied.

He had one solace outside of his music, and that was reading. He believed it his solemn duty as an artist to feed his intellect with the best thought of every age. Because his early education had been neglected, he knew little Latin and no Greek; but he seized every German translation he could get of the great ancients—Homer, Plutarch, Xenophon, Plato, Aristotle, Euripides, Horace, and Ovid. He loved Shakespeare, and he was well acquainted with Moore, Byron, and Sir Walter Scott. Of the Germans he knew intimately the works of Schiller, Lessing, Klopstock, and the others of the group who contributed to the *Sturm und Drang* period of German literature. He read Immanuel Kant in later life; but above all he adored Goethe, the man who towered over German literature—whose youthful *Werther* signaled the opening of *Sturm und Drang,* and whose mature *Faust* lighted the way of the romanticists of every country in Europe. Beethoven read him almost daily.

The dark period in the composer's life was not completely barren. There were occasional flashes of his old inspiration, momentary but brilliant, as exemplified by his Seventh and Eighth symphonies, which were both composed in 1812. The Seventh Symphony must be ranked among a small group of Beethoven's grandest works. The temptation to agree that it is "the most beautiful symphony ever written" is strong indeed. Here Beethoven propounded no cosmic problems; he let loose no dramatic conflicts of the soul. He simply took the spacious frame of the symphonic form and filled it to the brim with melodic, harmonic, and rhythmic ideas of the first order. Richard Wagner called the Seventh Symphony an "apotheosis of the dance." Every one of its four movements could almost be called a study in pure rhythm, so compelling is the feeling of pace, of irresistibly propelled motion, that pervades the work from beginning to end.

The Eighth Symphony, when it first appeared, was a matter of considerable disappointment to Beethoven's followers. He had fed them on the strong meat of his *Eroica*, Fifth, Sixth, and Seventh symphonies until they had gotten to like it; now they complained when he seemed to serve them up milk toast from an old eighteenth-century bowl. The Eighth Symphony remained unloved for a long time (it was actually an early custom to interpolate the immensely popular Allegretto of the Seventh, to give it a lift) and even today it suffers a certain measure of neglect. It might be called a study in high spirits—in whimsical, almost nonsensical humor. For this purpose Beethoven deliberately harked back to the symphony of Haydn, scaling down both the size of the work and its emotional voltage. There is no slow movement; all four sections are bright and gay. Even the usual Beethoven scherzo becomes a scherzando, a light-footed harlequinade. The last movement is musical humor in essence, for it is a boisterous collection of the composer's best jokes. A friend once asked Beethoven which one of his symphonies was his favorite (there were then only eight), and he replied, "The *Eroica*." One would like to hazard the guess that the symphony that he most enjoyed writing was the Eighth.

XII

After the lean years had passed, Beethoven entered upon the closing phase of his life, a decade, beginning in 1817, during which there was a mysterious return of his creative strength. The music of this last period is often called the most difficult ever written; it challenges both the technical equipment and the intellect of the greatest interpreters, and it reaches heights of music aesthetics which had never before been scaled and which remain not entirely explored to this day. The works are comparatively few in number, but some of them are monumental—the Ninth Symphony, the Missa Solemnis, the *Hammerklavier* Sonata and the Sonata Opus 111 for piano, the last five string quartets.

For a long time the quartets especially were considered utterly incomprehensible. Early quartet players were so baffled that they refused to play them at all.

One of the chief reasons for the difficult character of these works is the fact that they bear scars of a lacerating mental conflict through which they were brought to fruition. Beethoven in this period was actually in a kind of transitional stage. He was in a spiritual agony, trying to shape his music into new contours, to push it out beyond all known borders; frustration tortured him when the solution of his problems eluded him.

The Ninth Symphony itself gives ample evidence of that struggle. Beethoven began it in 1817, five years after he composed the Eighth, and he worked on it off and on for about six years. When first performed (in Vienna, on May 7, 1824), it stunned the audience by its magnitude. It runs for an hour and ten minutes, and the last movement requires, in addition to the usual symphonic orchestra, a large chorus of voices and four vocal soloists, for it is a setting of Schiller's *Ode to Joy*. This gargantuan size, plus the loftiness of the composer's aims, helped for a time to place the work on a pedestal beyond critical reach. In our own times there are some who regard this symphony as a hybrid, an unsuccessful attempt to fuse the symphonic and choral styles; they insist that the voice parts sometimes become dreadful screeching because Beethoven was deaf and no longer remembered their proper range; that Schiller's poem is not worthy of a setting as inspired as Beethoven attempted in his last movement, and that that movement itself is an anticlimax. There is an element of fact in all of these criticisms of the Ninth Symphony, but the truth is that the flaws do not essentially weaken its gigantic structure.

There is no greater first movement in all symphonic literature than its stupendous opening. Only the first movements of the *Eroica* and Brahms's First Symphony may stand comfortably beside it. "A Titan wrestling with the Gods," was Wagner's description of Beethoven; and it was never more apt than in this furious and storm-racked tragedy with which the Ninth Symphony begins. As for the

Scherzo, it is the greatest of all Beethoven's scherzos. It is his masterpiece in a form in which he had no rivals.

At the opening of the final movement Beethoven faced a problem of extreme difficulty: how to achieve the "joint" between the three purely abstract and wholly symphonic movements and his oratoriolike finale, with its solo voices and its chorus. He solved the problem, and with an episode that is the high point of the entire work. His finale opens stormily, leading to agitated recitatives for the basses alone, ominous and protesting figures that are like a great voice delivering angry speech; ghostly sections of the first three movements come and go like wraiths on the wind; a magnificent choralelike theme unfolds itself at length; there is a return to the stormy mood of the opening, and then the protesting orchestra is suddenly interrupted by the first sound of a human voice—a ringing challenge from the baritone that pierces the orchestral gloom like a shaft of light. Thereafter the entire apparatus of soloists, chorus, and orchestra is set in motion, publishing the stanzas of Schiller's poem. It is an undeniable fact that these ensuing sections are not of equal merit. For one thing Beethoven makes indifferent use of his soloists; nothing that they do either singly or as a quartet approaches the baritone's opening recitative. On the other hand, there are many superb moments in this finale that are as powerful as any to be found in symphonic literature. The work as a whole succeeds in projecting an impression of epic grandeur.

Further evidence of the metamorphosis through which Beethoven's art was passing during his last years is to be found in his last four piano sonatas. These are the Sonatas Opus 106 (the *Hammerklavier*), Opus 109, Opus 110, and Opus 111, which were composed between 1818 and 1822. Here is contained music that transcends everything he ever composed for the instrument. Here also is the majesty of sheer size. The composer has returned to forms that he had already magnified and is expanding them still further to the limits of their endurance. The *Hammerklavier* Sonata is simply mammoth—a taxing experience for both the performer and the listener. In all these sonatas, moreover, there is a complexity that had been lacking in

keyboard music since the death of Bach. They have the
density, the weight and force of an immense concentration of ideas that is remindful of Bach's polyphony. Beethoven returned especially to the fugue, a form that had
fascinated him all through his life. The closing movements
of three of his last five piano sonatas are fugal. He also
begins to break down certain fundamental restrictions of
the sonata form itself. He had long since ceased to observe
the orthodox rules about the number of movements, and
had written sonatas with three, four, and sometimes only
two movements. Now at times he ignores the very boundaries of the movements; it is often hard to tell when one
movement leaves off and another begins. There are sudden and unaccountable changes of tempo and mood, as if
the composer were working according to no known procedure but with rhapsodic freedom. It becomes more and
more difficult to predict what the next measure or the
next note may be. Above all, there is present the constant
pressure of a compelling emotion. This is especially true
in certain of the slow movements. No music touches more
profound depths of pathos, of grief nobly restrained, than
these elegies of Beethoven's last years. In the last piano
sonatas there are several notable examples—those of the
*Hammerklavier* Sonata, and the Sonatas Opus 109 and
Opus 111.

The net result of all these qualities is that combination
of aesthetic perfection and a vaguely unsatisfactory diffuseness that appears again and again in art that is passing
through a stage of transition. It is an easy matter to point
out in the piano sonatas passages that are totally unpianis-
tic, places where the music becomes so abstract that the
capabilities of the instrument are ignored; it is easy to find
disturbing thickness in chords in the bass, ugly combinations of tones spread too far apart, unfortunate use of a
polyphonic style for which the piano as a percussive instrument has little aptitude. Most glaring example of all is
probably the fugue that ends the *Hammerklavier* Sonata,
a movement that many of the most ardent Beethoven admirers have put down as unplayable, tortured, and even
monstrous. There is no use denying these blemishes; they

exist as an integral part of Beethoven's mature art, just
as certain weaknesses of character were part of the man.
They merely reiterate the fact that of all great artists he
was one of the most uneven. He was the archiconoclast,
the rule-breaker, the experimenter, the eternal pioneer in
music. And he was completely unpredictable. Moreover,
nothing could seriously detract from the achievement that
Beethoven's thirty-two sonatas represent as a whole—the
Shakespearean abundance and range, the congregation of
ideas, and the protean variety of their presentation. These
are the things that have held even the severest critics of
Beethoven enthralled. These and the fact that one man
could have taken the slight frame of the eighteenth-
century sonata and built it as he did into such a labyrinth
of magnificent rooms.

## XIII

The Missa Solemnis (or Solemn Mass), in D, is Beethoven's largest work. It was originally planned for the
installation of Archduke Rudolph as Archbishop of
Olmütz, and Beethoven began it in 1818. At that time he
was also working on the Ninth Symphony. The installation occurred in 1820, but the Mass was not ready. It
had grown in the composer's mind to such proportions and
was causing him such creative agonies that another three
years went by before it was finally finished. Even then
Beethoven hated to let it pass irrevocably to the publishers,
but kept revising it constantly. He changed the tympani
parts in the Agnus Dei so many times that he wore a hole
in the thick manuscript paper. However, he was able to
capitalize (quite literally) on the delay, by indulging in a
shakedown of six different publishers, to each of whom
he had promised the publication rights. Then, having
closed an excellent deal with a seventh, he delayed publication still further while he sent around petitions to
various European courts, offering manuscript copies of the
Mass at fifty ducats each. Thus he was able to use his most
sacred work as a means of squeezing money out of the
two classes of persons he hated most—publishers, whom he

once described as "hellhounds" who licked and gnawed his brain; and the "princely rabble" whose system of patronage he loathed and helped destroy, but nevertheless dipped into with a free hand throughout his life.

The only other work in music to which the Missa Solemnis might be compared is Bach's B minor Mass. Both are scored for chorus, soloists, and orchestra (although Bach's orchestra, of course, is a mere eighteenth-century rudiment of Beethoven's elaborate symphonic band). Both works outgrew their original proportions and became far too big for actual use in a church service. Beethoven himself confidently believed that the Missa Solemnis was his greatest work, but today not many accept his estimate. Judged as a whole, it falls below his finer symphonies and string quartets.

Actually, Beethoven began his task with comparatively little practical experience for the thing he was attempting. A previous and much smaller Mass in C, the weak *Mount of Olives* Oratorio, and a few unimportant cantatas almost sum up his liturgical works. Moreover, his whole art had been dedicated to the development of a dramatic and intensely personal style that was the exact opposite of the ecclesiastical idiom. As a result, the Missa Solemnis became a battleground upon which some of the composer's most agonized creative struggles took place. The opening Kyrie is undistinguished and melodically dry, and so is the Gloria. Not until he reached the Credo did the composer really get into his stride. The Crucifixus and the Et vitam venturi are full of splendor, and there is a brief instrumental prelude to the Benedictus that is the inspirational peak of the entire work. The Benedictus itself is a lovely violin solo and is in the style of an Ave Maria; but the Agnus Dei is again a mixture of the great Beethoven and the commonplace. The composer apparently had a hard time deciding whether to end brilliantly for effect or quietly as the text demands, so he fell into an anticlimax between the two.

With the Missa Solemnis and the Ninth Symphony finally out of the way, Beethoven had but a few years left of life. They were years of misery and mental anguish. He found little comfort in the honors that were heaped upon him from all sides. By this time he was the most famous musician in Europe, with his works in demand everywhere and his financial security assured. England tried to lure him for a visit, to pay him the homage she had lavished upon Haydn; Vienna acclaimed him and had relieved him of the duty of paying taxes. At the first performance of the Ninth Symphony he received an ovation greater than that reserved for royalty. But the vivid colors of life had drained away, and his mind was all grays and blacks. His health began to break; there were premonitions of death. At times he reached a detachment from the world like that of Rembrandt in the last poverty-bitten years of the painter's life, but he never achieved the serenity of spirit that glowed in Rembrandt's face. Promethean struggles still possessed him; while walking in the country he shouted to himself, waved his arms, and gesticulated wildly at unseen foes; oxen were frightened and fled. It was not uncommon for strangers to believe him insane.

He turned again to the string quartet, and in the course of three years he wrote five. They were his last works—"the last of life for which the first is made." In the sober nomenclature of music they are known simply as String Quartets Opus 127 in E flat, Opus 130 in B flat, Opus 131 in C sharp minor, Opus 132 in A minor, and Opus 135 in F. They are unlike any other of Beethoven's works. Deliberately he turned his back on the grand style of the bigger symphonies and sonatas, the overtures and the colossal Mass. He quenched the passions that had so often set his works ablaze. For these string quartets there was to be no music "but what is grave and doric." All is subdued, ascetic, and introspective. The grayness of the composer's mind tinges even the brightness of some of the allegros. Emotion is present as always, but it flows inward and at great depth. In certain of the slow movements Beethoven surpasses even himself, notably in the Adagio with which the C sharp minor Quartet begins—a bitter, slow-moving fugue that Wagner called "the most melancholy thing in all music." Never was art less concerned with brilliance, ornament, or opulence of expression; never did it speak more profoundly from a medium so compressed and austere.

For a long time these last quartets remained so many enigmas. In some respects they defied laws that had come to seem as fundamental as those of nature: e.g., the C sharp minor Quartet, instead of having the usual four movements, has seven, and they are to be played without pause. For the last movement of the B flat Quartet Beethoven originally wrote a fugue, but it was so complex and of such length that it dismayed those who first tried to play it. The publisher begged Beethoven to substitute another movement for it, which he finally did. The so-called "Grand Fugue" now stands alone, a work of exhausting size and content, clearly too big for its medium.

About all five quartets there clings to this day a certain strangeness. No longer disquieting, they are rather infinitely fascinating, for they hold something of the unearthly distortion that elongated the faces and bodies of El Greco's saints into an embodiment of spirituality and suffering. We now see within them in clear outline the end of the lifelong struggle of the composer against an enemy fate. He had lost that struggle, and he knew it. In the words of W. J. Henderson, "Fate was too strong for him, for she robbed him of the power to hear his own art. Tantalus standing in the midst of the waters of Hades and forbidden to drink was no more a tortured spirit than the failing Beethoven going down into the graveyard of a soundless old age." In these last quartets may be found both the iron courage and the pathos with which he bore that resolution of his destiny.

It was in the year 1826 that Beethoven's nephew Carl shot himself in the head in an attempt at suicide. The shock to the composer was a grievous one; later he was to feel the real sharpness of the serpent's tooth when the young man publicly stated that his uncle had tormented him to desperation. Meanwhile Beethoven took him to his brother Johann's home in the town of Gneixendorf, to recuperate. The composer had aged terribly and his own health was bad, but that did not prevent him from working. At Gneixendorf he finished the last movement of the

B flat Quartet, the one substituted for the fugue; he began a quintet, and there were other larger projects in his mind, including an opera, an oratorio, a Requiem, and a tenth symphony.

Early in December he returned to Vienna. On the journey, either from riding in an open wagon or from sleeping in a drafty room in a cheap inn, he contracted a cold. He was put to bed in his lodgings in Vienna, desperately ill from what the doctors called "inflammation of the lungs." He passed the first crisis, but then the doctors found evidence of jaundice, "hard nodules on the liver," and finally dropsy. There began a ghastly four-month struggle with death. The sick man's body swelled and at times the pain was excruciating; but his sufferings served only to put him into violent rages, "mighty explosions of temper," which the doctors feared would carry him off. With the grotesque fumbling that then passed for medical science they gave him frozen punch to drink, put him in enervating sweat baths, and tapped him four times for dropsy. As the water was drawn the composer remarked, "Better from my belly than from my pen."

On a day late in March it became evident that the end was near. He signed his will and received the last rites of the Church. To those at his bedside he murmured, "Plaudite, amici, comedia finita est [Applaud, friends, the comedy is ended]," and a few hours later he lapsed into a coma. Even yet the iron will was not broken; for two more days of unconsciousness the struggle went on. Then on March 26, 1827, there occurred a scene so melodramatic as to seem apocryphal, though it is well authenticated. It was late afternoon and snow lay on the ground outside. Suddenly the watchers at the side of the dying man were startled by a flash of lightning and a violent peal of thunder. Beethoven, who had been unconscious for hours, roused himself and opened his eyes; he even raised his clenched fist as if in a last gesture of defiance. Then he fell back, and the struggle was ended.

# Schubert
## 1797—1828

In Heaven a spirit doth dwell
  "Whose heart-strings are a lute";
None sing so wildly well
As the angel Israfel.
And the giddy stars (so legends tell)
Ceasing their hymns, attend the spell
  Of his voice, all mute.

EDGAR ALLAN POE, Israfel

I

On a winter day in 1827, when Beethoven was on his
deathbed, someone tried to beguile him by showing him a
collection of songs in manuscript, written by a young
Viennese named Franz Schubert. The sick man was told
that these were only a portion of the thirty-year-old composer's output of more than five hundred songs, and a
cascade of piano pieces, chamber works, symphonies,
Masses, and operas. Beethoven was enthralled by the
beauty and originality of the Schubert songs: "for several
days he could not tear himself away from them; he passed
many hours daily over *Iphigenia, Grenzen der Menschheit,
Die Allmacht, Die junge Nonne, Viola*, the *Müllerlieder*,
and others. He cried out several times with joyful enthusiasm: 'Truly in Schubert there is the divine spark.' . . ."
Sometime during the ensuing days the two men are supposed to have met. If they did, Beethoven looked from his

deathbed upon his successor among the reigning monarchs of his art, the first and one of the greatest of all the composers of the coming romantic movement, and the most inspired melodist who ever lived.

Beethoven saw a young man of insignificant, almost ludicrous appearance. Schubert was five feet one in height, with a roly-poly figure and sloping shoulders. His face was round and pudgy, with thick lips and a short nose. Even his eyes, which shone with a clear brightness expressive of the man's inner spirituality, had to be marred by ugly spectacles.

His meeting with Beethoven fulfilled one of the dreams of Schubert's life. At the public funeral of his master he was one of those who carried torches before the coffin. After the ceremonies Schubert sat in a tavern with his friends. He proposed a solemn toast, "To him we have just buried"; and then, in a moment of sudden and melancholy prescience, another: "To him who will be next." They drank—to Franz Schubert himself; for within two years he too was dead.

## II

The romantic movement, to which Franz Schubert contributed in such prodigal measure, was far more than an efflorescence of new ideas in the arts. It was a tide so strong that it burst the confines of the arts and flooded every corner of civilized man's activity. It affected morals and manners, politics, religion, even science. It passed from being an inspiring idea in the minds of a few creative artists into a way of life for several generations of Europeans and Americans. The present age, which arose from its dead ashes, is too much inclined to view that movement with disdain. We are close enough to remember at first hand its decadent and overripe end, the exaggerations and absurdities of its Victorianism, and the tight-laced corsets of a preposterous conventionality in which the movement had at last become encased. It is well to remember that the beginnings of romanticism were far different from its end.

The movement gained impetus from the writings of Jean-Jacques Rousseau, whose doctrine of naturalism was one of the two torches (the rationalism of Voltaire was the other) that set the fires of the French Revolution and ultimately burned down part of the eighteenth-century political system. Out of that conflagration came the ideal of freedom, equality, and the "rights of man"—a vast liberation of the human mind from ancient political and philosophical prisons.

Men of the arts were soon to take their cue from the statesmen and the sages. By the beginning of the nineteenth century the literary men especially were in rebellion against the dogmas of an outworn classicism. Down went the dusty walls of the Latin and Greek academicians, and the dry conventions that had kept creative minds in a closed garden. Out into the world the artist looked, free at last to choose for his uses any subject under the sun. Some of them turned to the past, and there began a re-creation of medieval history, celebrated in tales and ballads, novels and epic poems. In England the novels of Sir Walter Scott were a mixture of historical fact and poetic fancy, of love, adventure, and romance. E. T. A. Hoffmann in Germany and Edgar Allan Poe in America produced tales of imagination and horror, grisly excursions into the fantastic and the nightmarish; the Brothers Grimm turned to simple fairy tales and folklore. Some writers found inspiration in the beauty of nature and the simple life, others went down to the sea in ships. Cooper's theme was the struggle of a people against the wilderness and the savage; and later Herman Melville made grandiloquent epic out of a man's revenge against a great whale.

Inevitably it was the emotion of love that motivated most of the new romancers, especially in England where Coleridge and Wordsworth, Byron, Shelley and Keats, Tennyson and Browning burned their passions at undreamed-of temperatures. Shelley shocked his country not alone by his wild conduct but also by the searing intensity of his love poems; they were more frightening to a classic age than even the splendors of *Prometheus Unbound* or the violence of *The Mask of Anarchy*. In France it was with the novel that the romantic age reached one of its finest flowerings. Few other countries could rival the royal line that included Stendhal, Mme. de Staël, Dumas, Gautier, George Sand, Victor Hugo, and Balzac.

Germany had the most resplendent single figure of all, in the first flush of that age—Johann Wolfgang von Goethe —who was poet, dramatist, philosopher, novelist, and one of the universal minds of his time. Goethe's long life (1749–1832) bridged the two ages of classicism and romanticism. He called himself a classicist, and at times he opposed the excesses of the romantic movement; nevertheless, he was at once the sire and the midwife of that movement in Germany. As a young man in his twenties he had helped inaugurate the *Sturm und Drang*; his *Sorrows of Werther* filled the minds of half the young intellectuals of Germany with sentimental dreams of lovesickness, frustration, and suicide. His mature *Wilhelm Meister* became the model for countless romantic novelists, as his lyrics, ballads, and poetic dramas inspired the poets.

Goethe's life, his very self, was a romantic ideal. The lofty mind, serene and powerful, seemed to span the entire field of human knowledge—from the arts and philosophy to jurisprudence and medicine, from mysticism to occult philosophy, from the sciences of morphology and optics to astrology and alchemy. Handsome as a young god, born to the refinements and securities of life, he moved through an enlightened existence with deliberation and grace. He took the beauty of Italy in his stride; at Weimar he played the Platonic role of philosopher-statesman. With true romantic disdain of commonplace moralities he had one love affair after another, not omitting the scandal of an illegitimate son. Truly, "his life was his greatest work."

There was one of Goethe's creations that cut more deeply than any other into the romantic mind of the nineteenth century—his dramatic masterpiece, *Faust*. For almost sixty years first one and then the other of its two parts lay athwart his consciousness, struggling to be born. The work was an epitome of its author's own mind, with its churning of myriad ideas, its conflicts of philosophical thought. *Faust* became the great catalyst of its age, used by men in every other art to quicken their own imaginations.

Across the spectrum of romanticism, to which all the arts, the philosophies, the sciences, and even the personalities of individual men contributed, there appears one band of color more resplendent than all the rest—the art of music. The men who created romantic music came upon the scene after Beethoven, a procession of geniuses, one upon the heels of another, not only from Germany but also from neighboring countries where sparks from the blaze of German music had begun to fall—Schubert, Berlioz, Schumann, Chopin, Mendelssohn, Liszt, Wagner, Verdi, Brahms, Mussorgsky, Tchaikovsky. The work of all these men was originally made possible by Beethoven himself. He was like Goethe—the connecting link between the past and the future, a classicist whose work contained the germs from which the romantic ideas were to grow. The first truly romantic composer was Schubert.

### III

Franz Seraph Peter Schubert was born in a small suburb of Vienna on January 31, 1797, the son of a schoolteacher and the grandson of a Moravian peasant. The family was almost as large as that of J. S. Bach; there were thirteen children by two wives. Franz was the twelfth child. His father had to contend with the struggle against poverty that is often the reward of members of his profession. He found time to become an amateur cellist, and his famous son's first music teacher.

As a child Franz Schubert's talent was phenomenal. He picked up violin playing from his father, piano playing from an older brother, singing and harmony from a local choirmaster. He amazed them all by an intuitive knowledge that gave him a grasp of a subject before he was taught. He began composition at the age of ten.

In 1808 he won an appointment to the Imperial Convict, a school that was to be his home for the next five years. This was one of those child prisons where, in return for their singing in a choir, the boys were boarded, lodged, and taught. The building was spare and cheerless; in winter the rooms were icy. The schoolmasters were often cruel to the point of sadism, and there was never quite enough to eat. There exists a letter written by Franz Schubert, when he was fifteen, to his brother Ferdinand. His request is a pathetic one. "You know from experience how sometimes one wants to eat a roll and a few apples, and all the more when after a modest dinner one can look forward to a wretched supper 8½ hours later. This continually persistent wish troubles me more and more. . . . How would it be if you were to let me have a few kreutzers each month?"

Fortunately, there was the compensation of music at the Convict. The school orchestra was a good one, and at his post among the violins Schubert became acquainted with the easier works of Haydn, Mozart, Beethoven, and Cherubini. At the age of twelve he was emotionally stirred by Mozart's G minor Symphony, saying that it shook him to the depths without his knowing why. Soon he began to compose in earnest. He was too poor to buy music paper, but an older boy in the school gave him the money and then he used up paper by the ream. One of his teachers reported, "The lad knows everything already; he has been taught by God."

By the time Schubert was sixteen he had written half a dozen string quartets, and just before he left the Convict, late in 1813, he finished his first symphony. The next year he attempted his first opera. From the top gallery of a Viennese opera house he had heard Cherubini's *Medea*, Spontini's *Vestale*, and Gluck's *Iphigenia in Tauris*. In a few weeks he completed a long three-act work called *Des Teufels Lustschloss* [*The Devil's Pleasure Palace*]. In later years he gave the rearranged manuscript of this opera to a friend, whose servants (in 1840) used the pages of the entire second act to light a fire.

After he left the Convict, Schubert was nearly drafted into the Austrian army. It was the year 1813, and the European headsman was once again stalking the land. Unless a man could buy his way out, he faced a fourteen-year term in the service. Schoolteachers were exempt, so

Schubert took the easiest way and became an assistant teacher in his father's school. There he spent three years of drudgery at a business he loathed. Every moment that he could spare went into composition, and soon his production of music became nothing less than prodigious. Music seemed to pour from his pen with artesian abundance and without effort. Songs occupied him chiefly. In the two years between 1814 and 1816 he composed about two hundred and fifty. He wrote as many as eight in a single day. "When I finish one," he said simply, "I begin another."

The wonder of Schubert's genius was that his facility was geared even in his youth to superb creative ideas. One of his songs of his seventeenth year is *Gretchen am Spinnrade* [*Margaret at the Spinning Wheel*], from Goethe's *Faust*. It is his first masterpiece. It is also the beginning of a new phase in music—the modern German *Lied*. The poet's verses depict Margaret seated at her spinning wheel, her mind obsessed with longing for her lover. The first experiences of passion have ensnared and bewildered the unfortunate girl. Thoughts of the handsome man, the touch of his hand, of his lips, set her head reeling with desire; she is sick with the wish to die in his arms. The vividness with which Schubert translated this scene, with all its emotional and psychological implications, makes this song a prime example of art compressed into small means.

Late the next year (1815) two of his friends came to Schubert's lodgings and found him pacing the floor, reading aloud Goethe's ballad, *Erlkönig* [*The Erlking*]. The composer was "in a state bordering on frenzy." He had no piano, but he seated himself at a table and "in the shortest possible time the splendid ballad was on paper." He had created one of the world's greatest songs. Goethe's poem has a wildly dramatic beauty and a moving pathos that constitute balladry at its finest. It is the story of a father who rides through the night and the storm, clasping his child in his arms. The frightened boy imagines that the Erlking is following them, trying to lure him away. His father comforts him, but soon the voice becomes threatening and the boy cries out in terror that the Erlking has seized him. The father spurs on his horse until, trembling and exhausted, he reaches his home. But the child in his arms is dead.

Schubert's song is again a masterpiece of vividness and economy. The dramatic ride through the wild country-side, the eerie voice of the Erlking, the pleading of the child and his father's attempts to calm his fears, the des-perate dash for home, and the heart-breaking end—every implication of the words is painted in music. The pound-ing gallop of the horse's hoofs seems to continue without a break, until the last three measures; yet over that urgent pulse are heard four contrasting voices—the boy, the Erl-king, the father, and the poet himself describing the scene. The boy's is high-pitched and hysterical, the father's is low, the Erlking's barely whispered. These shifts in regis-tration and personality are achieved through a series of smoothly wrought modulations, which also serve to increase the excitement of the scene by moving higher and higher through a variety of major and minor keys.

If *Erlkönig* were not in every respect a great song, it would still be a landmark in music by reason of its har-monic scheme. Boldly the young composer set key against key with the daring of a painter placing unrelated tints together, yet fusing them so that they flow one into the other with liquid smoothness. The result was a richness of coloring that was rarely found in the music of the eighteenth century. It was one of the first manifestations of a metamorphosis in the science of harmony which was to bring about, under the hands of Schubert, Chopin, Liszt, and above all Wagner, a complete change in the face of modern music.

IV

It is now accepted as a practical truism that the song as a modern art form begins with Schubert. There is more accident than mystery in the fact that this appealing branch of the music art should have bloomed so late, and that so many of the masters of music before Schubert (particularly the Germans) should have ignored it. Because of its primitive origins and its kinship with folk music, the song was disdained by early composers of serious music, whose energies were bent instead upon church music and upon the development of more complex and hence, to them, more interesting forms.

There were a few isolated attempts by important composers to make art out of the song. The great English lutanist of the early seventeenth century, John Dowland, sang and accompanied himself on the lute in a virtuoso manner, and with notable public success. He published four volumes of his songs with lute accompaniment. An Italian contemporary of Dowland's, Giulio Caccini, also published (in 1601) a collection of songs for the lute, in a book famous among musicologists, *Le Nuove Musiche*. In his preface Caccini claimed to be the inventor of songs "for a single voice to the accompaniment of a single instrument."

Bach wrote but a handful of secular songs. His inspiration (aside from the purely abstract forms) came almost entirely from liturgical works. Handel's reservoir of melodic ideas was poured into operas and oratorios. Even Mozart, the most versatile of all composers, wrote but thirty-four songs, the merest drop in the bucket of his output. Mozart did, however, make one noteworthy contribution to the art of the song. By this time there had grown up in Germany two general types of serious songs, a division that exists to this day. The first was the *Volksthümliches Lied*, the simpler type based on the folk song, in which the same melody was used for each stanza of the poem. The second was a more sophisticated type, the *Durchcomponiertes Lied* (meaning, literally, "composed through"), in which the melody paid no attention to the form of the poem, stanza, or otherwise, but varied itself with complete freedom in order to mirror the thoughts expressed by the words. In 1785, Mozart set to music a short poem by Goethe, *Das Veilchen* [*The Violet*], and this is generally regarded as the first perfect example of the *Durchcomponiertes Lied*. All the implications of the words, both pictorial and emotional, are expressed with fidelity in Mozart's music.

With *Das Veilchen* the modern art song begins at last to put forth the tender leaves of hope. Beethoven unquestionably helped its growth. He wrote many songs, and the very fact that a composer of his eminence took an interest in the form was enough to give it a needed dignity. But Beethoven was not really the man to do it complete justice. Words were usually an obstacle instead of an inspiration to him. What the song as a serious form needed was a composer whose ear was attuned to the golden ring of great poetry, a man who could feel profoundly the pure beauty of words. Beethoven was not such a man, nor was Mozart, nor Haydn. But young Franz Schubert was. Poetry enthralled him. His ecstasy over Goethe's *Erlkönig* has been described. It was not by any means unusual.

There is the greatest unevenness in the words to the Schubert songs. They range from the best of Goethe and Schiller and Shakespeare to potboilers, on an aesthetic level with the words of the modern popular tune. This does not prove, however, that the composer himself was lacking in taste. It is more likely that he used the poorer samples along with the best simply because they were the only ones available to him. Books in his age were still a luxury; such a thing as a good, moderately priced anthology of verse was unknown. Much of the time he was so poor that he could not buy music paper, much less books. When he could not get good poems he used poor ones, and when he could get neither he reset poems he had already used. In his lifetime Schubert wrote more than six hundred songs; some two hundred (or about one third) are repetitions of lyrics previously used. Of Goethe's famous poem, *Nur wer die Sehnsucht kennt*, he made no less than six different versions over a period of a dozen years. Sometimes his repetitions include no more than slight corrections of the original, but many times the later version is an utterly different treatment. That he knew good poetry from bad is proved by the Goethe songs. He wrote seventy-one songs to fifty-nine of Goethe's lyrics, and their general excellence is unsurpassed in the entire catalogue of his vocal works.

To discover precisely what Schubert did for the song as an art form it is necessary to go no further than his so-called "song years," from 1815 to 1817, when hundreds of songs fell from his pen in a spring freshet of abundance. They include besides *Gretchen am Spinnrade* and *Erlkönig* almost thirty other of his great Goethe songs, among them *Heidenröslein*, *Wanderers Nachtlied*, *Rastlose Liebe*, *Erster Verlust*, and a group based on verses from *Wilhelm Meister*. Here also are *Der Tod und das Mädchen*, *An der Mond*, *Memnon*, *Gruppe aus dem Tartarus*, *An Schwager Kronos*, *Ganymed*, *An die Musik*, and *Der Wanderer*.

In spite of their creator's youth, these songs bear not the slightest trace of immaturity; but instead a wealth of melodic and harmonic beauty, originality, subtlety, exquisite workmanship, and an unerring sense of musical translation. Schubert could already project in tone not alone the dramatic feeling, atmosphere, and emotion of the poems as a whole, but also the niceties of thought contained in single words. To appreciate his accomplishment one need take but a sheaf of half a dozen of the best of these songs, almost at random, and then take note of the enormous span of creative thought that they bridge.

*An der Mond* [*To the Moon*] and *An die Musik* [*To Music*] are essays in pure melody. The former is a lovely night piece, tinted with the pale grays and silver of moonlight. It unfolds two melodies of piercing sweetness, clearly anticipating the nocturnes of Chopin. *An die Musik* is the composer's hymn of joy to his own art, which has sustained him in his hours of gloom and carried him heavenward on the wings of inspiration.

*Heidenröslein* is a little melody after Goethe's famous poem. The words are artlessly naïve, recalling the verses of Burns. A boy spies a wild rose growing on a hedge, and is captivated by her morning freshness. He tries to seize her, and is stabbed by her thorns. As a point of contrast it is interesting to turn to a song written two years later (in 1817), the celebrated *Der Tod und das Mädchen* [*Death and the Maiden*]. Here is simplicity, too, and brevity, but of an entirely different order. The words are a mere fragment of dialogue, in which a young girl begs Death to pass her by. "I am still young!" she cries, and Death is filled with compassion for his victim. In a monotone that hardly rises above a whisper he calms her fears. He is not wild or gruesome, nor has he come to frighten or to punish. His errand is the merciful blessing of sleep. Here is a case where the composer's genius lay in what he omitted. He needed only a handful of measures, two themes of utmost simplicity, and an accompaniment that is a model of restraint; yet with these few means the macabre idea grips the imagination. The composer himself was haunted for years by the solemn theme that is the voice of Death. A decade later he used it for the Variations in his Quartet in D minor.

*Rastlose Liebe* [*Restless Love*] is a passionate and fiery love song. The words were a memento of Goethe's youthful adoration of Charlotte von Stein, one of his numerous inamoratas. The wild ecstasy of love has swept the poet's life like a storm, giving him no respite from its blissful torments. How can he escape from the love that is at once the agony and the crown of his life? Schubert set this lyric to music when he was eighteen years old, the same year that he wrote *Erlkönig*. The song was also a product of one of his clairvoyant states, when he was so moved by the verse that the music came to him in one blinding flash of inspiration. This moment in which *Rastlose Liebe* was born was so vivid that he remembered it for years afterward and spoke of it himself with astonishment.

Among the flood of songs of Schubert's nineteenth year is one of his most famous works—the lordly *Wanderer*. The poetic idea is typical of the German sentimentality of the time. A homeless one has wandered, careworn and heartsick, searching for the land of his desire. But always that country of green fields and rose blooms has eluded him; to his sighs of "Where? where?" a voice within him answers, "'Tis always there, where thou art not." In Schubert's hands the idea takes on the grandeur of a lofty drama.

*Gruppe aus dem Tartarus* [*Group from Tartarus*] is an inferno in tone. The words are Schiller's. We descend into Hades, an abyss of horror in which the wail and shriek of the damned fill our ears. Upon the banks of Cocytus stand a desperate company, their brows knotted with anguish, their hollow eyes staring at an approaching ship. Is it to be deliverance at last from an eternity of pain? Schubert patterned his music on the chaos of the frightful scene, basing it on unrelated harmonies that move chromatically up and down, filling it with clashing discords and grating dissonances. What the composer's contemporaries thought of this song we can only guess; nothing like it had ever been heard before. But its chromaticism and its discord, its dramatic furies, were not forgotten. They were to echo again, decades later, all through the music of Wagner, Liszt, Strauss, and their contemporaries.

From the above half-dozen examples, chosen from his several hundred, it is possible to gauge what Schubert accomplished with the song. Relatively speaking, it hardly existed in his time; with one stroke he created it and almost exhausted its possibilities. All his finer songs had important implications for the future. There were two main forcing beds from which the romantic movement in German music blossomed: one was the music of Beethoven, the other the songs of Schubert.

The crux of the romantic movement was a new connection between music and purely literary ideas. Nearly every exemplar of romanticism, from Schubert to Richard Strauss, lived in a creative atmosphere saturated with ideas borrowed from literature. These men took the abstract forms of the eighteenth century and revivified them by crossing them with poetry, legend, drama, folklore, religion, and even philosophy. Schumann made his piano music the mirror of a picturesque array of literary fancies; Berlioz took the pure abstraction of the symphony and gave it a program; Liszt created the tone poem; Wagner changed opera into music drama, in which the play was given at least a theoretical rank of importance with the music. The basic impulse of all these manifestations can be found in the songs of Franz Schubert.

No one need expatiate at this late date on the genius of Schubert as a melodist. It was one of the most astounding gifts ever bestowed upon a creative musician, worthy of rank with Beethoven's powers of thematic development and Bach's command of polyphony. In Schubert's songs it flowered with junglelike profusion. Moreover, the Schubert melodies are not only abundant but also characteristic; we can recognize them instantly as his. They can be sweet, exquisite, tender, lovely, melancholy—and yet they never cloy. They can be noble to the point of sublimity, and without the slightest trace of strain. One fact about the Schubert melodies, however, too often goes unnoted: they were supported by the composer's almost equal gift for harmonization. Schubert was the first composer with a modern feeling for harmonic freedom. He seemed to have divined the open sesame of modulation; he could move from key to key almost at will. As a result, his harmonic schemes are so rich in color contrasts that they make the works of his late eighteenth-century predecessors seem washed out and plain. The effect, in music history, is like passing from the view of pictures in black and white to the splendor of stained glass windows.

One other technical feature of the Schubert songs should not pass unnoted—the variety and range of their accompaniment material. Every poem seemed to suggest some new treatment of the piano part. Often it becomes almost symphonic in texture; invariably its role in expounding the idea, painting the scene, and arousing the emotion of the poem, is hardly secondary to that of the voice itself.

v

When he was twenty years old Schubert could stand schoolteaching no longer. He wanted to devote his life to music. The idea was long opposed by his father, who knew what misery lay in store for a musician as impractical and retiring as his son. But young Schubert was not to be swayed, and he gave up his position at the school. From there on his life was like a boat cast adrift. He had no money and no income except an occasional pittance from music lessons or the sale of a song. How he managed to exist during the next ten years remains a mystery. Most of the time he lived off his friends.

There had grown up around him a group of young intellectuals, some of whom had been his fellow students at the Convict. They were bohemians of a sort—writers, painters, actors, and musicians. They met in the genial atmosphere of the Viennese taverns. Schubert was one of the leading spirits, and he seems to have been particularly admired and beloved. One of his warmest admirers was Michael Vogl, who was a famous operatic star of the time. As a schoolboy Schubert had heard him sing at the Viennese opera houses. Vogl was fabulously endowed for his profession, with a glorious baritone voice, a gift for dramatic acting, a Hollywood face and figure, and a brain. In his dressing room he read the works of Plato, Epictetus, Marcus Aurelius, and Thomas à Kempis. He became an ardent Schubert champion and the first important artist to sing his songs in public. He introduced *Erlkönig* to the world at a public concert in Vienna, in 1821. On several occasions Vogl took the composer with him on summer trips to neighboring Austrian towns. The actor's generosity gave Schubert an opportunity to enjoy the countryside and his first glimpses of mountain scenery, and it probably saved him from starvation. On another occasion (in the spring of 1818, when he was twenty-one) Schubert's friends had to come to his rescue by securing for him a position as music teacher to the two young daughters of Count Johann Esterhazy. The composer spent the summer and autumn months at the Esterhazy country estate in Zseliz. His teaching duties were not arduous, he had ample time to compose, and his surroundings were pleasant. In his letters he spoke well of the Esterhazys, but remarked, "I have been spared any invitation to the dining room." He lived and associated only with the servants—the coachmen, the chef, the nurse, and the chambermaid.

After the Zseliz interlude the composer returned to Vienna. The fact that his personal life was disorganized and his income practically nil seemed to have no effect whatever upon his work. He could compose anywhere, at any time, for hours at a stretch if he was lucky enough to find solitude; if not, while carrying on conversations with friends, and even at the tables of noisy taverns. The works poured out in an endless stream—songs by the hundreds, symphonies, chamber works, piano pieces, overtures, Masses, operas, and operettas. Very little of this mass of work saw the light of publication during Schubert's lifetime. The music publishers paid almost no attention to him; when they did buy an occasional piece, it was for sums that were criminally small—often as little as a gulden (about ten cents) per song. Schubert did not seem to care what happened to his music. He gave away many of his manuscripts. It is fortunate that one of his admirers, Josef Hüttenbrenner, became a self-appointed librarian for Schubert, collecting and preserving his manuscripts, and even recovering many that had either been given away or simply had been taken by chance acquaintances.

Much of Schubert's time at this period was taken up by his persistent attempts to write operas. Beginning with his earliest effort at the age of seventeen, *Des Teufels Lustschloss*, he wrote no less than eighteen works for the stage. Some of these were never completed and exist only as sketches or fragments; others are lost. Not one of them ever succeeded. Modern attempts to revive and reconstruct the Schubert operas have always revealed the same fundamental defects. A few of the librettos are good; but the others strike an all-time low in a field where ineptitude is often taken as a matter of course. In spite of his lyric sense and his genius for translating into music the emotion and drama of words, Schubert had only a weakly developed sense of stage situations and of theatrical conventions.

## VI

In the fall of 1823 Schubert received notification that he had been elected an honorary member of a music society in the town of Graz. In his reply he promised to send the society a score of one of his symphonies as a token of his gratitude. A year went by before he finally delivered the pages of two movements of a symphony in B minor to Josef Hüttenbrenner, who passed them on to his brother Anselm, an officer in the Graz music society. Anselm then did a curious thing. He stored the manuscript away and said nothing about it to anyone. He kept it for more than forty years. Finally, in 1860, his brother happened to mention its existence to a conductor named Herbeck. This man persuaded Anselm Hüttenbrenner to give him the manuscript, and he produced the work for the first time, in Vienna, on December 17, 1865. Thus one of the most celebrated works in the whole literature of music—the *Unfinished* Symphony—was at last given to the world. By that time Schubert had been dead for thirty-seven years.

The manuscript of the *Unfinished* Symphony bears the date October 30, 1822, indicating that Schubert was only twenty-five years old when he composed a work that comes as near to claiming the attributes of aesthetic perfection as anything yet created in the music art. It was his eighth attempt at the symphonic form. Unlike Beethoven, who waited until he was thirty, Schubert had followed Mozart in plunging into these musical deeps while still an adolescent. His first symphony was written when he was sixteen and a pupil at the Convict; he wrote five more before he was twenty-one.

For the most part the early Schubert symphonies are typical late eighteenth-century products. Even though the composer had heard most of the eight symphonies that Beethoven had then written, he was not sufficiently impressed by them to attempt any imitations. As a youth he had disliked Beethoven's "revolutionary" style. His lack of creative daring is strange. At this time he was pioneering with all sorts of new ideas in his songs, but very few of these ideas creep into his early symphonies. Instead it is the impress of Mozart that is felt constantly—the elegance and grace, the insistence upon symmetry and formal balance. At times one might easily mistake them for works of Mozart; except when there appears in the melodies a certain mellow richness, and in the harmonies an unexpected brilliance of coloring, by means of which we recognize instantly the hand of Schubert.

In 1821, Schubert made elaborate sketches for a seventh symphony, in E major. He never finished it, even though he got enough on paper to permit several modern musicians to attempt reconstructions of it. The next year he tried another, but once again the effort was laid aside in an uncompleted state. This was the so-called *Unfinished* Symphony in B minor which he sent to Graz; and fortunately the composer did not follow the sketchy procedure by which he had laid out the rough general plan of the E major Symphony without filling in the details. The first two movements of the B minor Symphony are complete down to the last note. The composer dropped the work after sketching a hundred and thirty measures of a third movement.

The very opening measures of the *Unfinished* Symphony indicate what a remarkable advance Schubert had made over the style of his previous symphonies. He was no longer imitating; he had struck a style of his own. There is a quality of grandeur and tragic solemnity in the entire first movement of the *Unfinished* Symphony that is lacking in his early symphonic efforts. For this purpose Schubert borrowed certain elements of dramatic structure and style from Beethoven, but invested them with ideas of his own. He also succeeded at last in finding expression within the symphonic framework for his own especial gift—beautiful melody supported by enriching harmonies. The *Unfinished* Symphony is one long procession of superb melodic ideas, colored by some of the most exquisite harmonic hues ever devised. The orchestration is in every way equal to the material it illuminates. In the second movement the use of solo woodwinds is lovely beyond description. For a time the music seems to lose contact with life; it becomes unearthly, spiritual, angelic.

Why Schubert abandoned this masterpiece as he did remains a mystery. It seems inconceivable that it would be a matter of indifference to him if a work of such magnitude remained truncated. He obviously broke off his third movement because it lacked the inspiration of the first two; possibly other attempts at completion failed the same way. The composer's problem was made especially difficult by the mood that binds the first two movements together—a gentle sadness that pervades not only the minor modes of the first but, by some unexplained alchemy, also the major modes of the second. To continue that mood through two more movements would have been out of the question. The problem was to create another mood that would end the work and yet harmonize with what had gone before. Even Schubert, with all his fund of inspirational material, did not find it. It is likely that he came then to the same realization that the listener does who has heard many performances of this symphony: that the work is not unfinished at all. To have gone on, merely for the sake of obeying one of the laws of musical structure, might have meant detracting from the supreme beauty of what had already been accomplished. In a symphony every movement exists both for its own special virtues and for the beauty of contrast, of dramatic emphasis, of unified style that it sheds upon all the other movements. If a composer of Schubert's greatness could find nothing to say beyond the two movements of his *Unfinished* Symphony then we may be certain that the work was, in every aesthetic sense, complete.

### VII

Shortly after the composition of the *Unfinished* Symphony Schubert became ill. He was taken to a hospital in Vienna; his hair fell out and for a time he had to wear a wig. During the following year he was plunged into terrible despondency. One after another his operas had failed; his songs were making headway in popular favor, but he had foolishly sold certain of their publication rights for almost nothing. For almost ten years he had known little else than poverty and the charity of his friends. And now, with all his privations, he was sick. "Picture to yourself," he wrote, "a man whose brightest hopes have come to nothing, to whom the joy of love and friendship is but anguish, whose inspiration for the beautiful threatens to fail, and then ask yourself if such a man is not miserable and unhappy. . . . Every night when I go to sleep I hope never to wake again."

The ultimate wreckage of Schubert's life and of his immeasurable talent was so tragic a set of circumstances that writers have too often fallen into erroneous generalizations about its basic causes. Since art began there have been artists who lived and practiced in comfort or even luxury, and others who starved. The precise economic value of the artist and his work is a problem that no age has ever solved. A case like that of Schubert was so glaring that we are likely to look back upon it over the range of years and assign wrong reasons for its happening—to assume that he suffered because the people of his time must have been indifferent to music, or because there was a wholesale lack of appreciation of art and the problems of the artist.

It was not the people of Schubert's time but the economy that was out of joint. He had the misfortune to be born into one of the catastrophes of modern history—the Napoleonic wars. He reached manhood in the decade after Waterloo, a time when Europe was floundering in a morass of woe. Millions of lives had been destroyed or ruined; commerce was paralyzed. Peasants and workers who were not driven to starvation by the ruination of the old economy were being caught in the wheels of the new industrial system. Misery was spread over the whole face of Europe, and with it a corroding despondency. The blazing light of revolutionary hope had gone out; Bonaparte had been beaten at vast cost of blood and treasure only to return the Bourbons to the seats of power. It was no accident that in 1818 Schopenhauer published *The World as Will and Idea*, a work of philosophy ridden with pessimism as by a disease.

In the midst of these depressed times, musicians like Franz Schubert suffered a double calamity. A few years before they had been living under the patronage system. For all its meanness, that system had at least kept many of them alive. Now great social and political storms had swept it away, but as yet nothing had been devised to take its place. The artist had won his social freedom, but years would pass before new economic machinery could be set up to make him even moderately self-sufficient. That machinery would take the form of the public concert, widespread music publishing enterprises, with royalty payments and the protection of copyrights. But in Schubert's time these existed only in embryo.

In a world like that after Waterloo the first demand for any man is the tough armor of self-preservation. It is one of the enigmas of human life that a man like Schubert, so laden with genius, should have been sent into the world practically defenseless. The help of his friends was not enough. He needed a patron; he needed a wife. It would not have been too much to ask for Schubert a woman like Catherine, the wife of William Blake, whose life was a slavish dedication to the service of her husband's art. But Schubert never married. His reticence constituted a barrier that he never got over. There were women in his life, but next to nothing is known of his relationships with them.

In recent years there have been musical-comedy versions of Schubert's life, with various romantic episodes embroidered into the plot. These episodes are as specious as the popularized adaptations of his music are vulgar. The most we know is that when he was seventeen he fell in love, for the first time, with a girl named Theresa Grob whose family lived near the Schuberts in Vienna. She had a lovely voice, and Schubert some years later said that she was "not beautiful and had pockmarks on her face," but she was "good—good to the heart." He admitted that he had loved her deeply, but he had no prospects whatever, so her family persuaded her to marry a well-to-do baker.

When he was twenty-four Schubert spent a second summer with the Esterhazys at Zseliz. The count's younger daughter Caroline was now seventeen, and some biographers believe that the young composer fell in love with his pupil. The evidence is slight. She once reproached him for not having dedicated any of his music to her; he replied, "Why should I, when everything I ever did is dedicated to you?" This may have been simply a gracefully extravagant compliment. If it was more than that, the composer must have known that his love for a woman so far above his rank was hopeless.

In the summer of 1823, at the time of his worst mental anguish, Schubert produced one of his most famous vocal works—the richly sentimental song cycle, *Die Schöne Müllerin* [*The Beautiful Maid of the Mill*]. The composer happened to pick up a small volume of verses, the *Müllerlieder*, by Wilhelm Müller, an obscure young professor at Dessau. Müller was a minor poet who wrote verses full of sentimentality and artificial melancholy, in which mills, streams, and other rustic scenes were the background for lovesick youths in the throes of unrequited love. The *Müllerlieder* recount the love of a wandering young apprentice miller for a miller's fair daughter. The idyl is shattered by a green-clad hunter who captures the maid's heart. The despairing youth seeks death in the millstream.

Schubert was instantly taken with the possibilities of the Müller poems, and from them he created a cycle of twenty songs. In themselves, the *Müllerlieder* are hardly more than a collection of inoffensive valentines. But in Schubert's settings they become as authentic in their representation of simple rustic beauty as the verses of Burns; their sentiments seem as deeply felt as those of Housman.

In spite of the doleful end of the story (and the fact that the composer was in the hospital part of the time while he composed them) the Mill songs contain some of the most exuberantly happy music that Schubert ever wrote. The first pieces of the cycle especially are full of the wild ardor of young love. Spring is in the heart of the youthful miller; it sings from the rushing brook and from the roar of the flashing mill wheel; it floods the scene like May sunshine streaming through green branches. Schubert made some of these songs almost folklike in their simplicity; they wear the mask of peasant innocence. But theirs is a case of art that conceals art.

It has long been one of the clichés of music criticism that Schubert could not write successfully in the larger forms. The notion still persists that he was incapable of anything but a kind of spontaneous composition. He has even been regarded as a wonderful simpleton who had no control whatever over the inspirational geyser that spouted from his brain. It is supposed that when he did try to guide this font of ideas into the larger areas of design his work became diffuse, sprawling, and lopsided. Under this theory works like his *Unfinished* Symphony and the great C major Symphony, his D minor String Quartet, are regarded as accidents—as exceptions which do not disprove the general rule.

No blanket denial can be made of these criticisms of Schubert's work, for the reason that some of them are true. At times he was a careless craftsman, taking the line of least resistance, filling up his reams of music paper with notes not too scrupulously conditioned by self-criticism. It is undoubtedly his piano music that has given most credence to a disparaging view of Schubert's work as a whole. His smaller pieces contain some of the loveliest music he ever wrote, while the larger ones are noteworthy for their mixture of good and mediocre. The short pieces include the famous *Impromptus* and *Moments Musicals*, miniatures that were written late in the composer's life. They introduced a new idea into piano music: the brief one-movement piece, poetic in mood and songlike in melodic style. Schubert simply transplanted the song idea to the piano, and thus he was the father of the *Song without Words* and that vast progeny of piano pieces in similar vein with which the later nineteenth century was overrun. Being so close to the basic style of the song, it is obvious that here Schubert could not fail. Especially in the *Moments Musicals* his touch is unerring and exquisite.

The larger works—that is, the sonatas and the *Wanderer* Fantasia in C major—are problematical. For more than a century pianists neglected them. They were generally dismissed as garrulous and diffuse, as a hodgepodge of many loosely strung together melodies instead of the logical development of a few. The modern view, however, is quite different. There are at least half a dozen of the sonatas that are magnificent. It goes without saying that they are full of splendid melody. Schubert simply could not write other than melodiously. Harmonically they are even more interesting. Taking advantage of the freedom offered by the instrument, the composer flooded them with ingenious and kaleidoscopic key coloring. Moreover, some of these pieces have a breadth of dimension and an underlying dramatic force which indicate that Schubert as he grew to manhood had begun to understand the aims of Beethoven. They speak in the grand manner. Certain of them stand out above the rest—those in A minor (Op. 42) and D major (Op. 53), which date from 1825; the brilliant G major (Op. 78) written the next year, and misnamed "Fantasy" by an obtuse publisher; and the three "Large Sonatas" in C minor, A major, and B flat major, written in 1828, the year of the composer's death. To these must be added the spacious *Wanderer* Fantasia, so named because the opening theme of its slow movement derives from the famous song.

There is a revealing fact to be pointed out here. The sonatas that are poorer in quality than those mentioned above are all products of the composer's earlier years. They are hardly more than boyhood attempts. The great ones clearly demonstrate Schubert's maturing mastery of the larger forms.

## VIII

After his first spell of serious illness Schubert was never again a well man. He was subject to recurring periods of sickness and to acute melancholia.

One of the respites from his despairs was a trip with Vogl into Upper Austria in 1825. On this occasion Vogl sang for the first time Schubert's newly created songs from Scott's *Lady of the Lake*, including the *Ave Maria*. The two men were royally entertained by musical friends; they went on to Linz, to Salzburg, and to Gastein. There the composer wrote his tremendous *Die Allmacht* [The Almighty], another song of epic grandeur and solemnity; and there too he may have composed the mysterious *Gastein* Symphony. This work (if he ever really wrote it) is lost; but like Kidd's treasure it still plagues and fascinates the believers in its existence.

In March 1827, Beethoven died, and Schubert bore a torch at his funeral. His melancholy at that event has been noted. A few weeks before he had begun work on another cycle of songs based on poems by Wilhelm Müller, and called *Der Winterreise* [The Winter Journey]. Müller too may have had premonitions of death; before the year was out he was dead at the age of thirty-three. The cycle of the *Winterreise* is Schubert's sovereign achievement in the art of song. Certain of his other songs may singly surpass the finest in this cycle, but as a group those of the *Winterreise* are peerless.

Schubert himself knew that his pieces would be disquietingly strange to his contemporaries. He said to a group of his friends to whom he first sang them, and who sat gloomy and puzzled at the end, "I like them all more than any of the other songs, and the day will come when you will like them too." He knew that this cycle was the hardest task he had ever set himself in song—a twenty-four-part dissertation, of enormous variety and range, upon a single theme of human woe.

The story of *The Winter Journey* is a far different one from that of the *Mill* cycle. Again it is a lover whose progress is followed, but this time the man's mind is unhinged by the unfaithfulness of his loved one. He plunges out into the bitter cold of a winter night, wandering aimlessly, hoping to find respite; but every aspect of the pale December landscape, every sound that he hears, pulls his mind back like a weighted wheel to his inward agony. A weather vane reminds him of his sweetheart's affections, which veer with every gust of the wind; he searches for her footsteps in the snow; he recalls the words of love he had carved on the bark of an old linden tree. The eerie will-o'-the-wisp leads him on until he finds shelter in a charcoal burner's hut. There he dreams of past happiness until the crowing cocks waken him to his cold bed in the freezing winter dawn, and to further wandering and suffering.

Through twenty-four separate songs the lugubrious tale is unfolded. There is hardly a weak song in the entire cycle, although a few have stood out above the rest in popularity. Most famous is *The Linden Tree*, which is Schubert with all his tenderness, his unblemished sentiment, his simplicity that defies imitation. There is little doubt, however, that the masterpiece of the cycle is the last—*Der Leiermann* [*The Organ Grinder*]. It is a matter of wonderment, fascination, and mystery. "Given a thousand guesses," wrote Richard Capell, "no one could have said that the last song would be at all like this." At the end of a village street the madman meets an old beggar. Ragged and barefoot, he stands on the icy ground, grinding away on a wheezing organ. His cup is empty; "no one listens to him, no one looks or cares. Snarling dogs pursue him, still a smile he wears." At last the madman has met his destiny. "Old man, shall I go with you?" he cries. "Will you set my songs to music?"

*Der Leiermann* is one of the sparest songs ever written. A single empty fifth in the bass drones like a barrel organ through the entire piece; above it the whining, jangling little tune of the hurdy-gurdy repeats itself again and again, alternating with the voice. Only three score of measures, with the barest handful of notes to each measure —and yet the song crowns the *Winterreise* cycle with a perfection that baffles and haunts the listener.

The year 1828 was Schubert's last and, like the closing year of Mozart's life, it was crowded with creative activity. It was his "great year" in every sense, when his prodigious outflow of work was governed by an assured mastery in every form that he touched. He wrote his great Mass in E flat, three of his best piano sonatas, the String Quintet in C major which is one of the most resplendent works in the whole range of chamber music, a group of songs that include some of the profoundest of all his vocal works, and finally the C major Symphony which now stands shoulder to shoulder with the *Eroica*, the Fifth, and the Seventh symphonies of Beethoven. In the face of these achievements there can be little left of the notion that Schubert was incapable of the workmanship required of the builder in the higher forms.

The C major Symphony was composed in the month of March 1828, but Schubert did not live long enough to hear it performed. When it was first tried out in Vienna, the orchestra gave it up because it seemed too involved and difficult. The first performance did not occur until 1839, when Mendelssohn performed it at the Leipzig Gewandhaus. After that occasion a young composer named

Robert Schumann wrote, "I say quite frankly that he who is not acquainted with this symphony knows but little of Schubert. . . . Herein is revealed the finest technical skill, life in every fiber of the music, the finest gradations of coloring and care for the minutest detail; the whole structure is shrouded in the cloak of romanticism which has now become familiar to us in Schubert's compositions. It has, too, the same heavenly length as, say, a four-volume novel by Jean Paul. . . . No symphony has made such a strong impression on us since the days of Beethoven."

When Schumann spoke of "heavenly length" he used a phrase that was often to be quoted in later years with ironic intent. The C major Symphony is in truth a gigantic structure—four long movements which run to more than forty-five minutes in performance. There were few who, like Schumann, could encompass its tremendous arc without repeated hearings. In 1842 a Paris orchestra refused to go on with it after rehearsing the first movement. Mendelssohn tried it out with the London Philharmonic in 1844, but had to abandon it. There was a famous scene. When the English players came to the wild triplet figures in the last movement they burst out laughing and had to stop.

If Beethoven's Seventh Symphony may be called an apotheosis of the dance, this C major of Schubert is in an equal sense an apotheosis of song. Schubert had learned how to take the small materials of his songs—the lovely melodies, the prismatic harmonies, the vital rhythms—and expand them into the macrocosmic world of the symphony. Moreover, the composer's power to evoke compelling emotion, so often displayed in his songs, is here given the scope and opportunity worthy of its strength.

Schubert worked harder on this symphony than on any other work. The original manuscript is full of corrections in the composer's own hand, proof that he had realized the value of Beethoven's meticulous workmanship. The last movement is the greatest single movement that he ever wrote, and one of its technical features is a dramatic device so simple and yet worked out with such effect that

Beethoven himself would have envied it. This is the use of a motive built upon a single note repeated four times. Soon after the opening of the movement these four notes appear, breathed softly in the horns, so guilelessly as to seem little more than a rhythmic pulse. As the movement unfolds they begin to take form and importance; their irresistible throbbing begins to dominate all else, making itself felt even when the notes themselves are not the dominating melody. At the stunning and climactic end they reach at last their victory over the entire emotional scheme of the work—as four tremendous Cs, stamped out in unison, fortissimo, like the master cadence of some universal revelry.

## IX

Late in the summer of 1828 Schubert became so ill and so despondent that his brother Ferdinand took him to his house in the suburbs of Vienna. There the composer lived quietly for a time, unsuspecting that the hour had grown late. On the last day of October he suddenly rose from his table at an inn and exclaimed that he could not eat, that his food tasted like poison. He did not realize that the poison in his veins was typhus. On the twelfth of November he wrote a letter (it was his last) to a friend, saying, "I am ill. I have had nothing to eat or drink for eleven days now, and can only wander feebly and uncertainly between armchair and bed. . . . Please be so good as to come to my aid in this desperate condition with something to read. I have read Cooper's *Last of the Mohicans*, *The Spy*, *The Pilot*, and *The Pioneers*. If by any chance you have anything else of his, I beg you to leave it for me at the coffeehouse. . . ."

After that he never left his bed; though he talked at length of plans for another opera, and he sat up to make corrections in the proofs of his *Winterreise* songs. Immersed in those pages of gloom and frustration, he performed his last earthly task. He became delirious, crying out to his brother, "Do not leave me in this corner under the earth." Ferdinand tried to explain that he was in his own bed, in his own house, but the dying man insisted, "No. That cannot be true. Beethoven is not here."

The end came on the nineteenth of November 1828. He was thirty-one years old. One final wish at least was carried out, for they buried him at Währing, a few feet from the grave of Beethoven.

The official who made an inventory of the composer's effects recorded a list of his clothes and the bedding—the remnants of a personal life that had never known the meaning of abundance or of comfort. Noted too was a quantity of "old music"—in reality some five hundred of the composer's manuscripts. These heaps of pearl were valued at the equivalent of about two dollars. At first the dust of neglect lay over them and many other of Schubert's scores, the same dust that had choked and smothered the composer himself throughout his life. Years went by before much of it saw light. The famous discovery by George Grove and Arthur Sullivan of the lost music of *Rosamunde* was made as late as 1867.

One group of works at least did not share that fate of prolonged silence. This was the collection of fourteen songs which a publisher brought out some six months after Schubert's death, under the title *Schwanengesang* [*Swan Song*]. These pieces had been written in August 1828 and were the composer's last. Included are songs of undying fame and unexampled greatness. One is the lovely *Serenade*, its exquisite texture still whole, in spite of years of hard treatment that would have worn a poorer fabric to shreds. There is also the wildly despairing *Aufenthalt* [*My Abode*], and the last of Schubert's many brook songs, *Liebesbotschaft* [*Love's Message*]. Six of the group are settings of verses by Heinrich Heine. These include *Der Atlas*, an expression of tragic power and great depth of feeling; *Die Stadt* [*The Town*], and *Am Meer* [*By the Sea*], songs whose subtlety and originality hint strongly of an impressionism that was yet three quarters of a century in the future; and finally *Der Doppelgänger* [*The Double*]. In these Heine songs burned the coals of prophecy. Without them the progress of the German *Lied* during the nineteenth century would have been utterly different.

The urge is strong to pronounce *Der Doppelgänger* Schubert's greatest song. The poet stands in the dead of night in a lonely street. "In that house my loved one once dwelt. She is gone; the place is deserted. But there stands a man, staring at the empty house, wringing his hands in despair. I shudder; the moon comes out and I see his face. It is myself! Thou ghastly fellow, thou shadow of my own grief, why do you enact my sorrows of many a night so long ago?"

This is one of those songs, like *Der Leiermann* and *Der Tod und das Mädchen*, in which the composer seized upon an idea that would have left any other musician of his time helpless, and proceeded to give it a setting that is a marvel of aptness and economy. The accompaniment is especially stark. It revolves around four chords that strongly suggest the Dies Irae. Above their tolling the voice describes the weird scene in recitativelike phrases. Schubert, the master of harmonic progression, broke all bounds here. The modernity of his chords is astonishing, and like the clash of iron. It would require no wrench of the imagination to place this song fifty years into the future and straight into the hands of Mussorgsky.

Thus the man who was "very nearly the greatest of all composers" ended his career—with his eyes upon a horizon far beyond the range of any of his fellows.

# Berlioz and Liszt
## 1803—69        1811—86

### I

No age or place ever produced a denser concentration of
individualists, each intent upon the free proliferation of
his own ego, than Paris during the years 1830–40–the
bright morning of the romantic era. The city swarmed
with wild men of genius, with exotic personalities as brilliantly colored as so many tropical birds. Romanticism had
come of age, and 1830 formally celebrated its adulthood.
In that year the stupid Bourbonism of Charles X met its
end in revolution; in another quarter the riots over the
production of Victor Hugo's *Hernani* signaled the victory
of the new romantic drama over a dogmatic classicism. In
that year Berlioz, "mad Hector of the flaming locks," composed the *Fantastic* Symphony, a musical landmark which
was also a testimonial to his unrequited (later all too
completely requited) passion for an Irish actress. Hugo
was beginning his long career as dramatist, novelist, and
poet; Balzac was toiling away his anchorite existence in an
attic, already started on the stupendous task of the *Comé-
die humaine*, which was to burn his body out at the age
of fifty but leave him the master of all French novelists.
Gautier was there, brilliant stylist and passionate romantic; Dumas, the French Scheherazade; Sainte-Beuve, the
greatest critical mind of the nineteenth century; George
Sand, the woman who dressed like a man, smoked cigars,

and performed man's work of writing novels; the German, Heinrich Heine, a poet "who dipped his pen in honey and gall, who sneered and wept in the same couplet," and Mérimée, Stendhal, Lamartine, Musset, and Chateaubriand. Delacroix was there, a man of bold imagination, intellect, and courage, whose work became a lasting ornament to French painting; and Delaroche, Vernet, Corot, Ingres, Ary Scheffer, Théodore Rousseau. The roll call of musicians was no less impressive. Besides Berlioz and Chopin there was Liszt, then in the zenith of his flaming youth ("the wild, lightning-flashing, volcanic, heavenstorming Liszt," Heine called him), conquering the piano and women with the same Jovian ease; Rossini, the strangest of geniuses, who stopped work when he was thirty-seven at the height of his career and lived to be seventy-six; Meyerbeer, the man who made opera "grand," i.e., added the elements of spectacle, pageantry and bombast to the fundamentals of music and drama; Thalberg and Kalkbrenner, the rivals of Liszt as piano-taming virtuosi; Auber, Hérold, and a score of other men, once lions but now mere small type in music's footnotes.

The time was one of excess and extravagance. Individualism had boiled over until it dripped down into the fantastic, the exotic, and the downright foolish. To be an apostle of romanticism it seems that one had first to be odd. A strain of morbidity also ran through the minds of half of these romantics. They were filled with obsessions, illnesses of the flesh and of the spirit—and they gloried in them. Dumas wrote that "it was the fashion to suffer from the lungs; everyone was consumptive, poets especially; it was good form to spit blood after every emotion in any way sensational, and to die before reaching thirty." It was also the fashion to weep, faint, or otherwise carry on during theatrical performances. When Lesueur, an operatic composer and Berlioz' teacher, first heard Beethoven's Fifth Symphony, he was left so emotionally disorganized that when he started to put on his hat he could not find his head. When Alfred de Musset listened to lines by Racine, he would take his head in his hands and blanch with emotion. This same young poet admitted that, after his affair with George Sand had ended with her in the arms of the Italian Dr. Pagello, he spent four months shut up in his room in incessant tears.

It was the day of the grand passion and the *idée fixe*. Men's minds seemed to be conditioned less according to rational patterns than in imitation of some literary figure —the more morbid the better. If one did not fancy oneself a Werther with suicidal melancholia, one might be a Faust in the throes of a soul struggle or a Manfred hiding in his bosom some nameless sin of sins. Lord Byron himself had been one of the most popular literary figures in Europe; he had personified Werther, Don Juan, and Manfred all rolled into one; he was poet, adventurer, cynical sensualist, and possibly murderer. His very death was a piece of romantic idealism—an Englishman dying for the cause of Greek freedom.

If anyone could be said to personify that age—to typify (paradoxically) an era that was all untyped individualists —that man was surely Hector Berlioz. The first French romantic composer, and one of the most original musicians who ever lived was also a character who could serve as a model for some of the choicest aberrations of abnormal psychology. His life was a long train of misfortunes of every sort, caused by his work, the world, and women. Had he lived a hundred years later, he would have spent hours pouring his troubles into the ears of psychiatrists. Being denied that luxury, he wrote them instead in his celebrated *Memoirs*. That fascinating, overheated collection of fact and fancy is far from the most accurate book ever written by a great musician, but it is surely a masterpiece of revelation of both the author and his age. Berlioz never hid the truth about himself; on the contrary, he told all—and with a passionate and disarming abandon.

Born in Côte Saint-André, near Grenoble, in 1803, he was the son of a provincial doctor who sent him to Paris when he was eighteen years old to study medicine in spite of his desire to compose music. The sights of the dissecting room filled him with horror, at the time when his first experiences in the opera house had raised his musical ambitions to fever heat. He gave up medicine, but remained in Paris and became a composer. He almost starved to death during his early years of study, but when he was twenty-six he wrote the *Fantastic* Symphony, one of the most daringly original works in music.

The genesis of this piece was a theatrical performance in Paris at which Berlioz saw Shakespeare's *Hamlet* for the first time, and an Irish actress, Henrietta Smithson, who was a sensation as Ophelia. It was love at the very first glance. The composer wrote in his *Memoirs:* "I became possessed by an intense, overpowering sense of sadness, that in my then sickly, nervous state produced a mental condition adequately to describe which would take a great physiologist. I could not sleep, I could not work, and I spent my time wandering aimlessly about Paris and its environs. During that long period of suffering I can only recall four occasions on which I slept. . . ." As a means of getting the attention of the actress and impressing her, he wrote his symphony and got it performed in Paris. After some years of desperately unhappy amorous adventure he married Miss Smithson, and the marriage was a failure more excruciating than the courtship. Berlioz loved at least five different women in his lifetime, all with consuming ardor, but in true romantic fashion lost all of them. After divorcing the actress he married another lady who made him miserable when she tried to sing his songs. When he was an old man he decided that he had in reality loved but one of them—the first love of his adolescence. He sought her out finally, an old white-haired lady of sixty-seven with four grown sons, who remained only bewildered when he insisted that he had loved her for almost fifty years, even though in that time he had seen her but once.

Berlioz' music brought him even less happiness than his love affairs, because he was a prophet without honor in his own country. His originality and his genius were misunderstood in France, where he was generally regarded as a wild man. Certainly he did little to allay the fears of the conservatives, for he was an eccentric man, passionately sure of himself and his destiny, who became at last, through frustration and disappointment, embittered, disillusioned, and cynical.

There is a strong temptation to dwell upon the life and personality of this composer (it would be an impossibility for anyone to write a dull biography of him), but it is nevertheless his music that remains the more fascinating part of him. The *Fantastic* Symphony is a piece of musical pioneering of the first order—like a sudden tearing aside of a curtain to reveal in an instant the entire scene of musical romanticism as it was to develop during the next half century. It is the first "program symphony" (anticipated, it is true, by Beethoven's *Pastoral*), the first modern symphony with a fully developed literary plot. Brilliant, flamboyant, saturated with Byronic passions and ornamented with Poe-like grotesquerie, the *Fantastic* Symphony broke away completely and for the first time from the austerities of German classicism.

Its program was published by the composer as follows, in a preface to the score: "A young musician of morbid sensibility and ardent imagination poisons himself with opium in a fit of amorous despair. The narcotic dose, too weak to result in death, plunges him into a heavy sleep accompanied by the strangest visions, during which his sensations, sentiments, and recollections are translated in his sick brain into musical thoughts and images. The beloved woman herself has become for him a melody, a recurring theme [idée fixe] which he finds and hears everywhere." The five movements of the symphony are also plotted in detail. I. Dreams and Passions: in which the young musician recalls the melancholy yearnings and joys he experienced before seeing his beloved, the "volcanic love" with which she inspired him, and his moments of "delirious anguish." II. A Ball: at which he sees his beloved in the midst of a brilliant fête. III. Scene in the Fields: two shepherds piping; he is tranquil until *she* appears and he has a horrible presentiment that she may prove false. Thunder sounds in the distance, then silence. IV. March to the Scaffold: he dreams that he has killed his beloved, is condemned, and led to the execution block. At the end the idée fixe reappears for an instant, interrupted by the stroke of the ax. V. Dream of a Witches' Sabbath: he is in the midst of a frightful company of ghosts, magicians, and monsters who have come for his obsequies. Even her theme is made grotesque as she takes part in the diabolic orgy. The witches dance to a parody of the Dies Irae.

The young man of twenty-six who dreamed this morbid and fantastic dream did not create an unflawed masterpiece. The work is uneven—at times tragically so—but it teems with ideas. A new imagination, powerful and original, is at work, and the sparks fly in all directions. Moreover, the piece was only the first of a long series of efforts that contained more of revolution and image-breaking. The *Harold in Italy* Symphony (1834) was another symphonic adventure, based on Byron's *Childe Harold's Pilgrimage*. The entire work is built around an elaborate part for solo viola (supposedly the voice of Childe Harold), making it a kind of romantic concerto. The "dramatic symphony"—*Romeo and Juliet* (1839)—is an even more elaborate exposition of a literary work, a seven-part structure for chorus, orchestra, and soloists, describing various scenes from the play. *The Damnation of Faust* (1846) is a hybrid, half opera and half oratorio, based on a free interpretation of Goethe's drama. Meanwhile, in 1837, Berlioz had composed his Requiem, a work notorious in the history of music for its employment of the most gigantic of all orchestral forces. The score calls for a string section of more than one hundred players, twelve horns, four cornets, twelve trumpets, sixteen trombones, six ophicleides, and sixteen kettledrums—besides a host of woodwinds and percussion, and a chorus of more than two hundred voices. This, moreover, was only a fraction of the army of performers which the composer had originally planned for the work.

Heinrich Heine, who knew the composer in Paris, said of him: "He is an immense nightingale, a lark as great as an eagle. . . . The music causes me to dream of fabulous empires filled with fabulous sins." The empires of Hector Berlioz remain so many fantastic pieces of architecture reared against the sky of romantic music; and they remain, too, after a hundred years, a center of controversy. No music over so long a period has been so berated, belittled, defended. In all the criticism of Berlioz' work one word appears like a recurring theme—uneven. For all the boldness and vehemence of his style, he could not escape inequality of inspiration. It was not that he ever descended into the meretricious or the cheap; his bombast or his dullness results not from a failure of his taste, but from an unaccountable thinning of his ideas. He did not seem to know whether an idea was good or empty.

As a result it is the big works of Berlioz, those which represented his greatest ambitions and his most daring leaps into the future, which suffer most. The best of them are all repositories of music that is splendidly vital and enduring, but hardly one is a complete and rounded masterpiece. Individual movements, shorter pieces, fragments from some larger whole—these are often superb; for example, the *Roman Carnival* Overture, in which melodic verve and orchestral color are fused into a scintillating whole that never for an instant falters; or much of the oratorio, *L'Enfance du Christ*; or the famous short pieces from *The Damnation of Faust*, or the *Queen Mab* Scherzo from *Romeo and Juliet*, or certain sections of the *Fantastic* Symphony, and of the sadly neglected opera, *Les Troyens*. In the course of the long, sustained efforts, however, Berlioz' strength fails him and his breath gives out. Often his weakness is melodic. He lacked a large fund of interesting thematic ideas. His harmonic invention, moreover, was sometimes inadequate to the boldness of his other schemes. Although avoiding the commonplace, his harmonies sometimes sound awkward, not convincingly realized, too thinly spread or too dull to support his long melodic lines.

Thus the music of Berlioz is often that of the revolutionist who has not quite the strength to make his ideas stick. Other men copied them, improved them, and made them completely successful. Part of Berlioz' weakness came undoubtedly from his own character. He lacked the balance wheel of self-criticism, a governor on his cyclonic temperament. There is also something of the amateur about him; he is brilliant but erratic.

Berlioz' contributions to music, despite his faults, were of high importance. One of the foremost was his work in establishing the new spirit of romanticism in music. It is true that he was practically ignored during his lifetime in his own country, but in Germany and later in Russia his influence was enormous. He helped set the new style that broke away from eighteenth-century classic abstractions into vividly colored pictures and stories in music. He injected a stronger emotional force into this art, and a new element of strangeness and fantasy.

Technically his contributions were even more potent, especially in that field in which his pre-eminence has never been denied—orchestration. Berlioz was the first composer with a modern conception of instrumentation as a means of virtuosity for its own sake. He experimented with the various instruments, singly and in combination, in order to draw from them colors and timbres that his predecessors had never suspected. He added new instruments, including the harp and English horn. From all of them he made new demands of virtuosity and tonal range. It is significant that Berlioz never learned to play the piano. The orchestra was his personal instrument, and he thought directly in terms of it. His *Treatise on Instrumentation*, published in 1844, is the classic work on the subject. All great orchestrators who came after him—Liszt, Wagner, Rimsky-Korsakov, Strauss, Stravinsky, Ravel, and a host of others—owe him a debt.

II

If the personal life of Hector Berlioz typified the slow, melancholy descent into frustration and defeat that may so often befall a revolutionary artist, the life of Franz Liszt presents a dazzling contrast. Famous from the moment when he performed in Paris as a child prodigy, he went on to become the sovereign pianist of all time and one of the most brilliant figures in the gallery of nineteenth-century romantics. Liszt seemed to bear a charmed life. The gifts of grace were all his. Strikingly handsome, with a magnetic personality and a capacious mind, he was as commanding a figure in intellectual circles as in the salons of the rich. Audiences went mad over his playing and women adored him. His love affairs with various princesses and countesses, his illegitimate children, were the talk of Europe. This generous, proud, magnanimous artist, as warm-hearted as he was supremely gifted, went through life gathering all the honors and triumphs his age could bestow.

He was born in Hungary in 1811, the son of a minor official in the service of Prince Nicolaus Esterhazy. In young manhood, after his first successes as a prodigy, he joined the Paris romantics and became the friend of Chopin, Berlioz, Paganini, and George Sand. From Paganini's wizardry on the violin he conceived the idea of a new kind of piano playing, and at one stroke changed piano performance from a refined dissertation into a grandiose oration.

Writes Sacheverell Sitwell: "There were, it is beyond doubt, hypnotic powers in his playing. Something of a great actor like Keen or Irving, something of the Hindu fakir, were embodied in his art. It died with him; and we are bound to believe that nothing so transcendental will ever appear again."

Liszt's public career as a virtuoso came virtually to an end in 1847, and from the next year until 1861 he was at Weimar, as Court Music Director of the Grand Duke. This was a period during which he became an ardent propagandist for the new romantic music, giving historic public performances both orchestral and operatic, including the *première* in 1850 of Wagner's *Lohengrin*. It was also the period of his own greatest fertility as a composer, when he turned out a vast flood of music. From 1861 until 1870 he lived in Rome, where he took minor orders in the Church and became the Abbé Liszt. In the last decade of his life (he died in 1886) he taught a new generation of pianists who were to become the lions of the first decades of our own century; and with his last creative efforts he composed a final group of piano pieces that still sound daring in their harmonies and sonorities.

What remains today of the torrent of Lisztian music

that had once hypnotized Europe? A great part of it has melted away. First to go were hundreds of the transcriptions, by which Liszt had turned other composers' works of every conceivable nature into piano vehicles for himself. They often epitomize both his own fabulous technical equipment and his public's disregard for the canons of taste. He could translate brilliantly a Bach organ fugue, or exquisitely a Schubert song, or incredibly the complexities of Isolde's *Liebestod*. As easily he could toss off reams of rubbish, efforts that would create hysterical laughter among audiences today.

His original works often show the same contrast of the brilliant and the meretricious; nevertheless he was one of the most potent of romantic innovators. His finer piano works—the two concertos, the *Hungarian Rhapsodies*, the *Etudes Transcendantes*, the *Paganini Etudes*, the *Années de Pélerinage*, the B minor Sonata—are still living examples of his gift for iridescent harmonies, richly sentimental melody, florid design, dramatic power and declamation, and, above all, his profound understanding of the instrument itself. His *Faust* and *Dante* Symphonies, although not wholly successful, still recall vividly the spirit of musical romanticism that tried to re-create in tone the artist's adventures in great poetry and the drama.

Liszt's most enduring single invention was the symphonic poem. His idea came undoubtedly from the overture as that form had been developed by Beethoven, i.e. a single orchestral movement that relates in tone the general scheme of a drama that is to follow. Berlioz had developed the same idea on a much bigger scale in his program symphonies, a form that Liszt imitated in his *Faust* and *Dante* symphonies; but Liszt alone set the style for the shorter type of piece, and he coined the title, "symphonic poem." His procedure was to depict a fairly brief poetic idea or story, usually prefacing his score with a program note that set forth the meaning of his piece. He wrote thirteen symphonic poems in all, including *Orpheus*, *Prometheus*, *Tasso*, *Mazeppa*, *Hunnenschlacht*, and—most famous of all—*Les Préludes*.

# Chopin
## 1810—49

I

It was in mid-September 1831 that Frédéric Chopin arrived for the first time in Paris. He was twenty-one years old—a thin, sickly young Pole with a pale face, a long nose that curved like a scimitar, and large, sensuous lips. He was a sad young man; for he was bewildered, alone, and without money in a strange city that knew nothing of his talents as pianist and composer. His loneliness was aggravated by homesickness of the most poignant sort. Only a few weeks before a calamity had befallen his native land: the Russians had captured Warsaw. The thought of that devastation and the possible fate of his family and friends had left his mind in torment. He looked upon the gaudy French metropolis with mingled emotions. He wrote:

"There is the utmost luxury, the utmost swinishness, the utmost virtue, the utmost ostentation; at every step advertisements of venereal disease; shouting, racket, bustle, and more mud than it is possible to imagine; one can perish in this paradise, and it is convenient, from this point of view, that nobody asks how anybody lives. You can walk in the streets dressed in rags, and frequent tip-top society; one day you can eat the most hearty dinner for thirty-two sous in a restaurant with mirrors, gilding, and gas lighting, and the next you can lunch where they will give enough for a dickeybird to eat, and charge three times as much. . . ." He noted the hordes of "shabby individuals with wild physiognomies," but also the "host of interesting people here, belonging to the various professions."

Chopin did not know it then, but he had found his spiritual home. Paris was to be his headquarters for the remainder of his life. His work there was to make him one of the most influential creative musicians of the century, and the supreme composer for the piano.

Chopin became music's outstanding specialist. His range was not panoramic, but confined; his frail body and essentially limited mental scope reduced his interests to a narrow field. That field was a single instrument—the piano —but he understood it so profoundly that in a comparatively few years of work he almost exhausted the things that a composer could do with it. Chopin was one of the most original of musicians. He was also a stylist, who left his individual mark on everything he wrote.

He was born in a village near Warsaw, on February 22, 1810. His mother was Polish but his father was a Frenchman, who taught the French language for a living and held a professorship in several important Polish schools. Frédéric's unusual musical talent was discovered when he was six years old, and thereafter his family gave him the advantage of the best teaching available in Warsaw. He was so precocious at composition that many thought he would outstrip Mozart, but he was also such a remarkable pianist that it was not certain which way his future lay. When he was nineteen he heard Hummel, a noted pianist of the day, and Paganini, who set the violin afire with virtuosity. That decided him on being a pianist. Before he went to Paris he had given concerts with mild success in Warsaw, Vienna, Prague, Teplitz, and Dresden.

He was an odd man. For one thing there was ingrained in his soul a deep strain of melancholy. His whole life after childhood was colored by it; his music, of course, was drenched and tear-stained by it. Part of his mental suffering was the result of a sensitive mind in a sickly body. The last half of his life was a struggle against tuberculosis. Another possible cause of his moodiness was his attachment to his native Poland, the country he had to leave as a young man never to return, and which he saw mangled under the wheels of war.

Psychologically there was something within him that was badly warped. He never married, but all through his life he suffered from the frustrations of love. There exist passionate love letters that he wrote as a boy of eighteen to another young man. Later he fell in love with a young girl singing student at the Warsaw Conservatorium, Constantia Gladkowska. He was so shy that he scarcely dared to meet her, much less tell her of his love. Constantia became the means of turning him into a morose and brooding man, lonely of mind and disconsolate of spirit. There is no doubt that he dramatized and half consciously enjoyed his frustration.

When he was twenty-four he fell in love with Maria Wodzinska, the nineteen-year-old daughter of a Polish count. She was a flighty, coquettish girl who led him on; but her family objected to her romance with a musician and a sickly one at that. A few years later their engagement petered out. After Chopin's death all the letters of Maria and her family and a faded rose she had given him were found carefully wrapped in an envelope marked, "My sorrow."

These affections, however, were merely a prelude to the great love of his life, which began in Paris in 1838, when he was twenty-eight. This was his affair with George Sand. It lasted for eight years. Its final rupture brought first his creative career and then his life to an end.

II

Chopin's talent as a pianist was one of the most remarkable and one of the rarest in the history of the instrument. He was a brilliant technician, but he suppressed that side of his art for the exquisite and the subtle. Lacking the physical strength of Liszt, who could (and often did) smash the insides of a piano at a blow, he developed instead a marvelous fluency and a control of tonal color that was unique. Some critics complained of his extreme pianissimos that hardly rose above a whisper and of the intense refinements of his style but most listeners were impressed. They had never heard tones of such singing quality or such ethereal delicacy drawn from the instrument.

The young man's first few months in Paris were hard sledding. He gave a few concerts that were financial failures. But at least they gained him the admiration of certain influential musicians—especially Mendelssohn and Liszt—who introduced him to important musical and social circles. Chopin soon realized that the concert platform was not for him. It was not alone that his playing was too intimate for large rooms. "The crowd intimidates me," he later wrote to Liszt; "its breath suffocates me; I feel paralyzed by its strange look, and the sea of unknown faces makes me dumb." He gave up the idea of making money as a virtuoso, and for a time he even thought despondently of going to America. Then suddenly his prospects changed. His reputation as a pianist began to bring in pupils—the well-paying kind from the Parisian aristocracy. Soon, with an income assured, he began to live exactly as he pleased.

Chopin was the sybarite of composers. He loved luxurious surroundings, elegant clothes, aristocratic people. When he chose an apartment, it had to be in the best neighborhood, away from bad smells, smoke, or the sound of blacksmiths. He spent money lavishly on his furnishings, selecting everything with the care of an interior decorator. He loved flowers, and it gave him a sense of exquisite pleasure to have his rooms pervaded by the fragrance of violets. Beside his bed there had to be volumes of poetry. The small and beautifully ordered existence that he carved out around himself suited him ideally. He wanted no intruders, but only a few favorite pupils and his chosen friends, most of them socially prominent Poles. Each day he taught for a few hours, in a precise, efficient way. He liked teaching. Clothes were both a delight and a problem. He wore velvet waistcoats (generally black), patent leather shoes, and white or yellow gloves; but the rest of his costume was somber. His standard was that difficult one for which members of the Conservative Club everywhere strive—an unmistakable elegance that contrives to avoid the slightest hint of loudness. He got himself a carriage so that he could go about the mud of Paris in a manner befitting a gentleman. The orbit of his movements was narrow—the opera (which he adored), a few concerts, the houses of wealth and society to which his playing gave him entree. In these last places he was happy and at home. He could not bear coarseness or vulgarity in people any more than he could in clothes, and in the polite society of aristocratic ladies his sensibilities were less likely to be assaulted. He was decidedly a prude. Once he almost broke up his friendship with Liszt when he discovered that in his absence the pianist had used his rooms for an assignation. Mme. Sand wrote that Chopin "never contemplated without dread the idea of leaving Paris, his physician, his acquaintances, his room even, and his piano. He was a slave to habit, and every change, however small it might be, was a terrible event in his life." He had constructed a charming hothouse existence, ideally suited to his proud, sensitive nature, and he proposed to enjoy it to the full. Fortunately, it was an existence that also suited his creative needs. It permitted him to devote the best of what little energy he had to composition.

### III

A mere listing of Chopin's works is curiously revealing. In the first place it is a meager output: a dozen thin volumes will house his entire life's work. Coming after such producers as Bach, Handel, Mozart, Beethoven, and Schubert, Chopin seems almost like a loafer. Rather he was a perfectionist. He never set a note down carelessly, and he never tired of polishing and changing. As he worked over his manuscripts, he tortured himself with doubts about the minutest details, unable to make up his mind.

His output was otherwise restricted. The great composers who came before him were generally producers in a wide variety of forms—symphonies, operas, church music, chamber works, and pieces for various solo instruments.

Only the piano interested Chopin. The rest he almost totally ignored.

Even in his special field of the piano he composed with
a disdain of conventions. Up to his time most serious
piano music had consisted of sonatas and concertos. These
were the large classic forms in which a composer was expected to express his ideas for the instrument. Chopin
wrote only three sonatas and two concertos. The bulk of
his piano works came under titles that were new and
strange in his time for a composer of serious purposes.
These are the names that he chiefly used: Mazurkas, Polonaises, Waltzes, Rondos, Impromptus, Etudes, Nocturnes,
Scherzos, Preludes, Fantaisies, and Ballades. All of these,
except the Ballade, which he invented, were established
musical forms when Chopin took them over. But in every
case the basic idea was subjected, under his hand, to "a
sea change into something rich and strange."

There was another reason, beyond the desire for individuality, for Chopin's preoccupation with these unconventional forms. Early in his career he had difficulty writing
in the old matrices of the sonata and the concerto. His
first piano sonata, written when he was eighteen, is a premature birth—dead before it ever breathed. The two piano
concertos, both written before he was twenty, are much
better; but they are played today only because of their
fine piano parts. The orchestral material is amateurish and
weak. Chopin was slow in getting his ideas to work on a
grand scale. Instead he devoted himself to the thing he
could do best—the exploitation of small instrumental
forms. In this field his accomplishment was surpassed by
only one other composer—the omnipotent one in forms
both great and small—J. S. Bach.

Chopin was fortunate in discovering something else in
his early years as a composer—his own characteristic style.
It is one of the most individual of all musical styles,
stamped on almost every measure as his trademark, and
recognizable instantly as his alone. It might well have
taken him years to evolve. Nevertheless, even a piece like
the Variations on Mozart's *Là ci darem la mano*, Op. 2,
for piano and orchestra, a product of his eighteenth year,

contains in astonishing measure the essentials that were to serve him throughout his career. (This is the piece that called forth from Robert Schumann one of the most famous remarks in music history: "Hats off, gentlemen, a genius!") It is often said that of all important composers Chopin seemed to develop the least. Of course he *did* develop. With every work that he turned out his musical ideas became subtler and more original, his technical devices more brilliant, his handling of material more assured. But it was all within the confines of the general style that he cut out for himself when hardly more than a boy.

Chopin's style had many ramifications, and even certain peculiarities, but none of them was arbitrary. Almost everything that he did stemmed directly from his intuitive knowledge of the piano and all its possibilities. It was a mastery for which the instrument itself had been waiting for more than a hundred years. The piano is by far the most successful musical instrument ever invented—successful in the sense that it is not only a resplendent producer of musical sound, but an immensely practical one as well. It is Chopin's distinction that he was the first composer who understood what the piano could do.

Everyone knows that the name "piano" derives from the original name, "pianoforte," which meant literally "soft loud," and which indicated a range of dynamics impossible on clavichords and harpsichords. But that was not the only point of the pianoforte's early significance. The inventor, an Italian named Cristofori, had produced something else —a mechanical device that was the real revolutionary nub of his new instrument. For years before him builders of clavichords and harpsichords had been trying to solve the problem of a successful hammer action for keyboard instruments. In clavichords the strings were struck by small brass wedges; in harpsichords they were plucked by quills. These devices permitted a free vibration of the strings, but in both instruments (in the clavichord especially) the tone produced was weak and thin. Builders knew that a hammer of some kind striking the string would produce a richer, purer tone; but what eluded them was a method

of getting the hammer to escape from the string the instant
after it struck, thus allowing the string to vibrate freely.
The problem seems simplicity itself; nevertheless it remained unsolved until Cristofori worked it out with an
ingenious mechanism. His was also a fairly complex mechanism, as anyone may see by looking at its modern counterpart in any piano action today.

Once he had worked out his clever hammer device,
Cristofori also strengthened the frame of his instruments
so that he could stretch the strings much tighter. This
meant that they could withstand heavier hammer blows
and thus sustain their tones longer. And there, in essence,
was the triumph of the pianoforte: a clear, ringing, sustained tone that got away from the twang of the plucked
tone of the harpsichord; and a range of dynamics that
neither the harpsichord nor the clavichord could approach.

Cristofori's invention dated from 1711. Musicians being
among the most conservative of all the artistic species, it
is not surprising that many years went by before the pianoforte made any impression at all. Bach knew very little
about it until as late as 1747, when he played on the
pianofortes that a German builder named Silbermann
made for Frederick the Great. It was not until Mozart's
time that the new instrument began generally to supplant
the older ones. Beethoven was the first important composer
who realized that the piano required a new kind of music
especially constructed for it. His greater piano sonatas,
with their exploitation of the singing tone of the piano,
their use of chordal masses and a wide range of dynamics,
would have been as insipid on a harpsichord as modern
stereophonic records played on an old acoustical phonograph.

Beethoven went far, but it remained for Chopin to go
the final step and to free writing for the piano from the
last vestiges of the clavichord-harpsichord style. Like Liszt,
he recognized the piano as a contrivance capable of an infinite variety of beautiful sonorities. He did not try merely
to adapt those sonorities to suit preconceived musical
styles; he also worked in the opposite direction, creating
new technical ideas in music that would exploit the piano

tone to the full. The style he thus developed was so perfectly suited to the instrument, and went so far in sounding out all its possibilities, that for more than fifty years after him no composer made any important advance beyond it. Claude Debussy, early in the present century, was the first to produce important new ideas for the piano which did not stem directly from Chopin.

## IV

Around the turn of the present century, James Huneker, one of the most discerning of modern American music critics, whose understanding of Chopin's music was as penetrating as his love for it was unaffected, was moved to write an essay called *The Greater Chopin*. "The old Chopin," he said, "is gone for most of us. . . . The E flat Nocturne is drummed by schoolgirls as a study in chord playing for the left hand, and the mazurkas—heaven protect us!—what have not these poor dances, with their sprightly rhythms, now wilted, been subjected to; with what strange oaths have they not been played? . . . Poor Chopin! devoured by those ravening wolves, the concert pianists, tortured by stupid pupils and smeared with the kisses of sentimentalists, well may you cry aloud from the heights of Parnassus, 'Great Jove, deliver me from my music!'"

What Huneker was protesting against, with all the vigor of his articulate and colorful pen, was the last and worst stage of the late nineteenth-century Chopin craze. For a time almost as much Chopin music was played by pianists on recital stages as that of all other composers combined. Fortunately, as Huneker was at pains to point out, there are two Chopins: the inferior one who was almost destroyed in the orgy of overplaying, and the "greater Chopin," as Huneker called him, whom age cannot wither nor custom stale. In his essay Huneker went through the composer's works and made his selections, separating the sheep from the goats. It is the best evaluation of the Pole's music that the present writer knows, and it can be recommended to music lovers with only this reservation: if one is lucky enough not to have heard too much Chopin, one may still find beauty and freshness and melodic charm in many of the lesser pieces that overplaying has ruined for others— yes, even in pieces like that poor tortured *Fantaisie Impromptu* whose insides were ripped out to make *I'm Always Chasing Rainbows*. But one would be wise not to linger over them too long. There is too much of loveliness and splendor, of far more enduring satisfaction awaiting in the greater Chopin.

To begin with, there are the Etudes. Now the very word "étude" is synonymous with some of the flattest, dreariest words in the language, i.e., "study," "practice piece," "exercise." It is the last form in the world in which one would expect to find sentiment, poetry, drama, or the play of strong emotions. But that is precisely the use which Chopin made of it. He wrote twenty-seven Etudes, two sets of twelve (published as Opus 10 and Opus 25) and a final set of three. They have been called music's most triumphant wedding of pedagogy and art. It is remarkable that Chopin wrote most of them while still in his teens and early twenties.

Each Etude is based on some problem of piano technique, but unless a listener is told this, he would never suspect the core of pure mechanics which lies under the veil of art. He would never imagine, for example, that the melting, heartbreaking song of the E major Etude (Op. 10), or the equally sorrowful lamentations of the C sharp minor (Op. 25) are in reality testing grounds for the pianist's touch—for his ability to sustain a singing tone and a smooth legato style. Or that the eerie, faintly sinister G sharp minor (Op. 25), which races and whistles and sighs like autumn wind in a chimney, is the most famous exercise ever devised to make the pianist play thirds in the right hand at dazzling speed. Or that the titanic C minor (Op. 10), though it may indeed be a "Revolutionary" Etude from the fact that Chopin probably composed it when in torment over the fall of Warsaw to the Russians, is nevertheless a test of dexterity for the pianist's left hand and a means of teaching him to conserve his strength through many measures of sustained violence.

So cunningly is the mechanical problem disguised that the listener can hear every one of the Etudes and never suspect that the pianist is actually practicing arpeggios which stretch beyond an octave, or speedy passage work, or dexterity in thirds and sixths, or strengthening figures for the third, fourth, and fifth fingers of the right hand—he will not suspect it, that is, unless the pianist has the soul of a machine. From the pianist's viewpoint it should be admitted that the Etudes in the aggregate are works of appalling difficulty. Inside every one, and apart from the main technical problem, there bristle numerous minor problems and pitfalls—of rhythm, phrasing, accent, pedaling, etc.—thrown in here and there to trip the unwary. Anyone who can play all the Etudes and play them well may qualify as a concert pianist of distinction. They are the backbone of all modern piano technique. But that fact alone is not what keeps them alive. They would be so much sterile Czerny were it not for the rich investiture of poetry with which Chopin clothed them.

The Etudes are the first of Chopin's works which exhibit in full panoply his magnificent use of harmonic color. It is one of the more diverting contradictions of genius that this man, who was as prim and timid as a girl in his personal life, had the boldness of an Arctic explorer when he set his musical ideas to working. In the field of harmony he was a rule breaker second only to Wagner. Like Schubert, he had extreme agility in modulation; he could leap from key to key with ease, and he had a highly developed sense of the sheer beauty of key contrasts. But while Schubert's harmony was chiefly diatonic, i.e., based on the natural notes of the scale of a particular key, Chopin began the extensive use of chromatic harmony, which means modulation through the sharps and flats not at all related to the key. In this respect he was the ground breaker for Wagner, and all the teeming chromaticism that has flooded modern music since *Tristan und Isolde*. Chopin also loved the use of dissonance, and he threw aside so many of the old theoretical rules of harmonic procedure that the pedants of his time came to the comforting conclusion that his early training must have been deficient.

V

Chopin had a passion for the dance. At least a quarter of his compositions are based on three dance forms—the polonaise, the mazurka, and the waltz. He worked at them almost continuously throughout his creative career. Even though only a few of these many pieces reach the high altitudes of the composer's inspiration, they are nevertheless among his most ingratiating works. They represent a side of Chopin which is treasurable because it is unique.

The polonaise was not a folk dance. It originated in the sixteenth century among the Polish nobility. Furthermore, in the words of Franz Liszt, "this dance is one of those rare exceptions designed to show off not the women but the men, to exhibit manly beauty, to set off noble and dignified deportment and martial yet courtly bearing." It is too bad that more concert pianists do not prepare their performances of the Chopin Polonaises by reading the description of this dance and its origins contained in Liszt's book on the life of Chopin. It is a vivid picture of a vanished glory—the once-proud aristocracy of Poland when she was one of the most vigorous states in Europe. It makes plain the fact that the polonaise began not as a dance, but as a march, a processional. In the great houses of the Polish nobles the assembled company would pass in review to the strains of stirring music. "A rhythmical, regularly cadenced, undulating step was secured, and the entire form of each dancer swayed with graceful wavings and harmonious poisings."

In the Polonaises of Frédéric Chopin these brilliant rhythmical pageants are re-created in tone, and the martial spirit of the country he worshiped rises from the cinders of the past. Some of the Polonaises are sheer exultations in march step—especially the one in A major, and the celebrated *Drum* Polonaise in A flat major. In these pieces Chopin pushed the piano to its limits for sheer volume of sound. The A flat Polonaise requires prodigious endurance. Only the greatest pianists should attempt it; the rest succeed only in giving the piano a thorough pounding, exhausting both themselves and their listeners.

Not all the Polonaises ring with victory. The dark side of Chopin's nature, which appeared in every form that he touched, crops out in such essays as the Polonaise in E flat minor, and the altogether superb one in F sharp minor. Under the gloomy surface of their melodies and their prevailing minor modes smolder defeat and despair. Deep below is a red-eyed fury, ready to burst forth in savage revolt. Someday, these pieces seem to imply, someone is to pay for the ruination of Poland and her monstrous injustices.

The Chopin Polonaises are the most thoroughly masculine music ever written for the piano. Yet they came from a man who was a physical weakling, with a marked psychological leaning toward the feminine. The Polonaises prove beyond doubt the duality of his nature. The body was epicene and the temperament febrile, but somewhere inside of him there was enough masculinity to serve a gladiator.

The Mazurkas are the feminine counterparts of the Polonaises. They are much more modest, intimate, and subtle. The original form was a national Polish dance, and in his translations into piano music Chopin used many native Polish melodies. He wrote more than fifty Mazurkas, and in mood they range from the rollicksome and completely carefree to the extremes of melancholia. Most of them are a blend of different moods, the alternations of sadness and gaiety so typical of Slavic natures.

What Chopin used in his Mazurkas was a procedure since copied by many modern composers: that of taking the essential idioms of some simple, often primitive form, and translating them into his own highly refined style. In the Mazurkas he used the authentic Polish melodies and their infectious, unpredictable rhythms; the odd harmonic touches, typical of their folk origin, though grit to the taste of his Western contemporaries; the capricious changes of mood, and above all the *tempo rubato*. This last means simply that the player disregards a strict metronomelike tempo and hurries or lingers over certain notes of a musical phrase. It was by no means a new thing in Chopin's time, but he used it so freely that he aroused the especial fury of the pedants.

The waltz was a new thing in Chopin's time. At first it was even a matter of scandal. In an age of square dances the sight of two young persons holding each other in close embrace and flying around a ballroom to this giddy new rhythm was enough to make the righteous blush. But the young bloods had their way. Aided and abetted by the fabulous Strauss family, the waltz soon became the craze of Europe, and the old square dances were doomed.

Like the Mazurkas, the Chopin Waltzes are a refinement of the original simple idea. Huneker called them "dances for the soul, not the body"; and Schumann said that the ladies who dance them should at least be countesses. Unfortunately they are also among the composer's most popular pieces, which means that they have been worn thin by students who use them as finger exercises and virtuosi who toss them off as facile encores. This writer, for one, would relish the now impossible experience of coming upon some of them for the first time—say the Valse brillante in A flat major (Op. 34, No. 1), which is as glittering as a chandelier of glass; or the A flat major (Op. 42) with its clever insinuation of a rhythm in double time over the prevailing three-quarter—an altogether captivating piece.

Even in so vivacious a form as the waltz Chopin could not repress his inbred pessimism. Several of these pieces are in the minor mode, of which two (the A minor and the C sharp minor) are the best of the entire group. The C sharp minor is great Chopin, a product of his last years. The original shallow framework of the waltz is completely obscured under a mood of dreamy, reflective sadness. At every point it avoids the commonplace.

VI

The piano nocturne as a form was invented by a fat, wine-drinking Irish composer named John Field, who was born in Dublin in 1782. His originals are almost forgotten today, though they had a considerable vogue in Chopin's time. Field did not care for his Polish rival's essays: "He has a sickroom talent," was his sneering remark. It is clear that Chopin himself felt the limitations of the nocturne, for as he matured as an artist he tried hard to improve and vary the form itself. Realizing the monotony of his slow-moving melodies, he devised middle sections in a contrasting vein—sometimes even in violent opposition to the prevailing nocturnal mood, as if his brooding had been interrupted by sudden emotional storms. For example, the C sharp minor Nocturne (Op. 27, No. 1), a distinguished work at which no one may sneer, builds up to a climax of massive power. So does the noble C minor (Op. 48, No. 1), possibly the finest of all the Nocturnes.

More obviously than any others of his works the Nocturnes point to Chopin's command of his melodic lines. Everyone knows that he was a first-rate inventor of melodies, but not many realize that the instrument for which he wrote them is far from being the ideal melodic medium. The piano is a percussive instrument. Its striking action of hammer against string, even though a great improvement over the old claviers, is still subject to the danger of monotony. Its tone, though pure and lovely, cannot be sustained; it begins slowly to die an instant after hammer and string meet. Chopin understood the piano so profoundly that he was able to turn these weaknesses almost into virtues. Even in his earliest compositions he began experimenting to find ways and means of sustaining the interest in his melodies over long stretches, a feat easy for the violin but difficult for the piano.

At first he used the ornaments that were the common devices of his time—the little turns and trills which the old composers in harpsichord days had to fall back upon to keep important notes in their melodies alive. Chopin improved and elaborated on them; and because he was passionately devoted to opera he also borrowed ideas from the florid cadenzas of Italian coloratura singing. He developed a whole new language of ornamentation, until his music was studded with little turns, trills, sudden runs that dart up and down the piano, tiny cadenzas that are like sprays of raindrops. To this day these decorations are the most purely Chopinesque features of his music. But they were far from being mere feminine fripperies— jeweled necklaces to set off a musical gown. They served the very practical purpose of breaking up the monotony of his melodic lines.

Another device that Chopin used for propping up melodic interest was the introduction of melodic material in the accompaniment, or even a secondary line of melody between the chief melody and the bass. This last he evolved from his lifelong study of Bach. Among the Nocturnes it is best exemplified by the E flat (Op. 55, No. 2), which is decidedly polyphonic in style. At points where the interest in the melody is likely to droop it is suddenly revived by the appearance of another melodic line just below it. This device, and the enrichment of his accompaniments, became increasingly important as Chopin's art developed. Together they give weight and density to many of the masterpieces of his last years.

VII

Chopin's affair with George Sand is one of the enigmas of music history. It is also one of the curiosities of that dim and murky region of human affections where even the emotions of normal individuals do not always assume the shapes of reason and expectation. The composer was a prime neurotic, but Mme. Sand was an even stranger agglomeration of psychological contradictions. She was undeniably one of the most extraordinary women who ever lived. Born Aurore Dupin, she was a descendant of the French militarist, Marshal Saxe, who was an illegitimate son of Augustus II of Saxony. Various other bars sinister ran in her ancestry, a fact that did not deter her family from steering her at eighteen into a loveless marriage with Casimir Dudevant, a dissipated and boorish country squire. She stood it for eight years, then cut loose and went to live alone in Paris. After writing one inconsequential novel in collaboration with a young man named Jules Sandeau (from whose name she evolved her nom de plume, George

Sand) she turned out another novel, *Indiana*, by herself. This book was the wildfire best seller of its day, and it swept its author into fame overnight. Thereafter, to the end of her long life in 1876, she worked with incredible industry, writing more than a hundred books.

With fame came an even greater measure of notoriety. Mme. Sand simply could not live conventionally. She was the great-grandmother of all the feminists who established woman's freedom in a modern world. Even in such minor matters as dress she refused to be bound. When she found that she could roam the streets of Paris unmolested in the dress of a Latin Quarter student, she continued to wear men's clothes whenever she pleased. Later she took to cigars and a hookah. Her divorce action against her husband created a lurid scandal; but she bore it stoically, valuing independence more than reputation. Intellectually she was the peer of most of the men she knew; therefore she demanded the right to live with the same freedom that men enjoyed. This freedom included, according to the viewpoint she developed not long after coming to Paris, the right to love. Her numerous affairs were more scandalous than all her other oddities put together; but the thing that her critics (particularly the male ones) were never able to forgive was her assumption of what had always been man's inalienable right—the privilege of terminating a love affair. Before she met Chopin she and the young poet Alfred de Musset had been through a scorching affair. When she left him for an Italian doctor, Musset almost died of damaged pride and Sand herself was very nearly wrecked emotionally.

None of George Sand's affairs brought her lasting happiness. Her longest association, eight years, was that with Chopin. Throughout her life there ran like a band of scarlet the continual pain of disillusionment and frustration in love.

In January 1838 Balzac spent several days at her country place at Nohant. He recorded his impressions in a letter. "I found Comrade George Sand in her dressing gown, smoking an after-dinner cigar, in front of her fire in an immense room. She had on lovely yellow slippers ornamented with fringe, bewitching stockings, and red trousers. So much for her state of mind. As to physique, she had doubled her chin like a monk. She has not a single white hair in spite of her frightful misfortunes; her swarthy complexion has not changed; her lovely eyes are as brilliant as ever; she has the same stupid air when she is thinking, because, as I told her after studying her, her whole countenance is in her eyes. . . . She leads about the same life that I do. She goes to bed at six in the morning and gets up at noon; I go to bed at six in the evening and get up at midnight. Naturally, I conformed to her habits, and for three days we gossiped from five o'clock in the evening, after dinner, until five in the morning. . . .

"She is a bachelor, she is an artist, she is big, generous, loyal, chaste; she has the features of a man. Ergo, she is not a woman. . . . It is a man she would like to be, so much so that she left her womanhood and is no longer a woman. A woman attracts and she repels, and, since I am very masculine, if she produces that effect on me, she must produce it on men who are like me. She will be unhappy always. . . . A woman must always love a man greater than she, or she must be so blinded that it is the same as though he were."

The meeting of Mme. Sand and Chopin had occurred about a year before Balzac's visit. The composer was twenty-seven; the novelist was six years older. As two celebrities they had anticipated meeting each other, but after their first encounter Chopin remarked, "What a repellent woman that Sand is! Is she really a woman? I'm ready to doubt it." In the summer of 1838 the composer, who had been ailing, was invited to Nohant to recuperate. Before many weeks had passed the most famous infatuation of the age was well under way.

It was also one of the most inexplicable of affairs. The customary explanation relied upon by most writers is that Chopin, the high-strung, sensitive, effeminate man was naturally drawn to a masculine, strong-willed woman six years older than himself and ready to assume a maternal control over him. But it was not as simple as that. Many contemporary writers describe her as definitely unprepossessing in appearance—a short, dumpy figure, with a swarthy complexion like an Indian, a nose too large, and a coarse mouth. As Balzac said, only her eyes—enormous pools of liquid blackness—gave her face distinction. Of beauty such as a man of Chopin's tastes would be expected to admire there was none. Moreover, the composer's fastidious nature recoiled from many of her unwomanly habits, particularly the cigars. He was a hidebound conservative in clothes, in etiquette, in his choice of friends, in his personal conduct—in everything except his music. She was disdainful of conventions of every kind—personal, social, or political. Even in the matter of religion it shocked him to learn that she did not believe in a literal hell. Nevertheless, these two polar natures were drawn together by the most powerful of all human attractions.

There is no doubt that at first Mme. Sand adored Chopin. She called him her angel; she took care of him as she did her own children. She ordered eight of the best years of her life to suit him. His love for her was even greater. It is plain that he literally could not live without her. Yet at first he was somehow ashamed of his infatuation, and was concerned that his family and friends might learn of the liaison. He never dedicated a single one of his works to her.

No one has ever explained these inner mysteries of the Chopin-Sand affair. Nor has anyone ever doubted this result of it: that during those years the "greater Chopin" came into being.

The beginning was marked by disaster. Mme. Sand decided to spend the winter of 1838–39 on the island of Majorca, and she persuaded Chopin to accompany her and her two children. He went expecting to find a tropical paradise where he could recover his health in the warm Mediterranean sun. But very soon after they arrived the rains came, and with those torrents all comfort vanished. The composer developed bronchitis. Soon rumors spread among the islanders that he had tuberculosis; threats were made against his life. The Sand party had to leave their villa and take refuge in an abandoned Carthusian monastery in the near-by hills. It was a great, sprawled-out pile of stone, some of it dating back to the fifteenth century—a labyrinth of cells, with walls three feet thick, lofty ceilings, and small Gothic windows. Sand and her two children and Chopin occupied three of the cells. The misery of their situation was indescribable. What food they could get was wretched, and the peasants would not work for them, fearing the composer's disease. Chopin, established in a cell (shaped, he said, like a coffin), struggled to go on with his life and his art. He had a broken-down piano part of the time, and he worked at his Preludes, several Nocturnes and Polonaises, the F major Ballade, the C sharp minor Scherzo, and the B flat minor Sonata; but his health grew steadily worse. Then his nerves gave way. The gloom of his surroundings—the somber, ancient building isolated in a sea of verdure and drenched in never-ending rain—was depressing enough by day; but at night unnamed horrors and the fear of death clutched him. Mme. Sand wrote: "On returning from my nocturnal explorations in the ruins with my children, I found him at ten o'clock at night before his piano, his face pale, his eyes wild, and his hair almost standing on end. It was some minutes before he could recognize us."

After three months they decided to return to France before it was too late. On the voyage back to the mainland the composer had incessant hemorrhages, and at Barcelona he lost bowlfuls of blood before a French warship's doctor finally stopped the flow. They got him to Marseille, a walking shadow, but definitely reprieved from death. His health mended slowly, and they returned at last to Nohant.

There can be no exaggerating the effect, both upon Chopin and Mme. Sand, of the dreadful Majorca experience. It undermined the composer's health; he never again was a well man. More than that it bound him to Sand with hoops of steel. All through the sojourn her labors for him and for her children had been heroic, and she stood them with courage and fortitude. He was never to be free of his reliance upon her.

Soon a routine of life developed for them: summers at Nohant, the rest of the year at Paris. In the city they did not actually share the same house, but Chopin always

lived very close to Mme. Sand. Every day, after his hours
of teaching and composition, he appeared at her apartment
to assume his accustomed place in her salon. She was then
the most famous woman in Europe, and he had also become a public figure. Everyone of artistic or social importance wanted to meet them and be seen at her apartment. There Liszt, Delacroix, Heine, and Balzac mingled
with the composer's wealthy and aristocratic friends. Chopin had little vitality, and people were annoyed by his
coughing; but in spite of the fact that his life energies
were draining away, his creative powers had reached their
flood tide.

### VIII

The Preludes are clearly a bridge between the lesser
Chopin and the greater. Most of them were written and
their publication contracted for before he went to Majorca; he finished and perfected them during the three
months on the island. At first there were twenty-four, one
in each major and minor key. A twenty-fifth, in C sharp
minor, was written a few years later. Thus the title "Prelude" was taken from J. S. Bach's *Well-tempered Clavier*,
which contains preludes and fugues in each of the major
and minor keys. Once he had set down the title upon his
page, Chopin's fancy released itself from any fetter of
classicism, soaring into poetry of the most romantic sort.

The Preludes are remarkable, first of all, for their brevity. Some of them cover no more than a single page; one,
the C minor, is only twelve measures long. This fact, and
the wide range of styles and moods that they cover, puzzled Chopin's contemporaries, who could not discern what
new form he might be aiming at. One biographer felt that
the Preludes were no more than a group of rough sketches
from an artist's portfolio, some of them unfinished. The
exact opposite was true. In most of them Chopin's aim was
simply to show what he could accomplish with a single
musical idea—not at length but in brief. Each prelude is
like a solitary precious stone upon which the composer
brought to bear the delicate skills of the lapidary. From

the facets of each there flashes some particular phase of
his varied art: his gift for melody, his scintillating harmonic coloring, his ornamentation, his skill at sounding
out all the stops in the piano's range of sonorities. In addition, each one has its own emotional color—and here too
the variety is remarkable. We sample moods of gaiety,
sadness, serenity, brooding, fury, despair, and others too
subtle to categorize.

Nothing that Chopin wrote has caused more wrangling
among music critics than his B flat minor Sonata. This is
the work whose slow movement is the familiar Funeral
March. The pedants used to dismiss it as not a sonata at
all, for the reason that its first movement disregards certain
formal rules of structure of the sonata form, and because
the three remaining movements did not seem to be related as they should be. Schumann said that here Chopin
"bound together four of his maddest children," and that
the Funeral March did not belong in the work at all. Even
Huneker thought that "in reality, these four movements
have no common life."

The public, undismayed by these dicta, has taken the
B flat minor Sonata to its bosom. It is one of the most
popular of the Pole's works, and for a long time it was the
most frequently played of all sonatas in piano literature.
The reason is not far to seek. It contains some of Chopin's
most dramatic, passionate, and spaciously wrought music;
and it gives the player opportunity for pianism that is
brilliant without descending into self-conscious display.
So far as quality is concerned there is only one genuinely
weak spot—the lyric middle section of the Funeral March.
The rest is Chopin not far from the top of his powers.
Few care any more that the first movement omits the first
theme entirely from the recapitulation, or any other detail of pedantic significance. The music moves with a wild
and clamorous rush that is irresistible. Powerful emotion,
perfectly controlled, makes up for any irregularity in formal
structure. The Scherzo is tremendous—full of explosive
energy and relieved by an unhackneyed lyric section. The
Funeral March is uneven, but in the tolling bells of its
opening and close there is masterful tone painting. Seldom

has music achieved such a deep and utter black. The closing Presto is one of the most original things that Chopin or anyone else ever wrote—a weird, enigmatic movement, filled with premonitions of terror. Throughout its entire length the two hands play single notes, an octave apart. These octaves race up and down the keyboard at headlong speed, until individual notes and even harmonic structure disappear as in a gray mist. The movement reminded Anton Rubinstein of night winds sweeping over churchyard graves.

What really binds these four mad children together is a matter of mood—a shroud of gloom and death, of tragic and furious desperation which hangs like a pall over the entire work. There are moments of lyric respite; but the essential morbidity is never absent for long.

Chopin's third and last sonata, the B minor, appeared in 1845, when the composer's health was rapidly going downhill and only a few more works of authentic greatness were left in him. The B minor Sonata lacks the dramatic impact and the black moodiness of the B flat minor. Instead there is more polish, and a slightly nearer approach to the canons of strict form. There is also a finer lyricism: Chopin did not often surpass the lovely second theme of the first movement, or the entire Largo, with its long-drawn-out melodic lines that have the reposeful beauty of an elegy. The Scherzo is all foam and sparkle, instead of the cleaving, slashing blows of the Scherzo in the previous work. The last movement, compared with the startling Presto of the B flat minor, is almost conventional; but it winds up the piece with a fine technical display for the performer.

IX

Chopin's genius for originality, for taking a form previously established and giving it a new imprint entirely his own, was nowhere better displayed than in his Scherzos. He wrote four solo pieces under this title, to which should be added the two in the Sonatas, making six in all. The old classic use of the scherzo was to inject a mild element of humor into music. The word originally meant "a jest." Scherzos were light, airy pieces in rapid tempo, from which all seriousness was banned. With Beethoven the form took on bulk. His scherzos were huge bellows of Falstaffian laughter, roaring like gusts of wind through his symphonies. Among romantic composers Mendelssohn wrote some of the most charming scherzos. His were often fairy pieces, light as thistledown, like the incomparable one in his *Midsummer Night's Dream* music. Two of the Chopin Scherzos lean to this type—the one in the B minor Sonata, and the superb Scherzo in E major (Op. 54). Curiously enough, these two were the last of his six. It was in the first four that he set the old form completely upside down.

His First Scherzo, in B minor (Op. 20), was an early work, written when he was twenty-five. What fierce corroding ironies were working in his soul when he named this piece "scherzo" we may only guess. It begins with two shocking chords—and then a blast of passion is let loose. No music Chopin had then written, not even his *Revolutionary* Etude, had ever twisted the euphony that was supposed to be music into spiritual warfare so violent. Nothing is left of the classic notion of a scherzo except the breathless speed with which the piece moves. There is an idyllic middle section, a needed contrast of pure melody from the grinding dissonances; but it does not hold forth for long. The end of the drama is more terrible than the beginning: "Seize on him, Furies, take him to your torments!"

The Second Scherzo, in B flat minor (Op. 31), is a far more popular work; it is much more pleasingly melodic and its emotions are constrained within more reasonable bounds. The Third Scherzo, in C sharp minor (Op. 39), stands at the top of the group. It sprang from the Majorca nightmare. Huneker wrote: "It is a somber and fantastic pile of architecture, and about it hovers despairing and perpetual night. It is a tale from Poe's 'iron-bound, melancholy volume of the magi,' and on its gates might be inscribed the word 'spleen.'" Great imagination went into this C sharp minor Scherzo, and a sure grasp of all the complex mechanics of pianism. It has the malignant strength of the B minor Scherzo, but the hysteria is absent. Chopin the harmonist is here at his best, splashing his colors with immense verve and daring. Virtuoso pianists relish this scherzo, because it gives them opportunity to draw many brilliant arrows from the technical quiver: furious octave work, massive power, beautiful sequences of chords, and the most gorgeous arpeggio display in all piano music.

The Ballades are a pure Chopin invention. He had no precedent for their form. These pieces have the further distinction of having been composed to a literary scenario of some sort, which was another innovation for Chopin. The union of music with literary ideas, while it fascinated all other romantic composers, did not appeal to him. Even though his music is poetic, dramatic, lyrical to the core, it is still abstract. The Ballades are the nearest thing to an exception. That Chopin wrote them inspired by works of the Polish romantic poet, Adam Mickiewicz, is certain. But of what the story or even the symbolism of each might be, we have no inkling.

Every one of the four Ballades is a strong work, and the Fourth, in F minor, is very likely Chopin's masterpiece. It is that fortunate case of an artist cramming onto a single canvas the choicest things he owned in all the various departments of his inspiration and technique. Its melodies are as distinguished as any he ever wrote, with no trace of the marshmallow sweetness that sickens some of the Nocturnes. The harmonic scheme is a continual shifting of multicolored lights, relucent and fascinating— the most convincing proof we could ask of Chopin's place as a harmonist of the first rank. Many other details force themselves upon the attention, but none more than the splendor of the accompaniment material. The left-hand part is enriched and varied with such a wealth of interesting detail that it often takes the center of the musical stage. Here again Chopin was the innovator. He was marking the turn away from a long established homophony, with its formula of melody supported by chords, and was breaking up his chords into a new kind of linear counterpoint.

The F minor Ballade has but one rival for top ranking in the catalogue of Chopin's works—the glorious F minor Fantaisie. This work has so much in common with the Ballades, in style and spiritual content, in the refulgence of its ideas, that it may well be classed with them. It has the same breadth of design and the same cohesion. Chopin was again wielding the big brush and his muscles were equal to the task. There is a somber magnificence about the entire work; and, at times, grandeur.

The F minor Fantaisie and the F minor Ballade are twin suns, dominating the galaxy of pieces that marked Chopin's final efforts as a composer. The Fantaisie was written in 1841, the Ballade in 1842; and round about them, in all the other forms in which he worked, Chopin was turning out masterpieces. Just before them came the F sharp minor Polonaise, the C minor Nocturne, the A flat Ballade; after them came the thunderous A flat Polonaise, the E major Scherzo, a group of his finest mazurkas, the Berceuse and the Barcarolle, and his last nocturne— the redolent E major (Op. 62, No. 2). By 1845 his strength was going fast. That year the B minor Sonata was published, his last work of epic dimensions. There was still one more single movement in the grand style—the Polonaise Fantaisie of 1846. This was the work about which the usually astute Liszt made a notorious error of judgment. Although praising it in part, he thought that it stood, "on account of its pathological contents, outside the sphere of art"—a cryptic reasoning which simply meant that he did not like it but did not know just why. Very likely what disturbed him was the somewhat rambling form of the piece. Chopin used the polonaise form as a mere jumping-off place for excursions into unfamiliar territory, both wonderful and exotic. He leads us on through half a dozen different themes and multifarious changes of key, as his moods veer with the wind. Today—used to the waywardness, the perversity, the often deliberate incoherence of the modern tone poem—we follow Chopin through his adventurous polonaise with ease and delight. If there is a hint of diffuseness in this splendid work the reason may possibly be found in the personal life of the artist, which was then moving toward a crisis. The affair with Mme. Sand, the supporting structure of his entire emotional existence, had begun to crumble.

X

The last chapter in the Chopin-Sand affair is the most confused and obscure of the entire story. Chopin left her in 1847, but no one can fix with certainty the precise reasons or the blame for the breach. The culminating episode was a complex family quarrel at Nohant, which involved Mme. Sand and her son and daughter. Chopin, who was in Paris at the time, took sides with the daughter against her mother. Mme. Sand was distressed by his attitude, and she wrote him a letter that he may have taken as his dismissal. We do not know the contents of that letter, for Chopin destroyed it after showing it only to his friend Delacroix. The painter noted in his *Journal*, "I must admit that it is atrocious. The cruel passions, the long-suppressed impatiences are having their day." Chopin did not return to Nohant that summer, which was the sign that everything was over between them.

The affair had been disintegrating for several years. The composer's friends insisted that Mme. Sand had long been tired of him and that she finally jockeyed him into the position of having to make the ultimate break. It was widely believed that she deliberately caricatured him in her novel, *Lucretia Floriani*. Lucretia's lover, Prince Karol, a man with a neurotic and excessively jealous nature, was supposed to be Chopin. The composer had read the book before the quarrel and did not seem to recognize the portrait, until kind friends afterward pointed it out to him.

Mme. Sand's defense was that she had made herself the slave of his whims and his jealousies, but that she could not show him preference over her children. "For seven years," she wrote in confidence to a friend, "I have lived as a virgin with him and with all others. I have become so weary of passions and so disillusioned that even without

effort or sacrifice I have grown old before my time. . . .
I know that many people accuse me, some of having exhausted him by the violence of my senses, others of having
driven him to despair by my coldness. I believe you know
the truth." Her pleas in defense are persuasive, until it is
remembered that she was both a facile writer and a smooth
rationalizer of her own actions, and that even her admirers
never classed her as a high priestess of the truth.

They met only once again. In March 1848 he passed
her on the stairs in the house of a friend in Paris. She
wrote, "I pressed his trembling and icy hand. I wished to
speak to him; he slipped away." In that brief moment he
told her that she was a grandmother—that her estranged
daughter had borne a child.

It would have been merciful if Chopin's life had ended
when the rupture with Mme. Sand first occurred. His most
vulnerable part, his pride, had been hurt beyond all help.
He composed no more. He did not want to live. But for
three more years he had to crawl toward death. When the
Revolution of 1848 made it necessary for him to leave
Paris, one of his pupils, a wealthy Scottish lady named Jane
Stirling, persuaded him to go to London. He spent eight
months in England and Scotland, lionized by society, but
so ill that he shocked everyone who saw him. He was
dreadfully emaciated and pale; his back was bent and he
coughed incessantly. He suffered such fatigue that at times
he had to be carried upstairs. In spite of his misery he
played a great deal, even giving several concerts. His last
public appearance as a pianist occurred in London in
November 1848. The occasion was a ball for the benefit
of Polish refugees. Most of those present wanted to dance,
and when Chopin played, nobody listened to him.

Finally he dragged himself away from the chilling fogs
of England and went back to Paris, but almost another
year went by before he was released from his sufferings.
Meanwhile his money ran out and he was haunted by the
fear of poverty, until Miss Stirling sent him secretly a gift
of twenty-five thousand francs. A story was circulated that
a few days before he died (October 17, 1849) Mme. Sand
tried to see him but was turned away by his friends. Care-

ful research has revealed, however, that she was not in Paris at the time. On his deathbed Chopin was heard to murmur, "She told me that I should not die except in her arms."

## XI

Throughout his life Chopin was a jealous guardian of one thing above all else—his reputation as a composer. He made it a rule never to publish anything that did not measure up to his own high standards. Before he died there were in existence numerous manuscripts of works that he considered unworthy—many of them efforts of his student days. He begged that they be burned. His dying wishes, however, were not carried out; five years later most of them appeared in publication. They consist chiefly of mazurkas, waltzes, and polonaises, and the ill-fated *Fantaisie Impromptu*. With very few exceptions they prove that the composer's powers of self-criticism were astute. So far as their interest to musicologists is concerned, the publication of these pieces was justified; otherwise most of them should be ignored. Identification is easy. The last work that Chopin himself published, the Sonata for Piano and Cello, is marked Op. 65. Any work with an opus number higher than that, or any published posthumously without an opus number, is suspect.

# *Schumann*

## 1810—56

### I

Lytton Strachey remarks about one of his "Eminent Victorians": "It was as if the Fates had laid a wager that they would daunt him, and in the end they lost their bet." The life story of Robert Schumann reads as if the Fates had laid some such bet upon him, too, and that he had surmounted their obstacles one by one—but in the end they won their bet. They daunted him at last, but only with the cruelest weapon that a man may be brought to face.

The shocks of misfortune with which Schumann had so often to contend had naturally a profound effect upon his mind and character. They had a corresponding effect upon his art, and thus upon the history of music itself. For Schumann was one of those artists who do not create in a vacuum. The work of few composers falls more readily into "periods"—into categories clearly defined by external events that were shaping the course of his life. We may trace in his music the books that he read, the friends that he made, the scenes of life and nature that his eye had fallen upon and loved. More than any other romantic composer he used as the tissue of his art his own highly personalized emotional moods.

On that account the position of Schumann's music in a modern world is full of contradictions. Being, as he was, an archromanticist, we have every right to expect that he would now be as outmoded as an antimacassar. This is an age which is supposed to regard sentiment with the same abhorrence felt by the devil for holy water. It lumps together the novels of Bulwer-Lytton and Disraeli, the poetry of Byron, the *Songs without Words* of Mendelssohn, and all the other pressed flowers and scented album leaves of romanticism and pronounces them unfit company for a civilization that includes atom smashers, dissonant counterpoint, and the science of geopolitics. And yet Schumann, with all his unabashed sentiment, his avowal of such romantic inspirations as young love, spring, and the beauty of flowers, goes right on living and blooming—like a patch of violets in the middle of a motorcar assembly line.

It is not hard to find reasons for his music's vitality. The chief one is what might be suspected at once: he was a first-rate melodist. Schumann produced his tunes in abundance and in great variety, and yet he knew how to give them a distinction that always raised them above the commonplace. All of his musical procedures had this element of individuality—of saying a thing in a way not quite expected. He was thus an innovator, an experimenter; but never in the large, bold sense that Beethoven was. Rather he was a phrasemaker in music, just as he was in literature. Among musicians he was one of the most able writers about music, and music history and criticism are now studded with quotations from his pen. He was also the master of the small idea in music—the piquant, whimsical touch, the epigram. It was therefore a collation of felicitous detail, projected over the whole field of his art, that gave his music an outstanding character.

II

Robert Alexander Schumann was born on June 8, 1810, in Zwickau, a town in Saxony. The general region was one of natural beauty and fertility. Musically it was fertile too, for besides Schumann it nurtured Handel, the Bachs, and Wagner. It seemed also to be an ideal spot for war.

In 1806, Napoleon routed the Prussians at Jena; in 1812 thousands of his troops streamed through Zwickau, followed one gala day by the Emperor himself, on his way to Poland; and then on another day, a year later, the people of the town (including presumably the three-year-old Robert Schumann) could hear the thunder of cannon from Leipzig, where, at the tremendous Battle of the Nations, Napoleon was being pounded to his doom. That year there was a famine in Zwickau, and typhus, and the horror of maimed and dying soldiers filling the hospitals.

August Schumann, the father of the composer, owned a book-publishing business in Zwickau. He was a fortunate parent for a future man of the arts, for he was a person of intellectual distinction himself. He wrote numerous books, and he was one of the first to publish cheap, well-printed pocket-size editions of the classics; he produced books on business, statistics, geography, and military history, and he made and published translations of English poetry. He was immensely interested in Robert's education. Not certain which way the boy's talents might lie, he encouraged him to study both literature and music. At one time he even tried to get the eminent Carl Maria von Weber to give his son music lessons.

It was Robert's first serious misfortune that he was robbed at the age of sixteen of his father's sympathy and encouragement. August Schumann died in 1826, worn out from overwork at the task of translating Byron's *Childe Harold* and *Beppo*. The boy was a long time getting over the shock. His education now fell into the hands of his mother and a guardian, who straightway proved their obtuseness by deciding that he should study the law. No doubt they thought it the only logical profession for a young bookworm who spent hours poring over Homer, Sophocles, Plato, and Tacitus. At any rate, in the spring of 1828 young Robert Schumann enrolled as *studiosus juris* in the University of Leipzig. This was the second major misfortune of his life. He had no more business trying to plow through the sand dunes of Saxon law than John Keats had trying to be a surgeon.

As a result he remained aloof from the noisy students

at the university, took long walks in the near-by country, and stuffed himself with a diet of Greek and Latin classics and the bloated novels of Jean Paul Richter. Whether he realized it or not, he was going through one of youth's worst ordeals; he consoled himself by becoming an intellectual snob. He consoled himself otherwise, too. There was a man in Leipzig named Friedrich Wieck, who was a piano teacher of unusual ability. It was not long before Schumann was taking piano lessons from Wieck and spending many hours in his home. He even lived there for a time. One of Wieck's children was the nine-year-old Clara—a wonder child whose virtuosity as a pianist was already astonishing.

"My whole life," the composer wrote later, "has been a twenty years' war between prose and poetry—between law and music." From the beginning the law fought a losing battle. After a year in Leipzig, the young man decided to try a course at Heidelberg, and on the way he made a short detour through the Rhineland. It was spring. When he came to the river for the first time he closed his eyes in an ecstasy of expectation, and then, "It lay before me—calm, still, grave, and proud, like an old German god, and with it the glorious, blossoming, green *Rheingau* with its hills and valleys and the whole paradise of vineyards." He had a wonderful time; he encountered strange people; he threw off the guise of aloofness and diffidence. And then at Heidelberg, in the very citadel of jurisprudence, the law career of Schumann met its deathblow. He studied there under the renowned Professor Thibaut, who had a massive reputation in the law. Thibaut was the author of a monumental codification of the Roman law; but deep under the crust of his legal learning lay a totally incongruous stratum—a passion for music, especially the art of Palestrina. One almost discerns the hand of Providence at work here: Schumann, led against his will to the law, and then finding the one professor in ten thousand who was also a music authority. In Heidelberg the young man spent far more time at the piano than at the pandects, so the next year he wrote to his mother and begged to be set free. "Jurisprudence so ossifies and freezes me," he

pleaded, "that no flower of my imagination will ever again
long for the world's spring." He asked that his mother be
guided by the opinion of Friedrich Wieck, and Wieck
agreed—Robert Schumann *did* have the makings of a great
pianist. He suggested, and the young man's mother finally
agreed to, a six months' trial.

The twenty years' war was over.

### III

Quite naturally, the man to train young Schumann as a
piano virtuoso would be Wieck himself. This pedagogue
deserves attention, for he was to play, through Schumann
and his own daughter Clara, an important part in the un-
folding of nineteenth-century music. Wieck was forty-three
when Schumann met him for the first time, and he had
a past that a modern psychiatrist would examine with
interest. He came from poor parents and had had to fight
every inch of the way for an education in the ministry.
During many of his adolescent years he was actually hun-
gry. In early manhood he suffered painfully from a skin
disease of the face. As a minister he preached but one
sermon—and then left the Church forever. He became a
tutor, and finally a teacher of music, the thing he really
wanted to do. Music thus gained an inspired pedagogue,
while the Church lost what would have been a bigot and a
fanatic. When he was past thirty Wieck married a girl of
nineteen. She stood him for eight years, bore him five
children (one the famous Clara), and then divorced him.
He must have been a singularly repellent man. He was
opinionated and vain, sure of himself and his own ideas.
The cruelty in him manifested itself in the form of rudeness. He was a meddler, who loved to put other people to
rights, always using the most acid of insults to do it.

Wieck had reason to be proud of his ability as a teacher.
He understood the psychology of teaching; he was progressive in his ideas, and his musical taste was fine. At
first Schumann admired him. The young man wrote, "You
have no idea of his fire, his judgment, his attitude to art;

but if he speaks in his own or Clara's interest, he becomes quite savage."

Wieck did not have much chance to prove what he could make of Robert Schumann's talent, for a short time after his career as piano student began the young man did a foolish and tragic thing. At Heidelberg he had been practicing on a small dumb keyboard, carrying it with him everywhere. Impatient as usual, he tried still another short cut to finger dexterity. Unknown to Wieck, he used a device that held one of the fingers in a stiff position while the others were exercised. The idea was to gain greater independence and strength for the weaker fingers. The exact opposite happened. One day in the spring of 1832, Schumann suddenly realized that the fourth finger of his right hand was lame. At first he was so shocked that he did not dare to go to a doctor. After months of anguished waiting he came at last to the realization that his finger was practically paralyzed and that his career as piano virtuoso was ended before it had even begun.

Schumann's bravery in the face of his many adversities remains one of the most admired aspects of his character. He was never braver than at this moment—a youth of twenty-two facing the ruination of his life's ambition. He spoke very little about his misfortune, and at first he minimized it in his letters. Certain details of the device and the injury it caused remain a mystery. He seems to have decided almost immediately to become a composer. The broken career and the maimed hand were pushed into the background of his consciousness, to be forgotten but to fester. He flung himself into composition.

At first he began his studies with a theorist named Dorn. He went at them with immense zeal, but the lessons did not last long. The young man was so wayward and so disdainful of orthodox procedures that Dorn soon threw him out. Schumann did not seem to care. He declared that the best way to learn was to study the old masters; he went to the works of Bach (which he adored) and analyzed them down to the last sixteenth note. Soon his own magnificent first works for the piano began to appear. *Papillons* he had composed before he gave up the law, but in the eight years beginning in 1832 he produced the Paganini Etudes, the C major Toccata, *Carnaval*, the Symphonic Etudes, the *Davidsbündler Dances*, *Scenes from Childhood*, *Kreisleriana*, the C major Fantasie, *Faschingsschwank*, three sonatas, a host of pieces under the titles *Fantasiestücke*, *Blumenstück*, *Novelletten*, and many more.

These are all piano works, and they remain among the best ever composed for the instrument. The thing to be noted about them at once is that they are chiefly short works, or collections of short pieces bound together by some poetic idea. This was in the true romantic vein—music fertilized by the literary or the pictorial germ. Thus *Papillons* was inspired by the last scene (a masked ball) of Jean Paul's *Flegeljahre*; *Carnaval* was a scene at a fair, a phantasmagoria of real and literary figures; *Kreisleriana* was a representation of Johannes Kreisler, the eccentric Kapellmeister of E. T. A. Hoffmann's novel. Even if Schumann did not have definite stories or pictures in mind when he actually composed some of these works, he often attached them to the music afterward.

*Carnaval* is typical of his works of this period, beside being one of the masterpieces of romantic piano literature. It is made up of twenty short pieces, each with a fanciful title. Some are persons at a ball—Pierrot, Arlequin, Pantalon, and Columbine; others are real people—Chiarina (Clara Wieck), Estrella (a certain girl named Ernestine whom Schumann once loved), Chopin, Paganini, and Schumann himself under two of his pen names, Eusebius and Florestan. Still others are moods or romantic episodes, rather than people—Aveu is an avowal of love, Reconnaissance a scene of recognition, Promenade a walk at a German ball—and so on.

There is also a technical bond among the members of the cycle. The entire work is built upon a foundation of four notes (A flat, E flat, C, and B flat) which the composer used in three different sequences, and which he indicated in the work itself as Sphinxes. Schumann thought originally of calling the whole thing *Frolics on Four Notes*, and he was bemused by the fact that the German letters that represent the four notes are ASCH—the name of a small Bohemian town where the young lady Ernestine lived. Actually this matter of the four notes is of scant importance to the enjoyment of *Carnaval*, even though their clever use can be traced, sometimes with difficulty, through the whole scheme. What they do indicate is the whimsical trend of Schumann's mind. Musical puzzles and acrostics delighted him; he loved to be mysterious in a sly way. It was one of the aspects of his humorous, warmhearted nature.

There is more than humor and fantasy and poetic charm in *Carnaval*. As pure piano music it is also magnificent, a wholly unexpected product to come, as Opus 9, from the pen of a young man of twenty-four. It indicated in its time a new and powerful individuality. Schumann's entire pianistic style had here begun to blossom. Admittedly, it is not the most popular or the most brilliant pianistic style, but that in the long run has been one of its virtues. In his time the trend in piano music was toward brilliant technical display and lavish color. Schumann cared for neither. He avoided the luxuriant ornamentation of Chopin, and the hectic coloring; he avoided Liszt's combination of grandiloquent melody and dazzling trapeze work. With virtuosity as such he would have no truck. He said of his own music that it contained "a fine thoughtfulness that I would not sacrifice for all Liszt's magnificence"; and of Liszt's, "I sometimes find too much tinsel upon it."

Thoughtfulness is indeed the kernel of Schumann's pianistic art. It is never merely facile. Its aesthetic delights are found not easily, but only after digging in. There lies another of its differences from Liszt's music. Liszt must be interpreted by a player with his technical equipment plus his emotions. Lacking either, it becomes meaningless music. With Schumann there must be added a third element—the intellect. For the performer (or the listener) with a brain he offers inexhaustible pleasure. But it is not on the surface; it is underneath a style which used to be called crabbed and perverse, but which we now know to be one of the most fruitful in modern music.

IV

The last piece in *Carnaval* is called *March of the Band of Davidites against the Philistines.* The Davidites, or *Davidsbündler,* were Schumann's mythical champions of a new order in music, as opposed to the old fogies and the ignorant. In Leipzig they were personified by a group of young intellectuals who banded themselves together under the composer's aegis to combat the "Philistines." They felt that the general level of taste in music was low, and that the German periodicals devoted to music were conservative, dreary, and venal. In 1834 they founded the *Neue Zeitschrift für Musik,* with Schumann (then only twenty-four years old) as editor. He remained its guiding spirit for ten years, and during that time it became the most famous musical journal ever published.

It has been noted that Schumann was passionately addicted to the works of Jean Paul. This novelist has long been one of the deflated balloons of German literature, but Schumann ranked him with Bach as a creative artist—a considerable overestimate. The composer's *Neue Zeitschrift* articles are replete with whimsies borrowed from Jean Paul's voluminous works. One was Schumann's habit of writing under the noms de plume Florestan and Eusebius, who were taken from the characters Vult and Walt in the novelist's *Flegeljahre.* Florestan was the impetuous, hotheaded enthusiast; Eusebius was restrained, introspective, and gentle—as they are so charmingly mirrored in *Carnaval.* Schumann also introduced various of his friends under fanciful titles: Chiara was Clara Wieck, Felix Meritis was Mendelssohn, and Master Raro was Friedrich Wieck.

Schumann's altogether unique style of writing, backed by his progressive ideas on music, made an instant impression on the public, and it was not long before the *Neue Zeitschrift* was known all over Germany. It had a fine effect in raising the general standard of music taste. Schumann deplored Italian opera, which was then overwhelmingly popular, and thus indirectly he helped pave the way for Wagner. He fought hard for Bach, who was still practically unknown, for Schubert, and for the greater works of Beethoven. He was one of the first to praise Chopin. His great discovery, made in his later years, was the genius of the young Johannes Brahms.

v

Schumann's romance with Clara Wieck is one of the tenderest of nineteenth-century love stories. All its various phases—the slow awakening of love between them, their long separation, the fulfillment of their hopes, their romantic personalities, even the tragic end of their union—all wove themselves into a tale that a Victorian novelist could hardly have surpassed.

When Schumann first entered Friedrich Wieck's house as a dreamy-eyed *studiosus juris* of eighteen, Clara was a little girl of nine. She was already a remarkable pianist, and in a few months she was to make her first public appearance in Leipzig, at the historic Gewandhaus. She was an adorable child, unspoiled and unaffected, for her father had the good sense to foster her talent without straining it. He never exploited her, as Leopold Mozart did his son Wolfgang. After the Leipzig appearance, Wieck took her on many tours of German cities, and even as far as Paris. Soon she became the most celebrated prodigy of her day, but her wholesome childhood was never allowed to suffer. She loved music, and piano practicing was as natural to her as play.

At first Clara and Schumann paid little attention to each other. The tall, handsome student was in fact very hard to know. He was shy and taciturn, given to long, moody silences. In company he would often stand in a corner by himself, lost in thought, his lips pursed as if to whistle some theme that might be running through his head. Once he went boating with a young lady and sat for an hour without uttering a word. Then suddenly he pressed her hand and said, "Now we understand each other perfectly." His silences and his moroseness were not a pose; they may have been the first manifestations of the derangement that later took root in his brain.

As Schumann gradually came to know Clara, he began to watch her career with interest; he romped with her, told her stories, wrote her occasional playful letters. In later life Clara said that she had begun to love Schumann when she was twelve, but it was several years after that before he suddenly realized his own feelings. One night, shortly after her sixteenth birthday, Clara and her father were preparing to leave on a long concert tour, and a disconsolate Schumann came to say good-by. As he left their house, she followed him down, holding a lamp to light the way. At the foot of the stairs he turned and suddenly took her in his arms.

That romantic scene on the stairs was followed by the cruelest of awakenings. To the lovers' amazement, Clara's father objected—and with all the pathological obstinacy that his nature could summon. He ordered Schumann out of his house, forbade Clara to see him or to receive any of his letters, and even took her to Dresden to separate them. Of course Schumann followed her, and when Wieck heard of it his anger became a blind insanity. He threatened to shoot the composer if he dared go near his daughter again. The next four years became a nightmare for the two lovers. Clara tried dutifully to carry out her father's wishes, and for months at a time she and Schumann heard of each other only indirectly. Wieck meanwhile began spreading slander about the composer, aiming to blacken him in Clara's eyes. It is clear that he did not want her to marry anyone; he feared, of course, that it would ruin her career. He said, "The idea of Clara with a perambulator is preposterous."

The four years of separation were a torment to Schumann, the worst thing that could have happened to one of his unhealthy mental state. So far as his character and his art were concerned, however, the effect was different. Clara, and the struggle for her, made a man of him. He cast aside his priggishness and his intellectual affectations. His seriousness was now real, his emotions less tinged by sentimentality. In his music he worked from a depth of inspiration that he had never reached before. To these years belong the C major Fantasie, *Kreisleriana*, the *Novelletten*, the *Davidsbündler Dances*, the *Fantasie-stücke*, *Faschingsschwank*, and the *Scenes from Childhood*. Schumann said that he composed the last work because of a remark made by Clara—that in some ways he seemed to her like a child. With the subtle simplicity that hides art, he created a dozen or more of these little pieces, each like a tiny drawing that captures for a moment some attitude of an evanescent childhood.

The C major Fantasie was the first product of the composer's separation from Clara, for it was written in 1836. It is his finest piano work, and it has a double significance: as a piece of pure romantic writing it may stand with the best of Chopin, and as an example of spacious tonal architecture, with the Beethoven sonatas. It is in three big movements. The first is rhapsodic and impassioned, with many changes of mood and style. The second is a magnificent march. The third is the slow movement, one of the most serious and deeply felt that Schumann ever wrote. The impress of Beethoven is marked. Schumann had at first planned this work as his contribution to a monument to Beethoven, to be erected at Bonn, but then the original idea got lost somehow as the music evolved. He later wrote Clara that she was its inspiration—which is a good example of the way the creative ideas of composers sometimes wind up in territory entirely different from that in which they began.

In the Fantasie Schumann's peculiar and somewhat involved style of piano writing reached its maturity. The composer's intense study of Bach shows itself clearly. In certain places there is a strong impression of polyphony—not at all of the eighteenth-century type, but an entirely new kind, of which Schumann and Chopin were to be the early exemplars. The left hand no longer plays a mere subordinate part. Its chordal structure is continually broken up into secondary themes and inner voices, which must be separated from and balanced against the chief melody. The right hand is often given two different melodic strands instead of the usual one. These and numerous other technical problems serve to make the Fantasie one of the most difficult of Schumann's works, both for the hand and the intellect of the performer. It is a virtuoso piece that makes no concession to mere display.

In August 1837, Clara gave a recital in Leipzig. Schumann was in the audience. He had been separated from her for months and was no longer sure of her feelings, but after she played his own Symphonic Etudes there was no room for doubt. Love had found a way to convey its secret messages. Clara herself said, "I had no chance of showing you my inmost heart. I could not do it in private, so I did it in public." The next day they became formally engaged. But the struggle with Wieck had only begun. For three years more he tried to put them off with evasions and postponements, until Clara was forced to leave his house and strike out on her own. She was still a minor and under his control, which finally made it necessary for Schumann, as a last and terrible resort, to bring his case before a court of law. Wieck meanwhile went about spreading vile slanders, accusing the composer of drunkenness and even attacking the morals of his daughter. It is known now that he might have had a real grievance had he objected to Schumann on the grounds of incipient mental disease; but of this he made no mention, probably because no one at that time suspected it.

The lawsuit dragged on for a year, but when the decision finally came, it was in Schumann's favor. He was completely vindicated. The lovers were married on September 12, 1840, the day before Clara's twenty-first birthday.

VI

The year of Schumann's marriage is more in music history than the anniversary of a romantic event in the life of a great composer: 1840 was what Schumann himself called his "Song Year," for in that short space of time, and in a perfect blaze of inspiration, he turned out more than a hundred songs. Among them are many which belong with the finest in the whole range of German *lieder*.

It is often considered strange that Schumann, with his love of poetry and his own exceptional literary endowments, should have waited until he was thirty before writing songs. The answer is found in his own statement, made as late as 1839: "I have always considered songs as being on a lower level than instrumental music, indeed I have not looked upon song as a great art"—an attitude typical among composers before his own and Schubert's time. Once he had gotten over these toplofty ideas of his youth, he went at song writing with frenzied intensity. In the course of a single day, early in 1840, he turned out twenty-seven pages of music. He was then working on the group of songs (Op. 25) which he presented to his bride on the eve of their wedding. He called them *Myrthen*, myrtle leaves being the equivalent of orange blossoms for German brides. It is doubtful if any man ever matched this wedding gift of Robert Schumann's, for *Myrthen* contains such masterpieces as *Widmung* [*Dedication*], *Der Nussbaum* [*The Almond Tree*], *Die Lotosblume* [*The Lotus Flower*], *Du bist wie eine Blume* [*Thou Art like a Flower*], and *Du meine Seele* [*Thou Art My Soul*].

After *Myrthen* the stream of beautiful songs continued, both singly and in cycles. Practically all of the hundred or so that he produced in that year are worth while; at least half of them are superlative. The *Liederkreis* [*Song Cycle*], Op. 39, contains among others *Intermezzo*, *Waldesgespräch* [*Lorelei*], and two lovely night scenes, *Mondnacht* [*Moonlight*], and *Frühlingsnacht* [*Spring Night*]. Opus 42 is the celebrated cycle of eight songs, *Frauenliebe und Leben* [*Woman's Life and Love*]. The verses by the poet Chamisso recount the various phases of a woman's love life—her meeting with her beloved, the courtship, betrothal, and marriage, the birth of her child, the death of her husband. The great *Dichterliebe* series, a group of sixteen songs after Heine, contains, among many sovereign examples, *Ich grolle nicht* [*I Chide Thee Not*].

In the final evaluation of Schumann's contributions to the art song he can be compared only to Schubert's, for only Schubert surpassed him. Schumann built solidly upon the foundations of his predecessor, but he also made important advances. He set a new standard in the care he took with a poet's words. He paid scrupulous regard to prosody (a thing Schubert did not always do), and he fitted his music to the poetic idea with such skill that the one seems to be the very image of the other. Hardly less inspired was his treatment of the piano part. Something unusual could be expected here, for Schumann was already a master of piano writing before he attacked the song. His piano parts (especially in the greater songs, like the *Dichterliebe* series) are so varied, so rich in independent ideas that they can hardly be called mere accompaniments. They become rather a collaboration. The composer's attitude toward the piano is plainly indicated in his frequent use of elaborate postludes, in which the instrument continues for a number of measures after the voice has finished.

For the singer most of Schumann's songs are a challenge. The composer had plunged headlong into song, with very little preparatory study of the human voice, and his procedures are not always what vocalists call "grateful." In addition his songs are an intellectual test, just as his piano music is. The singer who can master them may lay claim to a considerable distinction. Sometimes they yield up their secrets only after long searching and the hardest kind of study, for Schumann's mind was a subtle instrument, not at all the vessel of naïve sentimentality that many used to suppose. He was never more subtle than in some of his songs.

After the astonishing freshet of the Song Year the composer said that he was satisfied with what he had accomplished, but that he did not think he would ever write songs again. Unfortunately, he did write many more. A decade later he turned out still another hundred or so, but the contrast in quality with the first series could not be wider if they had been the product of two different brains. As a matter of fact they were, for by that time the composer's mental faculties were going fast and he had left but a few more years of sanity.

## VII

From the beginning of 1840 Schumann had been working at top speed, under the forced draft of a furious inspiration. At the end of the year he suddenly dropped his songs and turned to the orchestra. During 1841 he produced nothing but orchestral works—his symphonies in B flat and D minor, sketches for a C minor Symphony that he never completed, the Overture, Scherzo, and Finale, and what later became the first movement of his Piano Concerto. Then in 1842 came another switch, this time to chamber music. In that year he composed his three string quartets, the Piano Quartet, the Piano Quintet, and the *Fantasiestücke* for violin, cello, and piano.

With the completion of his Song Year, Schumann had come to a fork in the road. He took the turn away from his purely romantic procedures, from music impregnated by poetic ideas, and went over in the direction of classicism. Now it was the abstract forms which absorbed him, and though his music was still saturated with his essentially romantic style, the literary fancies of his former days were conspicuous by their absence. Gone were Florestan and Eusebius and the other whimsies of Jean Paul; gone were Chiara and the *Davidsbündler*, the masked balls, the carnivals, the sweet-smelling garlands of romantic song. They were left behind with the composer's own romantic youth.

Schumann's First Symphony in B flat was begun late in 1840, a few months after his marriage to Clara. He worked at it with such concentration that it was finished before the end of the following February. He called it his "Spring" Symphony. The D minor Symphony which he completed the following September was actually his second, but because he revised it ten years later it was published as his fourth. These two symphonies, and the two that Schumann wrote in later years, have gained a unique reputation in symphonic literature. They are almost as famous for their shortcomings as for their virtues. Poorly balanced orchestration is their prime defect. Practically all of Schumann's works in this medium have been edited and refurbished by later experts; to this day many conductors continue to make extensive alterations of their own in the scoring.

Schumann's weakness as an orchestrator resulted partly from his method of work. He composed best in sudden bursts of inspiration, when the urge to get his ideas into concrete form, regardless of obstacles, simply could not be resisted. He began the B flat Symphony knowing almost nothing about instrumentation. His dogged perseverance and his boundless enthusiasm carried him rough shod over every handicap. In the face of these shortcomings, one might wonder why the four Schumann symphonies have not gone the way of those by Ludwig Spohr. Instead they are still established fixtures in the repertoire of every symphony orchestra, and through the years their pages show no signs of yellowing around the edges. They continue to give delight for the same reasons that the composer's piano works do. First-rate melodic ideas, beautiful schemes of harmonization, rhythms that are fresh and buoyantly irresistible, a sense of romantic ardor suffusing the whole—these are the essentials, here as in every other phase of his art. These and the ability to avoid the commonplace and the expected. Even when he transgressed rules of technical practice, Schumann made up for it with style and good taste.

Almost everything that has been said of Schumann's orchestral works of the year 1841 can be repeated for the chamber music of 1842. The composer went at his new task with the same intensity, and to the exclusion of everything else. He wrote his three string quartets in a space of eight weeks; the last, in A major, was struck off in five days. He also plunged into this new medium without any too much preparation, although he said that he first shut himself up for a spell and studied the Beethoven quartets. Because of his haste, he had to make many revisions in his quartets in later years. Nevertheless, one of these quartets, the A major which he wrote in such incredible haste, is a masterpiece. It is the Schumann of the greater piano works and the songs, simply translated into a new medium.

The Piano Quartet (for piano, violin, viola, and cello), and the Piano Quintet (for piano and string quartet) represent one of the composer's most successful musical innovations. In combining these two different mediums he had few precedents. He had to feel his way. The Piano Quartet is entirely successful; the Quintet is both great and famous. Here Schumann hit upon an ideal union for piano and small string group. Pedagogues have found various ways in which he might have improved his handling of the two mediums, but few could suggest improvements in the music itself.

### VIII

The marriage of the Schumanns has always been regarded as the perfect one. In the joint diary that they kept, in their letters during the periods of separation, there is no mistaking that their union was the life and soul of each. Schumann's happiness is clearly indicated in his immense creative activity during the first three years. He composed as a man possessed and inspired. Clara's affection for her husband was a blind adoration. She could see no weakness in his character, no flaw in his art. In the course of a decade and a half eight children, four boys and four girls, were born to them. Nevertheless, Clara found the time and energy to make many public appearances. Often they were a matter of necessity, as the strain on their finances increased.

Clara's true greatness, both as woman and artist, began with her marriage. She grew out of a girlhood of simple sweetness into a woman of unbending strength of character, equal to the strain of a long public career and a burden of personal sorrow that few are called upon to bear. On sheer merit she won a place beside Liszt, Thalberg, and the other virtuosi, at that time no small feat for a woman. Schumann's chief contribution to her development was in the improvement of her musical taste. He helped her weed out of her repertoire the flashy tinsel pieces of Herz, Thalberg, Henselt, and even Liszt; he taught her instead the gospel of Bach and the Beethoven of the big sonatas. This was a procedure clearly against the popular taste; it was in fact an unheard-of thing when Clara first played an entire Beethoven sonata at a public concert. One of her happiest privileges was the introduction to the public of many of her husband's works.

Schumann's long period of intense creative activity, which had begun with the Song Year, came to a climax in 1843 when he produced a huge cantata, *Paradise and the Peri*, for solo voices, chorus, and orchestra. It was an exhausting task, and it left the composer in a disturbed mental state. The next year he and Clara set out on a four months' tour of Russia, to bolster up their finances. A Russian journey in midwinter was full of unforeseen difficulties—wretched inns and coaches, long drives by sleigh through regions of endless desolation inhabited only by wolves, cold that was excruciating. In that land of iron twilight and brooding icy darkness a deep melancholia settled upon the mind of Schumann. He was mulling over an epic idea, music for Goethe's *Faust*. When they returned to Leipzig he set to work, only to suffer a complete nervous collapse.

Once before, when he was a young man of twenty-three, Schumann had suffered an illness almost as alarming. There had been one particular night of horror when he had gone to the edge of suicide, and for weeks afterward he had been afraid to be alone. Now his mental depression was even worse. He could not sleep, he was tortured by all sorts of imaginary terrors, and he wept incessantly. Clara took the only advice that the doctors could offer—a change of scene—and late in 1844 the Schumann family removed to Dresden.

The precise nature of the disease that slowly disintegrated the composer's brain and nervous system is not known; modern diagnosticians are still left in doubt. But the record of the next twelve years, until his death in an asylum, is a story of almost unbelievable suffering and of heroic fortitude. The effect upon his art constitutes in itself one of the tragedies of music history. It is true that to the earlier part of this period belong several of his finest works—the last two movements of the Piano Concerto, the symphonies in C major and E flat major, the *Manfred* Overture—but for the most part what he produced were ghost pieces, done in a dull whiteness and removed from the body of his genius. He wrote enormous quantities of music, and in almost every known form—for various chamber combinations, piano duets and solos, organ pieces, over a hundred songs for solo and mixed voices, several huge choral works, an opera, a Mass, a Requiem—but the melancholy fact is clear that much of the time he wrote not under the press of inspiration but as a distraction from the tortures that were swelling within his brain.

Schumann was practically an invalid when they arrived in Dresden, in December 1844. He suffered not only from mental depression, but also from a mysterious skin trouble that he described as "a hundred places itching and twitching." As a hope of distraction Clara persuaded him to try exercises in fugue writing. They would both take the same fugal subject, work it out alone, and then compare and correct their efforts together. For Schumann this became a fascinating game and a means of getting back on the way to temporary health.

It was in Dresden that Schumann encountered Richard Wagner at close range. They had known each other casually in their student days in Leipzig, and Wagner had contributed several pieces to the *Neue Zeitschrift*. In 1844, Wagner was thirty-one years old, and he held the post of Kapellmeister at the Court Theater in Dresden. There he had produced his *Rienzi* and *The Flying Dutchman*, and he was now preparing for the *première* of *Tannhäuser* in 1845. The social intercourse between the two composers was something less than a spectacular success. Schumann recoiled from the neurotic, egotistical little man with an enormous head, who talked incessantly about himself, his music, and his grandiose ideas on art and aesthetics. Wagner in turn complained that he could get nothing out of a man who went for hours without uttering a word. When Wagner presented him with a score of his forthcoming *Tannhäuser*, Schumann studied it and pronounced it clever, but unmelodious and full of technical mistakes. After he heard it performed, however, he withdrew his criticism and admitted that it had moved him deeply. It almost goes without saying that Wagner did not care for Schumann's work. He thought it stodgy and unadventurous. The two composers by this time were traveling in opposite directions. Wagner was moving forward; he had in fact hardly made a beginning in the revolutionary procedures that were to influence every composer who came after him. Schumann had already made the turn back toward the past. He had begun as a pure romantic, but now he was immersed in the old classic forms. Compared with Wagner's, his influence in the future was to be small. After the death of his heir, Johannes Brahms, it would almost disappear as a moving force in music.

The first work of importance that Schumann was able to complete at Dresden was his Piano Concerto. He went back to a Fantasia in A minor for Piano and Orchestra, which he had written four years before, and added to it a second and third movement. Clara played it for the first time at the Leipzig Gewandhaus in January 1846; and on that occasion she had the honor of introducing to the world one of the most beloved works ever written in that form. In this concerto the many diverse elements in Schumann's art are brought together in perfect fusion. It is primarily a showpiece (as every concerto is by its very nature), yet it is written in impeccable taste; it is so romantic in style that its ideas flow with rhapsodic freedom, and yet it has a splendid underlying structure of classic form; it is as fragrantly sentimental as a packet of old lavender, but it remains one of the least dated works in nineteenth-century music. For once Schumann delivered a piece of orchestration that requires (for him) a minimum of tinkering to make it sound like something, while the writing for the piano is magnificent throughout.

Felicities of melody and style are strewn lavishly through the score, but there is one that cannot go unnoted—the cadenza at the conclusion of the first movement. The original purpose of a cadenza, as it developed in early eighteenth-century concertos, was to give the soloist an opportunity to display his skill at improvising. Down to the beginning of the present century the art of extemporization was part of the equipment of every musician of consequence. The test supreme was the cadenza in a concerto, when the soloist's dialogue with the orchestra came to a dramatic pause and he was permitted to take off on a daring solo flight. Unfortunately, the result was more often than not a blotch on the face of the piece as a whole. Beethoven indicated his opinions on the subject by writing out his own cadenzas for his E flat Piano Concerto. It was Schumann who really put an end to the custom of free improvisation. He produced for his Piano Concerto a cadenza that remains the model, both for inspiration and taste, and one of the few that is a joy rather than an ordeal for the listener. The fact remains that even written cadenzas, though an improvement on improvisation, are still too often a mistake. A good one is the hardest part of a concerto to write, and more musical rubble has been dumped into this form than into any other, not even excepting arias for coloratura sopranos. Schumann's, by contrast, is spun so beautifully from the main ideas of the work that it becomes not a separate and disturbing entity, but a part of the texture of the concerto itself; yet its style is such that a capable pianist can make it sound very much like an improvisation.

While he was at work on the concerto, Schumann remarked in a letter to Mendelssohn that for days "trumpets and drums have been sounding in my head—trumpets in C. What will come of it all I do not know." Once he had gotten the concerto out of the way, the composer set down on paper those clear-sounding trumpet Cs, and around them he wove the noble opening measures of a symphony —the Symphony in C major. If ever a work of art was produced "amidst inconvenience and distraction, in sickness and in sorrow," it is this crown of Robert Schumann's symphonic endeavors. It required many months of labor, and again and again the composer had to put it aside when his mental and physical pain became unbearable.

The C major Symphony is more than Schumann's best; it is the best symphony produced by any composer in the whole half century that stands between Schubert's C major and the C minor of Brahms. In the orchestration the composer's sins are not beyond forgiveness or repair; and in one movement, the Adagio espressivo, he achieved a piece of instrumentation that is actually inspired. It is well that he did, for this Adagio is a creation of profound and moving loveliness. It has superb lyric contours; it is the type of long-breathed, impassioned singing which Schumann could do so poignantly. Looking backward into his profuse past, and then into the bleakness of his future, one may perceive that this slow movement was the point of his highest development.

After the C major Symphony, Schumann turned again to his massive project, the *Scenes from Faust*, and these occupied him, along with many other works, until 1853. Meanwhile, in 1848, he fell a prey to the distraction that afflicts so many composers who ought to know better. He tried his hand at writing an opera. Like Beethoven and Schubert, he was doubtless attracted by the handsome perquisites that only a successful opera can offer, but like them he ended up on the hard rocks of failure. His *Genoveva* was produced in Leipzig in 1850 but it enjoyed only a *succès d'estime*. Today it is merely another tombstone in the overpopulated operatic graveyard.

More fruitful than either *Genoveva* or the *Faust* scenes was the music that Schumann composed to Byron's *Manfred*. In spite of the fact that Byron did not intend his dramatic poem for actual stage presentation, the composer made an attempt to adapt it, with appropriate music. The attempt was a failure, and the work as a whole found few performances after Liszt staged it at Weimar in 1852. (There was a presentation in America that must have been memorable—that of the Philharmonic Society of New York, in 1869, when the entire score was played and Edwin Booth read the text.) What survives of Schumann's *Manfred* today is a single magnificent fragment—the Overture. In addition to being the composer's best piece of orchestration, it is musical portraiture of a high order. The composer himself, like Manfred, had already "supp'd full with horrors"; so it is not strange that he was able to cast into this somber music much of the essence of human despair.

## IX

In 1850 a well-meaning friend of the Schumanns persuaded them to move to Düsseldorf, where the composer was offered the post of conductor of an orchestral and choral society. By this time he had gained a considerable reputation in Germany, and his appearance with his celebrated wife created a stir in the Rhineland town. They were feted and serenaded, and it appeared at first as if the new post would be one of congeniality.

At Düsseldorf Schumann produced his last symphony, the *Rhenish*, in E flat. This work was inspired by a trip to the city of Cologne, a few miles up the Rhine, and specifically by a ceremony that he witnessed at the great Cologne Cathedral. The occasion was one of the most solemn and gorgeous of all church services—the elevation of an archbishop to the rank of cardinal. Schumann's imagination took flight. In a sudden renascence of his old romantic spirit, he struck off the handcuffs of the classic rules and constructed a symphony in five movements instead of the usual four. The fourth movement he marked, "In the Character of an Accompaniment to a Solemn Ceremony." This is the so-called "Cathedral Scene"—a slow-moving, choralelike chant in the brass and woodwind, in effect a romantic impression of the ancient church ritual. The appearance of so unorthodox a movement in a symphony puzzled Schumann's contemporaries; even the faithful Clara admitted that it was not quite clear to her. Today it remains one of the composer's more impressive symphonic movements, and the only dismay it engenders is with the brass players, who are called upon to unsnarl some knotty problems of technique. The rest of the symphony is notable for its copious use of folklike tunes and rhythms, supposedly reminiscent of the Rhine Valley.

The composer's revision, in 1851, of his early D minor Symphony was his final work of consequence. He went back in memory to the first year of his marriage, to those halcyon days of midsummer when he had worked hard on this symphony to finish it in time for Clara's birthday. At its first performance it had fallen flat, and he had refused to publish it. So now he took it up again, and with a mature hand recast it. One of the changes that he made was to omit a guitar from the Romanze; in place of this youthful indiscretion he substituted strings pizzicato. The symphony appeared as his fourth, although in point of time it was actually his second. Certain innovations of form, rather than of musical content, have made the D minor Symphony a kind of lesser landmark. The four movements are not separated by pauses; they are intended to flow one into the other in a continuous stream. Moreover, some of the themes appear in various guises in several of the movements. One of them is a kind of motto theme, and is woven through the work with considerable technical skill. Schumann's aim was obviously to achieve some kind of organic unity among the four parts of a symphony, a problem that had bothered composers for a long time. His was a fairly simple solution (he had a precedent, of course, in the last two movements of Beethoven's Fifth Symphony); but it is noteworthy that at first he thought of hedging on his rash procedures by calling the work a *Symphonic Fantasia*. Since the D minor Symphony was published, these innovations have become a common practice with symphonic composers.

The post at Düsseldorf proved to be the worst thing that could have happened to Schumann. He had no natural gifts for the task of conducting, and yet he attempted to take over a musical organization that had a fine background of leadership and training. After a fairly successful first year a chill of disappointment spread over the musical circles of the town. Clara soon sensed it, but she shut her eyes to it and to her husband's growing disabilities. By this time a new torture had been added to his sufferings: he imagined that a single note was sounding continuously in his ears. His speech had become thick and his bodily movements slow. His attempts at conducting became an ordeal for the chorus and the orchestra. At times he would stand before them with raised baton, and then remain lost in thought, forgetting to start; or he would continue to conduct long after the music had stopped.

"My music is silenced," he finally wrote in the spring of 1854. The sound of notes ringing in his ears had become so intolerable that he had to give up all but sporadic attempts at composition. With the last vestiges of his failing mentality he turned to a literary project that had been in his mind for years. He began compiling his *Dichtergarten für Musik* [*The Poet's Garden of Music*], an anthology of allusions to music by the great poets of the ages. It was never finished. Every noise that he heard now sounded to him like music, "a music more beautiful, more finely colored in instrumentation than has ever been heard on this earth." One night he imagined that Mendelssohn and Schubert came to him, bringing him musical themes.

On the twenty-sixth of February 1854 there was a carnival in Düsseldorf, and in spite of a heavy rain the streets were filled with people dressed in the grotesque costumes of a masquerade. A man appeared in the crowd, wearing a long green dressing gown and slippers. He was bareheaded, and the rain was dripping from his hair. He ran out upon a long bridge and flung himself into the Rhine. Men in a passing boat got him out of the water; and then they recognized the music director, Dr. Schumann. A week later he was taken to an asylum at Endenich, near Bonn.

Schumann was kept there for more than two years, until his death on July 29, 1856. Clara was not permitted to see him until two nights before he died. His sufferings had changed him so that she was scarcely able to recognize him. But he smiled at her, and with a last effort put his arm around her.

She wrote, "I would not give the memory of that embrace for the world's treasures."

X

The chronological facts of Schumann's life would seem to indicate that he was one of those artists who mature early, do their best work in their twenties and thirties, and then reach a point of sterility in middle age. But in his case we cannot be sure, because his mental deterioration coincided with the decline in his art. There is no way of knowing whether or not, granted health, he could have gone far beyond the great work he had accomplished before he reached forty. If he had, there is interest in the speculation as to what he might have achieved—what splendid works would have followed the C major Symphony, the Piano Concerto, and the *Manfred* Overture—instead of the pile of dank, unloved scores that he did produce. We have a slight hint, for Schumann died leaving an heir. In a sense, it was Johannes Brahms who carried on where Schumann left off.

The two composers met only a few months before Schumann's attempted suicide. Brahms, a shy, unknown youth of twenty, came to the Schumanns' house in Düsseldorf with a letter of introduction. His eyes were a brilliant blue, and his straight blond hair fell almost to his shoulders; underneath a shabby exterior there was something of the aspect of a young god. He had hardly touched the piano and the opening measures of his own Sonata in C major before the older man sensed the faint current of divinity. For weeks after that the Schumanns could not get enough of this wonderful young man and his music. Schumann then made the boldest prediction in music history. He had not written for the *Neue Zeitschrift* for ten years, but now he contributed an article called "New Paths." It was his last literary effort, and his most potent, for it announced to the world the genius of Brahms. Schumann made no reservations: Brahms, he said, was the great new talent for which music had been waiting; he was not an artist who had to go through slow stages of development, but one who sprang, like Athena, fully armed from the head of Zeus. It was a stroke of unparalleled prescience, for Brahms was still hardly more than a boy and he had written but a handful of songs, piano pieces, and chamber works. "New Paths" made a stir all over Germany. It caused great irritation among the champions of Wagner and Liszt; it was a source of embarrassment and even a handicap to Brahms himself.

Writing elsewhere of his "young eagle," Schumann said, "I should dearly like to be at his side on his flight over the world"; but he did not live long enough to witness more than the first trials of those sturdy pinions. However, the effect of Schumann's musical ideas upon Brahms was profound. In the stream of music the one body flows directly into the other. Young Brahms inherited part of the older man's style, his romantic ardor, and to a minor degree certain of his weaknesses. Brahms's supreme accomplishment was along that road which Schumann had taken shortly before death stopped him; he arrived, from beginnings of romanticism, at the loftiest classicism of the later nineteenth century.

More than his music, Schumann bequeathed to Brahms the devotion of Clara. She outlived her husband by almost forty years. For a time, after her bereavement, she and Brahms were inseparable companions. He worshiped her, and thus it became her privilege to inspire a talent greater even than that of her beloved Robert.

# Wagner
## 1813—83

### I

The ship was the *Thetis*, a tiny merchant vessel bound for
London from the Prussian harbor of Pillau, on the Baltic
Sea. She made ready to sail one day in July 1839 with a
captain, a crew of six, and two passengers. These last were
a young German opera conductor and his wife. They had
come aboard secretly, and they hid themselves below decks
until the ship cleared. They had no passports. The cockle-
shell of a ship was overcrowded without them; nevertheless
they brought along a huge Newfoundland dog that had to
be hauled up the ship's side. The crew of the *Thetis* looked
upon them with disfavor and even superstition.

The young man was strikingly odd in appearance—only a
few inches over five feet in height, but with an enormous
head. His nose was large and Teutonic, his forehead broad,
his mouth a straight firm line that any reader of character
would know meant determination of a high order. Most
salient feature of all was his eyes. They were a brilliant,
luminous blue, and so piercing and alive that everyone
who knew him remarked about their fascination. He was
an intensely nervous man, and he talked too much. His
wife was a pretty young woman, a few years older than
he—quiet, pleasant-tempered, and modest. She had been an
actress.

The couple came from Riga, the Livonian city far up

the Baltic Sea, where for two years the young man had been the conductor of the town opera. It had been a dreary experience and he had finally lost his job. They had to get out of Livonia (which was then under Russian rule) like two criminals escaping from prison, for the reason that they did not dare apply for a passport. That would have brought down upon them a horde of creditors, the young man having contrived during his short stay in Riga to run up bills and borrow money from a remarkably large number of friends, acquaintances, and tradesmen. They fled in a coach down to the Prussian border, and at a lonely outpost got themselves smuggled across the frontier, even racing across the final dividing ditch at risk of being shot by Cossack sentries. At Pillau they got aboard the *Thetis* for an eight-day voyage to London, but their final destination was Paris.

The young man's real ambition in life was not conducting but composing operas. To anyone but himself his prospects of success in Paris could not have appeared bright. He was going to the most celebrated operatic center in Europe, where even French composers had to have extraordinary luck and ability to get their works performed; yet he was an unknown German who had written but two operas and part of a third. Only the second had been performed; it was given but once and the performance was a fiasco. Nevertheless, he was certain that the unfinished work (it was based on Bulwer-Lytton's novel, *Rienzi*) was sure to be a success in Paris—once he could get there, finish it, and bring it to the attention of the authorities of the Paris Opéra.

Obviously this young man was blessed with self-confidence and assertiveness in copious quantities; he was, in fact, so sure of himself that at the age of twenty-two he had bought himself a large red notebook in which he carefully recorded all the details of his life for reference in future years when he would be writing his autobiography.

The voyage of the *Thetis* lasted not eight days, but three and a half weeks, and it was a horror that the passengers never forgot. As they coasted through the Skaggerak and into the North Sea they were beset by storms so violent

that several times they were driven off their course. The
captain had to seek shelter in Norwegian fiords, and once
the little ship almost foundered when she struck a reef.
The two passengers were in torment from seasickness and
fear. During one thunderstorm the poor wife went almost
insane with terror, and she begged her husband to tie her
body to his so they would not be separated when they
drowned.

They reached London at last, on August 12, 1839; and
the *Thetis*, sturdy little ship that she was, brought safely
to port one of the most precious cargoes that she or any
other ship of her time ever carried. For her passenger was
Richard Wagner—the young Wagner, carrying in his enormous head the seeds of the intellect that was to become a
*sequoia gigantea* among the creative minds of the nineteenth century. This was Wagner standing in the doorway
of the most incredible career in music—a life in which the
contrasts of privation and luxurious indulgence, of steady
year-by-year defeat and final overwhelming victory, of personal venality and unswerving artistic idealism, were combined to an extent that would stagger the imagination of a
Hugo. This was Wagner, whose art would become the
crowning phenomenon of the entire romantic movement.
More words would be written about him than about any
other composer of his age; whole libraries would be devoted to his life, his ideas, his works; the controversies
that they would raise would be unmatched in violence and
would not be resolved within a space of a hundred years.
What he accomplished in music, the extent of the metamorphosis he caused both in its technique and its aesthetic, was so profound that it still defies final evaluation.

II

His life at its very inception is a matter of controversy.
He was born in Leipzig on May 22, 1813, supposedly the
son of a police actuary named Karl Friedrich Wagner. Six
months later the father died, and the mother married Ludwig Geyer, an actor. There is strong evidence that Geyer
was Wagner's real father. Whatever the truth, Geyer's in-

fluence upon Wagner as a child was important. He was a man of more than ordinary intellect. Besides acting with one of the better German theatrical troupes, he wrote plays, and also made a fair name for himself as a portrait painter. Geyer died when Richard was eight years old.

The most significant grain of fact in the boyhood of Wagner was his early passion for poetic drama. He read the plays of Shakespeare and decided to become a dramatist. He then wrote a play in which all twenty-two characters were killed off, so that in the last act he had to bring them back as ghosts. His interest in music was secondary until he happened to hear some of Beethoven's orchestral works. He was so moved that he decided that his play would need incidental music and that he would write it himself. He went so far as to borrow a textbook on music from Clara Schumann's father, Friedrich Wieck, who had a lending library in Leipzig at that time. Later he began to study music theory in earnest, but he probably learned most from his studies of Beethoven's scores—the piano sonatas, quartets, overtures, and symphonies. He was so mad about Beethoven that when he was seventeen he copied out the full score of the Ninth Symphony and made an arrangement of it for piano—a long and arduous task. No other such arrangement then existed in print, so he offered it to Schott, the publishers, who rejected it.

When he was twenty-one, Wagner got a job as conductor of a small opera company in the town of Magdeburg. It was one of the numerous fifth-rate, faded, half-bankrupt troupes that traveled among the less important German towns that could not support theaters of their own. The more dismal features of life with this company did not depress young Wagner's ambitions; it was in the following year that he purchased his red book for the autobiographical notes. He also finished his first opera, *Die Feen* (The Fairies), which was never produced during his lifetime; and he began work on his second, *Das Liebesverbot* (The Ban on Love), which was a perversion of Shakespeare's *Measure for Measure* into an operatic comedy in the style of the contemporary Italians.

When he was twenty-three Wagner married an actress

named Minna Planer. This was one of the most unfortunate mistakes that the history of the marriage institution has to record. Wagner was attracted to Minna with an infatuation that is common among highly sexed, wildly imaginative men. He pursued her until she finally gave in to marriage. Not long afterward she ran away from him. He was in misery for months, imploring her to come back; when she did, he freely forgave her affair with another man.

There had been previous indiscretions in Minna's life. When she was sixteen a man named Einsiedel entered the pages of history by seducing her. She bore a daughter, Natalie, the shame of whose parentage was concealed by Minna by the simple expedient of passing the child off as her sister. Wagner knew this, but he too kept the secret for years. Natalie herself did not learn the truth until she was an old woman.

These irregularities in Minna's life had little or nothing to do with the failure of her marriage to Wagner. She was a plain sort of woman of limited intelligence who would have made an average German hausfrau. With every year that passed, her husband's mentality expanded, until not only his ideas and his music but also his simplest actions became incomprehensible to her. Minna was consumed by jealousies and Wagner by irritations that ruined her life and festered his.

After two years at Magdeburg, the opera company collapsed into bankruptcy. One of its final performances was the dismal *première* of *Das Liebesverbot*. Wagner took up his next post at Königsberg, far off in East Prussia, and from there he went on to two years at Riga. The crows of despair were sitting on the young man's battlements all through these years of hack conducting in grim old eastern towns. It seemed that he was being pushed farther and farther from the European musical center of gravity into the dank spaces of Prussia and Russia; he was beginning to stagger, too, under a load of debt. The only thing that kept him going at Riga was his work on the opera *Rienzi*. By the summer of 1839 he had almost completed the first two acts—and then he made his great resolve. He had lost his job as conductor, so he decided to give up his conducting career entirely and devote his life to the composition of operas. The flight from Riga and the voyage on the *Thetis* were thus his first leap into the dark. It was the most critical single decision of his entire life.

### III

The reason why Wagner chose to go to Paris rather than back into Germany had to do with the unsatisfactory state of operatic affairs in his native country at that time. All the German operatic composers were on the horns of a two-pronged dilemma. The German public not only refused to believe that its own composers could write as good operas as Italians or Frenchmen, but it also refused to see that they were paid decently for their work if they did prove it. From the time of Mozart on, German composers had been trying to break the strangle hold of Italian opera in their country; the idea of an opera that would be a "truly Germanic work of art" had haunted Mozart years before it did Weber, Marschner, and Wagner himself. Weber's *Der Freischütz*, first produced in 1821, was remarkable both because of its new "romantic" style and because its subject matter was as natively German as beer and black bread. It created immense enthusiasm, but it could not change overnight habits of thought that had prevailed for generations.

Wagner himself became one of the strongest forces in the awakening of the German people, in the later decades of the nineteenth century, to a realization of their national strength, both political and intellectual; yet it is ironical that as a young man he actually had to leave Germany because he felt it was useless to try to get a hearing for his work in his native land. Brooding over his unhappy job at Riga, he came to the decision that the only way he could get his *Rienzi* produced in Germany would be to get it produced first in Paris. The Paris Opéra was then the most powerful institution of its kind in Europe; if *Rienzi* were to be performed there, every opera house in Germany would demand it with sheeplike acquiescence. Wagner also hoped that it would get him out of debt. At the Paris Opéra a composer was paid a royalty on every performance of his work, but in Germany the opera houses paid him only a single fee (usually miserably small) which gave them the right to perform his work forever after without royalty.

And so Wagner and Minna and the Newfoundland dog betook themselves to Paris in the fall of 1839 as a roundabout means of assaulting the recalcitrant managers of the opera houses of Germany. As it turned out, they had far better have stayed at home. Wagner accomplished none of his aims in Paris, but he suffered two and a half years of privations so cruel that he spoke of them forty years later with tears.

The chances were heavily against him at the Paris Opéra. At that time fashionable prestige with the aristocracy of Paris, liberal perquisites from the state to pay for its extravagances, a management with a notable lack of artistic foresight or conscience, and a method of operation that made it (in Ernest Newman's phrase) "one third temple of the Muses, two thirds antechamber to a seraglio," had drained the Opéra of any true artistic purpose. In the endless coils of its intrigue, musical and social, a new personality or an unfamiliar idea had no more chance than a rabbit in the embrace of a snake. Dominating the entire institution was Giacomo Meyerbeer, son of a wealthy banker of Berlin, who had come to Paris in 1826 and, within a decade, given it two of the biggest successes in French operatic history—*Robert the Devil* and *The Huguenots*. Meyerbeer's particular brand of opera was what the public of Paris craved in copious quantities, and it was the style that young Wagner was trying hard to imitate in the writing of *Rienzi*.

By a lucky chance Wagner got to see Meyerbeer himself. The older man listened while Wagner read him the libretto of the first three acts of *Rienzi*; he found it admirable, but of the music he praised only the composer's handwriting. Later Wagner got an audition for *Das Liebesverbot* before a committee of the Opéra which included Eugène Scribe, Meyerbeer's prolific and enormously successful librettist. Wagner himself accompanied the singers on a piano, but after the gentlemen had listened solemnly they told him in effect to sell his papers elsewhere.

It was not long before the poor young German was struggling desperately for his next meal. He wrote articles for the Paris musical journals and did hack jobs for a music publisher. These included making arrangements of entire operas for various instruments—for piano (two hands and four hands), for two violins, for voice and piano, and even for the cornet. At that time the cornet was a new instrument, enjoying a poisonous vogue in Paris similar to that of the saxophone in America decades later. Wagner plowed through reams of stuff of this kind—labor that was backbreaking and stultifying.

At the same time he was struggling to finish *Rienzi*. He worked at home in a miserable apartment, going out every fourth day for exercise. He went around Paris in worn-out clothes and shoes full of holes; there is strong evidence that he was jailed for a time for debt. The dog Robber disappeared, a sore blow to Wagner, who was pathologically fond of animals, but Robber doubtless had to find a home where the rations were more plentiful. The composer himself became ill of a gastric disorder that was to plague him for the rest of his life.

In November 1840 Wagner completed *Rienzi*. Realizing that a Paris production was out of the question, he sent the score to the Dresden Opera. At the same time he addressed a letter to the King of Saxony, imploring him to order its performance. Months went by, and in the spring of 1841, Wagner wrote a sketch for a new opera, *The Flying Dutchman*, based on a legend of the sea that had been churning in his mind since the voyage of the *Thetis*. Then in June came the electrifying news that *Rienzi* had been accepted for performance in Dresden. The lift to the young man's spirits must have been enormous. He set about the task of composing *The Flying Dutchman* with terrific concentration, finishing it before the year was out. The music was actually composed in a space of seven weeks during August and September 1841.

In April 1842, after two and a half years of concentrated misery, Wagner and Minna sat weeping in a coach that took them through the gates of Paris. Ahead of them was Dresden—and the real beginning of Wagner's career.

IV

The *première* of *Rienzi* took place on October 20, 1842, after many postponements. The task of producing it was an enormous one, and Wagner was lucky that the Dresden Opera spread itself lavishly. More than five hundred new costumes were made for the principals and supernumeraries, new stage settings were built, and the singers included two famous German stars—a *Heldentenor* named Tichatschek, and Mme. Schröder-Devrient, who was the Flagstad of her day. The composer himself supervised every minute detail of the production.

The *première* turned out to be a success so immense that even Wagner, archoptimist about anything concerning his own work, was stunned with amazement. As the long five-act work began, he sat like a man in a trance, his eyes glazed and his face green with fear. He had grossly underestimated the length of the piece; it began at six in the evening and did not end until midnight. But with every act the enthusiasm of the audience increased, until the end was a triumph. The opera continued to run for months, and the news of its success spread all over Germany. People even traveled from neighboring towns and cities to see it.

In *Rienzi* Wagner's purpose had been to imitate the master of the Paris Opéra, and it has often been said that in *Rienzi* he "out-Meyerbeered Meyerbeer." The truth is that the music of *Rienzi* falls far short of Meyerbeer's best. The only thing of outstanding merit is the Overture which, for all its slam-bang style, is a shrewdly constructed piece. It has dramatic drive, piles climax upon climax with skill, and shows imagination if not much taste. Thereafter the score is a collection of clichés, most of them Italian rather than Meyerbeerian. The general form is conventional—arias, duets, trios, quartets, and choruses interspersed with recitatives. No character, not even that of Rienzi, comes to life.

What made *Rienzi* a success was not its music, but its combination of music and spectacle. Wagner was attracted to Bulwer-Lytton's story of Rome in the fourteenth century because it gave him the chance to load his stage with the very stuff that had made opera in Paris "grand." The work is a three-ring circus of stage effects. There are scenes before the Church of St. John Lateran, in the Capitol, and in the Roman streets; there are processions of monks and priests, pageants of ambassadors, troops of soldiers, mobs of men, women, and children; there are trumpet calls, organ playing, chanting in the distant church (a forecast of *Die Meistersinger*), and great bells tolling (a forecast of *Parsifal*); there are a ballet, an off-stage battle, and a funeral march; at one point Rienzi makes a grand entrance on a horse, and at the end of the last act the Capitol falls in flames. This was Wagner the showman gorging himself (and his audience) with scenic splendor and masses of people—to the accompaniment of roaring choruses and some of the loudest orchestration written up to that time.

With a success like *Rienzi* on its hands, the Dresden Opera naturally wanted more of Wagner, so in great haste preparations were made for the production of *The Flying Dutchman*. Its *première* occurred on January 2, 1843, only ten weeks after that of *Rienzi*. It was a failure. After four performances it had to be withdrawn, the public demanding *Rienzi* instead. What had happened was the first appearance of the difficulty that was to dog the composer most of the days of his life. Wagner's art never stood still; from *Die Feen* to *Parsifal* it grew and changed and intensified, which meant that his life was a continual process of educating musicians, singers, impresarios, and the public itself to an understanding of what he was about. They had scarcely begun to appreciate one phase when he was ready with something new.

*The Flying Dutchman* is miles beyond *Rienzi*. It is a fascinating study in the embryology of music, for it contains the rudiments of practically all the ideas that Wagner would later use to revolutionize opera. It also exhibits many of the idiosyncrasies of his mature style, of which there was theretofore no trace in his music.

The libretto itself is indicative of a complete reversal of the composer's ideas. *Rienzi*'s subject was historical (in the manner popularized by Meyerbeer); *The Flying Dutchman*'s is legendary, and many of the details of its story are Wagner's own invention. The basic legend is that of the Dutch mariner who swore an oath that he would double the Cape of Good Hope in the teeth of a storm. For his blasphemy he was doomed to sail the seas forever until he could find a woman willing to sacrifice her life to save his. Wagner's opera begins with a landing by the Dutchman on the coast of Norway, a respite he is permitted every seven years. He meets Senta, a girl who has been deeply moved by his story. She promises to marry him. The Dutchman later learns that Senta was betrothed to another man and has broken her vows; believing her fickle, he sets sail again in despair. As his ship sails away, Senta throws herself into the sea, faithful to him even to death. The ship then disappears and the spirits of Senta and the Dutchman she has redeemed are seen to ascend heavenward.

In the handling of this story Wagner made his first step toward the ideal for which he was to wage a lifelong campaign—the changing of opera into what he called "music drama." His overpowering impulse, as it began to develop in *The Flying Dutchman*, was to make the drama the focal point of the artist's effort, with the music simply a means of expressing the emotional, poetic, and pictorial details of the story. The failure of *The Flying Dutchman* in Dresden was owing to the bewilderment of both the public and the performers at Wagner's first tentative steps toward this new idea. The new opera had none of the circus pageantry that had glutted *Rienzi*; it had a few choruses, but they were justified by the dramatic situations; there was comparatively little singing of the purely theatrical order. Instead of the glare and bombast and pseudo-Roman brilliance of *Rienzi*, it exposed a short, swiftly moving drama played by a few characters amid the gloom of a Norwegian fiord.

The music of *The Flying Dutchman* is incomparably finer than anything the composer yet had done. The musical mind of Wagner had never really entered the story of *Rienzi*. The music of that opera is remote from any real suggestion of the characters or their setting of fourteenth-century Rome. It is stencil stuff that opera composers of that time all used to represent certain dramatic situations. But in *The Flying Dutchman*, Wagner actually got his music to expressing, unmistakably, and with swift original strokes, the essence of his drama. His score is saturated with the sounds and smell of the sea, the darkness of the north, and the fury of the storms that pursued the Dutchman; it depicts the characters and follows their story vividly.

The score also contains the real beginnings of Wagner's scheme of leitmotivs, or "leading motives," which later became the nervous system of his entire musical style. He devised short musical phrases that were suggestive of a character, or a mood, or a dramatic situation; he used them again and again in the course of his opera, weaving them into the texture of the music whenever the character or mood or situation rose to a dominant place in the drama. Wagner had used leading motives in a fragmentary way even in his three earlier operas, but in *The Flying Dutchman* they take real shape and importance. The first of them is a masterpiece worthy of his maturity—the bold blast of the horns in open fifths with which the Overture begins—a motive suggesting the Dutchman himself.

*The Flying Dutchman* is still not a popular opera, largely because it has been dwarfed by the works that came after it, and because its musical texture, although full of originality, is still crude. Wagner was in the throes of a struggle to cast off the influence of the Italian lyrical style and develop one of his own. *The Fying Dutchman* is a mixture of both. By far the finest thing in the work is the Overture, which is a superb concentration of the drama that follows. In a few pages the composer outlines the despairs and yearnings of the condemned mariner, the compassion of Senta, their ruined hopes, and their final redemption—all framed in the roar and fury of the sea and the screaming of the wind. When this stunning seascape was first exposed, on the second day of the year 1843, the audience that had come expecting other things did not suspect that a revolution had been let loose in the theater.

## V

Shortly after the production of his two operas, Wagner was made Kapellmeister of the Dresden Opera. His yearly salary was fifteen hundred thalers (about two thousand dollars) for life. Had he been a differently constituted man he might have used this job as a sinecure, gone on composing *Rienzis* and ended up the German equivalent of Meyerbeer. Already he was being lionized in Dresden, and his fame was spreading through Germany with stories of the success of *Rienzi*. He accepted the post of Kapellmeister, but only with misgivings. *The Flying Dutchman*, failure though it was, had given this thirty-year-old, slowly developing genius a sudden realization of the strength that lay in the thews and sinews of his imagination.

He remained for six years in Dresden, hard at work but fundamentally an unhappy man. With every year that passed, his frustrations grew; his mind, gathering strength as it developed, reached out in all directions—wanting to change, to improve, to re-create. He had no patience with the routine performances of Italian works at the Dresden Opera. He wanted to conduct only the finer German works—those of Gluck, Mozart, Beethoven, and Weber. When he performed *Iphigenia in Aulis*, he refurbished it completely, ridding it of a half century of conventional excrescences. He tried to revitalize the personnel of the orchestra and to reseat it; he wrote a long report to the King of Saxony with plans for a more efficient operation of the entire institution. His plan was turned down as too visionary, when as a matter of fact it was both sensible and practical. To this restless, bitterly sincere, furiously energetic little man the opera house was not merely a glorified vaudeville show, but a temple where a new art could be made to flourish. When he could not pull the men who ran it out of their conventional ruts he was balked and maddened.

The unflattering portraits of this composer with which biographies are now loaded begin with him at Dresden: Wagner the exhausting talker about himself and his ideas; the nervous, intense, and irritable man with the eyes of a fanatic and the cruel mouth of a zealot; the paragon of conceit who was so opinionated that the slightest disagreement with his ideas excited and exasperated him.

Wagner's great work during the Dresden period was the composition of *Tannhäuser* and *Lohengrin*. The idea for *Tannhäuser* first came to him in Paris. On the journey from there to Dresden in the spring of 1842, he and Minna passed through the little town of Eisenach, to the south of which is located the Wartburg, the illustrious old castle where the medieval minnesingers were supposed to have held their song contests. At that moment Wagner conceived the idea for the third act of his opera. After the production of *The Flying Dutchman*, he set to work, first writing a poetic libretto of his own.

According to Wagner's story, Tannhäuser, a young minstrel, has lived for a year with the pagan goddess Venus. Satiated with sensual pleasures and knowing that his soul is endangered by his sins, Tannhäuser breaks away from Venus and returns to the country of the Wartburg. He rejoins the minstrel knights and takes part in the celebrated Tournament of Song. But he scandalizes the company with an outburst in praise of the profane love he enjoyed with Venus. The knights threaten to kill him, but he is saved by the pious Elizabeth, who loves him. He goes to Rome with a band of pilgrims to seek forgiveness from the Pope, but later returns a doomed and broken man. As he dies at Elizabeth's bier, evidence is brought of a miracle at Rome that is the sign of his redemption.

After a poor *première* at the Dresden Opera (October 19, 1845), *Tannhäuser* suddenly turned into a success. The public of Dresden liked it as well as they had *Rienzi*, and within a few years it was a drawing card all over Germany. Today, after a hundred years, it is still popular in operatic repertoires.

It is all too easy to underestimate *Tannhäuser*. This is largely because it cannot stand anywhere near the immense works of the composer's maturity. But a work of such vitality cannot be dismissed. *Tannhäuser* has first of all a fine dramatic structure. Wagner had developed as a dramatist since the days of *Rienzi*. He had learned how to use and, even more important, how to conserve his effects. *Tannhäuser* has a bacchanal, a march, a song tournament, and many imposing choruses. At bottom these are Meyerbeer's grand-opera effects, but Wagner worked them into his story with reality and justification, and he used them with restraint. As for the music, old-fashionedly romantic though much of it is today, it supports the drama with remarkable fidelity. No other composer of his time could have painted these pictures in music as surely and as brilliantly as Wagner did. And few would have even attempted to portray as he did the psychological states of mind of the various characters.

In *Tannhäuser* appears, for the first time in this composer's music, one of the most salient features of his entire art—sensuality. Wagner the man was a sensualist to the core. His nature was permeated both by the desires of sex and the sybaritical pleasures of life—the caressing sounds and perfumes and textures that appeal to the born voluptuary. It was thus no accident that drew him to paint in music the scenes of the Venusberg and their hold upon Tannhäuser; it was the strongest side of his whole nature bursting at last into expression. Never before *Tannhäuser* had music expressed passion with such urge and vividness. It is the most powerful and original feature of the entire score. For Wagner it was only a beginning. He had in reserve ideas that would make even the fires of Venus and her sirens and the bacchantes seem cool by comparison.

*Lohengrin* was finished about three years after *Tannhäuser*. Wagner's method was the same as in the previous work. He chose a Germanic legend, manipulated it to suit his purpose, and wrote from it his own poetic libretto. The scene of the opera is Antwerp in the tenth century. Elsa of Brabant is accused by Count Telramund of murdering her brother. She is saved when Lohengrin, a knight in shining armor, appears in a boat drawn by a swan. Lohengrin offers to protect and marry Elsa on condition that she never ask his name or where he came from. He then defeats Telramund in a trial by battle. But the latter plots vengeance with his wife, Ortrud. After the marriage Elsa makes the fatal mistake (prompted by Ortrud) of breaking her promise and asking her husband's identity. Lohengrin sadly tells his story: he is the son of Parsifal, one of the knights of the Holy Grail. As he leaves Elsa forever, his swan is changed into her brother, who had been a victim of Ortrud's sorcery.

The story of *Lohengrin* is less convincing than that of *Tannhäuser*. Its Germanic sentimentality and its medieval superstition, overlaid with the sugar of chivalry, are now faintly ludicrous; while the character of Elsa is too insipid to inspire much sympathy. Even so, the opera is still a long stride beyond its predecessor. The score of *Lohengrin* is by far the richest musical texture that Wagner had yet spun. It glows with exquisite harmonic schemes and finely spun melodic threads; the whole piece has a shimmer, a golden aura suggestive of its subject. The vocal writing and the handling of the orchestra are masterly throughout.

In this opera Wagner moved still farther toward his music drama ideal. A system of leitmotivs is fairly prominent. The set numbers of the old-style opera have practically disappeared. Instead the music moves in one continuous flow as it follows the action on the stage. There are still vestiges of the old recitative and of the aria (in "Elsa's Dream" and "Lohengrin's Narrative"), and the composer did not forget the purposes of the Paris Opéra in his many brilliant choruses, the wedding scene, and the bombastic introduction to the third act.

The Prelude to *Lohengrin* must be set apart from everything the composer had written up to that time. It is a masterpiece, the first appearance of the mature Wagner working under inspiration of the highest order. To set the mood of his story, the composer depicts a vision of the Holy Grail as it descends from the heavens, dazzles the eyes with its ethereal beauty, and then disappears. To gain this effect, Wagner worked out an ingenious tech-

### JOHANN SEBASTIAN BACH
Portrait by Elias Gottlieb Haussmann, painted in 1723 and lost for almost 140 years. The only known portrait of the composer as a young man. (Courtesy of Mrs. Emma Reifenberg)

GEORGE FRIDERIC HANDEL
Portrait by Thomas Hudson (1701–1779). (Courtesy of
The Metropolitan Museum of Art, New York, Gift of
Frances Neilson, 1946)

**FRANZ JOSEPH HAYDN**
Portrait of the composer during one of his London sojourns, painted by John Hoppner. (Courtesy of The Bettmann Archive)

WOLFGANG AMADEUS MOZART

LUDWIG VAN BEETHOVEN
The composer in his middle years. Portrait by Willibord
Mähler. (Courtesy of The Bettmann Archive)

FRANZ SCHUBERT

FREDERIC CHOPIN

From a rare daguerreotype made about three years before
the composer's death. (Courtesy of Courtlandt Palmer)

ROBERT SCHUMANN

RICHARD WAGNER

Parigi 9 Aprile 1896
Boldini

GIUSEPPE VERDI
Painting by Boldini.

JOHANNES BRAHMS

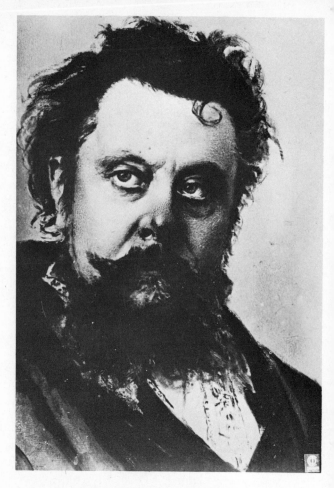

MODEST MUSSORGSKY
Painting by Repin. (Courtesy of The Bettmann Archive)

PETER ILLICH TCHAIKOVSKY
Painting by Kusnetzov. (Courtesy of The Bettmann
Archive)

ACHILLE-CLAUDE DEBUSSY
Painting by Marcel Baschet (Rome, 1884).

RICHARD STRAUSS
Conducting in the 1930s. (Courtesy of The Bettmann
Archive)

IGOR STRAVINSKY
(Courtesy of Boosey and Hawkes)

nical design. The piece is based on a single prolonged crescendo and a shorter diminuendo. The music begins in the
highest reaches of a few violins; as it drifts slowly downward toward the middle and bass registers, the other instruments gradually make their entrances, enriching and
broadening the entire scheme into a blazing climax, and
then moving upward again to thin out and disappear in
the high strings. The golden tapestry that Wagner created
with these means is one of the richest sounds in music. It
is the first of a long series of tone pictures with which the
later works were to be studded.

Wagner finished *Lohengrin* in August 1847 (he wrote
the Prelude last), but the work was not produced at
Dresden. Nor was the composer present at its *première* at
Weimar, in 1850, under Liszt's direction. He did not hear
a performance of the opera until 1859, twelve years after
its completion. What happened meanwhile was a complete unheaval of the composer's life which drove him out
of Germany, a political exile hunted by the authorities.

The Revolution of 1848 had gone off all over Europe
like a series of firecrackers, finally reaching Saxony in the
spring of 1849. For many months the young Kapellmeister
of the Dresden Opera had been one of the leading spirits
of a group of liberals who were drumming for an overthrow
of the monarchy. He had written pamphlets and made
speeches, and when the storm broke in Dresden, Wagner
risked his life for several desperate days in the barricaded
streets. But the revolution was crushed, and among the
warrants that were posted for the arrest of the ringleaders
was one dated May 16, 1849, for the "Royal Kapellmeister,
Richard Wagner."

He was never caught. He and Minna had fled to
Switzerland.

VI

The early years of Wagner's exile from Germany are the
great interregnum of his career as a composer. With the
completion of *Lohengrin*, he had created the finest romantic opera yet written in Germany. There was not

another composer alive who could offer him any real competition in his field, and he knew it. Yet he did something that must have seemed incomprehensible to his admirers, and, to a woman like Minna, sheer insanity. He stopped writing music altogether. For six years he composed nothing at all. Instead he devoted his time to the writing of a huge body of prose works.

His political banishment had nothing to do with this radical action. It appeared later that he was in a long period of gestation during which his next musical work— a gigantic creation—was slowly taking shape in his mind. That work was *The Ring of the Nibelung.* He was not yet ready for the task. It was too enormous and too far outside the boundaries of any known concepts of the musical art. Wagner could not remain silent about it; he had to talk. He had also to find a valve for the release of his enormous mental energy. And so several of the six years between the completion of *Lohengrin* and the start on *Das Rheingold* were taken up with a geyser of literary work, most of it elaborate theorizing on the subject of music, opera, and the drama.

Anyone reading the life story of Richard Wagner can only regard this six-year period with admiration for both the man's courage and his intellectual strength. It is one of the things that compensate for the thick defamatory coating with which his character is plastered today. That there was an unpleasant side to Wagner the man is undeniable, and the fact that the calcium lights of modern research play heavily upon it today is largely his own fault. In the later years of his life he sat down with his second wife (Cosima Liszt von Bülow Wagner) and dictated his autobiography, *Mein Leben.* This large, two-volume work was published in 1911, long after his death. It proved to be the worst mistake that Wagner ever made. He could not foresee that the fashion in biographies would change and that the public would prefer about the great dead not a velvet-lined Victorian eulogy but a dissection performed by a psychiatrist with a hatchet in his hand. He could not foresee that hundreds of biographers, critics, and musicologists would seize upon his words, compare them with other records, and prove him not only an egomaniac but a liar as well. His autobiography is in fact flooded with untruths, evasions, and misinterpretations about many of the people he knew and many of the vital events in his life. It has raised enormous clouds of controversial dust, making the real truth about him difficult to discern. The English biographer, Ernest Newman, whose work is a model of thoroughness and impartiality, spent years at the task of clarifying the Wagner data contained in other biographies, in the composer's own writings, and in his thousands of letters; and even Newman leaves many issues in Wagner's life in doubt.

Wagner's detractors have made the most, probably, of his debts. He was the high priest of borrowers. Nobody has ever been able to figure out exactly how much he borrowed in his lifetime, but it must have been several hundred thousand dollars. He seldom repaid. He borrowed at Magdeburg and Riga and Paris, and on up to Bayreuth. He borrowed from his relatives, from his friends, and from singers in the opera companies; he borrowed from Liszt, and from the husband of at least one lady with whom he was in love; he persuaded another lady to give him a regular income. Finally, as a grand climax to the art of raising money, he borrowed huge sums from one of the European kings. Reading his letters, one might think that half his time was spent at this melancholy and often desperate business.

One of the chief reasons for Wagner's money troubles (as so many writers have been careful to point out) was his pathological extravagance. His creditors were always aghast at the luxuriousness of the houses and apartments he chose to live in; his homes were always lavishly furnished, and generally there was a lovely garden. At Dresden he had a magnificent library and an expensive piano, which he had to leave behind him when he escaped. When Liszt visited him at Zurich, the pianist was startled by the splendor of the furnishings, the thick carpets, and heavy silk draperies—strange surroundings for a man with no visible income. The Wagner wine cellar was always full, with plenty of champagne. Whenever he brought out a new opera or book or poem, a small edition was expensively printed and bound for distribution among his friends. He loved gold watches, and he spent a small fortune on his clothes. He could not bear to have coarse fabrics next to his skin, hence his large wardrobe of silk underwear, velvet dressing gowns, coats, and caps.

There was a reason for this craving for luxury, beyond pure sybaritical desire. Partly it was Wagner's curious means of stimulating inspiration for his music. Composition, as he described it, was a kind of dream state, in which he was submerged in a twilight world removed from reality. Wrapped in a brocaded dressing gown, in a richly furnished room that was softly lighted and heavy with perfume, he was in a Nirvanic state in which the world's harshness could not touch him. "This was Wagner's way," writes Newman; "for other men it may be opium or wine, or tobacco." Thus for all the thousands of dollars that he squandered on luxuries he repaid the world a thousandfold with what he produced. It was either borrow or—literally and artistically—starve. If he had fewer moral scruples than Mozart and Schubert, the art of music is infinitely richer for the fact.

Wagner's relations with the women in his life are another rich vein for opprobrium. His treatment of Minna was often inexcusable. Her worst troubles with him began shortly after the flight from Dresden. He fell in love with an Englishwoman named Jessie Laussot, who was married to a Swiss. Wagner visited her at Bordeaux and tried to persuade her to elope with him to the Near East. A few years later began his famous infatuation for Mathilde Wesendonck, the wife of one of his wealthy benefactors. This affair tortured Minna to the point of insanity. The next major affair was with Cosima, who was the daughter of Liszt and the wife of Hans von Bülow, two of Wagner's dearest friends. Cosima left her husband, lived with Wagner, and bore him three children before they were finally married.

The root of Wagner's troubles with women was in all probability frustration. He was highly sexed; he craved the companionship of women; his desire for an Ideal

Woman who would feed his ego was one long romantic dream. Yet it remained a dream unfulfilled until after he was fifty years old and had seduced young Cosima away from her husband.

## VII

Wagner was one of the most penetrating thinkers in the history of art. He knew this—a fact that often made him insufferable as a man. He was as surely one of the greatest musicians and one of the most capable operatic dramatists. He also imagined himself a great writer and poet, but in this he was mistaken. His prose works are seldom read today. They contain some of the most important ideas on art hatched in the nineteenth century, but as literature they are heavy going.

"Wagner's essays are of astonishing intelligence," writes Thomas Mann, "but they are not to be compared, as literary and intellectual achievements, with Schiller's works on the philosophy of art—for instance that immortal essay on Naïve and Sentimental Poetry. They are hard to read, their style is both stiff and vague, again there is something about them that is overgrown, extraneous, dilettante. . . ."

The most important of Wagner's prose works are *Art and Revolution* (1849), *The Art Work of the Future* (1850), and *Opera and Drama* (1850–51). His most notorious piece was a tract called *Judaism in Music*, in which he tried to prove the Jews a subversive influence in music. This was partly inspired by his dislike of Mendelssohn's music and his hatred of Meyerbeer, who he imagined was thwarting the production of his operas.

The underlying theory of *Art and Revolution* and *The Art Work of the Future* is a need for an entirely new art which shall regenerate and free humanity. The Greeks, Wagner felt, had such an art in their drama, which was a synthesis of several arts—music, literature, painting, sculpture, the dance. Moreover, it was not a commercialized project; it was rather a religious festival, "the expression of the deepest and noblest consciousness of the people." Only a revolution in modern society could bring about this regenerating, unified art work which (according to him) was the salvation of the "free Greeks."

From these realms of pure theory (and more than a dash of fancy) the composer got down to something more concrete in his next piece, the lengthy tract, *Opera and Drama*. This was his first exposition of the new "music drama" idea that had long been agitating his mind. Wagner had felt for years that there was something fundamentally wrong with the aesthetics of opera. He got down to the nub of it in one sentence when he said that the error of opera lay in the fact that "a means of expression (music) has been made the object; and that the object of expression (drama) has been made the means." In other words, composers heretofore had thought of their dramatic story only as a convenient scaffolding upon which their music might be built. What he wanted to do was to make a powerful dramatic story, clothed in the splendor of poetry, the real object of his endeavor, with the music simply one of the handmaidens that would point up and intensify that drama. To accomplish this would require a radically new approach to the various elements of opera. A new type of poetry would have to be written, a special kind of drama, and an entirely different kind of music. All the old stylized forms and practices—the set numbers, the arias, the choruses, the old divisions into scenes, etc. —would have to be thrown out of the window; instead the music would have to flow along continually with the drama in order to give it the movement of reality.

Especially pregnant for the future were Wagner's ideas for the orchestra. He felt that it should not confine itself merely to helping along the particular words that were being sung; rather it should express in the broadest way the mood behind the words. In short, the orchestra was no longer merely to accompany; it was to be the main protagonist of the drama, expounding all phases of it with symphonic freedom and fullness.

Many of the ideas that Wagner expressed in these prose pieces sound stale today because they are long since an accomplished fact. Midway through the nineteenth century, however, they were still the dreams of a visionary. They required someone who would not only create the music dramas themselves but also school a new generation of singers and musicians to interpret them, educate the public to appreciate them, and even build a new kind of theater in which to produce them. It was to this gigantic task that Richard Wagner now applied himself.

While he was busy writing about his theories for the music dramas of the future, Wagner was also casting about for a fit musical subject on which to begin. For a long time he had been attracted to the idea of Siegfried, the hero of the *Nibelungenlied* in the Norse mythology. In 1848 he had made sketches for an opera based on Siegfried's death, but he laid it aside and wrote a long prose sketch on Jesus of Nazareth. After that he went back to *Siegfried's Death* and decided to expand it, leading up to it with another opera called *Young Siegfried*. Then he realized that he would have to go still farther back and use even more of the legend. He ended up with not one music drama but four—or, as he termed it, a trilogy with a prologue. *Das Rheingold* was the prologue, and the trilogy consisted of *Die Walküre*, *Siegfried*, and *Die Götterdämmerung*.

This vast project underwent many changes in the composer's mind before it crystallized into the final story. As he progressed backward with the main plot he made many changes in the details of the legend. There were various prose sketches of great length before he reached the final poetic libretto. This libretto was finished in 1852 and the composer published it—a small edition distributed among his friends. He was immensely disappointed with its reception. He could not understand that to everyone but himself his verse without music was simply an empty shell.

Undaunted, he held one of his readings. He called together a group of his friends in a hotel in Zurich and read them the entire poem on three successive evenings. As his interest in his own ideas gradually became an obsession with him, these readings became standard practice. Once he actually read the whole of *Opera and Drama* to a group of friends. Twelve evenings were required. It is a tribute to the man's personal magnetism that his audience, far from quailing before so fearful a dose of literary medicine, actually went away clamoring for more.

At this time a new and modern force was taking a hand in the shaping of Wagner's career. This was the force of publicity. *Lohengrin* had been produced in 1850 by Liszt at Weimar, and with historic success. Everywhere in Germany people were discussing both the successful operas —*Rienzi, Tannhäuser,* and *Lohengrin*—and Wagner's radical prose pieces. A serious misunderstanding arose. Many were bewildered when they could find no trace of the composer's theories in his operas already produced; it was not clear that they applied to works as yet unwritten. The war that then broke out over Wagner was by all odds the most violent in music history. Every conservative critic, every opera manager, musician, and singer with tory leanings went after him, all feeling that their comfortably accustomed order was threatened by a madman. On the other side he was defended by a few intelligent champions like Liszt, and by the general public itself. For Wagner's operas were their own best advocates. Wherever one was well produced, its popularity grew in leaps and bounds.

Meanwhile the composer himself struggled on at Zurich, desperately lonely in his mental isolation, standing before the most stupendous task any musician had ever attempted. By the middle of 1853 he had as yet made no beginning on the music of *The Ring.* Much of the time he was physically ill. He had tried all sorts of treatments in Switzerland, including a ghastly water cure and an even worse sulphur cure; but he could not seem to find the peace of mind that might induce the dream state essential to inspiration. And then one afternoon the sick, neurotic man dropped upon a couch, exhausted after a long walk. Instead of sleeping he fell into the curious state of catalepsy that is supposed to have accompanied his finest inspiration. It seemed, he said, as if he were engulfed in a torrent of water whose rush and roar sounded like "the chord of E flat major, surging incessantly in broken chords." The triad of E flat major never changed; it persisted until he awoke in terror with the feeling that the water had rushed high above his head. And then he recognized at once what his subconscious mind had finally delivered: the orchestral Prelude to *Das Rheingold*.

A short time later he set to work, translating his vision into the incredible opening of *The Ring*—one hundred and thirty-six measures on the tonic chord of E flat major that plunge the listener to the twilit gloom at the bottom of the river Rhine.

### VIII

At first he moved with swiftness. *Das Rheingold* was completed in about seven months, between November 1, 1853, and May 28, 1854. He worked so well that he imagined he could finish the entire project in three years. But with *Die Walküre* he began to hit snags. It required the better part of two years, and he did not get to *Siegfried* until 1856. There was a long interruption in the spring of 1855 when he went to London to conduct eight concerts for the Philharmonic Society. The fee was two hundred pounds, and he needed it badly, but it turned out to be the hardest money he ever earned. He loathed London. The critics excoriated his music and his conducting, so he decided they were all Jews in the pay of Meyerbeer. For some time he had been reading the philosophy of Schopenhauer; now he plunged into the *Divine Comedy* of Dante—exacerbating treatment for a lonely, homesick man. The root of his trouble was his enforced detachment from *The Ring* and, even worse than that, his separation from Mathilde Wesendonck.

The Wesendonck story is a long one. (Many of the associations of this volcanic man were long and involved, and whole volumes have been written about his relations with Mathilde, Minna, Cosima, Liszt, King Ludwig II, Nietzsche—to say nothing of Bülow, Meyerbeer, Berlioz, Jessie Laussot, and a score of others.) Mathilde Wesendonck and her husband Otto, a wealthy partner of a New York silk house, had met the composer during his early days at Zurich. The Wesendoncks were soon hypnotized by his personality. Before long, Wagner was a continual guest in their home, followed by the step inevitable: Wesendonck began giving him financial help of various kinds, including finally a house for him and Minna adjoining the lovely Wesendonck villa.

Mathilde was twenty-three when they met; the composer was thirty-eight. She had beauty, intelligence, and sensitivity; she yearned for an understanding of art and music, but her mind, she said, was "a blank white page." Upon this Wagner proceeded to write, in characters bordered with fire. He expounded Beethoven's music to her; he told her of his own theories and his visions; he read her all his prose works. Every evening he would play for her what he had composed in the morning. On the manuscript of *Die Walküre* are cryptic inscriptions testifying to the composer's infatuation. He composed five exquisite songs to poems by the young lady, which he called studies for *Tristan und Isolde.*

The precise limit to which this love affair proceeded remains a mystery. Wagner's was a transfiguring passion, but mingled with Mathilde's affection for him is more than a trace of feminine shrewdness. She knew that every hour spent with Richard Wagner was a step toward immortality, but she was not prepared to sacrifice her home, her children, and the protection of her wealthy husband. For several years she pursued a course between the two currents, with that wiliness by which some women can make diplomatists seem like amateurs at their own business.

By this time Wagner had progressed to the middle of the second act of *Siegfried*, and his huge task had begun to weigh him down. He despaired of ever completing *The Ring*, or of producing it once it was finished. Meanwhile, a new idea had begun to crowd into his mind—the legend of Tristan. At last, in midsummer, 1857, he made a decision that would have broken the spirits of smaller men. He stopped work altogether on *The Ring*. "I have led my young Siegfried into the lovely solitudes of the forest," he wrote to Liszt; "there I have left him under a linden tree, and, with tears from the depths of my heart, said farewell to him."

He hoped the interruption would be a short one, but

twelve years passed before he met his young hero again.

Instantly he flung himself to work upon *Tristan und Isolde*. A prose sketch and a poetic libretto were each written in a few weeks; by the end of the year he had completed the music of the first act. Inspiration was going at drop-forge temperatures, and he might have set a new record of accomplishment, but as usual his luck did not hold out. In the summer of 1858 the dream of bliss with Mathilde was suddenly shattered by Minna. By this time even the townspeople of Zurich were gossiping, so Minna created an old-fashioned bourgeois scene and denounced Mathilde to her face. There was nothing for Wagner to do but get out. He left both Mathilde and Minna and went alone to Venice. In that one moment the break was made for a removal of the influence of both women from his life. At Venice he finished the second act of *Tristan und Isolde*, and then he went to Lucerne where the entire work was completed in the summer of 1859.

*Tristan und Isolde* is one of those works, like the *Eroica* Symphony of Beethoven, which exist both as supreme art creations and as forces that influence, regenerate, and fortify all the music that comes after them. This product of Wagner's unfulfilled desire inundated the minds of countless composers of his time and the decades following him, and now after a century it haunts them still. Wagner himself never surpassed it. *Die Götterdämmerung* is grander, more powerful in the puissant sweep and the impact of its Olympian style; but *Tristan und Isolde* is an unmatched concentration of beauty, and for originality it is peerless.

The story of this music drama is one of love thwarted by circumstances of honor. The knight Tristan is sent by his uncle, King Mark, to Ireland to fetch the princess Isolde so that Mark may marry her. Act I begins with the voyage from Ireland to Cornwall, during which Isolde recognizes Tristan as the man who had killed Morold, her betrothed. To avenge that crime and to avoid a loveless marriage with Mark, Isolde resolves that she and Tristan must both die. He agrees to drink with her from a cup of poison; but Brangäne, Isolde's maid, has secretly mixed a love potion instead. They drink, and instantly the unspoken passion between the two bursts into flame. In the second act, Tristan and Isolde meet secretly in her garden, and during a long summer night they declare their ecstasies and their despairs. With the coming of the dawn, King Mark and his courtiers unexpectedly return. The old king's reproaches are poignant and unanswerable; Melot, one of his courtiers, wounds Tristan. The scene of the third act is Tristan's ancestral castle in Brittany, where the knight lies dying under a lime tree in the courtyard. Dreams and deliriums are mingled with his longing for Isolde. She comes to him at last, and he dies in her arms. Isolde then sings out her own heart over the body of her lover.

The libretto that Wagner devised from this story is unprecedented first of all for its lack of dramatic action. For long stretches of time no movement occurs, and there are seldom more than two persons on the stage. Most of the drama is played in the minds of the two chief characters. The conventional chorus is reduced to a mere handful of measures in the first act, sung by a group of sailors. There are no elaborate stage effects whatever. This is Wagner's ideal of a drama expounded by means of music, and it is the purest realization of that ideal which he ever attained.

As for the music, it is so far removed from the operatic idiom of its time and even from its own composer's style in *Tannhäuser* and *Lohengrin* that it seems like the product of a different mind working in a different century. It is an astounding metamorphosis. The orchestra has taken over the center of the stage. It no longer accompanies the singers; it pours forth a continual stream of sound that is symphonic in richness and completeness. The chief melodic line is nearly always in the orchestra instead of with the singers. They generally sing a kind of obbligato that is simply one more melodic thread woven into the web of orchestral sound. There is hardly a trace of recitative or of an aria. Instead of the old-fashioned type of melody with its balanced symmetry of phrases and periods, its regular stops and half stops, there is set up an "endless melody" that seems to follow only the dialogue. In *Tristan und Isolde* there are no real cadences until the end of each act, and the only completely satisfying one is at the end of the opera.

By taking the place of importance away from the singers and giving it to the orchestra Wagner gave himself an enormous dramatic advantage; for the orchestra, with its unlimited range of tonal color and dynamics, has an emotional power far greater than that of any voice or combination of voices. By developing the leitmotiv idea, the composer had at hand still another new and potent device. It has always been a puzzle to modern theorists that the leitmotiv scheme lay around so long practically unused until Wagner took it in hand. Various composers before him had employed a recurring theme to label a certain character, or object, or state of mind; but they had done it only in a halfhearted fashion. Wagner himself had used hardly more than a dozen in *Lohengrin*, and they appear only sporadically in the course of the opera. In every one of his works after that they become the chief organizing force of the entire score. *Tristan und Isolde* has some thirty predominating motives and at least a dozen more of a secondary nature. They dominate the score from beginning to end, and provide the life germs from which the entire melodic scheme grows.

Some of the earlier Wagnerian motives are long and cumbersome, but in the mature works these themes are often reduced to a few notes—concise, swift, arresting. In an instant they telegraph to the mind of the listener a mental picture that might require whole paragraphs of words. A few in *The Ring* are actually onomatopoetic; e.g., those associated with the flowing of the Rhine, the roar of the Dragon, the sound of the forge, and most famous of all, the gallop of the horses in the *Ride of the Valkyries*. Others are strongly descriptive—like Loge's flames in *Die Walküre*, and the plodding of the Giants in *Das Rheingold*. The great majority are pure musical abstractions which, by the composer's alchemy, become a vocabulary of sound images and symbols. Those in *Tristan und Isolde* are almost all of the abstract type, and for conciseness of utterance, subtlety, and emotional expressiveness Wagner never surpassed them. They are remarkable both in themselves and in the way the composer wove them into his musical pattern. They are strong as steel or plastic as clay in his hands; he can present them alone or in combination; he can change them harmonically, rhythmically, and even melodically, and they still retain in some mysterious way their power and identity.

The harmonic texture of *Tristan und Isolde* could be a separate technical study in itself. When Wagner finished *Lohengrin*, the horizon of music was still bounded by the old world of diatonic harmony; with his music dramas after *Lohengrin* he was a Columbus opening up a new world of chromatic harmony. It was a world that a few other composers, notably Chopin, had touched upon but never really explored. The harmonic gulf that separates *Das Rheingold* from *Lohengrin* is wide. It is astonishing that the composer was able to make such an advance in this branch of technique during a long spell when he was not actually composing. With *Die Walküre* he went still further, but in *Tristan und Isolde* he is the master of a harmonic style the like of which the music world had never seen.

Wagner's arrival at this new style coincides with his exploitation of a new type of free counterpoint. The texture of his mature music is notable in the way it becomes increasingly polyphonic; there is a constant movement of various lines of melody in the orchestra, often made necessary by the combining of several leitmotivs. Bolder polyphonic procedure depended upon and engendered greater harmonic freedom and vice versa: the two developments complemented each other and permitted almost unlimited expansion in both directions. As he progressed, Wagner used an entirely new apparatus of chromatic modulations, breaking down inhibitions that had bound composers for centuries. He used all sorts of devices to modify and enrich the common chords, to avoid cadences and expected resolutions; he used dissonance with a lavish hand. Most important of all, he *dramatized* his harmony—his chords, chordal combinations, modulations, keys even—until it became as potent in his general scheme as melody itself. The result is a veritable chemistry in music—magical transformations of harmonic color which go on in endless series, one more startlingly rich than the last.

So much for the technical bases of Wagner's great music drama. On the aesthetic side one may only reiterate what has been the verdict of nearly a century: that *Tristan und Isolde* is one of the sovereign creations for the lyric stage. Wagner created two characters who will live with Romeo and Juliet; he brought them to life in a world of tone which, for emotional range, eloquence, and passion-drenched intensity, makes even poetry seem pale by comparison. From the incomparable Prelude to the closing *Liebestod*, measure after measure, the composer maintains the unyielding pressure of great inspiration. The opening of the second act and the ensuing love duet form a Shakespearean balcony scene prolonged with every artifice of musical skill until it becomes almost unbearable. Even finer is the third act, the reverse of the shield on which are graven not the ecstasies but the mournfulness, the shrouding despairs of love. A death scene has always been a cheap way to buy emotion, in opera as in literature; but the death of Tristan, and all the long, wonderfully prepared scene that leads up to it is musical utterance of the highest order. It has also the elevation, the nobility, and the poignancy that mark all great tragic drama.

If there is a blemish in *Tristan und Isolde* it is at least a famous one—the dreary complaint of King Mark as he interrupts the love scene in Act II. Wagner erred here. He forgot that the wronged husband or lover, if he would win sympathy, has only the recourse of silence. Otherwise he is a fit subject for comedy, as Balzac demonstrated with finality in his gallery of antlered ones. King Mark's position is not changed by the fact that the love of Tristan and Isolde remained, in Wagner's version, unconsummated.

IX

During the five years that followed the completion of *Tristan und Isolde*, the life of Richard Wagner dragged along the river bottom of existence. If ever an artist was put through an ordeal by misfortune, it was he. He had on hand three completed operas and part of a fourth. All were masterpieces, but there was no hope of getting any of them performed. His love for Mathilde Wesendonck had ended in frustration; life with Minna became a nightmare. His wife was suffering from heart disease, and the opium that her physicians prescribed for relief began to affect her mind, already warped by jealousy. She and Wagner lived together sporadically until a final break in 1862, after which he never saw her again. The composer carried on several desultory romances, one with Liszt's daughter Blandine, a sister of Cosima.

In 1861 an attempt was made to produce *Tristan und Isolde* in Vienna, but the project was abandoned after fifty-seven rehearsals. The press of Germany had always presented a granite front against the composer; now rumors began to circulate that his new works were not only monstrous but also unsingable.

The cruelest defeat of all was the failure of *Tannhäuser* in Paris, in 1861. This was the most notorious fiasco in the history of opera, and a blotch on the cultural face of the Second Empire. The composer had gone to Paris in 1860 with the vain hope of getting *Tristan und Isolde* produced there. He had an admirer at court—Princess Metternich, the wife of the Austrian Ambassador—who in turn had access to the curiously hazy mind of Napoleon III. To please her the Emperor ordered a production of *Tannhäuser* at the Opéra.

Almost instantly a powerful cabal formed itself against the foreign composer and his work. The objections centered ostensibly around the lack of a ballet in *Tannhäuser*. It was an unwritten law of the Paris Opéra that every work performed there must have a ballet, either during or after the second act. Beset by the management, Wagner rewrote his overture and first act to include a bacchanal. But this would not do. The Jockey Club, a group of aristocratic young subscribers who came chiefly to see their mistresses in the ballet, habitually dined late and did not arrive in time for the first act. They protested, but Wagner would not give in. For months the wrangling went on. The management spent some forty thousand dollars on a production that was in every way magnificent; there were one hundred and sixty-four rehearsals, fourteen with full orchestra. The whole venture was under Wagner's supervision and might have been a triumph. Instead the *première*, on March 13, 1861, almost ended in a riot. The Jockey Club deliberately sabotaged the performance. Their hisses, laughter, and whistling, mingled with the shouts of protest from those in the audience who wanted to hear the opera, created an uproar that drowned out the music. The same indecent demonstration of hate and stupidity took place at the second and third performances, after which Wagner withdrew the work.

For his labor and his heartbreak the composer received about three hundred dollars, the royalty on three performances. To the world he gave a new masterpiece. In his "Paris version" of the Overture and Bacchanal he had grafted onto his early work a piece of his mature inspiration of *Tristan und Isolde*. This Bacchanal is a red-hot coal of passion, an orgy of tonal sensualism that has no peer in music.

In 1862, in the midst of his worst miseries, the composer began work on *Die Meistersinger von Nürnberg* [*The Mastersingers of Nuremberg*], based on an idea that had been in his mind since 1845. For several years his work dragged on, with the composer too sick and distracted to give it full attention. Amnesty was finally granted him to return to Germany after twelve years of exile. He made a trip to Russia to conduct some concerts, and promptly squandered the money he made. A rich widow promised to give him an income and pay off his debts, so he celebrated Christmas by loading his friends with expensive gifts. Later the widow withdrew her kind offer, which left the composer looking straight into a debtor's prison. When his friends tried to commiserate with him he cried, "What's the good of talking about the future, when my scores are lying locked in the cupboard? . . . I'm not made like other people. I have finer nerves—I must have beauty and brilliance and light. The world owes me what I need."

By the spring of 1864, Wagner was at the end of his

rope. He was financially ruined and spiritually defeated. And then occurred the most incredible event of all in the life of this incredible man. One morning at a hotel in Stuttgart where he chanced to be staying, he received a visitor whose card bore the title: Private Secretary to the King of Bavaria. Wagner listened to a message that seemed like words spoken in a dream. Ludwig II, the nineteen-year-old King who had just ascended the throne of Bavaria, had been searching for him. The King was mad about Wagner's music. The composer must come to Munich; his debts would be paid, his music dramas would be produced; everything that he needed for happiness and security would be given him.

It was all true. Wagner rushed to the palace at Munich, and his meeting with the King was a moment of over-powering emotions. In the complex saga of the composer's life there is no episode stranger than this. Wagner found to his amazement that he was the young man's idol, that Ludwig was steeped in his music and his prose writings. Within a few weeks and in the course of innumerable meetings they mapped out a course of action: *Tristan und Isolde* was to be produced in Munich, and then *Die Meistersinger*; after that the Paris version of *Tannhäuser*, the completed *Ring*, and finally *Parsifal*. All this would require, they thought, not more than seven years. There were also to be an impressive national music school and a theater specially built to mount Wagner's vast creations.

That was the dream. Even though it was never realized by the two men together, the fact remains that Ludwig rescued Wagner and saved for the world three surpassing music dramas that might never have been written. He tried to perform an act of wisdom and generosity that would have occurred to few rulers in modern history; but he paid a heavy price for his idealistic effort. In his own character, as well as in Wagner's, were the flaws that ruined the plan before its realization had even begun.

Ludwig was a handsome young man with a certain intellectual keenness. Had this been joined with stability, it might have fitted him ideally for kingship. Instead he was emotionally unbalanced, abnormally sensitive and introspective. As he grew to manhood his frustrations made him morose and solitary. He had homosexual tendencies against which he struggled constantly. He looked upon Wagner and Wagner's music as his moral and spiritual salvation. As for the composer, he simply lacked the one ingredient necessary for a person in his unbelievably fortunate position—caution. Had he played his cards differently he might have appeased the statesmen and politicians who were watching the young King with anxious eyes, but that was not Wagner's nature.

The first fruit of the association was the *première* of *Tristan und Isolde*. The production, magnificently prepared by Wagner himself and conducted by Bülow, took place on June 10, 1865. It was a consummation of desires so long unfulfilled that the composer was beside himself with joy. He had not long to exult. By this time the political leaders of Bavaria were aghast at his influence over Ludwig. They began to make capital of the composer's extravagances and the drain he was causing on the state finances. Wagner had begun paying off his debts and had set himself up in a splendid house. He persuaded Ludwig to make Bülow court pianist, which meant that Cosima was able to come to Munich and take charge of Wagner's household. Soon gossip began to circulate about the composer and his friend's young wife. Within a year after the rescue, Wagner and his doings had become a national scandal, and it was freely rumored that the King was insane. Ludwig finally broke under political pressure, and late in 1865 he wrote Wagner a pathetic letter telling him that he would have to get out of Munich.

The composer went again to Switzerland. Although he did not know it, out of the wreckage of Munich his whole life would slowly resolve into a period of comparative security during which all the unfinished projects of many years would slowly converge into reality. He established himself in a lovely villa called Triebschen, on Lake Lucerne. There he spent the next few years on the composition of *Die Meistersinger*, attended by Cosima and helped financially by the King. It was one of the few happy times of his whole life.

*Die Meistersinger* was completed early in 1868, and it was first performed in June of that year, in Munich. Wagner returned to the city for the rehearsals, and at the *première* he sat with Ludwig in the royal box. Even though the performance was a great success, the press heaped abuse on both the work and the composer.

*Die Meistersinger* comes closest to *Tristan und Isolde* as the most nearly perfect work that Wagner ever wrote. As dramas the two are polar extremes in the art of their creator. *Tristan und Isolde* is supremely tragic, a "child of sorrow," Wagner called it; *Die Meistersinger* is a comedy—the best operatic comedy after Mozart.

The story is set in the old town of Nuremberg in the early sixteenth century. The hero is a young minstrel-knight, Walther von Stolzing. He tries to enter the song contest of the mastersingers of the town, because Pogner, a wealthy goldsmith, has offered the hand of his daughter Eva to the winner of the contest on St. John's Day; and Walther loves Eva. He rebels against the dogmatic rules of composition which the mastersingers have set for their contest. He is opposed by Beckmesser, the town clerk, a viciously stupid pedant; but he gets sympathy and help from Hans Sachs, the shoemaker, a man of kindness and common sense. At the contest Walther triumphs over Beckmesser and the narrow-mindedness of the mastersingers themselves when he delivers his splendidly rhapsodic *Prize Song*.

The allegory of *Die Meistersinger* is fairly obvious. Walther is Wagner himself, struggling against the critics, the pedants, and the conservatives of his day. Beckmesser was generally regarded as a caricature of Eduard Hanslick, the Viennese critic who was the composer's deadly enemy. So that this point might not be missed by anyone including the subject himself, Wagner once read the libretto of his opera to a group that included Hanslick.

By and large, *Die Meistersinger* is Wagner's best work as a dramatist. It is magnificently broad and sunlit, motivated by human affections and weaknesses and absurdities that have never failed to touch and delight the heart. As for the music, one must wonder at the magic by which the entire complex apparatus of the composer's art is suddenly switched around to serve a type of drama that was entirely new to him. The mood of *Die Meistersinger* is different from that of all his other operas, yet he works in it with the assurance of a master with years of the technique of comedy behind him.

The most noticeable technical difference between this work and its predecessor is the composer's return to diatonic harmony—in mood at least. Even though *Die Meistersinger* is the richest and most opulent diatonic fabric created up to that time, it nevertheless preserves in its chord and key relationships, a feeling of straightforwardness which is essential to the characters and their story. The "strange foreign" chords of *Tristan und Isolde*, the bitter dissonances, the exotic chromaticism would have been utterly out of place in this tale of a sweet old sixteenth-century town and its simple people. For sheer lyric beauty *Die Meistersinger* is Wagner's masterpiece. Its melodies are fulsome, distinguished; they are spread prodigally through the great score, singly and with all the wizardry of counterpoint until there seems to be no end to the composer's powers of lyric invention.

In the matter of character delineation *Die Meistersinger* again is Wagner at his summit. Here the portraits are lifelike even down to the members of the chorus: Walther and his manly impetuousness, the sweetly virginal Eva, carefree David, Beckmesser, the prototype of pedantic meanness and deceit, the pompous mastersingers themselves, and above all the wonderfully moving humanity of Hans Sachs. Whatever time may do to Wagner's art, whatever changes in the fashions of music may rob his work of its potency, this much will always be said: that he had the power to create in tone the images and the hearts of living people. He could bring them into existence and with piercing intensity paint the world around them until they began to own a part of reality. In *Die Meistersinger* even his enemies must give him his due, as he brings to life a piece of the vanished past, in that ancient sleepy town under the flooding moonlight.

X

After *Die Meistersinger* an inner harmony took possession of the composer's personal life. Cosima had left Bülow—left him a wreckage of nerves and ruined pride; from then on nothing that the world said could separate her from Wagner. She bore him three children, and in 1870 they were finally married. The composer left a record of his domestic happiness in the *Siegfried Idyll*. This and his early *Faust* Overture are his only important works for orchestra alone. It was composed secretly for Cosima, and on the morning of her birthday she was awakened by her husband and a group of musicians playing it in the hall and upon the stairs of Triebschen. It is an exquisite symphonic fragment, in part woven from themes that the composer also used in *Siegfried*.

With domestic bliss came the deep satisfaction of public recognition. In spite of the defeat at Munich, the world of art now sought out the composer at his retreat to pay him homage. Wagner never discouraged disciples, and among them there came a young professor of classical philology, Friedrich Nietzsche, whose adoration of the composer was fanatical. The Wagner-Nietzsche association burned brilliantly for a few years and then exploded, leaving one more mystery for the biographers to solve. Nietzsche had gotten too close to his idol, a dangerous proceeding for a fierce idealist who was also young.

At Triebschen the composer returned after twelve years to the uncompleted edifice of *The Ring of the Nibelung*. An immense labor still confronted him, but by 1871 he had finished *Siegfried* and started *Die Götterdämmerung*. The next five years were given over not only to the completion of that work, but also to the building of the theater where the trilogy in its entirety would be performed. To raise money for the project, Wagner Societies were formed all over Europe and in America; the composer raised part of it by giving concerts. He chose the site of the theater himself (on a hill outside the little town of Bayreuth in Upper Franconia); he supervised every detail of its construction, and he selected and helped train the singers and instrumentalists.

Several times the entire project seemed about to fail for lack of money. Once it was saved by King Ludwig, who had remained aloof, but finally came through with a gift of seventy-five thousand dollars. At the eleventh hour a vitally needed five thousand dollars came from the Exposition in Philadelphia which was celebrating the centenary of the Declaration of Independence. Wagner was commissioned to write a march, so he dashed off a potboiler called the *American Centennial March*.

On August 13, 1876, the doors of the new Festspielhaus at Bayreuth opened at last, and a cycle of the complete *Ring of the Nibelung* was begun. On that evening *Das Rheingold* was performed, followed on successive evenings by *Die Walküre, Siegfried*, and *Die Götterdämmerung*. The royalty of Europe, both of politics and art, assembled in the audience, and from the far corners of the world men watched the triumph of Richard Wagner.

It would be hard to magnify the immensity of his achievement. Twenty-seven years had separated the first nebulous imaginings and this final overwhelming realization; a quarter of a century of suffering and frustration, of defeats that had roweled through his heart and soul. If ever the world had an object lesson in the majesty of human perseverance, it had it those evenings in midsummer when Wagner first saw his trilogy unfold.

*The Ring of the Nibelung* stands alone in music. It is by far the largest single structure any composer has ever attempted. It is actually a threefold achievement—music, drama, and philosophical and moral allegory all rolled into one. An outline of the stories of these four music dramas would be too long to give here. Guide books that run to a hundred pages or more are not always complete. Suffice to say that the Ring itself is a symbol of the evil that ill-used power lets loose upon the world. In the first scene of *Das Rheingold*, the foul gnome Alberich steals a golden treasure from the Rhinemaidens and forges it into a ring that will bring to whoever holds it power over the whole world —provided he first renounces love forever. The Ring is taken from Alberich by the god Wotan, who craves world rulership; but the gnome in a fury of despair sets a curse upon the Ring and all who hold it. The working out of this curse is related in the four dramas, and it moves with the relentlessness of fate. The Ring brings ruin and death to all who possess it; it destroys the race of the gods; it causes the death of the hero Siegfried. In the closing drama, Brünnhilde, wife of Siegfried, at last frees the world from the curse of the Ring. As a final act of atonement before she seeks death on the funeral pyre of her beloved, she flings the Ring back into the Rhine.

The welding of this endlessly ramifying legend into four workable dramas was first of all a task of organization. That was precisely Wagner's gift. He could never follow the common practice of all other composers—taking some-one else's plot and working it into an opera. He had to execute the entire project himself. In *The Ring of the Nibelung* he spent years assimilating and organizing his material before he even started on the music. He had to arrange the vast story so that it would fall into four sepa-rate sections; each section must be an effective dramatic unit in itself, and each must fit into the arch of the entire tetralogy. He had more than thirty main characters to bring to life. He evolved almost one hundred leitmotivs that had to be woven through the four scores like threads through an enormous tapestry. How he kept the myriad details of this task in clear precise order in his brain, through a span of twenty-seven years; how he retained the grand line of his epic always in front of him as he toiled through endlessly detailed miniatures; how, as he wrote the billowing opening triads of *Das Rheingold* Prelude, he must have heard the last resolving chords of *Die Götterdämmerung*—these are the mysteries and the won-ders of his genius which would have to be admitted even if *The Ring of the Nibelung* were a failure as a work of art instead of a triumph.

The weaknesses of the tetralogy as a whole are obvious— and in a sense inevitable. Even though the four music dramas have an amazing homogeneity of style and color, they are distinctly unequal in workmanship and inspiration. They progress from a somewhat loose and even crude texture in *Das Rheingold* to the absolute mastery of style, inspiration, and technique in *Die Götterdämmerung*.

*Das Rheingold* is a far step beyond *Lohengrin*, but it is still a mixture of the early Wagner and the late. Disturbingly commonplace melodic ideas are mingled with some of the first examples of the composer's greater leitmotivs; a new boldness of harmonic invention appears, but there is still a reliance on old diatonic clichés, including the most overworked chord in every old opera composer's book —the diminished seventh. *Die Walküre* is a finer work. The composer is working with a more assured hand, especially noticeable in the mastery of his vocal writing and the balance maintained between singers and orchestra. The pace is deliberate and there is a prevailing gloominess of mood; nevertheless the piece remains the most popular of the four music dramas. This is largely owing to the third act, which contains a sequence of the composer's most brilliant murals—the *Ride of the Valkyries*, *Wotan's Farewell to Brünnhilde*, and the *Magic Fire* scene.

*Siegfried* has been called the scherzo of the tetralogy, for its mood is prevailingly cheerful. The exquisite peace of the forest pervades many of its pages. Here at last the great Wagner begins to emerge, the Wagner of *Tristan und Isolde* and *Die Meistersinger*. *Die Götterdämmerung* is a tremendous score—long, concentrated, with a projectilelike force that neither Wagner nor any other operatic composer ever matched. All the scenes, the characters, the emotions, and the musical apparatus of the entire tetralogy are here brought to their long-drawn-out climax. It must be accounted a stroke of rare fortune that Wagner was able to take on the work of composing *Die Götterdämmerung* at the moment of his ripest maturity. Had it been either too soon in his career or too late, the result might have been an anticlimax fatal to the whole project. Wagner was a master of last acts, a skill every dramatist must envy, for the final act is the hardest part of a drama to create. *Die Götterdämmerung* is his supreme last act, besides being the only one of the tetralogy in which his inspiration was wholly equal to the magnitude of his main idea.

Inequality then is a major blemish in *The Ring of the Nibelung* and there are others. All these pieces except *Das Rheingold* are overlong. The composer became involved in lengthy recapitulations of his plot, which he felt necessary to his story, but which even his musical skill could not float. They hang like dead weights upon a vessel. The work as a whole is overfreighted with story details, to say nothing of the composer's philosophical notions. The plot itself is full of inconsistencies; in places it is almost unintelligible.

Lastly, *The Ring of the Nibelung* is too big for the theater. No opera house has ever approximated the scenic grandeur inherent in the story and the music, and it cannot honestly be said that the ludicrous parodies that often result are the fault of stage directors and designers. All four music dramas are full of scenes and dramatic action that are simply beyond realization within the four walls of the conventional theater, e.g., the dim abysmal depths of a great river, the entrance of a group of gods into a majestic Valhalla, a hilltop aflame with magic fire, the wild ride of a company of Valkyries through storm-lashed mountains, the cataclysmic overflow of the Rhine and the fall of Valhalla—to say nothing of such impossible ideas as a pair of giants, the magic transformations of a *Tarnhelm*, the ride of the hero's wife upon a horse into a funeral pyre. Too often the wonder of what the music paints is daubed out by the ineptitude of what the eye beholds. Too often the illusion created by Wagner's magnificently wrought characters, the glowing nimbus of reality which the music gives them, is effaced in an instant by the surrounding cardboard of the theater.

The truth must be that Wagner's vision of *The Ring of the Nibelung* has never been realized. In all likelihood it never will be, unless some genius of a new art form based on the sound film will be able to recreate the work and bring its vast collation of elements into true focus.

## XI

In *The Ring of the Nibelung* Wagner's skill in writing for the orchestra reached its apex. He derived his orchestral style from two main sources—Beethoven and Berlioz. From Beethoven he learned symphonic treatment of dramatic ideas, intensity, a vitalizing style of attack; from Berlioz he had his first model for modern instrumental color. Out of these two he welded the orchestral style that is uniquely his own—a blend of heroic strength and warm, sensual richness.

The progress of the Wagnerian orchestration is a fascinating study for specialists. It began in his early works with the orchestra that most opera composers of the day were using—a fair body of strings with woodwinds and brass in pairs. With his ensuing music dramas there is a steady augmentation of forces until in *The Ring of the Nibelung* he is using both woodwinds and brass in groups of four, with several new instruments added—the English horn, bass clarinet, double bassoon, and bass trumpet. This permitted harmonic completeness through all the choirs of the orchestra. For *The Ring of the Nibelung* he also added a group of four special tubas, while the percussion and even the harps are augmented in proportion. To counterbalance this weighty aggregation he demanded a string choir of more than sixty players, and these he often subdivided.

The result was the most powerful body of orchestral force yet assembled in an opera house, but it was not used for force alone. It was used chiefly for variety—for an unending succession of beautiful tonal and dramatic effects. Wagner thought of the orchestra both as a large single unit and as an infinite number of small contrasting groups. His handling of the woodwinds especially was revolutionary, and the finest after Mozart. He established the modern usage of that choir as an unsupported unit, and he used solo flute, clarinet, and bassoon with the delicacy of a miniaturist.

It is astonishing how much of the man himself and his

essential character appears even in this technical side of his art. The sybarite who craved soft lights, exquisite sounds, caressing textures, all the sensuous pleasures of life looks out at us continually from this opulent orchestration—from its silky fineness, its lush, velvet smoothness, from the golden patina that covers all trace of harshness even in the extreme sonorities.

Hardly less remarkable than the richness of this orchestration is its clarity. In his time Wagner's scores were the most complex instrumental fabric yet woven; nevertheless they were the most transparent. A glance at his pages shows the formidable number of notes often sounded at one time, seeming to suggest an inevitable turgidity. Instead, by his knowledge of the instruments, their possibilities and combinations (a knowledge that he seemed to have intuitively), he gave his music the limpidity of crystal. Even in moments of polyphonic complexity the strands of melody move among one another with perfect smoothness and freedom.

With Wagner begins a new orchestral epoch for both opera and the symphony. It was not alone that he expanded the orchestra in size and resource beyond the standard set by Beethoven. He made it the virtuoso playing body that we know today. He made immense demands upon the players, requiring that all of them play with the skill formerly expected only of soloists. There are passages in his works that remain today among the most difficult in music. But his demands are never those of ignorance or ineptitude. They spring from the most penetrating knowledge of orchestral technique that this art has yet witnessed.

## XII

The first Bayreuth performances of *The Ring* turned out, as might be expected, a financial failure. There was a deficit of about thirty-five thousand dollars, and for six years it was impossible to open the theater for any further performances. Wagner had built himself (with Ludwig's help) a handsome house, called Wahnfried, not far from the theater. There he spent the remaining years of his life. He was an old man now, worn down by almost fifty years of constant struggle, troubled by a variety of diseases —erysipelas, dyspepsia, insomnia, and an ominous ailment of the heart. But his creative instincts still burned, leaving no respite for the tired mind and the weary body.

There remained the unfinished idea of *Parsifal*. Like all his other works, it had lain in his consciousness for years. On Good Friday, 1858, he had been deeply moved by the divine benison that seemed to rest upon the fields and the countryside near Zurich, and he had written the words to a scene that later became the *Good Friday Spell* in *Parsifal*. Even before that there are traces of the Parsifal idea in the abandoned *Jesus of Nazareth* of 1848. With *The Ring of the Nibelung* out of the way he set to work, and for five years he toiled slowly through this last great epic of his life. It was finished in the spring of 1882, and the following July the Bayreuth theater was reopened for its *première*.

It was inevitable that Wagner should write *Parsifal*. All of his dramas without exception are based on love, the impulse that ruled his life and his thought. In his last work he turned, like so many sensualists grown aged, to religion—to the triumph of renunciation over desire. In so doing he produced his most controversial work. *Parsifal* has been called sacrilegious and sanctified, blasphemous and reverential, dull and divinely inspired.

The story is derived from various legends of the Holy Grail. According to Wagner's version, a miraculous Grail and a sacred spear are contained in a castle, Monsalvat, in the mountains of Gothic Spain. They are guarded by a company of knights. But the king, Amfortas, has lost the spear. He had sinned, and now suffers from a hideous wound in the side which will not heal. He was tempted by Kundry, a weird creature who is the slave of the magician Klingsor. Amfortas' only hope comes from the words of a prophecy: that a guileless fool shall one day deliver him, a simpleton moved by pity and untouched by temptation. In the first act Gurnemanz, one of the older knights, encounters Parsifal, a strange, headstrong youth who is ignorant of his past life. Gurnemanz brings him to the castle, where he witnesses the solemn eucharistic ceremony of the knights. At the end he remains stolidly unmoved. In the second act, Parsifal is beset by temptations plotted by Klingsor. There is a magic garden with a group of lovely flower maidens and Kundry herself in the role of enchantress. When her attempted seduction fails, Klingsor hurls the sacred spear at Parsifal, who seizes it and makes the sign of the Cross. In an instant the garden and flower maidens are destroyed. After years of wandering, Parsifal once again finds Monsalvat. He comes on Good Friday morning as a knight clad in black armor. At the solemn ceremony, Parsifal heals the wound of Amfortas by touching it with the sacred spear. Parsifal is hailed as king.

Wagner looked upon *Parsifal* as a sacred work that would be profaned if it were ever performed in an ordinary theater. He decreed that it should be performed only at Bayreuth. At first a halo of inviolability remained around the work, but soon even the faithful began to be troubled by doubts. Moved as they were by much of it, especially the Grail scenes in which certain rituals of the Catholic Church were borrowed and subtly dramatized, they were nevertheless disturbed by the Magdalen-like figure of Kundry and the allegory of the scene in the third act where she washes the feet of Parsifal. Moreover, the juxtaposition of these Christlike conceptions and the seduction scene in Act II was often downright shocking. Certain of Wagner's old enemies finally came out and denounced him as a showman who had been notoriously anti-religious all his life and was now making capital of the mysteries of a great faith. Nietzsche was utterly revolted and maddened. In 1888 he published *Der Fall Wagner* [*The Wagner Case*] in which he excoriated as a hypocrite and a degenerating force in music the man whom he had once deified as its savior. Others declared that the music of *Parsifal* gave evidence only of the composer's senility.

One of the most penetrating estimates of *Parsifal* is that of Huneker. It was written early in the present century, when the general public was still puzzled and undecided about the work. Huneker damns the story of *Parsifal* from beginning to end. "Never has Wagner so laboriously built a book. It is a farrago of odds and ends, the very dustbin of his philosophies, beliefs vegetarian, anti-vivisection, and other fads. You see unfold before you a nightmare of characters and events" . . . while through it "has been sieved Judaism, Buddhism, Christianity, Schopenhauerism. . . . The plain fact in the case is this: *Parsifal*, despite all its wealth of legend, its misty, poetic allusiveness, its manufactured mysticisms, is simple old-fashioned opera." Huneker goes on to reduce all the oddly assorted details of the story to the lowest terms of a vaudeville show. But when he asks why the work still continues to impress and inspire multitudes of people he gives a candid answer: "The Music, always The Music."

And that in essence is the truth about *Parsifal*. Regardless of the sense or nonsense of the drama, regardless of whether the listener is impressed or repelled by this composer-cynic turned apostle, the music itself remains a font of beauty.

It is an uneven score. After a superb Prelude, the first act staggers under a load of narration that benumbs the listener. The flower maidens of act two are musically anemic. Clearly this is an old man trying to remember the fires of his youth, and one may only guess what the Wagner of *Tristan und Isolde* or the Paris *Tannhäuser* would have made of these seductive creatures. The work is too long and the pace often too slow; moreover, the music suffers from the fact that many of the characters it must bring to life are lacking in human interest.

Against these failings must be set music that belongs with the finest things in *Tristan und Isolde* and *Die Götterdämmerung*. In the two scenes in the Hall of the Grail, pageantry and church ceremonial are blended with choral and orchestral effects to create the grandeur of a cathedral. Even if Wagner was at heart the eternal showman, he justified himself with these masterpieces of musical scene painting. But there is more. The entire third act is a summation of his greatness as a composer. The richness of it all, the measure after measure of poignantly expressive melody that recalled to Huneker "embroidered altar cloths or Gobelin tapestry," and above all the incredible harmonies that seem to pierce to the very heart of human suffering, pity, renunciation—these are not to be found elsewhere in music. Here the very slowness of the pace and the lack of action become a virtue. For this music has a dying fall, as if the composer's life and art together were coming to their final resolution.

XIII

Wagner was spared the controversies that arose over *Parsifal*. A few weeks after the *première* performances, the tired old man fled with his family from the harsh German winter. They went to Italy, to Venice, where he established himself (sybarite to the last) in one of the finest palaces on the Grand Canal; there amid the splendor of silks and damasks and vistas of Renaissance marble he rested with Cosima and the children, talked for hours with old Liszt, who came for a long visit, and even dreamed of writing a symphony; and there, on February 13, 1883, he died. A moment came when the heart that had borne so much could no longer keep up with the spirit. He called suddenly that afternoon for a doctor and for Cosima. She tried to get him to a couch and to remove his jacket; his beautiful timepiece slipped to the floor. "My watch," he murmured—and spoke no more.

A few days later he was buried in the garden of Wahnfried, to the thunders of Siegfried's Funeral Music.

Within a few years the tragedy of King Ludwig's life had also played itself out. Deposed and declared insane, he drowned himself in a lake. Nietzsche, who had also loved the composer with a blind adoration, died in a madhouse. But Cosima, who loved him most of all, outlived him almost fifty years. She died in 1930 at the age of ninety-three; and in the course of those long years she had become a veritable dragon guarding what she thought was the Wagnerian treasure—maintaining the Bayreuth theater and presiding over the festivals, preserving the composer's ideas about his works, stoutly resisting change, fiercely suppressing criticism of her hero, always hopeful that she was perpetuating about him a legend as golden as his music.

It was a vain and useless hope. There are no longer any legends about him as a man; his works need none. Wagner's was a mighty intellect, and around it he had wrapped many robes and garments. One by one they have been stripped from him, as so many unnecessary trappings of an enormous egotism. No one classes him today as a philosopher. Thousands who enjoy his works never bother to explore the murky caves of philosophical and ethical allegory upon which he so painfully built them. He never was a poet, even though that was his fondest illusion. He did not really establish a new art form; even the four parts of *The Ring of the Nibelung* have each become simply operatic repertoire pieces. He did not even achieve his ideal of a true music drama. He improved the dramas, it is true, and he subordinated the singing, but he produced an orchestral symphony that dominated everything else.

Many of his theories then are gone, and his philosophizing, and his queer poetry, and his dubious ethics. What remains is infinitely the greater part—"The Music, always The Music." It is a mysterious fact (pointed out by Newman) that in all the flood of words that he wrote and spoke, almost none concerns the purely musical side of his art, and his mastery of its mechanics. Stupendous as that mastery was, he seemed to take it wholly for granted. And yet—another mystery—when his music and his theories came into collision, it was the music that triumphed every time. He never denied it the slightest advantage.

Even as a musician he seems to have labored under a misconception. He considered himself solely a music dramatist; he was in fact also a symphonist. His ancestor was Beethoven. The most enduring parts of his finest works are all orchestral. Besides the various preludes there are whole sections of *Tristan und Isolde, Die Meistersinger, Die Götterdämmerung,* and *Parsifal* in which the orchestral part is complete and the voices would hardly be missed. As a symphonist Wagner could not find inspiration in the old classic procedures, the development of a few themes, and the symmetrical balancing of one against the other. He needed the freedom of many themes. Nor could he draw them out of thin air. They entered his consciousness by way of some dramatic story, some pictorial idea, some moving emotion of the human heart.

The controversy over Wagner's music still goes on. Against the millions who worship his art there is a lesser but more articulate number whom it repels. They recoil from his sensuality and his Dionysian excess; they loathe him as a man; they deplore him as a crushing weight upon all music that came after him. No one can finally evaluate him. Only now are we beginning to understand that he, singlehanded, set the river of music to running in a new channel. He broke down the barriers of form; he freed melody and gave it a breadth and scope it had never had before; he wrought changes in the field of harmony that were the most profound in hundreds of years.

Naturally such a man would weigh upon the future. He hypnotized a whole generation of composers immediately following him, and even today others find it hard to escape the idiosyncrasies of his style. That is not Wagner's fault. The race of composers who followed him are with few exceptions his inferiors. This is especially true of the Germans. From where we stand today we may see that Wagner and Brahms stood at the end of the royal line that began with Bach, and that from the peak of the *Tristan* Prelude the slope of German music has been steadily downward.

# *Verdi*

## *1813—1901*

### I

It is easy enough to explain the continued popularity of
Verdi's operas the world over, but an honest evaluation
of his music offers difficulties presented by the work of no
other composer. In his own country his melodies are
known the way the words of Shakespeare are known and
revered throughout the English-speaking world. His art is
regarded—and rightly so—as the climax of the last three
centuries of Italian musical development, the brightest
sun in the entire galaxy of Italian opera. On the other
hand, many musicians in other countries, especially those
where the domination of German music has been strongest, have derided his work as stuff fit only for the masses;
they have called him a composer of "barrel-organ tunes,"
not to be mentioned in the same breath with the serious
composers of Germany, Russia, or France. Those who
damn Verdi often know very little of his art—his mastery
of vocal writing, his fund of melody, his knowledge of
stagecraft and dramatic effect, the steady progress of his
craftsmanship, and the growth of his artistic stature over
a period of half a century.

The year 1813 saw the birth of both men whose destiny
it was to dominate opera in their age—Wagner in Germany
and Verdi in Italy. The Italian was born in Le Roncole,
a village in the duchy of Parma. His father kept a small

inn and a grocery store. In the near-by town of Busseto was a wealthy wine and grocery dealer named Barezzi, from whom Giuseppe Verdi's father bought his goods. This kindly man took the boy Verdi into his home, treated him as a son, and gave him the beginnings of an education in music. When he was eighteen years old, Verdi went to Milan, and tried to enter the conservatory, but was turned down. He found excellent private teaching, however, and within a few years had a fine grounding in composition. In 1836 he married Margherita Barezzi, the seventeen-year-old daughter of his benefactor. Three years later his first opera, Oberto, was produced at La Scala, in Milan; but with that good fortune came also a crushing tragedy. Within a space of two years (according to some accounts it was only two months) he lost his beloved wife and both their small children. The shock of the three deaths in so short a time affected him for years afterward, leaving him embittered and at times deeply depressed.

Oberto was followed by a comic opera, Un Giorno di Regno, which failed. Verdi was in the depths of despondency, but his next work, Nabucco, was an extraordinary success. In the next seven years the composer turned out no less than twelve operas, including I Lombardi, Ernani, and Luisa Miller. Few of them are revived today, being crude and uneven compared with Verdi's later work, but they established him as the leading operatic composer of Italy. In 1851 he produced Rigoletto, followed in two years by Il Trovatore and La Traviata—three of his most famous scores, works that made him an international figure. Thereafter Verdi's production continued at a slower pace, with a gradual ripening of his powers. The next two decades brought forth I Vespri Siciliani (1855), Simon Boccanegra (1857), The Masked Ball (1859), La Forza del Destino (1862), Don Carlos (1867), and finally Aïda. The last opera was first produced at Cairo in 1871, and was commissioned by the Khedive of Egypt to celebrate the opening of the Suez Canal. It represented a climax in Verdi's career and was easily the most brilliant "grand" opera that had yet come out of Italy.

Verdi was an old man when Aïda was finished, and he

might easily have rested on his laurels. He had only one rival—Wagner—with whom he might contend for supremacy in the operatic world. In 1874 he composed his impressive Requiem, in commemoration of Alessandro Manzoni, the Italian poet; thereafter it seemed that he might end his days in the quiet of his villa near Busseto, where for years he had amused himself with farming and gardening. But in 1887, when the remarkable old man was seventy-four, he produced *Otello*; and six years later, in his eightieth year, *Falstaff*. These Shakespearean ventures, one a tragedy, the other a comedy, represent an astonishing accomplishment. At a time in his life when retrogression should have seemed almost certain, Verdi had produced his two masterpieces.

When he died in 1901 at the age of eighty-eight he had rounded out a career replete with romantic contrasts. He had come from the soil to achieve world renown in the arts; he had lived a life that began with the most anguished human sorrows and ended with the most enviable triumphs.

It used to be the practice of many musicians to deprecate Verdi's work by comparisons with Wagner's, when as a matter of fact these two men of polar personalities developed artistically in much the same way. Both began their careers by working with the materials of opera as they found them in their native countries; both improved and intensified those materials until they arrived, in their maturity, at the new stage of music drama. When Verdi produced *Otello* and *Falstaff*, he was widely criticized for having openly copied Wagner's new style. Unquestionably he must have been influenced by his German rival's ideas and theories, which were ringing through Europe in the late nineteenth century; but Verdi's last two operas are nevertheless a perfectly logical development of his own, not Wagner's, style. The Italian was simply following his own bent along a path that was similar to Wagner's and moving in the same direction.

Verdi's first models were the works of the triumvirate of early nineteenth century Italian opera composers—Rossini (1792–1868), Donizetti (1797–1848), and Bellini (1801–

35). Gioacchino Rossini's career was one that has both fascinated and baffled the music biographers. This son of a town trumpeter (who was also an inspector of slaughter-houses) began composing operas at the age of eighteen and was only twenty-four when he created *The Barber of Seville*, an immortal work, and the climax of the Italian *opera buffa* art. In the space of only two decades Rossini produced no less than thirty-eight operas and sixteen cantatas; he earned a huge fortune; he became the most renowned Italian opera composer of his age; and then, at the age of thirty-seven and at the height of a fabulous career, he retired from the operatic field. The remaining forty years of his life were a musical blank, except for the *Stabat Mater* and the unfairly neglected *Petite Messe Solonnelle*. Thus he earned the reputation of being "the laziest of geniuses." But this was a gross calumny, because his years of inactivity were a prolonged period of suffering from serious nervous disorders that had been brought on by his early years of overwork.

Rossini was one of the greatest masters of vocal writing. Equally he was a master of orchestral effect, and to this day composers pay their respects to his famous invention of the long-drawn-out crescendo. Coexisting with these skills were an intuitive feeling for stage comedy and a high sense of characterization. Thus Rossini's was a natural genius for the theater seldom surpassed in its history. Nor was it one-sided. His masterpieces of laughter, sparkling from every facet with infectious merriment, are indeed the height of *opera buffa*; but Rossini also excelled in *opera seria*, a form that the eighteenth century seemed to have exhausted. His last operatic work, *William Tell*, with its indestructible overture, was composed in 1829 for the Paris Grand Opéra. It has been called a mixture of music drama, *opera seria*, and grand opera, a work that embraced the past and foretold the future. A few years later Rossini witnessed the *première* of Meyerbeer's *Les Huguenots*, and, recognizing the emergence of a new genre, a mixture of grandiloquence and bombast with which he could not cope, he retired from the lyric stage forever.

Like Rossini, Vincenzo Bellini and Gaetano Donizetti

were primarily melodists who excelled in the art of vocal writing. Bellini is remembered today chiefly for his operas *Norma*, *La Sonnambula*, and *I Puritani*. His melodies are among the finest in the entire range of Italian opera—a blend of rare grace and sweetness, often tinged with melancholy. They greatly influenced Chopin. Donizetti's best-known operas are *Lucia di Lammermoor*, *Elisir d'Amore*, *La Fille du Régiment*, and *Don Pasquale*. He was an incredibly facile workman, composing sixty-five operas and operettas in a space of twenty-five years. He actually turned out an entire operetta in only nine days, and a single act in a few hours. Works of this type were still cut from the pattern that had ruled Italian opera for centuries: they were basically designed to provide vocalists with vehicles for splendid singing. Rossini had infused his orchestra with more brilliance and dramatic vitality, but in general the orchestra remained largely an accompanying medium, offering light and often inconsequential support for the voices, with comparatively little contrapuntal interest. In contradistinction, German opera from the time of Mozart had been exploiting the orchestra at the expense of the vocal lines. Its instrumental parts grew more weighty and complex as they gradually approached the symphonic texture of the mature Wagner. This type of music required greater powers of organization, deeper concentration, and hence more time to produce.

From beginning to end of his career Verdi remained in the Italian opera tradition, i.e., he is primarily a creator of beautiful vocal lines. The human voice dominates everything he did (just as the orchestra dominates everything Wagner did), and in his operas he created an enormous fund of melody designed to show off all the lights and facets of the vocal art. His music remains the vocalist's paradise, and an endless source of delight for all those who love the art of singing. Verdi's greatness as an artist, however, is proved in the way he refused to remain simply a singer's composer, but improved himself steadily in the manifold aspects of the operatic task. What he did with his melodies is typical. Everyone knows the banality and cheapness of some of his tunes. The composer himself has paid dearly for them; they have marred the reputation of one of music's best craftsmen. The fact is often overlooked that Verdi outgrew them as he slowly progressed. In the orchestra he began with the conventional oom-pah-pah accompaniments of the thinnest sort, but in his maturity he was creating instrumental textures of remarkable fullness, variety, and color. In *Falstaff* he achieved an almost perfect union of the voices and the orchestra, with the latter body supporting and illuminating the drama with remarkable musical commentary, but never overwhelming it.

Verdi's progress as a dramatist is also remarkable. He began his career at a time when almost any tragic drama, no matter how turgid or pompous, would do for an operatic libretto. The stories of the serious operas of Rossini, Donizetti, Bellini, Meyerbeer, and their contemporaries often impress the listener today by nothing so much as their absurdity. Donald Francis Tovey remarked that "if the famous 'Mad Scene' in Donizetti's *Lucia di Lammermoor* had only been meant to be funny it would not have been vulgar at all." Verdi went through this stage in his slow evolution. He wrote plenty of music that is marred today by the homage it must pay to ludicrous dramatics, and much that misses connection with what the drama was trying to say. Many of the lovely melodies would be just as effective if they were sung to entirely different words. From these beginnings Verdi progressed until he was a master of musico-dramatics, and the creator of a whole portrait gallery of human characters. *Otello* is a music drama in the completest sense, and one of the most effective ever written; while *Falstaff* is masterly in the way it mirrors, measure after measure, the subtleties of the characters' words and thoughts.

It is unnecessary to contrast Verdi and Wagner to the detriment of either. The main exterior difference between them remains, as has been said, the preoccupation of the Italian with the voice and the German with the orchestra. Beneath that exterior fact lie, of course, other more profound differences. Wagner was unquestionably the deeper thinker, and an artist of far greater range and influence.

Verdi was first of all a practical man of the theater who enjoyed creating popular successes as much as he relished the practice and improvement of his craftsmanship. He had no philosophical axes to grind; no grandiose, world-shaking art projects to construct. He simply composed the finest of all Italian operas. Outside Italy his effect on the music that came after him was limited, while in his own country opera continued to flourish but with a slow decline in power and fecundity. The Mascagnis and the Leoncavallos had isolated successes, but nothing remotely resembling Verdi's fifty-year stream of production. Only by Puccini was the tradition of Italian opera carried on with both popular and artistic success.

It used to be the fashion to dismiss the operas of Giacomo Puccini (1858–1924) as hardly fit for the company of Wagner's mammoth music dramas or Verdi's later masterpieces. No opera impresario would make that mistake today. *La Bohème* (1896) is now as firmly established in repertoires as *Faust*, *Carmen*, or *Tannhäuser*; while hardly less vital are *Manon Lescaut* (1893), *Tosca* (1900), *Madama Butterfly* (1904), *Gianni Schicchi* (1918), and the not-quite-finished *Turandot*. Puccini's gifts were precisely those required (but seldom realized) for success in the lyric theater. He knew how to write for the voice; he had an Italian sense of drama and knew how to translate theatrical values swiftly into music; and above all he had the gift of melody—vocal melody. An eclectic and a romantic, Puccini took exactly what he wanted from Verdi, Bizet, Wagner, and later Debussy; but his music always remained clear and simple, with the voices held always in the spotlight. When he created a fine tune he knew how to let the singers soar with it, even—to the horror of his more sophisticated detractors—underlining it with the instruments in unison.

The decline in Italian opera after Puccini brought a hiatus to that venerable art for the first time in two centuries. No true successor has yet appeared, unless time should prove that the Italian talent for music-in-the-theater has been transplanted to America in the person of the Italian-born composer, Gian-Carlo Menotti. Meanwhile, operatic decline is a phenomenon to be observed not alone in the country of origin. It is a world-wide condition in the present century.

# Brahms
## 1833—97

### I

A mere glance at the German music of the latter half of
the nineteenth century is sufficient to reveal that the entire landscape was dominated by the work of two men—
Richard Wagner and Johannes Brahms. In their own day,
however, that fact was far from evident. It is surprising
that during his lifetime Brahms made any show whatever.
Of the two, Wagner was by far the more fascinating
figure, an artist who dwarfed by comparison one after another of his competitors. Wagner's personality was the
kind that elbows its way to the center of the world's stage,
right into the most glaring beams of the spotlight, the
better to exhibit its colors. Wagner made it difficult for
every other composer of his time and every one who came
after him. He made it especially difficult for Brahms.

The essential difference between the two men was the
direction of their mental outlook. Wagner's imagination
was projected into the future, while Brahms sat steadfast,
immovable, and grave—his eyes firmly fixed upon the
past. His imagination was entirely retrospective. Technically speaking, he invented nothing; he changed nothing.
In certain respects he was like Bach, who, in summing up
the age of polyphony at its close, was left a lonely and
monastic figure, his work old-fashioned in a world which
had moved on toward newer standards. Brahms's music

might easily have suffered the neglect that Bach's did. What saved it was the institution of the public concert, by his time well established in Western society, and the rise of the commercial publisher—two factors that served to keep his work steadily before the public eye.

Brahms suffered at first because there are fashions in music and musicians, just as there are in dress and food, in politics and morals; and the fashion arbiters of Brahms's time were Wagner and Liszt. In his plushy retreat at Triebschen, living in blissful sin with another man's wife, and at Bayreuth, painting all four great walls of a new musical Jerusalem, Wagner had captured the admiration of Europe; and so had Liszt, the flamboyant pianist-composer holding court at Weimar. In contrast to these brilliant men Brahms lived in his dreadful bachelor flat in Vienna, lodgings that were a monument to bourgeois stodginess; Brahms, drinking beer and eating sardines out of a can, and writing the finest variations since the death of Bach. It is no wonder that his music was thought dour, he was so stubbornly dour a man himself. He was less influenced than any other important composer of his time by the most forceful creative idea then loose in his world— program music. He loathed Liszt's symphonic poems. He gave Wagner's music a grudging admiration, but he wrote no opera himself. He never let himself get close enough to the stage to write so much as a piece of incidental music to any drama. He loved poetry and was an inveterate reader of the classics, but he relegated his inspiration from words strictly to his songs and choral works. The rest of his music is as devoid of literary or pictorial connotations as the symphonies of Haydn. No other composer of his time leaned so heavily upon the classic procedures as Brahms did, and no one else could rival what he accomplished with them.

What his contemporaries often failed to understand was the fact that Brahms, though a master of formal structure, was still a romantic composer. Even at its most abstract the outward style of his music is invariably romantic; it is lyric in contour; it sings. But the failure of many people to realize that a man could excel at the classic forms and still avoid fossilization fastened a stigma upon Brahms's music that clung to it for years. His was the best-loved and best-hated music of the nineteenth century. As late as 1900, Philip Hale in Boston could say, "This way out in case of Brahms," and still retain the vestments of his critical reputation. Only during the past few decades has Brahms reached the ultimate heights; he is now a box-office attraction.

## II

Johannes Brahms was born in a tenement in the waterfront section of Hamburg, on May 7, 1833. He was not far removed from peasant ancestry. In many respects his family was worse off than the peasantry, for the squalor of their surroundings did not afford even the redeeming cleanliness of the earth and the open sky. The family of five was squeezed into a few miserable rooms, and the neighborhood itself was a red-light district frequented by sailors.

Brahms's father was a double-bass player, who worked his way up in the world until he became a member of the municipal orchestra. The composer's mother was seventeen years older than his father. She was forty-one at the time of her marriage—an unprepossessing little spinster with a badly crippled foot and a quarrelsome disposition. The mystery of that odd union is not explained, but it left psychological scars upon the mind of the celebrated son. Brahms's parents quarreled incessantly for many years, and when his mother was seventy-five she and his father separated and thereafter lived apart. The mother's affections seem to have been directed toward her son, who also adored her. On her death he composed in her memory one of his noblest works, A German Requiem.

Brahms's father wanted his son to become a professional musician like himself. When he discovered that the boy had unusual talent, he had sense enough to take him to one of the best teachers in Hamburg. From the age of ten Johannes began to appear in public concerts. His precocity was so remarkable that his father thought of sending him on a concert tour of America to make money as a piano prodigy.

About this time began the series of episodes that Brahms was to remember throughout his life as the dark tower of his existence. The Brahms family was so poverty-stricken that they permitted the boy to play for dances in some of the lowest dives of the Hamburg waterfront district. The thought of a child so young spending whole nights in beerhall brothels, applauded by drunken sailors and even fondled by prostitutes, was so shocking to Brahms's early biographers that these facts were suppressed for many years; but modern writers have accepted them as a cause of a deep-seated neurosis that later warped the composer's relations with all women.

Life was bitter for this boy from the Hamburg slums. He began giving music lessons when he was twelve. He was fourteen before he saw the countryside, and at fifteen he began a regular routine of drudgery, playing in dance halls and at parties in the poor neighborhoods of the city. By this time he had begun to compose, but his first creative efforts had also to be turned to moneymaking. He wrote quantities of cheap dance pieces and popular arrangements of opera melodies, using the names G. W. Marks and Karl Würth. These potboilers were the first published works of Johannes Brahms.

The first piece of good fortune in Brahms's life was his meeting in 1853 with a young Hungarian violinist, Eduard Reményi, who persuaded him to go on a joint concert tour of neighboring German cities. Young Brahms had never been out of the vicinity of Hamburg. He left his native city an unknown young man of twenty, without money, influence, or important friends; he was to return, eight months later, the most talked-of young musician in Europe, loaded with the praise of the foremost composers of the time.

In the town of Celle he performed a celebrated feat. He and Reményi were scheduled to play the Beethoven Sonata in C minor (Op. 30, No. 2), but it was found that the piano in the hall was tuned a half tone too low. Reményi refused to tune his violin down, and so, rather than disappoint the audience, Brahms obliged by transposing his part up a half tone. He played the entire sonata from memory in the key of C sharp minor. The difficulty of the Celle feat has aroused the wonder of musicians ever since. It has also aroused a certain suspicion—that Brahms was prepared for just such an emergency. All his life the composer had a passion for the art of transposition, and he often amused himself by playing Bach's preludes and fugues in various keys.

From Celle the two young men walked most of the way to Hannover, and there they met another Hungarian virtuoso, Joseph Joachim. This young man was a far greater artist than the flashy Reményi. He was already famous throughout Europe, and he became one of the most influential musicians of his era. Joachim was amazed by Brahms's talent. The young man from Hamburg had with him a number of his first serious compositions—his Piano Scherzo, Op. 4, his first two piano sonatas, and some songs. He had also a violin sonata, a piano trio, and a string quartet, works that are now lost because the composer destroyed them as unworthy.

From Hannover they went to Weimar. In that resplendent old town, in which the shade of Goethe still shed a radiance and even the dim ghost of J. S. Bach could be discerned, there now lived Franz Liszt. The meeting of Liszt and young Brahms was a minor drama of conflicting personalities. Liszt was his most magnanimous and charming self—elegant, effusive, hospitable in the grand manner. He invited Brahms to play, but the young man was too shy. Thereupon Liszt took up the manuscripts of the Scherzo in E flat minor and the C major Sonata and played them himself. He not only read them at sight but also kept up a running fire of conversation, mingling praise, criticism, and advice, just as he did on a later occasion when he first saw the Piano Concerto of young Edvard Grieg. Then he began to play his own great B minor Sonata, but before he had finished, so the story goes, young Brahms had fallen asleep in his chair. The truth of that last detail is often questioned; nevertheless it is not inconsistent with the character of Brahms as it later developed. Few artists have been more stubbornly independent, less willing to truckle, more deliberately boorish when it suited them to be perverse and difficult.

The next citadel that the young composer-pianist had to conquer was Robert and Clara Schumann. Brahms arrived at their house in Düsseldorf one day late in September 1853, met the coldly aloof Robert and was forthwith invited to play. This time he was not too shy, but after the first few measures of the C major Sonata Schumann stopped him and said, "Clara must hear this." When she came Robert went on, "Here, dear Clara, you shall hear music such as you have never heard before. Now, begin your sonata again, young man."

Before that day was ended Johannes Brahms had stepped out for the first time upon the world's stage. The Schumanns took him over completely. He was invited to stay in their home; Clara gave him advice about his playing; Robert could find no words of praise sufficient for his music. Schumann went completely overboard in the famous article he wrote a month later for the *Neue Zeitschrift*. His prediction in that piece, that Brahms was the coming Man of Music in Germany, has often been deprecated as a lucky hit in the dark, rather than a stroke of prescience. But Schumann knew what he was talking about.

### III

When Brahms returned to Hamburg after his visit with the Schumanns he was a profoundly unhappy man. He was upset by the contrast of life with his quarreling parents in their flat in the slums and the splendid, music-filled home of the Schumanns. His worst despair was an incurable longing. He had fallen in love with Clara Schumann.

The next spring, when Robert tried to end his life and the doors of the Endenich asylum closed upon him forever, Brahms rushed at once to Düsseldorf. He took a flat above the Schumanns', and for the next two years he sacrificed his career and his art for Clara's sake.

Aside from Beethoven and his Immortal Beloved, no romance in music history has left more unanswered questions than that of Brahms and Clara Schumann. Their attachment lasted for more than forty years, until Clara's death in 1896. During the first two or three years, especially during Robert's living death at Endenich, they were almost inseparable. Whether they were actually lovers, then or after Robert's death, is the great mystery of their sad romance.

That Brahms was desperately in love with Clara there is not the slightest doubt; but after the affair had begun to cool, his whole personal life and conduct gave evidence, increasing as the years went on, of a cankering frustration. Clara herself specifically whitewashed their love into a beautiful friendship in a passage in her diary addressed to her children and intended to set her cause aright after her death. She said simply that it was Brahms's sympathy and understanding that alone had borne her up during the days of her terrible sorrow, that their friendship was as perfect as it was unblemished, and that the small-souled and the envious who tried to make light of that friendship should go unheeded. It is hard not to believe Clara. She was a woman of deep devotions—to her Robert, her children, her art. Above all else she was sincere, with an unshaken belief in moral truth.

Sometime during those early years with Clara, Brahms made his great renunciation. He realized that marriage for them was impossible. The fourteen-year difference in their ages was not important; the simple economics of their lives was. She was a widow with seven children and no means of livelihood but her piano playing. To take over her burden would have meant sacrificing his own destiny as a composer. He chose not to sacrifice that destiny, and with that decision his whole career underwent a fundamental change. What might be called the drama of his life came virtually to an end. He never again experienced such brilliant and romantic episodes as those which crowded into the eight months of the year 1853, when Reményi, Joachim, Liszt, and the Schumanns found him and published him to the world. During that time he was propelled by circumstances and the influence of other people; now it was his own nature that would govern his life and his work. That nature was one of the most static ever to be joined to the buoyant art of music—a nature that hated change, decisions, breaks with the past. Brahms began to make for himself a life notable for its uneventful stodginess.

IV

He began his preparations for his career in a manner typically ascetic. For several years, at Düsseldorf and elsewhere, he produced very little new music. He was giving himself time to study and to think. Disturbing weaknesses in his technical equipment had made themselves apparent to him. In 1854, at Schumann's instigation, he had tried his hand at a symphony, but gave it up after sketching three movements. Some time later he put down the first seedlings for the opening movement of his C minor Symphony, not actually completed until twenty years later. These projects were too big for him, and he soon realized it, so he set himself a rigorous course of study in counterpoint, including the writing of canons and fugues of extreme difficulty.

To keep the pot boiling, he took a job for several months each year as music director of the court of Detmold. At this tiny principality he had to conduct a small orchestra and a choir, and give music lessons to the Prince of Lippe's sister. The court life was old-fashioned and stiflingly dull, but with little effort he could earn enough to keep himself going for a whole year.

Two of the works that stem from the Detmold period are the Serenades for Orchestra, in D major (Op. 11) and A major (Op. 16). The D major Serenade in its original form was scored for only nine instruments; then it was expanded, and still later revised a second time before its final appearance in 1860 as a six-movement piece for a sizable body of strings, woodwinds, and brass. In this and the succeeding serenade the composer was wading cautiously out toward the symphonic waters that he feared were too deep for him. The two pieces gave him the technical exercise that he was seeking, but for the listener they are not rich in musical vitamins. They are the least played of all Brahms's orchestral works.

The Serenades are important indirectly, because they offer an important clue to the workings of the composer's mind. To the end of his career Brahms never undertook a task without first preparing himself thoroughly, and he never published a work without giving it the benefit of long contemplation and the most exhausting criticism. Whenever he approached a form that had models of particular greatness in the past—the symphony, the concerto, the quartet—his caution became acute. Rather than attempt a headlong attack, he would sidle up to it, preparing the way first with excursions into adjoining territory. He hated to risk comparison with the achievements of Mozart, Haydn, Beethoven, or Schumann until he felt sure of his ground.

All through these early years Brahms was eager to produce some work on a large scale which would live up to Schumann's estimate of his powers. He had worked over the abandoned symphony, making it into a sonata for two pianos, and then the real medium for the work suddenly became evident to him—a piano concerto. He used the first two movements of the symphony and added a new finale. The result was his Piano Concerto in D minor, Op. 15, completed in 1858 when he was only twenty-five years old.

Tremendous mental effort had gone into this work. Brahms called upon a musician named Grimm to help him with the orchestration, and he sent his manuscript a number of times to Joachim for advice and criticism. If the birth pangs were agonizing, the actual delivery was even worse. On January 22, 1859, in Hannover, Brahms played the concerto for the first time in public, under Joachim's direction. It was received by the audience with disdain. Five days later, when he played it at the old Gewandhaus in Leipzig, a place where any young composer would have given his soul for a triumph, it scored another notorious failure. At the end there was a reverberating silence that must have chilled the blood of the young composer-pianist; a handful of people tried to applaud, but they were drowned out in a wave of hissing.

The D minor Concerto was neglected for many years. Most virtuoso pianists in the late nineteenth century considered it dour and unrewarding. It is in fact a somber piece, and strangely grave coming from so young a man. The bitterness of his youth, the tragedy of Robert Schumann, his own warped romance with Clara had found their way into his music. So, too, had much of Schumann's art. The older man's rhapsodic style, his individualistic piano figuration crop up again and again; but the imitation is by no means a blemish. The general style is Brahms's own. It is solid, melodious in an unpretentious way, technically difficult but never showy. The piano is not spotlighted; instead it carries on a serious dialogue with the orchestra. The slow movement proves that Brahms's study of Bach had borne fruit.

v

At the time of the failure of his piano concerto, Brahms's personal life was still in an unsettled state. He had hardly gotten over the worst of his frustrated love affair with Clara when he began courting a girl named Agatha von Siebold. She was the daughter of a science professor, and she offered the rarely combined attributes of beauty, intelligence, and an understanding of music. Just when everyone was expecting the announcement of an engagement of a pair so ideally suited, Brahms proceeded to jilt her—with not too gentle firmness.

At this time he was also having troubles with his family. His parents' home in Hamburg was a place of ugliness, with his mother and father quarreling incessantly, and his brother (who became known in Hamburg as "the wrong Brahms") trading on Johannes' generosity and fame. The young composer could not live in the same house with them, but had to take rooms in another part of the city. Hamburg itself seemed stale. Brahms tried to interest himself in the local orchestra, which was third-rate, and he assumed the directorship of a ladies' choir, for which he wrote a number of his early choral works. He was in the unfortunate position of a young man who had outgrown his family, his friends, and the city of his youth—all in a few short years. And yet, in spite of all this personal disharmony, he began enjoying a new-found happiness—the deep satisfaction of having struck his stride in his art.

For several years, leading up to his great year, 1862, new and splendid works had been in the course of construction. The gears of inspiration and technique had suddenly meshed. Besides the D minor Concerto he finished the B flat Sextet for Strings, Op. 18. This was only his second essay in chamber music (his second published one, at any rate), but it remains one of his loveliest creations in this field of music. Its outward charm lies in its flower bank of richly melodic and rhythmic ideas; but its real significance is found underneath, in the trellis of form upon which the composer built his ideas. This underlying structure is proof that Brahms had mastered, before he was thirty years old, the most difficult and abstruse phase of the music art. Formal design and the organization of material are, in all branches of art—music, literature, painting, sculpture, architecture—the aspect least obvious, the most imperfectly understood, and generally the last to be mastered by the artist himself. Brahms's strongest instinctive talent was his understanding of form. It was the thing he was able to grasp first, and to the end of his life his creative thinking was ruled by his concepts of what basic design should be.

The B flat String Sextet was the beginning of a sudden rush of works that startled even the most ardent Brahmsians like Clara Schumann and Joachim. In 1861 and 1862 came the immense F minor Piano Quintet, the first two piano quartets, five books of songs, and the Handel Variations for Piano. The F minor Piano Quintet is one of the masterworks of chamber literature. It is the opposite in style and conception from the B flat String Sextet. Instead of the sun and the warmth and the lyric buoyancy of the earlier work, the quintet is more like the D minor Piano Concerto—sultry, somber, full of violent passions. Of all Brahms's works it was one of the last to be widely appreciated.

As for the Handel Variations, their worth has never

been denied from the moment of their first hearing. Brahms wrote them in a manner unusual for him. They seemed to spring from his pen in a rush of inspired writing like that of Schubert, Mozart, or Handel himself. One day late in 1861, Clara Schumann went to visit Brahms in Hamburg and he played them to her for the first time. She was almost stunned by what she heard. Within a month she had mastered them herself (in spite of their technical difficulties), and she introduced them to the public at one of her Hamburg recitals. Nothing that Brahms wrote for the piano has been more highly praised. Even Wagner, who generally regarded his rival's music as so much bad-tasting medicine, had only encomiums for the Handel Variations when the composer played them for him a few years later in Vienna. They showed, Wagner said, what could still be done with the old forms by some-one who really knew how to manipulate them.

The original Handel theme is a fine old tune, eight measures long, perfectly symmetrical and plainly harmo-nized. From this simple beginning Brahms built an enor-mous structure of twenty-five variations, with a roaring fugue as a climax on the end. From the variety and luxuri-ance of the ideas it is hard to realize that these are so-called "strict" variations, i.e., the composer maintains both the basic phrase form of the theme and its general har-monic scheme in every one of his variations except the finale. Moreover, even though the work is made up of twenty-seven separate sections, these pieces are molded together and flow one into the other with such logic that the whole becomes one magnificent and unified design.

After the appearance of the Handel Variations there was little doubt in the public mind either of the technical ability of Brahms or the direction in which he was head-ing. At that time the composers of Germany were cleaved into two belligerent factions, and a noisy war was going on among them and their partisans. On the one hand were the followers of Wagner and Liszt, who rallied chiefly around the latter at Weimar and who were the romantic leftists of the day; on the other were the followers of the dead Schumann, who clung to a milder romanticism that was in reality a kind of neoclassicism. Brahms, having been named Messiah by Schumann, was clearly the leader of the latter group. In 1860 he even went so far as to publish, with three other musicians, a manifesto condemning the Liszt faction and their claims to a mortgage on "the music of the future." The attack backfired, and thereafter to the end of his life Brahms kept his mouth shut. He never again entered a public controversy, even though in private he excoriated program music, especially Liszt's invention of the symphonic poem. He stuck to the old variation and sonata forms, to chamber music, which was dying on its feet; he went right on with the time-tested methods of thematic development, and with the old uses of polyphony, and he infused them all with new life from the breath of his vigorous young lungs.

## VI

It was in 1863, the year of his thirtieth birthday, that Brahms's personal life fell finally into the groove it was to occupy for the rest of his days. For a long time he had wanted to go to Vienna. To a North German the Austrian capital, with its reputation for carefree, civilized living, was like a second Paris. Its glorious musical background was a tapestry through which the lives and works of Haydn, Mozart, Beethoven, and Schubert were woven like glowing threads. Late in 1862, Brahms went there for the first time and got his first taste of the city, its music, and its effervescent life. Later he returned and made it his permanent home. He loved Vienna, and it seemed that from the first the city liked him. When he gave his first concerts, there was a fine turnout of influential musicians curious to see what Schumann's famous protégé had accomplished.

At this time Brahms was still as much a pianist as a composer. From all contemporary accounts his playing was brilliant but uneven. Although he was a very short man, he was powerfully built, with heavy shoulders and strong arms. At the piano his pent-up emotions and his strength often carried him away; he was described as a bear hitting at the keyboard with great paws. Nevertheless, he could also play with the delicacy and tenderness of a woman. As he grew older, his playing became more eccentric and careless. For that reason he was himself partly to blame for the mixed receptions that his music received at early public performances. His own playing can often account for works like the D minor Concerto being received with acclaim from the audience at one performance and with a deluge of ice water at the next.

One of the first friends Brahms made in Vienna was the famous critic, Eduard Hanslick, who later became a fanatical propagandist for his music. The name Hanslick has survived even into our time and some of his reputation still clings to his name. In spite of the work he did trumpeting the greatness of Brahms, he was actually a malignant influence upon the music of the later nineteenth century. In his scalding diatribes against all program music, and against the works of Wagner in particular, he reduced music criticism to the level of religious bigotry. Hanslick was partly responsible for the two supreme musicians of their time, Wagner and Brahms, being pitted against each other constantly as enemies. Their first meeting in Vienna was their last; thereafter a gulf widened between them and their artistic careers. Hanslick did his best to widen it. He wrote as if a listener could not possibly love the works of both men, that he must perforce accept the one and damn the other—a piece of stupidity that required almost half a century to dispel.

Several years passed before Brahms finally got himself established in Vienna. He accepted a post as conductor of a choral society, the Singakademie, but after a few seasons he came to the conclusion that he was a failure at the job. His love of Bach led him to attempt performances of the Passions, motets, and certain of the cantatas, but he had neither the skill nor the inspiring qualities as a leader to grapple with those tremendous bodies. He quit his post, and for a while he drifted about uncertainly.

Early in 1865 word came that his mother was dying. He rushed back to Hamburg, but she died before he reached her bedside. For the shock and sorrow of his loss there could be but one assuagement; he must complete the great project that would be his mother's monument. Years before, after the death of Schumann, he had pondered these same bitter thoughts—of death and its sting, of the grave and its victory. Now, in full possession of his artistic manhood, he could finish the task. He produced what he called *A German Requiem*, for chorus, orchestra, and two soloists, the largest single work that he ever composed. Six of its seven parts were finished by the summer of 1866. Part V was added later.

Brahms's Requiem has no direct connection with the Requiem Mass of the Roman Catholic Church. The composer coupled the word "German" to the title to indicate a fundamental difference in style, if not of ultimate purpose. His text is not the Latin of the Roman Mass at all, but is a German translation of certain verses that the composer himself selected from the Old and New Testaments and the Apocrypha. He arranged them, wrote Lawrence Gilman, "to present in succession the ascending ideas of sorrow consoled, doubt overcome, death vanquished."

Since the words are the inspirational basis of the work, it is the vocal side of the Requiem which predominates. Brahms, the composer of great lieder, emerges here in full flower; the piece is in reality a series of superb, extended songs. The orchestra part is comparatively subdued, providing chiefly a rich underlying texture of polyphony. Brahms's peculiar lyric style saturates the work, the style upon which he built practically all his songs. The melodies are broad, with strong, simple outlines, long-flowing, often reminiscent of German folk song. Thus Brahms was following the dictates of his inner romantic nature in the creation of this work. It is not only a German Requiem, it is also a romantic one.

There are moments in the Requiem of great dramatic power, especially the magnificent Funeral March, "Behold, All Flesh Is as the Grass." Here the ultraconservative Brahms indulges in as theatrical a device as could be found in the instrumental book—a long and tremendously effective pedal point on the tympani. Otherwise he seldom departs from the somber mood of his subject, its tenderness and poignancy. The work as a whole remains one of Brahms's finest scores, consistently inspired and integrated by its exalted text.

The composer's bad luck with first performances dogged him again with his Requiem. The first three parts were given late in 1867 in Vienna, and the audience hissed—not so much the music as a performance that was ludicrously bad. The tympanist lost his place and ruined the seventy-two-bar pedal point on D. The composer bided his time, however, and on Good Friday of the following year a magnificent performance of the work (except Part V) was given in the Bremen Cathedral. Many of Brahms's closest friends were there to witness the triumph he knew would come; Clara Schumann arrived at the last minute and he walked with her down the long nave. The performance was an immense success and had to be repeated a few weeks later.

## VII

And now there emerged in outlines clear and unmistakable the figure of the great Brahms. He was thirty-five years old, in the prime of his life and his art. The fires under the forge were blazing, the ore was waiting. Slowly, but in steady procession, the great works began to come forth—the Haydn Variations, the concertos, the *Tragic* Overture, the four symphonies, the mature chamber works and songs, the last pieces for the piano.

The creation of this prodigious store of beauty required almost thirty years and the unswerving dedication of the artist's entire life to the task. Very soon after he settled in Vienna, Brahms fell into a routine of living from which he hardly varied, year after year. The summer was generally given over to composition, the winter to concerts at which his own works were featured. He invariably spent the summer months in the country, always choosing some lovely spot where he could work undisturbed, while indulging his passion for nature and his habit of walking. One of his favorite summer haunts as he grew older was Ischl, a watering place on the Salzkammergut, made incomparably beautiful by lakes, mountain streams, and snow-capped peaks. He made numerous visits to Switzerland, and in 1878 he spent the spring in Italy, the first of many pilgrimages there.

Invariably the central event of every summer was Brahms's visit to Baden, where Clara Schumann maintained her home. To support her family Clara had to make concert tours all over Europe. During the winter she often did not see her children for months at a time. When the summer came, they were reunited in a comfortable home near Baden. Brahms went there religiously, year after year. He gave music lessons to the children, and he played for Clara the new works that he was preparing for the coming winter season.

It was a matter of prime importance in Brahms's career that about this time he became financially independent. He was in fact one of the first nonoperatic composers to gain considerable wealth from his music alone. Once he became established, publishers all over Europe were hot for his works. They paid him large sums for publication rights and when he died he left an estate worth about a hundred thousand dollars. This meant that all through his most fruitful creative years he was practically free to do as he wished. And what he wished was the essentially selfish life of a bachelor.

It seems hard to escape the conclusion that Brahms's character was dominated by selfishness. The life that he chose was precisely the one he wanted, and in it there was no place for a wife or children, but only for a few friends who accepted him on his own terms. It is true that at times he was generous, giving away large sums to persons in need, and often imposing a strict secrecy; but about his own affairs he was as congenitally stingy as a peasant. He bought only the cheapest clothes, wore the same suit for years, and did not care that he looked slovenly. He ate only in cheap restaurants, and he always traveled third class. To avoid paying duty on his favorite cigars, he asked his friends to smuggle them in for him, and once he was fined seventy gulden for hiding Turkish tobacco in a stocking when he crossed the frontier. The composer's apartment in Vienna was a museum of bad taste that would have sent an aesthete like Chopin into convulsions. No hint of decorative beauty could be found in its plain walls, chromo pictures, Victorian upholstery, and uncomfortable chairs. There was no bath, and the living room had to be reached through the bedroom. The place was generally littered with music and books.

The price that Brahms paid for his denial of marriage and parenthood became more evident as he approached old age. Gradually he assumed all sorts of crotchety habits. He had a tongue like an adder, and he used it as cruelly against his friends as he did against some unfortunate stranger who made the mistake of praising his music to his face. Clara Schumann's children recalled that he often spoke to her with such deliberate rudeness that he brought tears to her eyes. He quarreled worst with some of his best friends—Hans von Bülow, with whom he broke off completely for two years after a bitter feud, and Joachim, whom he wounded deeply by taking the side of the violinist's wife in a divorce action. His was the case of a person of extreme sensitiveness, modesty, and even kindliness, who put on, with pathological perversity, the outward armor of rudeness. His sarcasm and his ill temper became a legend that has long outlived the finer attributes of his nature.

Just as his personal life was dominated by selfishness, so was Brahms's art ruled by caution. No composer, great or small, destroyed more than he did. He began this ruthless habit in his boyhood, and even through the years of his finest productivity reams of music went into his wastebasket. As a result the general level of quality in his work is exceptionally high. He published little that could be described as mediocre.

Brahms was the prime example of the northern genius whose talent is kept firmly on the track of common sense. He was also the northern type of romantic, whose passions were restrained by a coldly logical reasoning. Thus it is that his music, even at its richest and most vital, is actually unsensuous, as it is almost always serious. Few composers made more copious use of folk melodies; yet

he always used them prudently. His popular Hungarian
Dances are about as far as he ever let himself go in the way
of reckless abandon, but compared with Liszt's treatment
of similar ideas in the Hungarian Rhapsodies they are
tame.

In the matter of orchestration Brahms was so conservative that he used to be classed as a bungler. Berlioz, Wagner, and Liszt were doing for the orchestra what Chopin
did for the piano—composing music that purposely played
upon the sheer gorgeousness of sound that modern instruments singly and in combination could produce. These
composers raised the once-simple practice of orchestration
to an art in itself. Partly through caution and partly
through stubbornness Brahms refused to be pulled along
by the nose into using the discoveries of these men. This
was one reason why he was so slow to approach larger
orchestral composition. He waited until he had developed
a style of instrumentation which was his own, and which
was perfectly suited to his particular musical ideas.

There is no use denying that, comparatively speaking,
it is the "gray" colors that predominate in Brahms's orchestration. They are subdued rather than brilliant,
opaque rather than transparent. There is seldom a hint of
either sensuousness or violent contrast; there are no purple patches. But the notion that Brahms's orchestration is
"muddy" is a fiction perpetuated by several generations of
orchestral conductors who were themselves insensitive to
any modern orchestral coloration that differed from that
of Berlioz, Liszt, Wagner, Tchaikovsky, and Strauss. In
such hands it is not surprising that the Brahms symphonies
for years sounded smudged and dirty. A few modern conductors, however, have been at pains to work hard over
his orchestration, and they have proved how beautiful it
can be. It is bold and manly without being raucous; it is
full of delicate, even exquisite tints. Most important of all,
it says precisely what the music implies, no more, no less.
No idea in Brahms's music is overblown by the instruments out of all proportion to its importance; and there
is never any toying with sheer effect to give a musical idea
a subtlety it does not own.

The same is true of Brahms's piano music. If it is played like Chopin's it may remind the listener of the description of Carlyle's prose style—"coal arriving next door." Chopin set a standard that was followed by composers for years. He spread his chords out through the various registers of the instrument to give them the most perfect transparency. It is almost impossible to make his music sound other than clear. Brahms's trademark at the piano is the crowded thickness of his chords, especially in the bass. To avoid opaqueness the performer must use the utmost care in pedaling, and he must develop a touch of unique sensitivity. He must play Brahms's music as he plays no other.

In the field of harmony Brahms's caution is again marked, and again his reputation as a craftsman suffered for many years because of misconceptions. He was living in the age of Wagner, whose bold new chromatic harmony burst through the restraints of the old diatonic system like floodwaters bursting through an antiquated dam. Brahms lived for more than thirty years after the first performance of *Tristan und Isolde*, but during that time he hardly moved from his old diatonic position. Again a close study of his procedures reveals their justification. Brahms was a cautious harmonist, judged by Wagnerian standards, but he was, nevertheless, a very fine one. Curiously enough, his music is far less old-fashionedly diatonic than it sounds. He actually used a wealth of keys; he devised all sorts of subtle ways to vary outworn diatonic modulations; he got remarkable effects by boldly contrasting major and minor modes, and by uses of the old modal harmonies; he even liked astringent dissonances. The reason why we are not more conscious of the beauty of Brahms's harmonies is that he underplayed rather than overplayed their importance in his general scheme. Here again he was diametrically opposed to Wagner. Wagner, always the dramatist, squeezed every drop out of his harmonic effects. When he invented some new modulation of particular loveliness he was always sure to bring it into high relief, to work up to it with all the skill at his command so that it would fall upon the ear with an effect that would be breath-taking.

This Brahms could never bring himself to do. His ultimate
aim was always the purity and beauty of his general design,
never of an immediate effect. His music is studded with
beautiful modulations and harmonic highlights, but often
they go by so fast that the listener discovers them only
after repeated hearings.

### VIII

In 1873, Brahms was forty years old, and by that time
the thought that had so long baffled his admirers had become a burning question: Why had he produced no symphony? Everyone knew that he had the brawn for the biggest task in music—that is, everyone but the composer himself. That year he produced not a symphony but his last
preparatory study for one—the incomparable Variations on
a Theme of Haydn.

One cannot but admire him at this juncture—first for
his intellectual honesty and the self-discipline that he applied in staying his hand from the larger form, and second
for the courage that it took to produce instead the smaller.
The Haydn Variations were written at a time when the
fashion for program music was at its height, when picturesque titles, musical portraiture, and tonal delineations
of Shakespeare and Dante, Goethe and Byron were the
rage. Nevertheless, Brahms wrote his variations—a form as
outmoded as a peruke. What he produced was a work so
rich in architectural splendor and melodic grace that even
his worst enemies had little to say but praise. The piece
is about as far removed from the average cut-and-dried
variations as could be imagined. It is finer even than his
Handel Variations, for it is more compactly built, the
proliferation of its ideas from the central thematic stem
is more startlingly original, and the finale with its ground-
bass construction (foreshadowing the last movement of
the Fourth Symphony) is superior to the bombastic fugue
of the former work.

The Haydn Variations only served to set the Brahmsians to clamoring louder than ever for a symphony, but
they had three more years to wait. In September 1876,

when the composer was in his forty-fourth year, the work that had been growing in his mind ever since the days of his youth with Schumann came at last to completion. At Karlsruhe, on November 4, 1876, the C minor Symphony was played for the first time—surely one of the most dramatic moments in the composer's entire life, considering the length of time he kept the world waiting and what he had to offer when the time finally came. Since the deaths of Beethoven and Schubert half a century before there had been no symphony of such majesty as this one. The greatest of all classic forms had shrunk in those intervening years rather than grown; but the C minor Symphony of Brahms left no room for doubt that the classic symphony was still alive at the roots.

It is plain that Brahms was making one of the biggest efforts of his entire creative life. He was consciously striving for the grand style, for panoramic design, and for the lofty emotion that motivates epic poetry and tragic drama. This is a tall order in any art and for any artist, but that Brahms achieved it in this work is beyond question. The superb introduction to the first movement is like the lifting of a curtain upon some cosmic drama; the entire movement is full of dramatic stress and tension, the racing energy that is remindful of Beethoven in his great first movements. From the technical side this opening movement is a masterpiece of structural design—the sonata form expanded with perfect logic and proportion to a work of huge dimensions.

The slow movement is Brahms, the romantic, speaking. It is like some lovely, heart-searching song from which the words are absent. Its flowing lyricism is enriched at the end by the most saccharine of all instrumental devices—a violin obbligato; but Brahms uses it with no trace of oversweetness. The third movement has often been criticized as a letdown, and because it is not the bounding scherzo that convention might demand. Actually it serves as a needed respite, during which the emotional tension of the two preceding movements is purposely eased.

The last movement must rank with the Titans of the

art of music. Here, as in the first movement, the composer let himself go. Neither Beethoven nor Wagner, the archdramatists of music, could have improved upon the devices (at bottom purely theatrical) which this supposedly stodgy classicist uses with stunning effect. For example, the grave introduction that broods like a lowering of storm clouds over a landscape, until the sky is suddenly pierced by a lightning flash, clearing the air for the great horn theme. And again, the chorale in the brass that is first announced softly, and then is held in reserve all through the long movement, finally to be blazoned by the full orchestra at the climactic end. Few works in music are rounded off with such magnificent and satisfying completeness.

Brahms's First Symphony was recognized instantly as a work of very great importance, but it was not immediately loved by the public. Its austerities and its complexities mitigated against that. Only in the present century has it become a public favorite, with the drawing power of Beethoven's Fifth. During the composer's lifetime it was far overshadowed in popularity by his Second Symphony which he produced, with startling suddenness, the very next year after the First.

Except for its slow movement the D major Symphony is everything that the C minor is not—sunny, vivacious, a blend of idyllic lyricism and high spirits. The work is indicative of the change that life in Vienna, in fact the entire warm southern scene, had caused in the life of this coldly reticent northerner. It had thawed him out. Ten years before no one would have thought him capable of writing such things as his waltzes for piano, or the exquisite *Liebeslieder* Waltzes for mixed quartet—or for that matter the D major Symphony. In this last work there is but one lapse into seriousness, the Adagio. It is hard to realize today that this profoundly beautiful movement was once widely despised, that it was supposed to contain everything repellent in Brahms—a gray bitterness, an incoherence, and a drabness born of frustration, a willful disregard of melodic beauty and orchestral clarity. Times have changed, indeed, and the passage of time has invariably worked to the advantage of Brahms's greater works.

The D major Symphony also lacks a scherzo, but its Allegretto is a movement of charming grace and technical ingenuity. The composer takes a mere handful of notes and makes them serve, through various clever manipulations of accent, rhythm, and tempo, for an entire movement. This, of course, is the oldest leaf in the classicists' book—achieving unity and variety through the use of a limited number of basic ideas. It is a principle that was the cornerstone of Brahms's entire musical edifice. Every music student knows that in many of Brahms's symphonic movements it is possible to trace the relationship of all the melodic strands and to discover that chief themes, subsidiary themes, accompaniment material, sometimes even the most inconspicuous inner voices, are all derived from a few basic germs of melody. No note is wasted, and none is brought in unnecessarily. It is the constant and masterful use of this principle which gives Brahms's music its solidity and its wearing power. It lasts through endless hearings because, as Schumann said of Bach's music, it is made "for eternity."

In the matter of rhythmic variety Brahms surpassed every other symphonic composer of his time. Schumann had opened the way with new ideas of rhythm, cross rhythms, and syncopation, but his young eagle soon left him far behind. With Brahms rhythmic changes and complexities occur so often as to become almost a mannerism. He was especially skillful at making different rhythms sound against each other, giving the effect of a smooth current suddenly turning into a choppy sea. The purpose was more than a satisfaction of the composer's unusual rhythmic sense; his aim was to add flexibility, variety, and a lift in interest to his general scheme. It was one of the innumerable devices that he used to keep the attention of the listener riveted to what is going on in his music.

## IX

On the first day of the year 1879, at Leipzig, Brahms had another treat in store for the world. It was a new concerto, a form that he had not touched since the completion of the D minor Piano Concerto just twenty years before. The new work was for the violin, and it was first performed by Joachim, with the orchestra under the direction of the composer. Brahms was lucky to have his piece introduced by this virtuoso, for it requires precisely what the Hungarian possessed—a vast technique controlled by a superior intellect. For years there was a standing joke about this work: Bülow had called it a concerto not for but *against* the violin. Performers were dismayed by its intricate double-stopping, its wild leaps from low notes into the upper registers, veritable traps for intonation, and its endless problems of fingering. Appalling too was its size. Symphonic in length and texture, it required a giant to play it adequately, and to dominate the opulent orchestral part. As in Beethoven's concerto, the prevailing mood is one of serenity. There are few hints throughout its length of the gloom-ridden young northerner who wrote the D minor Piano Concerto; instead he is blithe as a songbird, and in the last movement he is positively jocund.

During the summer of 1880, Brahms was at his favorite spot in Upper Austria, the lovely spa at Ischl, and he was engaged in a most unusual task—the writing of two overtures. Even though in mood these two works might suggest the twin masks of Greek drama, neither one has any direct connection with the stage. The *Academic Festival* Overture was written as a tribute to the University of Breslau, which had conferred an honorary degree of doctor of philosophy upon the composer the year before. It is based on four student songs—a rather odd memento from the most serious of German musicians to the faculty of a university. If the learned gentlemen were inclined to look their gift horse in the mouth, they might have felt better upon remembering that a few years before when the University of Cambridge had offered Brahms a similar honor he had turned it down, because he would not go to the trouble of making the trip to England to receive it.

The *Academic Festival* Overture is not one of Brahms's masterpieces, although it is a lusty, well-made, and very popular piece. Its companion, the *Tragic* Overture, is masterly. Because its title suggested that it might have something to do with the stage there ensued a fox hunt among annotators and critics to trace down a possible source of inspiration. Hanslick thought it must have come from *Hamlet*; others were sure it was another delineation of *Faust*. The composer as usual maintained a dignified silence.

The next large work on Brahms's agenda was his Second Piano Concerto, in B flat major. This piece was the fruit of the composer's first two journeys to Italy. In the spring of 1878 he traveled south with two of his cronies: Dr. Billroth, a noted surgeon and accomplished music amateur; and Karl Goldmark, the composer of *The Queen of Sheba* and *Sakuntala*. Brahms had the time of his life. He had never seen the changing of spring into summer in surroundings so entrancing; his whole being responded to the prodigies of beauty spread before him by the vernal earth. Some time later he made sketches for his B flat Concerto, but then put them aside and left them untouched for three years. In 1881 he went again to Italy on a more extensive tour, and again the miracle of the southern spring set his mind working in the same inspirational grooves. He returned to Vienna, took up his task, and in two months the work was completed.

The first person to learn about the existence of this new giant was the composer's dear friend, Elizabeth von Herzogenberg. This lady was one of the half dozen or so whom he might easily have married. She had been his pupil, and after her marriage to another man she corresponded with Brahms for years. Their letters are a standard source of information about the composer and his works. The announcement of the B flat Concerto was made in a letter written July 7, 1881. It happens to be a much-quoted sample of the composer's peculiar type of elephantine humor. "I don't mind telling you," he said, "that I have written a tiny, tiny pianoforte concerto with a tiny, tiny wisp of a scherzo. It is in B flat, and I have reason to fear I have worked this udder, which has always yielded good milk before, too often and too vigorously." The piece referred to in these delicate terms is the largest thing of its kind in music—four enormous movements, a veritable symphony built around the piano.

How much the beauty of the Italian spring had melted the heart of this man from the north is apparent in every measure. Brahms seldom wrote with such felicity of mood. In all his music there is no finer melodic flight than the lovely, meditating romanza for solo cello in the Andante. The piano part is glorious throughout, but the performer must pay in advance for his triumph. He is put through a staggering test of endurance and skill, to say nothing of the musicianship required of him to convey the composer's aims. The orchestral part, too, is full of difficulties for the conductor, and for the first horn and first cello, so that an adequate performance demands the collaboration of several artists of the first rank.

All through these years of his finest productivity in the major forms Brahms was also busy turning out many works of smaller dimensions. Hardly a year went by without at least one group of songs, and at less frequent intervals a chamber work would appear. These latter are scarcely less significant than his symphonies and concertos. As a matter of fact, it would have been nothing less than a freak of nature if Brahms hadn't produced great chamber music, because he was so prodigally endowed with the three basic requirements for writing of this type—a lyric style, a command of polyphony, and a mastery of abstract form. Nevertheless he seems to have encountered immense difficulties, especially in the earlier years when he had to learn to trim down his burly, large-scale style to these comparatively delicate media.

String quartets gave him his worst trouble. He said himself that before he published his first (Op. 51, No. 1, in C minor) he had written more than twenty quartets, and he had also written two trios, two sextets, three piano quartets, a piano quintet and a cello sonata. Some of these pieces he kept on his worktable for years, mulling them over, tearing them apart, and putting them together again. His very first published chamber work, the Trio (Op. 8), for Piano, Violin, and Cello, was written in 1854 when he was twenty-one. Thirty-seven years later, when he was nearing sixty, he took the trouble to make a completely revised version of it.

For the listener, Brahms's twenty-four chamber works offer chiefly a difficulty of choice. Nearly every one has surpassing merit. In the aggregate they represent an enormous accomplishment, which from the historical viewpoint alone could hardly be exaggerated. Chamber music of Beethoven's lofty standard would have perished in the later nineteenth century had it not been for these works of Brahms.

As for the songs, they are the best evidence of the romantic spirit that lay at the heart of all Brahms's inspiration. There was hardly a time all through his creative life when this least "classic" of forms did not engage him. The sum of his work in this field is large—almost two hundred songs for voice and piano, and dozens of arrangements of German folk songs. As a writer of lieder Brahms stands with Schubert, Schumann, and Hugo Wolf. He carved out a style that was uniquely his own, and he did it as usual by subjecting his ideas to scrupulous self-criticism. Even the simplest of Brahms's songs, those which expose most clearly his affection for the German folk-song style, are distinguished by an unmistakable craftsmanship. He was never obvious in his procedures; there was never an idea, musical or poetic, that did not engage his best effort and his sharpest technical skill.

As a pure melodist he was not the equal of Schubert, whose themes have a spontaneous beauty that is baffling. Brahms's melodies are more artful, they have a way of moving in directions least expected, and generally they have the enormous span that is one of the hallmarks of this composer's style. That Brahms was himself a pianist with a special affection for the instrument is evident in practically every song. The accompaniments are rich in melodic and decorative ideas; sometimes they are so powerfully conceived that they steal the interest from the voice itself. It is with Schumann that Brahms has the closest affinity as a song composer, although he lacked the wild exuberance that at times seized the older man, and the subtlety, the cunning almost, with which Schumann could reflect in tone ideas in the text. Brahms was not always a scrupulous observer of words; it is often said that some of his songs would sound just as well with different words entirely.

In the main there were two wellsprings which fed most of Brahms's vocal inspiration. The first was German folk song, whose broad simplicity of style and whose spirit influenced his entire art. The second was his own romantic nature—the passionate, moody, deeply sentimental strain that burned always in the heart of this sad-faced northerner, but which as a man he hid from the world. A mere listing of the names of his many songs indicates his predilections for the whole catalogue of romantic ideas and affections, from the beauty of simple flowers to the wild ecstasies of love, from the dreams and yearnings of youth to the frustrated longings of age.

x

It is fruitless to try to evaluate the relative merits of Brahms's four symphonies. Each one has certain qualities unmatched by the others. Every listener has a right to his own choice. The real point of importance concerning them is the general level of inspiration which the composer maintained without a single break through no less than sixteen separate movements. The particular glory of the Third Symphony, in F major (finished in 1883, just after Brahms's fiftieth birthday), is its superb fusion of the two hemispheres of the composer's inspiration—the romantic and the classic. In mood he returns to the tragic austerities of the C minor Symphony. The serious note is seldom absent, from the first declaiming chords of the opening movement to the smoldering embers of the last, and there are wild bursts of passion throughout. The composer's singing style was never more in evidence, his melodies are ravishing, and in the first movement especially he achieves a variety of harmonic coloration that is sheer magic—for example, at the very outset the bold sweep of the main theme through F major, F minor, and D flat major, like the flinging of bright green and red and gold upon a canvas; and the transmutation of the second theme from A major to a dark C sharp minor at the beginning of the development section.

Again, this symphony lacks a scherzo. The third movement is almost a song without words, and it is so impassioned that one is likely to wonder what the cautious Brahms could have been thinking of to put so lyrical and so melancholy a declaration of love into the austere frame of a symphony. The final movement calls attention to this composer's peculiar mastery of the last word. Every one of his closing symphonic movements is crownlike in the way it rounds off everything that has gone before. That of the Third Symphony has the added distinction of being one of the composer's consummate pieces of musical design. It was a bold procedure, at the time this work was written, to end a symphony quietly, instead of with the expected triumphant declamation, but in this case the composer's logic is unassailable. Great winds blow through this closing movement, there are buffetings and the shocks of battle; but the end is peace.

Sleepe after toyle, port after stormie seas,
Ease after warre, death after life does greatly please.

The Fourth Symphony, in E minor, is Brahms's *King Lear*. Not because it relates any such tale of shattering horror, but because the manifold powers of the artist himself had here reached their climax, and in the particular sphere of his overshadowing greatness; and because thereafter he never attempted anything of such dimensions, intensity, or emotional range. The E minor Symphony lacks the theatrical note of the C minor—the lordly introduction, the ringing, rallying finale. This time the composer had no need in his design for purely dramatic devices. The first movement has no prologue; it simply begins. But before long the forces of conflict are surging and straining, and the climax at the end of the movement is violent. This first section has a saturnine cast, and somberness of mood pervades the entire work with the exception of the Scherzo.

The Andante is the richest slow movement in all Brahms. Condensed within the space of a few minutes in time is an unexampled weight of melodic beauty. This is no simple lyric flight. It is densely woven, heavy with emotion, decked in some of the rarest harmonic and orchestral hues that this austere northern master ever permitted himself. The third movement refutes the charge that Brahms could not write a genuine scherzo. This one has not the torrential energy of the great examples of Beethoven, but it certainly has gusto and vigor. It is the work of an aging man, yet it leaps and bounds like a young warrior trying out his flashing new arms in the sunlight.

For the last movement of the E minor Symphony Brahms held in reserve an idea that had been germinating in his mind for years. The form he used was one never before attempted in a symphony—the archaic chaconne. The basic theme is eight measures long, and it consists of eight great chords proclaimed at once by the wind choir fortissimo. The composer then proceeds to build thirty sections, each one eight measures long, and each a variant of the original eight—that is, of its melodic line, its bass line, and its harmonic structure. Only at the thirty-first section does he break the mold and extend into a coda that winds up the entire work. The key of E minor prevails throughout, except for a few of the central variations, which are in E major.

Now this is obviously a set of self-imposed rules that seem not only stultifying but severe to the point of self-flagellation. The chaconne, however, happens to be one of the theme-and-variations species, the form in which Johannes Brahms was the excelling master in his era. Years before as a young man he had expressed his belief that Bach's violin Chaconne was one of the greatest works in all music, one that both fascinated and awed him. (He once made a piano arrangement of it for the left hand alone.) Now at the zenith of his own powers he was showing what he could do with a similar technical problem. One of the secrets of the tremendous power of Brahms's movement is the total absence of the beads-strung-together impression which is so typical of most variations and which mitigates against emotional and dramatic force. It has instead the rise and fall of action, the emotional contrasts, the sweeping movement of one episode into another with all the impelling logic of a lofty drama. It is grandiose and compelling, and it gives no hint whatever of the ironclad technical matrix that is governing every inch of its progress.

XI

With the completion of the E minor Symphony in 1885 the twilight began to close in around Brahms's life and his art. He was not yet an old man, only in his middle fifties, but he suddenly began to take on the attributes of old age. He produced only one more large-scale work, the splendid Double Concerto for Violin and Cello in 1887; thereafter it seemed that some inner warning signaled the necessity for slackening his pace. Gradually his works became smaller and more intimate, but as yet there was no sign of a decline. In fact to these years belong some of his most mature chamber works—the F major Cello Sonata, the violin sonatas in A major and D minor, the C minor Piano Trio and the masterly G major Viola Quintet—and in 1889 came a group of songs which include such treasures as *"Immer leiser"* and *"Wie Melodien."*

With old age the composer became definitely an eccentric. He went around the streets of Vienna a corpulent, squat little man in grotesquely disheveled clothes—a low-comedy hat, wrinkled suit, and high-water pants. Often he wore neither socks nor a tie, and his cheap flannel shirt was covered by the famous beard, now grown white and patriarchal. The mustache was fiery red on one side and gray on the other. His thin, high-pitched voice became cracked like an old bell. A weariness began to appear in the brilliant blue eyes, and at times an anguished melancholy. He often spoke of his loneliness and the price he had paid in giving up a wife and children.

The composer's mental suffering began to appear in his music. It is noticeable in his last four chamber works, those featuring the clarinet. The composer had been a warm admirer of Richard Mühlfeld, the first clarinetist in Bülow's orchestra at Meiningen, and for him Brahms wrote a trio, a quintet and two sonatas. The Clarinet Quintet in B minor, Op. 115, is a great work, but the other three pieces are rather severe. There is not only a grayness of mood evoked by the reedy voice of the chief instrument but also a comparative thinning out of inspiration.

Early in 1892, Elizabeth von Herzogenberg died, and the shock to the composer was profound. Thoughts of the irretrievable past and of what he had missed in life began to torture him. He spent many hours at the piano, the instrument of his lost youth. From these spells of brooding improvisation came four groups of solo pieces, the last and some of the finest music he ever wrote for the piano. They are abstractions, even though they bear the somewhat romantic names of intermezzo, capriccio, romanza, ballade, and rhapsodie. They are also mood pieces, and though a few are gay and energetic most of them are minor both in mode and feeling. Some are as lyrically inspired as his finest songs; others are grave, bittersweet, hauntingly sorrowful. As always, the composer's piano style is singularly his own—devoid of display, solidly built, with more attention paid to polyphonic richness than to tonal coloring.

Within a span of two months, in 1894, Brahms lost three of his closest friends—Dr. Billroth, Bülow, and Philipp Spitta, the celebrated musicologist and biographer of Bach. The deaths of these men were a threefold blow, and in the spring of 1896, when Clara Schumann suffered an apoplectic stroke, it seemed that he had prepared himself for a last and terrible defeat. He wrote his *Vier ernste Gesänge* [*Four Serious Songs*], which have rightly been called a Hymn to Death. The composer selected his texts from the Bible, his lifelong study and solace. The first three are from Ecclesiastes, beginning with the words: "One thing befalleth the beasts and the sons of men; the beast must die; the man dieth also, yea, both must die."

The last is taken from Corinthians: "Though I speak with the tongues of men and of angels, and have not charity, I am become as sounding brass, or a tinkling cymbal." For the bitter words of the preacher, Brahms found an echo in his own soul. He knew again the terror and the agony that smolder in the Germanic mind at the thought of death. He wrote in the mood of his vanished youth, with the brooding pessimism and resignation that had colored his first sternly serious works. With these songs his art had deepened incomparably, to produce the finest works of their kind in the entire range of German lieder.

A week after he finished the *Serious Songs*, Clara Schumann died. The composer traveled to Bonn for her burial, and he arrived a broken and exhausted man. With Clara had passed not only the woman who had come nearest to his heart, but also the last link in his life with the great past—with Robert Schumann, who had cried out for him in the wilderness, with Mendelssohn, and Liszt, and Wagner. During that final summer of 1896 his music was to end too. Eleven chorale preludes for organ (published posthumously) were his last compositions, and the closing notes of these are a fantasy on the chorale "O World, I Must Depart from Thee."

On the third of April 1897, Brahms died. He had no close relatives left in the world, and very few friends who were dear to him. He bequeathed his entire fortune and his library to the Friends of Music Society of Vienna, whose artistic director he had been many years before.

## XII

Like Bach, Brahms had long outlived the age to which his work seemed to belong. From his earliest years he had watched the music of Wagner move steadily away from his, and as time went on the distance rapidly increased. When he died, practically all the younger composers were listening to the siren voice from Bayreuth; nobody of consequence followed Brahms. If his work was made to seem drab beside the flaming colors of *Tristan und Isolde*, more violent contrasts were to come. At the very time that he was composing his *Four Serious Songs,* Claude Debussy was working upon *Pelléas et Mélisande.* Between these two works lies a chasm. It would be difficult to imagine a greater contrast in style, technical procedure, and in the ultimate aims of the two composers. Debussy's impressionism, moreover, was only the first of even more revolutionary movements in music which came to fruition in the first three decades of the twentieth century.

The triumphant fact about Brahms's music is that during these very years, when it was besieged on every side by the novel and the revolutionary, it did not shrink in stature. It grew. More of his music is played today than ever before. When it appears on programs with the best of the impressionists, the nationalists, and the ultramodernists, it is seldom the Brahms score that yields first place in interest. He stands as solid as an oak—a living proof of the strength of an aggressive classicism.

In one sense at least Bülow was right in placing Brahms with the other two Bs. Like Bach and Beethoven, Brahms knew how to leaven his classicism with the richness of his humanity. In music, as in art, the danger of classicism is the drying-out process. Once the artist becomes preoccupied with pure design to the exclusion of his own personal emotions, once he surrenders to the rulemakers and the academicians and forgets that art cannot sever itself completely from nature, then he and his product are headed for decay. Beethoven rescued the eighteenth-century classic forms—the symphony, the sonata, and the string quartet—from the possibility of such a death. When he left them they were still the recognizable designs of before, but they were enormously expanded to accommodate the scope of his own imagination and personality. To regard Bach as simply an archformalist and technician in the abstract is to miss at least half of his greatness. A large portion of his music is an expression of his own religious fervor—a personal belief so strongly infused into his work that if the Christian epic were to perish in every other medium of human expression it could still be revived in all its grandeur from Bach's Masses, Passions, and cantatas.

So it was with Brahms. He used the devices of classicism not as an end in themselves, but to express the dictates of his own romantic heart. These were the two sides of his nature, and in his supreme works they were not at war but in perfect harmony.

# Mussorgsky
## 1839—81

I

Like a black thundercloud Russia had loomed for centuries
upon the horizon of eastern Europe. Down to the time of
Peter the Great little was known of this country outside
its own boundaries. A vast, amorphous object on the map,
it appeared to generations of western Europeans as an impenetrable murk of barbarism, ignorance, and mystery.
Cut off from the rest of the continent both by distance
and the iron rule of its despots, Russia was denied an
interchange of thought or of peoples with the countries of
the West. It was a prison house from which few men
and fewer ideas ever came out, only an occasional torture
shriek from its oppressed populace, to horrify and haunt
Western ears.

In the long and dismaying history of Russia's sufferings
the brief period of the Great Reforms, beginning in 1855,
was like a sudden rift in endless storm clouds. For several
decades the rest of Europe had been forging ahead with
the tremendous impulses of the industrial revolution; Russia alone remained in stagnation. By the end of the
Crimean War she was wallowing in defeat and despair.
Czar Alexander II, a cautious, phlegmatic man, sensed the
temper of his people. He was motivated by both a deep-
seated fear of revolution and a conviction, shared by the
educated classes, that something must be done. He moved

slowly, but within a decade there was accomplished the greatest work of reform that Russia had yet known. The cornerstone of the whole movement was the legislation of 1861 which began the emancipation of the serfs.

It is true that many of these economic and political reforms died a-borning, and that many of the hopes of thinking men were blasted when Alexander was killed by a bomb in 1881. Nevertheless, during those brief years the intellectuals, the liberals, the men of art, raised their heads at last. This period of the Great Reforms marks Russia's emergence as an important contributor to world art. In hardly more than a generation she produced one of the great literatures of modern times, the work of men like Turgenev, Dostoevski, and Tolstoy. She also produced Russian art music in a form that was to sweep the entire Western world by the originality, the vitality, and the brilliance of its style.

## II

The rise of Russian art music is a story as remarkable as a piece of romantic fiction. Except for an ancient church chant whose roots went back to Byzantine days, there was no important music in Russia before the nineteenth century. It was created almost overnight by the efforts of a small group of men. First came Michael Glinka, who was the forerunner of the movement. He was followed by the famous Five—Balakirev, Cui, Mussorgsky, Borodin, and Rimsky-Korsakov—whose activities centered in St. Petersburg; and by Tchaikovsky, who lived in the rival city of Moscow.

Glinka was born near Smolensk, in 1804, the son of a rich landowner. He spent much of his life outside Russia, and much of his musical training was foreign. His early piano instruction was from John Field, the Irishman from whom Chopin derived the nocturne form; he studied theory in Germany and Italy. Glinka loved Italian opera, and upon its framework he composed two operas that are landmarks in music history—A Life for the Czar and Ruslan and Ludmila. These are the first truly Russian operas of enduring quality. They are based on Russian stories, with music strongly flavored by Russian folk and church music. Glinka's life was in part a record of tragic failure. He had superior musical gifts, especially for melody and instrumentation; but he wasted much of his life in dissipation. He died at fifty-three, leaving a prophecy for Russian music rather than a fulfillment.

The Five, or "Mighty Handful," as they were also called, first banded themselves together in the early 1860s. Four of them (and this is the first incredible fact about them) were essentially amateurs. At first only Balakirev could have qualified as a professional musician. Cui was an army officer who became an authority on military engineering and fortifications. Borodin was a professor of chemistry of wide repute, and a doctor of medicine. Rimsky-Korsakov was an officer in the Russian navy, while Mussorgsky spent much of his life as a government clerk. As young men none of them had any important technical training in music. They all learned from Balakirev, who was their mentor and dictator. They met weekly in St. Petersburg, to play and sing, talk and criticize. What resulted from these meetings was something far more splendid than they could ever imagine. For these bold, opinionated, ignorant, inspired young men gave direction and purpose and style to the Russian nationalist movement in music, which they sired directly, and they also set the standards for nationalism which were taken up in other countries all over Europe and in the Americas.

Their first success was owing to the peculiar character, attainments, and limitations of Mili Balakirev (1837–1910). Rimsky-Korsakov's memoirs, *My Musical Life*, describe vividly the genius of this extraordinary man. It seemed that he was born with all the gifts that a musician could hope for. He was a fine pianist, could read music at sight as if it were mere words, and could improvise brilliantly by the hour. He had never studied harmony or counterpoint, but he knew correct harmony, part-writing, and even form intuitively. Though only twenty-four when the group first met, he had the musical erudition of scholars twice his age. His memory was phenomenal; he learned a thing the instant he heard it. Rimsky-Korsakov called him a marvelous "technical critic," for when the other four brought him their efforts at composition "he instantly felt every technical imperfection or error, he grasped a defect in form—at once." In his judgments he was severe, imperious, final. But he held all of them enthralled by his "alert fiery eyes," his personality, his lightning-quick mind.

Time has proved that with all his gifts Balakirev lacked the creative spark. His ideas flowed too fluently into improvisation. When he tried to set them into final form he was thwarted by an extreme caution. It seemed that the critic in him held the creative artist by the throat. As he grew older and his four disciples turned away from him to careers of their own, Balakirev grew morose and difficult. They would not see him for long periods, and at one time he seemed to suffer a mental breakdown of some kind. The list of his compositions is meager for so long and intense a career, and only a handful of them survive today—a few of his songs, his orchestral tone poem *Thamar* (on which he toiled for years), and the flashing virtuoso piece for piano, *Islamey*.

Of the remaining four, César Cui (1835–1918), had the least to say of permanent value. He was half French, his father having been a survivor of Napoleon's Moscow army who had remained in Poland after the retreat. Cui's distinguished career in the Russian army seemed not to impair his energies for music, for he composed in large quantities and in many forms—ten operas, numerous chamber and orchestral works, and a great many songs and piano pieces. Very few of them appear on programs today. Cui was also a critic and propagandist. His articles, some of which appeared in Paris journals, had the important effect of spreading the new gospel of Russian music abroad.

Alexander Borodin (1834–87) had, after Mussorgsky, the best musical gifts of the Five. It is one of the misfortunes of Russian music that his energies had to be divided between music and science. He composed only in the odd hours when his duties as professor of chemistry were not too pressing, or when he felt too ill to attend his classes. Even then this good-natured, utterly charming man was beset by a household as diverting as it was chaotic. Rimsky-Korsakov left an unforgettable account of the Borodins and their domestic circus—a house where no one seemed to care what time it was, and where they often sat down to dinner at eleven o'clock at night; where stray relatives continually moved in to take up residence, get sick, "or even lose their minds"; where pet cats ate off the table and sat on the backs of the guests; where Borodin himself had little privacy and practically no quiet—and yet lived with a devoted wife in complete felicity.

Between chemistry and a lack of organization in his private life Borodin left a catalogue of musical works almost as thin as Balakirev's. At his death in 1887 some of it had to be taken over by Rimsky-Korsakov for finishing, editing, and revision. But there is enough to indicate Borodin's genius—a number of songs of singular originality, the fine Symphony in B minor, two string quartets, the tone poem *On the Steppes of Central Asia,* and the opera *Prince Igor,* from which the *Polovtsian Dances* are classics of exotic melody, wildly barbaric rhythms, and splashing color.

Borodin exemplifies, better perhaps than any other of the Five, the advantages and the handicaps under which they worked. Because Balakirev himself understood the technical side of music with remarkable intuition, he discounted the need for technical training for any of his disciples. Thus Rimsky-Korsakov wrote his first symphony when (by his own confession) he was so ignorant of theory that he did not even know the names of the common chords, much less the rudiments of harmony or counterpoint. Borodin was not much better off when he tried to write his first symphony; and throughout his life he had little time for theory or such luxuries as the study of instrumentation. Intuition guided him, aided by a penetrating imagination and unfailing taste.

All of the Five except Rimsky-Korsakov were eager to set their faces against tradition. They refused to be constrained by the old classic German and Italian procedures that had ruled Western music since the eighteenth century; instead they admired the music of the freethinking romantics—Berlioz, Chopin, Schumann, and Liszt. Above all they wanted to move along the trail broken by Glinka—to a thoroughly nationalist music based on Russian folk tunes and church music, and using Russian historical subjects and the fantastic treasury of Russian folklore.

Rimsky-Korsakov (1844–1908) was the only member of the Five who refused to remain an amateur. After several years under Balakirev's spell he realized that his inspiration was drying up, so he broke away and committed the unpardonable sin of schooling himself in the technical side of music. While still ignorant of harmony and counterpoint, he accepted a professorship in the St. Petersburg Conservatory. He taught by studying the lessons first himself and then keeping a few steps ahead of his pupils. He taught himself orchestration by buying many of the instruments and learning to play them. He toiled through long exercises in counterpoint which would have revolted his fellows.

Before many years had passed Rimsky-Korsakov had become one of the most proficient musicians in Europe. He wrote a textbook on harmony and a manual of orchestration that is still a classic. Gifted with enormous capacities for hard work and a mind that was orderly and keen, he never tired of improving both his music and his methods. He was composer, conductor, teacher, and editor. He completed and revised various works of Mussorgsky and Borodin after their deaths, and he edited the works of Glinka. In the midst of this lifetime of industry he even found time to write his autobiography, the most absorbing work of its kind after Berlioz'.

Rimsky-Korsakov's temperament might sound like that of a methodical schoolmaster, but it is curious that his musical imagination was the most fanciful and often the most charming of all the nineteenth-century Russians. He loved the picturesque, the extravagantly bizarre. His thirteen operas are nearly all based on Russian legends or dramas, and the best of them (*Sadko, Snegurochka,* and *Le Coq d'Or*) are rich in fantasy, jeweled and brocaded like the gorgeous fabrics of the East. His master craftsmanship served him well. For one thing it helped him hide a fundamental weakness of melodic invention. Often his tunes are commonplace, but they are disguised by expert handling—by kaleidoscopic harmonies or an orchestration of marvelous clarity and brilliance. As an orchestrator, Rimsky-Korsakov stands with Wagner and Berlioz, and many modern composers have helped themselves freely from pieces like his *Russian Easter* Overture, *Capriccio Espagnole*, and *Scheherazade*—works that might easily be classed as études in orchestration.

During his lifetime Mussorgsky was the least understood and the least appreciated of the Five. Among the group itself there was a prevailing opinion that although he had unusual talent in music, he lacked intelligence. "His brains are weak," was Balakirev's bluntly expressed opinion. His music seemed so crude to many of his contemporaries that they classed him as simply a bungler who was never able to assimilate the finer points of harmony, counterpoint, and form. He was so little understood that after his death his best friend, Rimsky-Korsakov, tried to cover up what seemed to be Mussorgsky's musical ignorance. Rimsky-Korsakov edited many of the works for publication, "touching them up to make them more understandable to the public," ironing out the "technical mistakes." This well-meant act of a devoted friend had in the long run a totally different effect than anyone had foreseen. A new generation arose years afterward which found the originals far more inspired than the painted-over substitutions. The Mussorgsky who had been belittled as a bungler became one of the dynamos of twentieth-century music, with ideas powerful enough to galvanize some of the best musical minds of the present era.

An understanding of Mussorgsky's place in music today can only come when it is seen in relation to the entire broad scene of nineteenth-century music, and also in contrast to the members of his own small group. For he was unique—in his ideas, his methods, his inspiration, and his personal character.

III

Russian art music was something entirely new under the sun. It appeared at a time when the great galaxy of German music had reached its zenith and the downward swing had begun, and when the bright beam of Verdi was all that was left of a once-glorious Italian art. The old stars were beginning to set, as this aurora borealis suddenly appeared, flashing its brilliant multicolored lights across the night sky.

The Russian composers began with a rare advantage, for they had at hand the vast fund of Russian folk song, a storehouse of magnificent material of which the rest of Europe knew nothing. Ernest Newman made a penetrating observation on the fundamental difference between Russian and German folk music, as each affected the art music of its area. German folk and art music, says Newman, "have always been so intimately associated that it is hard to say where the one ends and the other begins. . . . The moods, prosody, the structure, the cadence of the folk song run, broadly speaking, through almost all German music, sacred and secular, vocal and instrumental, of the last three hundred years." In Russia, he points out, folk music existed long before art music, because there was no art music of significance until the Five and their immediate forerunners created it. It is to the eternal credit of Balakirev and his fellows that they realized the treasure they had at hand, and began using it in their own way instead of slavishly imitating German and Italian models.

Thus Russian music is, in the truest sense of a hackneyed phrase, the voice of the people. It sprang directly from the soil. For that reason it has flavors and characteristics more marked than the music of any other country except Spain. It is a faithful mirror of the men who made it and of their surroundings. There is reason, therefore, for the heavy reliance of this music upon the minor mode, and for the doleful contours of many of its melodies. They are perfectly expressive of the deep sufferings that generations of the Russian people have endured, and of the grim enormity of their natural surroundings—the steppes that seem to extend with the unbroken monotony of the sea, the ranges of wild mountains, the winter itself with its monstrous cold and its universe of snow. All these have acted to impress upon the Russian soul the helplessness of man in the face of indifferent forces of nature.

And then there is the note of Orientalism which crops out in Russian art as unexpectedly as it does in the faces of Russian men and women. Glinka and Borodin were among the first to make extensive use of the idioms of Eastern music, and their success was so marked that they had many followers among the Russians. Borodin especially captured with skill the combination of simplicity and subtlety in the Oriental melody, and the suave, languorous melancholia of its spirit; he showed how these could be translated into the more sophisticated medium of Western music.

Finally, there was the music of the Orthodox Church, an ancient art which Russia had originally derived with her Christianity from Byzantium, and which through the centuries had left its mystical imprint upon the Russian mind and character.

The use that the Five and their successors made of this diverse and wealthy material made a profound impression all over the music world. In England and Norway, in Spain and Bohemia, composers went scurrying to the highways and byways in search of folk material from their own soils, eager to emulate the brilliant achievement of the Russians. The cult of nationalism was under way.

Generally speaking, the procedures of four of the famous Five were basically similar, and through their work run common virtues and common faults. They worked best in the smaller forms; they leaned heavily upon color and harmonic richness; there is a strong sense of the pictorial about everything they do. They were less successful in the abstract and as builders in the large forms. Borodin's string quartets and his symphonies stand practically alone. The first requisite for success in all the larger forms of art is the same—organization of material; and the ability to organize, to plan, to map out on a big scale is a skill that seems in some mysterious way to have racial roots and sources. The early Russian composers clearly lacked it.

While Mussorgsky's work must be included in many of these generalizations about Russian music, it must be carefully excluded from others, for the reason that many of his aims were often totally at variance with those of his fellows. Even though he used the externals of nationalism as they did, he was not simply a nationalist. He was never beguiled by color per se. Very early in his career he discovered that the abstract forms appealed to him even less than they did to his four friends. As soon as he turned to opera and to songs he had found his métier. These are the two musical forms that are primarily concerned with the minds and the hearts of men—a significant fact. Human sympathy is the motivating force behind everything that is best in Mussorgsky's art. There is no Mussorgsky symphony, no string quartet, no sonata—almost nothing in the abstract. But his single finished opera, *Boris Godunov*, and his sixty-odd songs are beyond doubt the finest works of their kind produced in the entire first century of Russian music.

Mussorgsky's life was a chronicle of misery, of a kind not readily understood by Western peoples. We can perceive the unhappiness caused by disappointment and frustration and loneliness; but Mussorgsky was also pursued by a terrible melancholia, some of which seemed to spring from bleak periods of creative inertia, some from sources in the Russian soul which her greatest novelists have tried to fathom and explain. Toward the end of his life he was a man struggling against the worst of all adversaries—himself. Often he suffered simply from the way his mind reacted to the spectacle of other human suffering around him. It moved him to the profoundest depths of his soul, and he struggled fiercely to express what he felt in his art. Like Rembrandt and Van Gogh, Dostoevski and the Shakespeare of *King Lear*, he gazed into the abyss of life. Like Van Gogh, his own spirit lacked the tough insulating covering which must bring the artist himself through so searing an experience. The painter was driven insane; Mussorgsky drank himself to death.

IV

Modest Petrovitch Mussorgsky was born in 1839 in the village of Karevo, which lay a few hundred miles to the south of St. Petersburg. The Mussorgsky family were land-owners of the old Russian nobility, but the composer's maternal grandmother was a serf. By the middle of the nineteenth century they were land-poor. The composer's childhood was spent chiefly at the old ancestral country house where for years the Mussorgskys had lived the easy-going, monotonous life of a decaying gentry, isolated by vast stretches of plains and forests. His mother, whom he adored, was a woman of culture and sensitivity. She saw to it that he learned to speak French as all aristocratic Russians must (Turgenev, it will be recalled, learned French before he did Russian) and she encouraged the boy's talent for music. At the age of nine he was a remarkable pianist. The next year he was sent to a fashionable school in St. Petersburg which was operated along the lines of a German classical gymnasium. After that came several years in a cadet school, so that by the time he was seventeen he was ready to enter the Preobrazhensky Guards, a regiment formed by Peter the Great, in which many of his ancestors had served. Mussorgsky spent four years in the military service, and the only thing he learned from it was the drinking habit that later killed him. The ability to withstand excessive dissipation was a necessary part of the equipment of every young officer.

One day in the corridor of a military hospital he made the acquaintance of a young doctor, Alexander Borodin, who later became a fellow member of the Five. According to Borodin, Mussorgsky at that time was "very elegant . . . uniform spick and span . . . His feet were small and neatly turned outward. . . . His hair curled and scented with the utmost care, his hands exquisitely manicured. . . . His manners were elegant and aristocratic and he spoke with a slight nasal twang, employing a large number of French expressions, sometimes a little *recherché*." In polite company he delighted the ladies by playing the piano, "very sweetly and pleasantly, with some affected movements of the hands." He played pieces from *La Traviata* and *Il Trovatore*. Borodin's description is both vivid and curious, for it bears so little resemblance to the man Mussorgsky later became.

All during these years in the army Mussorgsky was passionately interested in music. His first meeting with Balakirev occurred when he was eighteen years old, and not long afterward their musical association began. About this time the young man suffered some kind of nervous breakdown. He was gripped by a paralyzing melancholia, brought on, he said, by "mysticism, aggravated by cynical thoughts about the Deity." Lord Byron was partly responsible. Mussorgsky and Balakirev both read *Manfred*, with results not uncommon among young intellectuals of that time. "I was so wildly excited by the sufferings of that lofty spirit," wrote Mussorgsky, "that I cried out, 'How I wish I were Manfred!'" And then, "I became Manfred for a time, literally—my spirit slew my flesh."

These words have a familiar ring. They sound like Hector Berlioz and all the other furiously romantic young men who lived in Paris in the 1830s.

When he was twenty years old Mussorgsky quit the military service so that he could devote his life entirely to music. He was now completely under Balakirev's spell, but it would be an exaggeration to say that the music he produced at this time showed anything more than moderate talent. He had tried his hand at a symphony, a few piano sonatas which have since disappeared, a couple of scherzos, and a number of songs. These early songs were lost for many years. In 1909 a French critic finally found seventeen of them in manuscript form in Paris. Mussorgsky also tried to write incidental music to a Russian version of *Oedipus*, but soon gave it up. The same year (1860) he started *A Night on the Bare Mountain*, the orchestral fantasy on which he worked on and off for years. It was revised by Rimsky-Korsakov after his death.

When Czar Alexander II issued the famous ukase of 1861 which abolished serfdom, Mussorgsky was one of those whom it affected disastrously. The family fortune, like those of many other moderately wealthy landowners, shrank to nothing. The composer's mother had to give up a fine house in St. Petersburg and retire to the old estate in the country. In spite of his personal misfortune, Mussorgsky sympathized wholeheartedly with the serfs, but it was not long before he began to feel the pinch. In 1863, when he was twenty-four, he was forced to go to work.

He got an appointment as an official in the Engineering Department of the Ministry of Transport. For the next eighteen years he toiled away at a dreary clerical job, a small cog in the enormous Russian bureaucratic machine. He worked every day from eleven to four, at a miserable salary. In the late afternoons and on Sundays and holidays he tried to compose. What little hope he may have had of escaping from these toils vanished in 1865, when his mother died. The old estate at Karevo had to be sold; the Mussorgskys' last hold upon the land of their forebears was relinquished forever. The composer had another nervous collapse, and it appears that at this time his long struggle against alcohol became chronic.

It would be hard to recognize in this intense, highstrung, neurotic man much else than a dilettante in music. He might well have served as a model for a type portrayed repeatedly by the Russian novelists of that period (Turgenev could have drawn him perfectly): a young man who talked passionately of his plans and ideals but never seemed to realize any of them; who started much but finished little; who stymied himself and his accomplishment in a maze of introspective thinking; who suffered from the prevailing disease of the Russian aristocrats—laziness; and, above all, whose entire being was saturated by devastating pessimism.

The first clear indication that Mussorgsky's genius was great enough to force itself through these weaknesses of his character came when he was twenty-four years old. He read Flaubert's newly published novel *Salammbô*, and set about with zeal to make it into an opera. He fashioned his own libretto and worked for more than a year on the music before he finally abandoned it. Fragments of *Salammbô* survive, and they offer a peculiar aesthetic problem for music theorists. In later years Mussorgsky lifted certain sections of this score and used them in other works of a totally different character—notably in his operatic masterpiece *Boris Godunov*. The composer completely reworked and revised these sections; nevertheless it must remain one of the enigmas of the creative processes of an artist that his inspiration for the molten passions and the sultry gorgeousness of Flaubert's Carthage could also be made to serve him perfectly for the story of a regicide in seventeenth-century Russia.

V

After the abandonment of *Salammbô* there followed a period of two years in Mussorgsky's life (1866–68) during which he gave up attempts at large-scale works and devoted himself to writing songs. He produced about twenty, and some of them are among the finest and most original art songs produced by anyone after Franz Schubert.

It is clear that Mussorgsky's whole equipment, both musical and temperamental, was perfectly geared to the creation of songs, yet he seems never to have fully understood that fact at any time in his career. His musical life was strewn with the ruins of large enterprises that he abandoned at various stages of incompletion. He lacked both the organizing skill and the creative endurance that labor in the big forms requires. *Boris Godunov*, his operatic masterpiece, is the one exception, and even it presented problems in structure which the composer struggled for years to solve. The song, however, was a totally different matter. It did not require sustained effort; the formal problems were comparatively simple (he simplified them even further); and the opportunities for freedom of expression were large. Moreover, the composer's sympathies were overwhelmingly urged toward certain of the materials out of which songs through the ages have been made, i.e., the minds, the emotions, and the hearts of men.

The Mussorgsky songs are noteworthy first of all for their variety. They are so widely dissimilar that it is hard to group them or classify them except in those cases where the composer himself arranged them in cycles. In subject matter they were absolutely unique in their time. Only a small number could be termed "love songs" of the sentimental type; the accepted subjects for songs of the romantic era—romantic affection, flowers, the beauty of nature—are seldom touched upon. In his technical procedures Mussorgsky was also wholly unconventional. Few of these pieces fall into the accepted "song forms," the stencil patterns that had been used by song composers for generations. Mussorgsky permitted himself complete freedom in following the lead of the words. He began ignoring old-fashioned notions about keys; he modulated freely (often with daringly harsh progressions); if he preferred, he would end a song in a different key from that in which he began it. Some of his songs had no final cadences at all. He did not even hesitate to rewrite the words of the poems that he used, often changing the sense of the original poem to make it conform to his own conception of the subject. He wrote the words of a number of his finest songs himself.

One of the works which typifies his methods—and his genius—is the famous "*Savishna* [*The Love Song of the Idiot*]." This is the plaint of the village imbecile for love and sympathy. The unfortunate creature, despised and mistreated by everyone, has secretly adored one of the prettiest girls in the village. He finally tells her—bursts out with a breathless, agonized declaration of his grotesquely hopeless passion. Mussorgsky actually witnessed such an episode when he chanced to be watching an imbecilic beggar from the window of a farmhouse. He was terribly moved, and he set down to his own words a song that is without a peer in music. The piece is cast in $5/4$ time, an unusual rhythm, to suit the droning contour of the words. The melody itself is hardly more than a single motive, repeated over and over, measure after measure, with no rests between—as if the wretched man were pouring out his words in a stream before he can be interrupted or laughed at. The harmonic scheme is equally distorted—a bitter clashing of open fourths and fifths.

"*The Orphan Girl*" is a song of the same vintage, totally different in style. Mussorgsky used as his melody for this affecting piece an actual tune sung by wandering beggar groups in Russia. Again he wrote the words himself, bitter words that describe a child (one of the hundreds who once roamed the streets of St. Petersburg) begging for a few pennies, that she may not die of hunger or freeze to death. Mussorgsky's words are devoid of sentimentality, as his music is a model of poignancy and restraint.

Along with his unbounded sympathy for his fellow men, Mussorgsky had a biting sense of humor. He saw deep into people's hearts, and he told freely not alone of the pathos of what he observed but also of the irony and the absurdity. "*Gathering Mushrooms*" is the tale of a young peasant woman who picks mushrooms in the forests and speculates on the possibility of poisoning her husband with toadstools so the way will be clear for her fair-haired young lover. The magnificent "*Hopak*" has a similar theme: a young Cossack woman dances furiously to forget her life with an old husband whom she hates. Still other songs, like "*The Ragamuffin*," "*The Goat*," and "*The Seminarist*," range from buffoonery to sophisticated satire.

Practically all of Mussorgsky's songs are a test for the capabilities of the singer. Vocal beauty, musicianship, intelligence are not enough. Above all the artist must be able to feel deeply and to project his emotion with the skill of an actor. In certain of the songs he must actually play several parts. Mussorgsky himself was an actor and mimic of unusual ability, and in the performance of his own songs he was incomparable. Among groups of his friends and at musical soirees everyone waited eagerly for him to sing. A performance of one of his new songs was an event.

In spite of their power and originality these songs were slow in reaching the general public, and for years after the composer's death they were neglected. The reason is fairly evident. Few of them conformed to the accepted standards of the age in which they were written. They were not "romantic" at all. Mussorgsky's work was in fact one of the signs and portents that the great romantic movement in world art was at last beginning to break up. It was giving way to the next major stage—that of realism.

Realism began and had its farthest-reaching effects in the field of literature. Here the urge of the artist to describe men and their world exactly as they are was a logical revulsion from the dream world of romanticism. It marked the next turn in the evolutionary art cycle that has taken place many times in history. The beginnings of the realism of the present age can be traced as far back as Rousseau's *Confessions*, but they become clearly discernible with Stendhal. Thereafter the slow, steady conquest of romanticism by realism is evident in the literature of every country. In France the change begins with Stendhal and Balzac; it extends through Flaubert to a climax in the extreme and often shocking "naturalism" of Zola.

If French realism was the most influential, it was Russian realism that touched the greatest heights. Gogol and Turgenev, Dostoevski, Tolstoy, Chekhov, Gorky—a long line of Russian masters drew out all the amazing range of colors in the instrument of life, painting not merely with photographic exactitude but also with all the subtlety, the depth, the fantastic range of introspective thought that the Slavic mind could bring to the problem.

It would be an exaggeration to say that Mussorgsky began any such clearly defined movement in music as these men were part of in literature. But when he was a young man the ideas of the realists were in the air, and he could not help but be influenced by them, attuned as he was with an almost abnormal sympathy to all human life around him. Painfully he groped to find some way of expressing in music what realism stood for in literature and in painting.

He wrote to Ilya Repin, one of the foremost of Russia's realistic painters: "It is *the people* I want to depict; sleeping or waking, eating or drinking, I have them constantly in my mind's eye—again and again they rise before me, in all their reality, huge, unvarnished, with no tinsel trappings."

## VI

One of Mussorgsky's close friends was the composer Alexander Dargomyzhsky. This man was older than the Five (he had been an intimate of Glinka), but he too was an advocate of Russian nationalism in music. He was also fanatically devoted to the new idea of realistic truth in art. In the middle sixties he began work on an opera called *The Stone Guest*, based on Pushkin's version of the Don Juan legend. Dargomyzhsky expressed his credo as follows: "I want the note to be the direct representation of the word—I want truth and realism." To this end he tried to discard all the old operatic conventions of aria, recitative, chorus, etc., and to set his entire opera in what he called "melodic recitative." He tried to set every line of Pushkin's text, without any alteration, to melody that was controlled at every point by the precise inflections of the words.

Dargomyzhsky was a keen thinker, but his musical talent was limited. He did not have sufficient inspiration to float so dogmatic a cargo of theories, and *The Stone Guest* (completed and orchestrated after his death by Cui and Rimsky-Korsakov) was a failure. Nevertheless, the work and its composer had a strong effect upon the Five, especially Mussorgsky, whose songs of this period are often miniature examples of Dargomyzhsky's theory. In 1868, Mussorgsky began a comic opera based on Gogol's *The Marriage*. He tried to follow faithfully Dargomyzhsky's doctrine of "melodic recitative" and realistic truth; he tried, too, to use Gogol's lines without alteration. After finishing the first act, he dropped the work entirely. This time it was not alone that he had wearied of his task. A new project had come up in the meantime which suddenly pushed everything else out of his mind. This was the idea for an opera based on Pushkin's historical drama, *Boris Godunov*.

The story of what happened to Mussorgsky's great opera, *Boris Godunov*, its original creation and its fate thereafter, is a strange tale indeed. Mussorgsky took up the project in the fall of 1868. He worked as he had never worked before, with furious intensity and uninterrupted zeal. Within two years he had completed the entire opera, including the orchestration. For him this was an especial triumph. It was the fifth opera he had attempted, the first to be finished. In jubilation he submitted it to the directors of the Imperial Theater in St. Petersburg.

The story of this opera followed Pushkin and was concerned with the culminating episodes in the life of Boris Godunov, the regent who ruled Russia in the turbulent days immediately after the reign of Ivan the Terrible. Boris was a man of strength and ability; but he had secretly ordered the murder of the six-year-old Czarevitch Dmitri, who stood between him and the throne.

Mussorgsky's first act centers upon the coronation of Boris, whose ambitions now seem realized. The Czar, however, is visibly oppressed by morbid thoughts of his crime. A pretender appears in the person of a renegade monk named Gregory, who claims to be Dmitri grown to manhood. He is supported by Poles and Cossacks who march on Moscow. Meanwhile the starving Russian peasants are driven to revolt by their sufferings. Boris no longer has the strength to face his adversaries; he is almost insane with remorse. He dies, after a pathetic admonition to his son to rule with wisdom.

After some deliberation, the authorities of the Imperial Theater rejected Mussorgsky's opera. They were repelled by the strangeness of the work, its grim character, its unconventional musical style, and its lack of an important woman's part. Mussorgsky had not felt the need for anything resembling love interest. The interest in his piece centered first around the character of Boris and the Czar's mental struggle against the thought of the blood that is on his soul; and second around the Russian peasants, whose hardships and bitter destiny are the backdrop against which the entire drama is played.

Mussorgsky was disappointed but not crushed. He set about revising his opera, and in 1872 he finished his second version. This, after considerable opposition, was finally produced, on January 24, 1874.

This second version represented a considerable alteration from the first. The composer shifted the order of several of his scenes, left out others completely, and recast others; he added several songs and episodes to relieve the prevailing gloominess of mood; most important of all he added the two so-called "Polish scenes," in which the character of a Polish princess (Marina) was brought in as the beloved of Gregory. This second version of *Boris* was the only one ever performed during Mussorgsky's lifetime. Its *première* at the Marinsky Theater in St. Petersburg enjoyed great success. There were the usual howls from the conservative critics and the pedants, but the public seemed to like it. Up to the time of the composer's death in 1881 it had something like fifteen performances. Then for reasons that are not entirely clear it was withdrawn for a time.

In 1896, when Mussorgsky had been dead fifteen years, Rimsky-Korsakov revived the work. Because he believed that his friend's music was a masterpiece marred by amateurish crudities, he made a sweeping revision of the entire score. He left out several scenes, he altered and amplified others radically; he shifted the keys, he changed many of Mussorgsky's harmonies, until hardly a measure had been left untouched. Finally, he reorchestrated the entire score. Rimsky-Korsakov believed that with his own masterly technical skill he was making his dead friend's work both brilliantly playable and musically above reproach. His version was in fact a magnificent success. In 1908 he made another version, in which he restored some of the cuts he had made in his first. This second Rimsky-Korsakov version was the one that became known in opera houses all over the world, and in which Chaliapin sang with unforgettable mastery.

Meanwhile, however, there had been more than faint rumblings of doubt. Rimsky-Korsakov was assailed by certain critics who knew the extent of his ministrations and suspected that he had entirely misconstrued Mussorgsky's intentions; but it was not until 1928 that the entire affair suddenly erupted like a small volcano. In that year the Soviet Government published a definitive edition of Mussorgsky's original score (his first and second versions together) based on the composer's manuscripts, which had lain for years in the Russian archives. On February 16, 1928, at the theater where his altered version had first been played in 1874, there was given a performance of his *original* score, the rejected version, for the first time on any stage.

There is no need to discuss here the relative merits of the two Mussorgsky versions, except to say that the first is doubtless the one of greater power and originality, and that the Polish scenes especially weaken the second. But as regards the Rimsky-Korsakov versions there can no longer be any doubt whatever. Even admitting his sincerity and the fact that his versions brought luster to Mussorgsky's name for many years, it can now be seen that Rimsky-Korsakov was guilty of malpractice. He simply had no conception of the fact that his friend was writing far ahead of his time. He remembered only that Mussorgsky had little technical training in music, whereas he (Rimsky-Korsakov) was a master of every branch of technique.

The changes that Rimsky-Korsakov made are worth noting for a more important reason than simple justice; in case after case they point to acorns of revolutionary procedure by Mussorgsky which grew in our time into oaks of modernism. For example, Rimsky-Korsakov always hated what he called Mussorgsky's "barbarous" harmonic progressions; so in *Boris* he smoothed them out wherever he could. Today, as used to rough progressions and dissonances as to dominant sevenths, we find Mussorgsky's chords superb in their dramatic effectiveness. His harmonic schemes are often hard, virile, grim—and marvelously expressive; while under Rimsky-Korsakov's hand they are mellowed into clichés. Mussorgsky's doubling is also hard and strong; Rimsky-Korsakov's is conventional and soft. Much of Mussorgsky's original score is without key signature; Rimsky-Korsakov recasts long sections of his into specific keys. This is an aid to sight reading, but it also demonstrates the difference in the thinking of the two men. Rimsky-Korsakov's procedure is affected by what he feels is the prevailing key, and he often makes unnecessary harmonic changes to keep the music consistent with the key he has chosen. Mussorgsky, on the other hand, is anticipating modern procedure in thinking outside key boundaries. His score is harder to read, but his mind is unfettered, and his harmony as a result gains greater freedom and boldness. Mussorgsky uses many changes of time signature, including odd rhythms like 5/4 alternating with 3/4. Wherever he can Rimsky-Korsakov irons them out to make them easier to read and to conduct, sometimes distorting the rhythmic pulse in doing so. Again, it was Mussorgsky who was writing toward the future.

It is clear that Rimsky-Korsakov knew Mussorgsky too well. Before the former's marriage the two men had lived together, and there were few weaknesses of Mussorgsky's mind and character that Rimsky-Korsakov was not aware of. At times in his *Boris* revisions he hardly gives his friend credit for common sense.

If the history of this opera is complex and perplexing, the conclusion to be drawn from it is a simple one: to have survived such a mauling the piece must have been blessed at the start with vitality of a wholly exceptional kind. No amount of retouching could destroy the superb inner quality of the music. *Boris Godunov* has in fact a character unique among works for the lyric stage. It was the first Russian opera in which the chorus played a part as important as the principals themselves. As an indication of his purpose Mussorgsky gave his second version the subtitle: "Music Folk Drama." He portrayed the Russian peasants with the humanitarian sympathies of a Tolstoy and the honesty of a Zola. These people surge through the somber drama, a ragged, hollow-eyed, desperate mob, goaded by their sufferings to revengeful cruelties. They are as far removed from the operatic chorus of Meyerbeer or Verdi or Wagner as McTeague is remote from Dorian Grey.

Only a great and compassionate heart could have struck so true and so deep a note as Mussorgsky did in these superb scenes. At times he used actual Russian folk tunes, but more frequently it is his own subtle imitations of that idiom which take hold of the listener with gripping force. The crown of his life's effort is the scene before the Church of St. Basil, in which an imbecilic boy, part of a starving crowd that begs Boris for bread, stands weeping in the snow, uttering a prophecy of the gloom of night that is to descend upon Russia.

Second only to the chorus is the character of Boris itself. The similarity between this masterful creation and that of Macbeth has often been remarked. Both are men of strength, driven to murder by an overwhelming ambition. Both pay for their crimes with the slow destruction of their minds and souls. It is sufficient praise for Mussorgsky's art to say that his handling of Boris is Shakespearean in its vividness and power.

The entire score of *Boris Godunov* burns with inspiration. In its greater moments it would be hard to find music less hackneyed; while the compression of its musical ideas is superb. Shakespeare could paint a scene or sum up a man's character in a single line; Mussorgsky does the same with a few measures, sometimes a few notes. Barring the Polish scenes, there is also a wonderful cohesion of style. Melodies, harmonies, rhythms all contribute to a mood that is unmistakably Russian in its prevailing melancholy and to a kind of somber gorgeousness that is like the beauty of old bronze.

### VII

Mussorgsky was thirty-five when *Boris Godunov* was first performed. Thereafter his life and character went slowly to pieces, until a premature death overtook him seven years later. The reasons for this tragic loss to music are not entirely clear, for we are still ignorant of many of the details of the composer's private life. We know many reasons why he suffered intensely—the disappointments connected with his work, his struggles against poverty and against alcohol, his loneliness—but there still seems to be something lacking in our knowledge to explain the depths of wretchedness to which he sank.

Almost nothing is known of his relations with women. Mussorgsky never married. He had a horror of the idea, for he once said, "When you read in the papers that I have put a bullet through my head or hanged myself, you may be certain that I was married the day before." In his youth he is supposed to have loved a young girl who died; and in later years he was devoted to the sister of a friend who sang many of his songs. But this latter affection seems to have been entirely platonic. If there was anything like romantic love in his later life the composer kept it to himself.

After the death of his mother Mussorgsky never again enjoyed the comforts of a home. He lived around with his relatives and his friends—a lonely, unsettled existence that left him without the roots of security. For two years he shared a small apartment with Rimsky-Korsakov, until the latter's marriage. Rimsky-Korsakov's memoirs describe bluntly the change that came over his friend after the completion of *Boris Godunov*—"a certain mysteriousness, even haughtiness, if you like, became apparent. His self-conceit grew enormously, and his obscure, involved manner of expressing himself (which had been characteristic even before) now increased enormously." He began the habit of sitting for hours in restaurants, consuming quantities of cognac.

Soon after the completion of *Boris Godunov*, Mussorgsky tackled the biggest project of his life, the opera *Khovanshchina*. The problems that this work present to the student of Mussorgsky's art are even greater and more complex than those concerned with *Boris*.

The story of *Khovanshchina* is also derived from Russian history—the struggle between two political and social factions at the end of the seventeenth century. It concerns the so-called Old Believers, religious fanatics who had set their teeth against the group who were trying to introduce Western ideas. Mussorgsky wrote his own libretto. He devoted himself passionately to the task, spending hours at research into this corner of Russian history. At first the composition of the music progressed rapidly, and the composer's enthusiasm was boundless; but gradually the idea began to get away from him. Never having a grasp of large-scale organization, he began to lose all sense of the proportions that his opera should take. He went on composing scene after scene, until the whole project became a morass in which he floundered around helplessly. For long stretches of time he stopped work on it completely while he tried his hand at other ideas. One of these was a comic opera, *The Fair at Sorochinsk*, based on a story by Gogol. After sketching out a large portion of this work the composer again lost interest and dropped it entirely. The realization that he now had two more large works in an unfinished state must have weighed upon his mind.

*Khovanshchina* was never finished. When Mussorgsky died in 1881 and Rimsky-Korsakov took over his manuscripts this opera was found in an unhappy state. Parts of it were complete, but others existed only as rough sketches; whole sections that the composer had played at the piano for his friends never had been written down at all; almost none of it was orchestrated, and the last scene was missing entirely. There was enough material for two operas instead of one. Rimsky-Korsakov devoted himself to the task of whipping this amorphous mass of music into a playable opera. He made many cuts in the score, piecing together what was left; he composed a final scene, and he orchestrated the entire work. His version was first performed in 1886, by an amateur company in St. Petersburg, after the Imperial Theater had turned it down. Thereafter the opera remained in oblivion until 1911, when the Imperial Theater revived it in a splendid production with Chaliapin in one of the leading roles. Since then it has enjoyed success in Russia, but elsewhere has never approached the popularity of *Boris Godunov*.

VIII

In 1873, while the ideas for *Khovanshchina* were first agitating his mind, Mussorgsky lost one of his dearest friends, a young architect named Victor Hartmann, who died at the age of thirty-nine. The composer was deeply moved. "Why should a dog, a horse, a rat, live on," he cried, "and creatures like Hartmann must die?" Later, when a posthumous exhibition of his friend's pictures and water colors was held in St. Petersburg, Mussorgsky paid tribute by composing a set of piano pieces that he called *Pictures at an Exhibition*.

Like so many of his works, this one took years to reach the public; and it finally did so in a form that the composer did not originally plan. Mussorgsky finished his *Pictures* in 1874, but the piece was not published until five years after his death. For years after that it was ignored by concert pianists. It was practically forgotten in 1923, when Maurice Ravel transcribed it for orchestra at the suggestion of Serge Koussevitzky. Its success in that form was instantaneous and sweeping; today *Pictures at an Exhibition* is in the repertoire of every symphony orchestra and is the most popular of all Mussorgsky's works.

Mussorgsky's piece begins with a charming introduction called *Promenade*, in which he represents himself as strolling leisurely through the gallery examining the various canvases. There are ten pictures in all, interspersed with recurrences of the *Promenade* theme, and they are titled: I. *A Gnome*; II. *An Ancient Castle*; III. *Tuileries, Children Quarreling at Play*; IV. *Bydlo, a Polish Wagon*; V. *Ballet of Chickens in Their Shells*; VI. *Samuel Goldenberg and Schmuyle, Two Polish Jews*; VII. *The Marketplace at Limoges*; VIII. *Catacombs*; IX. *Baba Yaga, the Hut on Fowl's Legs*; X. *The Great Gate at Kiev*.

It is obvious that in this work Mussorgsky would not have to face the problem that was so often his nemesis—that of extended form. The structure is simplicity itself, being merely a group of ten small pieces bound together by the theme of the *Promenade*. The composer might have been writing ten songs, except that his ideas came from pictures instead of the words of a poem. The pieces are not equal in merit, but the best of them are amazingly compact, displaying to perfection Mussorgsky's genius for painting a scene, describing a character, or expressing an emotion with the simplest means. Moreover, these pieces meet the test by which the program music of that time so often failed: they are self-sufficient. Even though they are wonderfully vivid and expressive when the listener is conscious of the idea in the background, that idea is not wholly necessary to their enjoyment. They have a fascination of their own even as music in the abstract.

Ravel's orchestral version of these *Pictures* is so brilliant that it makes Mussorgsky's original for piano seem almost drab by comparison. Nevertheless, the original is full of remarkable things that testify to the composer's prowess as a pianist and his understanding of the instrument. On the whole the work is eminently playable, while making use of few of the stock pianistic clichés or the standard tricks of showmanship. There are some remarkable inventions in pure sonority, many of them gained by Mussorgsky's unconventional doubling of his notes, especially those in the bass. A section like *Catacombs*, only thirty measures long, paints its scene simply but subtly, by means of a series of unconventional chordal progressions highlighted by cleverly contrasted dynamics. It must make any pianist deeply regretful that so boldly imaginative a composer left but a single large work for this instrument.

The same year that produced *Pictures at an Exhibition* also marked Mussorgsky's return to song. After Rimsky-Korsakov's marriage the composer had taken lodgings with a young poet, Count Golenishchev-Kutusov. The Count was twenty-four years old and as hard up as Mussorgsky, but his poetic gifts were exceptional. The composer set a number of his verses to music, and the result was an achievement in Russian song which has never been surpassed.

The first fruit of this association was the great cycle of six songs called "*Sunless*," written in 1874. These pieces are strange creations for a man of thirty-five and another of twenty-four, for they are full of the melancholia that suggests the close and not the noon of life. All six are mood pieces, usually expressing a pang of sadness at the thought of some vanished happiness. The first song (variously translated as "*In My Attic*," "*Within Four Walls*," and "*Interior*") sets the mood of what is to come: all is silence and loneliness in the little room; nothing is left for the poet but his brooding over moments of lost rapture, little but doubt and sorrow and suffering. The following five songs are called (again there are wide variations in translation) *"Thine Eyes in the Crowd," "Retrospect," "Resignation," "Elegy,"* and *"On the River."* In all of them there is the recurring theme of lost happiness, of the depressed mind and the defeated spirit.

There is little doubt that Mussorgsky found in his young friend's verses a mirror for his own tormented soul. The songs that he produced are as remarkable for their restraint as for the completeness with which they express a subtle poetic thought. From the technical viewpoint they exhibit a definite change in Mussorgsky's style. The melodies are more lyrical than had been his custom, and the composer has not limited himself to Dargomyzhsky's drastic theory of music rigidly controlled by the word. At times there is a total absence of nationalist flavor. But the hand of Mussorgsky himself is evident in almost every measure —in the amazingly bold and unconventional melodic lines, in the use of harmonies that must have shocked his contemporaries, and in the accompaniment material that is either richly ornate or sparse and empty to suit the composer's unrivaled sense of dramatic effect.

The cycle *"Songs and Dances of Death"* was another collaboration with Count Golenishchev-Kutusov. It consists of four songs: *"Trepak"* (or *"Death and the Peasant"*), *"Cradle Song of Death," "Death's Serenade,"* and *"Death, the Commander."* In the first song a drunken peasant, lost in the snow, dances a *trepak* until he falls exhausted, ready for Death. The second is a dialogue between Death and a mother who watches over the cradle of her dying child. The third is the serenade of Death under the window of a sick young girl. The last song depicts a battlefield covered with bodies. Death rides forth in the moonlight to take command—Death, the real conqueror, bids the dead men march in review before him. Mussorgsky had various other ideas for songs that he intended to include in this cycle, but only these four were ever finished.

The daring subject matter alone would set these *"Songs and Dances of Death"* apart, but it is the boldness of the composer's treatment that has made them overpoweringly great. Not since Schubert had so compressed a form as the song held music of such emotional power. *"Cradle Song* of Death" is like a scene from a music drama—infinitely pathetic, and yet by the composer's wonderful art expressed in hardly more than fifty measures of music. "*Death, the Commander*" is remindful of Schubert's "*Gruppe aus dem Tartarus*," for it is a scene of horror raised to the point of fantastic grandeur.

One other of Mussorgsky's songs belongs rightfully with these—"*After the Battle*," written in 1874 to words by the young Count. Again the scene is a battlefield on which lies a corpse. The dead man is forgotten by his victorious comrades; his torn body is the prey of vultures. Far away at home his wife sings a lullaby to their child, promising the father's safe return; but he lies alone.

The original inspiration for this song was a painting by Vereshchagin, who was famous for his realistic battle pictures. This particular scene of a corpse on a battlefield was so harrowing that it shocked Czar Alexander II. The picture disappeared, and for a time it was falsely rumored that Vereshchagin had destroyed it because of the Czar's displeasure. At first Mussorgsky was not permitted to publish his song; it did not appear until after his death. "*After the Battle*" is one of the most powerful preachments against war ever set to music, a piece of black realism that is remindful of Goya's ghastly scenes of war-torn Spain.

IX

The last of Mussorgsky's death songs was written in 1877. With the exception of the famous satire "*The Song of the Flea*" from Goethe's *Faust*, written in 1879, he had little more of value to say. The stream of his inspiration had been reduced to the merest trickle. Friends who had known him in the days of his youth were shocked by his wasted appearance. The once-dapper young army officer with the elegant manners and the immaculate uniforms was now a drunkard, going about in old clothes and actually threatened by starvation. Shame and pride kept him to himself. The other members of the Five were now great and famous; he alone seemed to have retrogressed. In the summer of 1879 a singer named Mme. Leonova asked him to tour with her as accompanist through the south of Russia. They went as far as the Crimea, and Mussorgsky seemed to enjoy the respite. Once back in St. Petersburg, he had not long to wait. Early in 1881 he collapsed and was taken to a hospital. Rimsky-Korsakov said that he had delirium tremens.

At first he rallied and many old friends came to see him. Repin came and painted his portrait. The picture is Mussorgsky as he looked barely two weeks before he died, and it is a masterpiece in its cruel realism. The hair and beard are uncombed, disheveled; the nose is discolored, the eyes hollow and staring. The composer wears a dressing gown that is too big for his shrunken frame. It belonged to his friend Cui, who sent it to the hospital. Mussorgsky looks like a man of sixty, but he died in his forty-second year—on March 28, 1881.

# Tchaikovsky
## 1840—93

### I

To Tchaikovsky must go the palm: he remains the most famous and the most popular of all Russian composers. That fact alone is a distinction not easy to ignore, especially in view of the vicissitudes through which this composer's music has passed since his death. There has been no one in music quite like him, and certainly there has been no music with so remarkable a history of fortune and misfortune.

He remains for millions the arch-Russian nationalist, even though during his lifetime his work was disdained by the Five and their followers as too watery, an emulsion of Russian and western European styles. The rest of the world took him up with avidity, until in the early decades of the present century the popularity of his music had reached the stage of a public craze. The institution of the all-Tchaikovsky program kept many a symphony orchestra out of the red, and many a conductor enjoyed an easy ride to fame on this composer's last three symphonies, his concertos, and his overtures.

Tchaikovsky, it is now quite evident, belonged among the most extreme manifestations of romanticism in music, and when that entire movement threatened to collapse in the years following World War I it seemed that his work might be buried under the ruins. Critics who had long preached against his excesses and his weaknesses doubled their efforts, until it became a rare thing for sophisticates to say a good word for Tchaikovsky. There arose a new generation of modernist composers to whom sentiment and romance were so much mildew on an age best forgotten, and for them the once-omnipotent Russian was an object fit only for ridicule. It seemed for a time that nothing was left to do for Tchaikovsky's music but to prepare the mortuary inscriptions.

Few of his detractors had reckoned with either the vitality of the man's music or the extent of the public's affection for the remnants of romanticism itself. Romanticism may be dying, but it is not yet dead. Today the people have returned to Tchaikovsky; their regard for him is a sobered and more temperate one, it is true, but with all his faults they love him still.

The man who created this remarkable and controversial music was one of the strangest characters in the history of music. His entire life was governed, and in part ruined, by an inner tragedy which he hid frantically from the world during his lifetime, but which found its way inevitably into his work. For many years the general public remained mystified and not a little fascinated by the spectacle of this man's secret sorrow, which gnawed at his soul and caused him to break out again and again in his music with wild sobbing and wringing of the hands. Part of the early popularity of Tchaikovsky's music was owing to this very fact—that he was the first composer to make outstanding use of the moods of melancholy, lamentation, and deep despair.

Tchaikovsky was born on May 7, 1840, in a town in the province of Viatka, which lies in the central part of Russia just west of the Ural Mountains. His father was working in that region as a mining engineer, but later the family moved to St. Petersburg. The Tchaikovskys were fairly well to do; the father made and lost several moderate fortunes. Peter Ilich was one of six children—a daughter and five sons, two of whom were twins. The famous son was at first headed for a career in mining engineering, but later his father decided that he should study law. Like

Robert Schumann, he loathed jurisprudence, but when he was nineteen he finished his course and took a government job in the Ministry of Justice. Meanwhile he had been trying his hand at music. He went so far as to take private lessons in harmony, but there is no evidence that he showed any special talent at that time.

In 1862 there occurred in St. Petersburg a musical event of prime importance—the opening of the Conservatory of Music, the first of its kind in Russia. It was under the leadership of the famous Russian pianist and composer, Anton Rubinstein. Time has not dealt kindly with this once-leonine figure who inherited the throne of Franz Liszt. We remember only his towering reputation as a pianist; his vast catalogue of compositions is now dust-choked and silent.

Rubinstein was born in Russia, but his career as pianist had taken him all over Europe. His basic musical concepts, like his training, were not Russian but German. Thus the St. Petersburg Conservatory reflected in its curriculum a reliance on the German type of teaching. For this reason the Five and their followers would have none of Rubinstein and his works. To them the Conservatory—any conservatory—was a sink of pedantry. This fact had an important bearing on at least one Russian who later became famous—Peter Ilich Tchaikovsky, who entered the Conservatory as one of its first pupils. A few years later, when he made the acquaintance of the famous Five, he was admired personally, but his scholastic training put his work outside the pale. The cleavage that existed between him and the Five had its inception at this point, and it widened as the years went on.

Anton Rubinstein had a younger brother, Nicholas, who was also a musician of immense talent and energy, although overshadowed by the more grandiose Anton. In 1866, Nicholas founded in Moscow a conservatory similar to his brother's in St. Petersburg. On the recommendation of Anton he offered one of the teaching jobs to Tchaikovsky, then one of the most talented students at the northern school. The young man had given up his government job and was trying to make a living by giving private music lessons.

Tchaikovsky took up his post in Moscow early in 1866. The next decade of his life was devoted to teaching and to the production of a long list of musical works, most of which are now regarded as unimportant and merely preparatory to the main creative efforts of his career. It was a difficult period in the young composer's life. He went through a long struggle in reaching an assured musical maturity, and he had to contend with periods of deep discouragement.

Tchaikovsky suffered from an abnormal shyness. In spite of a personal manner of exceptional charm he found it difficult to meet people; crowds, and especially audiences, filled him with terror. At his first attempt to conduct a group of his own compositions in public he was so unnerved that he did not conduct again for twenty years. He was also painfully sensitive to criticism. A bluntly expressed opinion about his works by someone like the Rubinsteins would shrivel him. At times he was self-critical in the extreme. He destroyed the scores of two of his early operas, *The Voyevoda* and *Undine*; and across one of his works he once wrote, "Dreadful muck."

Industry and methodical habits of work were assets heavily in his favor. Early in his career he learned the value of constant and unbroken effort, and for long periods of time he composed every day without fail. He once remarked, "I have patience and have trained myself not to surrender to inertia"—this in contrast to certain members of the Five who, he said, suffering from "lack of self-confidence and self-control, lay their work aside at the smallest difficulty." Soon he achieved great facility, and this in one respect was his undoing. Tchaikovsky composed too much and too easily for his own good. Had he taken more time, had he imposed upon himself even more rigid standards of self-criticism, the body of his work would not be flawed as it is—a splendid fabric marred with the gaping holes of mediocrity.

## II

One of the first products of the composer's early years in Moscow was his first symphony. This was followed in 1873 by a second, and in 1875 by a third. The First Symphony caused its composer agonies of creative labor. He suffered a nervous breakdown and spells of prolonged insomnia. The work bore a descriptive title, "Winter Dreams," and in the back of the composer's mind there was a vague poetic scene that had to do with winter journeys and cloud-hung landscapes. The presence of this descriptive program is a fact worth noting, for it has an important bearing on the big works that were to come. It gives an important clue to Tchaikovsky's creative processes.

The first work in which the composer definitely hit his stride came when he was twenty-nine years old. It was the Overture-Fantasy *Romeo and Juliet*—one of the finest works in his entire catalogue. For the idea of this piece and much of its general form the composer was indebted to Mili Balakirev. After a brief and stormy period as successor to Anton Rubinstein as head of the St. Petersburg Conservatory, Balakirev had moved in a huff to Moscow. There he became interested in Tchaikovsky. At his suggestion the latter undertook the fantasy on Shakespeare's tragedy, and according to his habit Balakirev took complete charge of the younger man's inspirational effort. He went into elaborate detail about the plan of the work, outlined the main themes, and even suggested the keys of the various sections. Tchaikovsky took full advantage of his friend's counsel. He also revised the piece twice himself, in 1870 and again in 1881, so that the work as we now know it is one of the most carefully wrought of all this composer's scores.

*Romeo and Juliet* is a score of passionate intensity, rich in melody, full of gorgeous harmonies, and making full use of the most glamorous orchestral sound. In spite of his personal shyness, there was never anything reticent about Tchaikovsky the composer; when an idea seized him he flung his inspiration upon the musical canvas with a wild abandon. His colors are all purple and gold and crimson, the shadows are deep and dramatic, the highlights brilliant. In *Romeo and Juliet* we come upon one of the first of the famous melodies that have since sung their way around the world—the dark, richly ornate theme for English horn and muted violas. It is followed by another even finer—a theme of exquisite tenderness, scarcely breathed by the muted strings. The entire section is worthy of the scene it evokes; it suits the incomparable words:

> JULIET:    Wilt thou be gone? it is not yet near day:
> It was the nightingale, and not the lark,
> That pierced the fearful hollow of thine ear;
> Nightly she sings on yon pomegranate-tree;
> Believe me, love, it was the nightingale.

> ROMEO:    It was the lark, the herald of the morn,
> No nightingale: look, love, what envious streaks
> Do lace the severing clouds in yonder east:
> Night's candles are burnt out, and jocund day
> Stands tiptoe on the misty mountain tops.
> I must be gone and live, or stay and die.

### III

Five years elapsed before Tchaikovsky produced another large-scale work of similar caliber. Meanwhile he was hard at work—at several operas, various short piano pieces and songs, two string quartets, his second symphony—and though many of these were adding to his reputation in Russia and abroad, the yield in comparison with his later efforts was not a rich one. In the first string quartet (D major, Op. 11) another famous melody was born. Tchaikovsky made use of a folk tune that he heard from the lips of a carpenter working in his house. It appears in the movement marked Andante cantabile, which became one of his most successful advertisements as a composer of lush melodies, richly harmonized, gilded with sentiment and melancholy. It has been played until it is now unbearable to many listeners. This is unfortunate, for despite its sentimentality it has the essential core of real melodic beauty. When all is said and done Tchaikovsky's skill as a melodist was one at which few have any right to sneer. Igor Stravinsky made that point clear in praising his predecessor's work, while admitting the wide inequality of many of his themes: "The point is that he was a creator of *melody*, an extremely rare and precious gift."

Tchaikovsky was thirty-four years old when he composed his Piano Concerto in B flat minor, Op. 23. This piece, now a fixed and brilliant star in every virtuoso pianist's firmament, had an inauspicious beginning. Tchaikovsky was not himself a piano virtuoso, and after completing the work he felt the need of expert advice on certain of its problems in piano technique. Naturally he sought the counsel of his friend and benefactor, Nicholas Rubinstein, who was one of the first pianists of Europe. Tchaikovsky played the work for Rubinstein on Christmas Eve, 1874 —an occasion that he never forgot. Rubinstein listened in silence, and at the end he delivered himself of a blast that froze his shy friend's very marrow. "It appeared," wrote Tchaikovsky, "that my concerto is worthless, impossible to play, the themes have been used before, are clumsy and awkward beyond possibility of correction; as a composition it is poor. I stole this from here and that from there; there are only two or three pages that can be salvaged, and the rest must be thrown away or changed completely!" It is a wonder that the shocked, hypersensitive composer did not destroy either his score or himself on the spot. Instead, he was "speechless with amazement and fury." He announced that he would not change a single note. He did, however, make extensive revisions some years later.

Whether Rubinstein's error in judgment was prompted by jealousy or an unaccountable obtuseness is hard to say. At any rate he talked himself out of a signal honor. He might have given the first public performance of what came to be the most sensational of all piano concertos. Tchaikovsky passed the work over to Hans von Bülow, who took it with him on a tour of America. Bülow first played it publicly in Boston, on October 25, 1875. The audience was so wild with enthusiasm that he had to repeat the entire finale.

The style of Tchaikovsky's famous concerto is derived, chiefly, from the piano concertos of Franz Liszt. The soloist performs prodigies of dexterity and strength; at times the piano and the orchestra are antagonists in a roaring war, and on the next page they are lovers sighing out their hearts in close embrace. The whole piece is dramatically constructed to shock an audience to attention by a magnificently imposing opening and to keep them on an emotional edge to the last note of a frantic finale. The popularity of this concerto has been enormous, and even today after three quarters of a century and more of battle it retains its vitality to an astonishing degree.

Anyone who heard the B flat minor Piano Concerto without knowing anything about the composer would in all likelihood gain a totally erroneous impression of his personal character. Tchaikovsky's musical style is one of such passionate intensity, vehemence, and at times even unrestrained violence that it would be natural to expect him to be one of the most masculine of individuals. The impression would be far afield from the truth. Tchaikovsky was not merely shy and gentle to an abnormal degree; he was definitely a homosexual. That was his terrible secret. After having been hushed up for many years, it is today a secret no longer, but is generally acknowledged and understood. The composer's abnormality would be of little importance in a discussion of his creative history, except that his own attitude toward it and his morbid fear of its discovery colored his whole life, and so his art.

Tchaikovsky lived in an age when an abnormality of this type had to be studied even by medical scientists with something like furtiveness. It could never be mentioned, much less discussed, in polite society. It was observed, of course, by people of sophistication, in circles like those in which the composer moved; but they generally regarded it either as a horror or a joke. Tchaikovsky's case was common gossip among many of his friends in Moscow. He lived in mortal terror that it would spread with his musical fame and become a public scandal. The only person to whom he could go for consolation was his younger brother Modest, who later became his biographer. Modest was also a homosexual, and the two brothers made cryptic references in their correspondence to the sword that hung over their heads.

By a stroke of irony it happened that, in the life of this man to whom women meant nothing, two women nevertheless played the dominant roles. One was a wealthy widow, Nadejda von Meck; the other was a young woman whom the composer made the ghastly mistake of marrying. Tchaikovsky's relations with these two women were among the strangest that might befall any man, normal or otherwise.

Nadejda von Meck was the widow of an engineer famous in the history of Russian railroad building. When he died, he left her an enormous fortune, which included a mansion in Moscow, a huge country estate, and two railroads. At this time Mme. von Meck was in her middle forties. She was a born autocrat, and after her husband's death she lived the life of a semi-recluse in her palatial Moscow home. Two interests ruled her life: her children (she had borne no less than twelve) and music. She was a generous patron of the Conservatory, and one of the few callers who were welcome at her home was Nicholas Rubinstein. Through him she became interested in the music of Tchaikovsky. Very soon this interest became a burning passion, and then Mme. von Meck and the composer began a correspondence. They wrote to each other constantly, at times almost daily, for fourteen years—from 1876 to 1890. In all that time they never once met.

Part of this correspondence was only recently published in English. It appeared in the book *Beloved Friend*, by Catherine Drinker Bowen and Barbara von Meck. The latter is the widow of Mme. von Meck's favorite grandson, who had possession of the correspondence until the Revolution of 1917, when it was seized with the rest of the Meck property. Much of it appeared for the first time in 1935, when it was published by the Soviet Government.

Tchaikovsky's letters to his "Beloved Friend" are an intimate picture of the man's character—in all except one detail. The specter of his abnormality is never once hinted at, and she seems never to have been aware of it; but otherwise he opened his heart and soul to her. His joys and his sorrows, his terrible despairs (both real and imaginary), the inmost secrets of his creative life in music, are all spread out in these hundreds of letters. Within a short time Mme. von Meck became Tchaikovsky's patron as well as his confidante. For years she provided him with a regular income; she sent him on trips abroad; she opened her purse with extra gifts whenever the composer asked for help. In short, she became the main prop of his life. He became so dependent upon her generosity and her sympathy that he suffered agonies if a week went by without word from her.

About Mme. von Meck's adoration of Tchaikovsky's music there was something almost pathological. Like many women of iron will, she was subject to odd and conflicting impulses. Music moved her deeply; Tchaikovsky's music left her devastated. And yet it was she who imposed the condition that they should never meet. The reason for this was never made entirely clear, but it seems unlikely that she feared Tchaikovsky the man would destroy her illusions about his music. She knew from his letters that he was a person of innate culture and unusual intelligence; everyone who ever met him remarked about that and about his personal charm and magnetism. It seems more likely that Mme. von Meck feared herself. She who had borne twelve children was left with an antipathy to the whole institution of marriage. She once wrote to Tchaikovsky the curious commentary: "It is a pity that one cannot cultivate human beings artificially, like fishes; people would not then need to marry, and it would be a great relief." Nevertheless, she had to devise an outlet for her passions and her longings. She achieved it by means of this strange love affair, which was both vicarious and remote.

There is little doubt that to the composer the arrangement was completely satisfactory. He must have realized that from this wealthy widow's adoration of his music to adoration of him as a man would have been an all too easy step. Then his situation would have been dreadful indeed.

Tchaikovsky knew precisely how dreadful, because another woman had enticed him into that very thing.

In the spring of 1877 a young woman named Antonina Miliukova, whom he had met casually, began to write to him. She indicated that she was madly in love with him and wanted to marry him. Tchaikovsky did not then realize that the woman was mentally deranged and that she imagined all men were in love with her. The composer finally agreed to marry her. He afterward explained this incomprehensible action by saying that she would otherwise have killed herself. Tchaikovsky also had a selfish motive that he did not divulge. In his dread that his own abnormality would become publicly known, he imagined that a marriage would somehow remove all source of suspicion. Once before he had attempted the same subterfuge and failed. When he was twenty-eight he had met a glamorous opera singer, Désirée Artôt. He was captivated by her beauty and her accomplishments, and he wrote his father of his intention to marry her. But quite suddenly she jilted him for another man.

Tchaikovsky may really have loved Artôt, for a time at least; but for Antonina Miliukova he had nothing even approaching affection. On the night of their marriage (July 18, 1877) as he sat with her on a train he realized that his wife was utterly abhorrent to him. He thought he would go insane: "When the train started, I was ready to scream." The story of the next three months was a Gehenna of mental torture that only a Dostoevski could have described. To avoid his wife, the composer would go out at night and walk the streets of Moscow for hours. One night he waded into the Moscow River up to his waist and stood in the icy water as long as he could bear it. He hoped to die of pneumonia and thus be spared the shame of suicide. Finally he fled to his brother Anatol in St. Petersburg, and there suffered a complete nervous collapse. Anatol got rid of Antonina by sending her with her mother to Odessa; then he took his shattered brother to a haven in Switzerland.

Tchaikovsky had not written Mme. von Meck a word about his plans until the day before he was married. The news almost killed her, but she concealed her feelings. Her replies were masterpieces of tact and sympathy. It was after the marriage broke up and he had written her in detail of the entire dreadful experience that she promised him an annuity of six thousand rubles to make him independent for life.

IV

The year 1877 had more significance in Tchaikovsky's life than the nightmare marriage. In the midst of this turmoil he had been at work on two major projects, the opera *Eugene Onegin* and his Fourth Symphony. The latter was the first of his three most famous symphonies, which were to form a crescendo of popularity, interest, and importance, as well as the inspirational climax of his entire career.

The Fourth Symphony, in F minor, is not one of Tchaikovsky's more nearly perfect scores, but it is surely one of his most effective. The opening bars are famous— a blaring of wind instruments, stirring and portentous, which seems to presage events of great moment. The movement that unfolds at length thereafter is melodious, colorful, and highly theatrical. Tchaikovsky himself described his inner "program" for this symphony, in a letter to Mme. von Meck. The introductory fanfare, he said, represented the *Fatum*, "the inexorable force that prevents our hopes of happiness from being realized . . . it is Damocles' sword, hanging over our head in constant, unremitting spiritual torment. . . . Despair and discontent grow stronger, sharper. Would it not be wiser to turn from reality and sink into dreams?" The varying moods of this first movement are thus an alternation, as in life itself, between "hard reality and evanescent dreams."

The three remaining movements are less convincingly explained by the composer, but the truth is that his whole program seems unnecessary. One is left with the feeling that Tchaikovsky attached his ideas to the music after it was written, rather than before. Musically the slow movement is a disappointment. There is a fine lyrical first theme, but the second is weak and repetitious. The third movement is an instrumental tour de force that has delighted audiences from its first hearing. The movement is made up of three contrasting orchestral colors—strings (pizzicato throughout), woodwind, and brass. Each group plays separately until the end, when they are joined. The themes are not in themselves exceptional, but the scoring throughout is original and charming. The finale is a whirlwind of melodrama. At the height of the battle's fury the brasses interrupt with the ringing fanfare of the introduction. It is a moment of great dramatic effectiveness.

So far as form is concerned, Tchaikovsky's music suffered from a fundamental weakness. Theorists soon observed that his symphonic themes do not show genuine organic growth. Rather, they move in sequences, as a series of melodic ideas contained in a row of boxes, but seldom progressing one into the other. The composer realized his weakness and admitted it. He said that in his music "the seams show." Fortunately, however, he had a redeeming virtue that rescued his best music from scrappiness and lack of cohesive movement. He had a remarkable sense of dramatic form. In this respect he was a true son of Beethoven (whose music he disliked, by the way). He had the born dramatist's feeling for rise and fall of action, for suspense, for climax; he could generate and control his forces and then unloose them until they swept everything before them in overwhelming momentum.

As an orchestrator Tchaikovsky ranks high among the direct heirs of Berlioz. He was one of those lucky composers who have an intuitive command of the instruments, so that he knew how to draw from them a maximum of expressiveness combined with a splendid clarity. Thus his orchestration is nearly always brilliant. Often it glows with rare and beautiful colors. He was not nearly as great an innovator as his French ancestor, but he contrived many clever effects that were widely copied after him.

The orchestra was Tchaikovsky's natural medium. Of all his large catalogue of works those centering around the orchestra are by far the most successful. A few of his songs and the string quartets are occasionally heard, but in other media the mortality has been heavy. Few pianists bother these days to look beyond his B flat minor Concerto. He composed a great deal for the instrument, but it was mostly in the small forms. He did not have the knack of piano writing, not being a notably good pianist himself.

It was Tchaikovsky's lifelong ambition to write a successful opera, and there was hardly a time when he was not occupied with some phase of the task. He finished eight operas in all, beginning with the abortive *Voyevoda* in 1868 and ending with *Iolanthe* in 1891. Most of them represent only a huge waste of creative effort. Tchaikovsky's trouble was a common one. Whatever gifts he had for the musical side of the task were canceled out by his ignorance of dramaturgy. His pieces were usually all melody and no drama. As a result his efforts in this field caused him some of his worst embarrassments. Several were dismal failures; others enjoyed only a succès d'estime. All died quickly, with the exception of *Eugene Onegin* (1878) and *Pique Dame* (1890), which were real successes during the composer's lifetime. *Eugene Onegin* especially has been a favorite both in Russia and abroad.

v

The years immediately following Tchaikovsky's marriage and the creation of the Fourth Symphony were transitional both in his life and in his art. In 1878 he resigned from the Conservatory, and thereafter he was relieved of the burden of teaching. To any other man his life would probably have seemed exceptionally pleasant. Mme. von Meck had made him comfortably independent, and he was free to devote his entire time to music. Her generosity also enabled him to make frequent journeys to Italy, France, and Germany; in the summer she placed her lovely country place at his disposal. His fame spread rapidly. But he was not a happy man. Instead he grew morose and solitary. He lived in constant fear that his wife (whom he called "the serpent") would blackmail him.

Part of his unhappiness came from his work. He had

achieved a technical assurance and a fluency of invention, but he knew that his inspiration had receded rather than advanced since the Fourth Symphony. The works of this period are seldom distinguished. The only exception is the Violin Concerto, which was written in Switzerland in 1878, immediately after the breakup of his marriage.

The Violin Concerto had a history much like that of the Piano Concerto in B flat minor. Tchaikovsky dedicated it to the celebrated violin teacher, Leopold Auer, who was just starting his long career as professor at the St. Petersburg Conservatory. Auer was not impressed by the work. He liked only the first movement; he thought the rest contained too much that was unsuited to the instrument. Three years went by before a violinist named Adolph Brodsky had the courage to conquer the technical difficulties of the piece and try it in public. He played it in Vienna late in 1881. The composer did not learn of this performance until some time later when he chanced to read a review of his piece by Eduard Hanslick who erupted volcanic lava over the entire work. Tchaikovsky was terribly hurt by the excoriating words; he remembered them until he died.

The Concerto ultimately became one of the most popular works ever written for the violin, but it used to be widely criticized. For example, the words of Fritz Kreisler, who was for years one of its most brilliant interpreters: "I think the concerto is a lovely work. It has, like everything by Tchaikovsky, an unending source of melodic invention. But it also shows, more than any other of Tchaikovsky's compositions, lack of workmanship." In an effort to correct some of its "faults" Kreisler made a revision of the concerto, which he performed with the Philharmonic-Symphony Society of New York in 1939. He made certain cuts, various changes in the instrumentation, and he rewrote completely the cadenza in the first movement. It is significant that the result seemed to add little to the stature of the work. Rather it proved that this concerto has been popular chiefly because of its sentimental melodies and its opportunity for acrobatic tricks of technique. It was a typical product of the later nineteenth century, a period in which the repertoire of the violin was degraded almost beyond recovery by sentimentality and display. That Tchaikovsky's concerto could succeed in spite of its lack of formal beauty is both a tribute to the vitality of his melodies and an indictment of the entire trend of violin composition during a period of a hundred years.

Shortly after the Violin Concerto came another opera, *Joan of Arc*, which enjoyed a mild success. The critics damned it. They were led by Cui, who said it was the worst thing Tchaikovsky had yet written. Four years later when *Mazeppa* was produced, Cui found that Tchaikovsky had achieved the impossible, in writing a worse opera than *Joan of Arc*. To this period also belong the first three orchestral suites, which contain movements of melodic beauty and charm; but the Second Piano Concerto (1880) is not in a class with the First. The "Italian Caprice" and the *1812* Overture were enormously popular works in their time, but their colors have long since faded.

The *1812* Overture used to be a favorite closing work on "all-Tchaikovsky" programs. It was the nearest thing to an explosion that had yet been devised for the concert hall. The piece was written on order for a mammoth exposition in Moscow, and was intended to depict the epic struggle between the French and the Russians in the year 1812. The first performance took place in 1882 in front of a cathedral in the Kremlin, and the original plan called for a huge orchestra augmented by a band of brass instruments, with the big bass drum part doubled by shots fired from cannon. Tchaikovsky detested the piece even while he composed it. He confided to Mme. von Meck that it "will be very showy and noisy, but it will have no artistic merit because I wrote it without warmth and without love."

In 1885, the composer established himself in a modest house near Klin. There he enjoyed the isolation and the closeness to nature that he loved. The place was furnished, it was said, in atrocious taste; but the composer was comfortable and as near peace as a man of his temperament could expect. He had a sign on his gate that bluntly told visitors that he received on Mondays and Thursdays from three to five. Otherwise he was "not at home. Please do not ring." Here he lived quietly, walked daily through the countryside, read philosophy, studied English, composed with regularity, and drank heavily every night. "For me," he wrote, "a man harassed with nerves, it is simply impossible to live without the poison of alcohol." Fortunately for him it never became the vice that ruined Mussorgsky. His capacity for liquor was enormous.

It was in this house in Klin that Tchaikovsky composed one of the most ambitious works in his catalogue—the *Manfred* Symphony. With better luck it might have been one of his finest. *Manfred* as we know it is a piece of vast proportions, overlong, stuffed with exasperating inequalities, and yet containing ideas which, had they predominated, would have raised this symphony to a rank of greatness.

The idea of writing a program symphony around Byron's dramatic poem was another scheme of Balakirev's. He had been hypnotized by the poem ever since he and young Mussorgsky had read it together, years before. He tried at first to interest Berlioz in the idea—certainly the right man for the fantastic nightmares of Byron's hero. Fifteen years after that, in 1882, he put it up to Tchaikovsky. As in the case of *Romeo and Juliet*, Balakirev provided a complete scenario. Tchaikovsky waited for three years before he made a start on the music, and even then he undertook the task with misgivings.

The composer indicated in his score the program of each movement, and in the main he followed Balakirev's plan. The first movement depicts the soul-tortured Manfred wandering in the Alps, "racked by remorse and despair . . . a prey to sufferings without a name. . . . The memory of the fair Astarte, whom he had loved and lost, eats his heart. Nothing can dispel the curse which weighs on Manfred's soul. . . ." The second movement depicts the Fairy of the Alps appearing to Manfred beneath the rainbow of the waterfall; the third is a peaceful Pastorale. The last movement paints the underground palace of Arimanes. "Manfred appears in the midst of the Bacchanal. Evocation of the ghost of Astarte . . . Manfred's death." Of course there would be an *idée fixe*. It runs through the work in the form of a motive portraying Manfred himself.

The multitude of ideas got completely away from Tchaikovsky, and he produced a score so long, sprawling in form, prolix, and variegated that the entire effort has generally been written off as a failure. This is unfortunate. For some of the *Manfred* Symphony is definitely worth rescuing. The fundamental fault, moreover, does not lie alone with the composer and his lack of self-criticism. Part of the blame must go to the form of the program symphony itself.

It is a significant fact that, since the prototype of all such works, the *Fantastic* Symphony of Berlioz, there has not been a completely successful program symphony. No one can deny the greatness of the Berlioz work, its originality, its sweeping, passionate vitality, its place as a landmark in nineteenth-century music; and on the other hand no one can deny that it is so uneven as to constitute one of the most baffling disappointments in symphonic music. The same composer's *Harold in Italy* Symphony is more weakly uneven, while the *Romeo and Juliet* was described by Wagner with brutal directness: "Piles of rubbish lay heaped up among the most brilliant inventions." The *Faust* and *Dante* symphonies of Franz Liszt are seldom heard on modern programs. The *Domestic* Symphony and the *Alpine* Symphony are long steps downward in the retrogression of Richard Strauss's art. What has defeated composers in so many cases has been the necessity of serving two masters—i.e., the literary scenario and the fundamental classic structure of the symphony itself. The two seldom jibe; generally they are at war. Tchaikovsky himself noted that fact when writing his *Manfred* Symphony: "It is a thousand times pleasanter to compose without a program. When I write a program symphony, I always feel that I am not paying in sterling coin, but in worthless paper money."

The composer knew what was wrong with his *Manfred*. Three years after its composition he confided in a letter that to him it was "a repulsive work, and I hate it heartily, all except the first movement. In the near future I plan to destroy the three last movements, which are musically simply trivial (except the final movement, which is impossible). So, from a piece of music that is much too long for a symphony, I shall make a symphonic poem." This was too drastic a judgment, but it is a pity that the composer was not spared to give *Manfred* a revision with the mastery he had gained in the closing years of his life.

## VI

In 1887 an event occurred that changed the later course of Tchaikovsky's life. He was finally persuaded to conduct a performance of one of his operas. The conducting experience of years before had seared his soul, and he undertook the task suffering agonies of nervousness. To his astonishment he was able to acquit himself so creditably that he received an ovation from the audience. As a result, he made a tour of western Europe, conducting various noted orchestras in performances of his own works. Thereafter he made several international tours, one of which took him to America. The shy, neurotic man to whom strangers, audiences, and crowds were so many nightmares, finally came out of his shell. At times he seemed actually to enjoy the public ovations. He was by no means a great conductor, but audiences everywhere took the occasion of his personal appearance to give evidence of their affection for his works. He had already become one of the most popular composers in the world.

The tour of 1888 took him to Leipzig, Hamburg, Berlin, Paris, and London. At the ancient Leipzig Gewandhaus, still the stronghold of German classicism, this foreigner and romantic interloper played his music with a quaking heart. But he was astonished. The audience recalled him twice, the Leipzig equivalent of an ovation. In the same town he met Johannes Brahms. His remarks about his German contemporary are remembered for their honesty rather than their perspicacity. He found Brahms the man quite likable: "Very simple, free from vanity, his humor jovial. . . ." But, "There is something dry, cold, vague, and nebulous in the music of this master which is repellent to Russian hearts. From our Russian point of view Brahms does not possess melodic invention. His musical ideas never speak to the point; hardly have we heard an allusion to some tangible melodic phrase than it disappears in a whirlpool of almost unmeaning harmonic progressions and modulations, as though the composer's special aim was to be incomprehensible and obscure. . . . It is all very serious, very distinguished, apparently even original, but in spite of all this the chief thing is lacking—beauty."

Shortly after his return to Russia from the first international tour, Tchaikovsky set to work on his Fifth Symphony, in E minor. It was written in about two months during the summer of 1888. For some time the composer had been brooding over the possibility that he was played out. He even wrote to Mme. von Meck of his fear that his inspiration had dried up and that it was time for him to quit. He worked hard on his symphony to prove to himself that his own fears were groundless. The first performance of the work left him more despondent than ever. When he conducted it in St. Petersburg later that year, and in Prague, it fell flat. "It is a failure," he wrote to his confidante. "There is something repellent in it, some overexaggerated idea of color, some insincerity or fabrication which the public instinctively recognizes." He went on to say that his Fourth Symphony was a far better work.

It is interesting to note after almost three quarters of a century how much of the composer's estimate of the Fifth Symphony fell wide of the mark and how much was damningly true. The work certainly was not a failure. It became one of the most popular symphonies ever written, one of the established showpieces of every orchestra's repertoire, and a bulwark of Tchaikovsky's hold on the affections of the music public. It has been played until every shred of novelty is worn away, the seams show, and the dramatic surprises are gone. Every critic knows how right the composer was when he spoke of overexaggeration, insincerity, fabrication—even the "something repellent." Nevertheless the Fifth Symphony is beloved wherever orchestras foregather, the world over.

The work is another laboratory specimen of the composer's mature style—which means a mixture of his virtues and faults in unexplainable juxtaposition. It has lyric richness almost to excess; it has brilliance, variety of mood, tremendous passion. It has also the composer's characteristic melancholia, and there is much use of the throbbing rhythms that so befit his moods of desperate sadness. There is orchestration of clarity, color, and resounding power; and finally, like pieces of glass set in a diadem, there are some classic examples of bad taste.

The symphony makes a good beginning, as Tchaikovsky so often does in his first movements. This one may be a patchwork of themes instead of a logical piece of sonata construction, but it has melodic interest, well sustained. The motto theme with which the work begins is radically different from the *Fatum* of the Fourth Symphony, being not a brassy fanfare but a soft, gloomily intoned melody for the clarinet. It runs through the entire symphony in various guises, becoming in the last movement the main declamation point of the entire work. Its use is so strongly stressed as to suggest some concrete idea behind the composer's inspiration. Tchaikovsky never admitted the existence of such a program, as he did in the case of the Fourth Symphony, but many commentators have supplied their own. It seems doubtful if one really existed.

The second movement of the Fifth Symphony presents another celebrated Tchaikovsky melody. It is given at first to the solo horn and is later entwined with an obbligato by the oboe. The movement is remindful of a Chopin nocturne, extended and intensified with all the swelling passions and colors of the great orchestra. It misses being one of the supreme nocturnes, for its chief blemish is two convulsive interruptions by the motto theme which are noisy and tasteless. The third movement is marked Waltz, and for this the composer has been doubly damned. The purists have said that a waltz has no place whatever in a symphony, and anyway this is not a real waltz at all. They may be right on both counts, but not many listeners would sacrifice this particular movement. It is unpretentious, melodious, and charming; and it serves to relieve the emotional tension of the surrounding movements.

It is hard to forgive Tchaikovsky for the last movement

of the Fifth Symphony. His purpose was to end his work with a resounding, triumphal finale; his method in part was to take the gloomy motto theme, turn it from minor to major, and proclaim it to the skies. It so happens that this is one of the hardest tests to which a composer may subject a theme—to have it sung fortissimo by the brass. Better themes than Tchaikovsky's have failed under this ordeal. Here the result is lamentable. The tune takes on neither dignity nor beauty, only the banal trumpery of an operatic march by Meyerbeer. The entire movement degenerates into an orgy of noise and triviality.

VII

With the Fifth Symphony out of the way, Tchaikovsky went on another international tour, early in 1889. All over the Continent and in England he was received with acclaim, but he was homesick and depressed the entire time. During the next year he composed one of his most successful operas, *Pique Dame* [*The Queen of Spades*], which created a sensation at its *première* in St. Petersburg. Then in September 1890 the brooding and the vague morbid fears suddenly burst over him in the form of a horrible reality.

He had gone to Tiflis, in the Caucasus, to conduct a concert and to stay with his brother Anatol. There he received a letter from Mme. von Meck. It informed him, in phrases that were strange and unfriendly, that the Meck fortune was in danger of collapse and that she could send him no more money. The composer was cut to the quick—not at all by any fears for his own security (for his music was at last bringing him an income), but by the tone of the letter, which was "tinged with inexplicable, ominous finality." He hastened to write his friend a long reply, assuring her that he would never again have to fear privation and that her own misfortune was his only cause for worry. He reiterated, as he had done a thousand times, his undying gratitude and affection.

He never heard from her again. When he returned to

Moscow a short time later he learned that her words were false: the Meck fortune was in no danger whatever.

Tchaikovsky was utterly crushed. In his bewilderment he grasped at every possible straw of explanation for his friend's action, but he found none. It seemed that after all he had been no more than this wealthy woman's diversion, and that when the bond of money between them was dissolved she no longer had any interest in him. His pride received a hurt from which he never recovered.

The real reason for Mme. von Meck's strange action is not known. Speculations have been various. It is possible that she may have learned in some way of the composer's abnormality, and that she was shocked. The authors of *Beloved Friend* believe that the answer is to be found in the lingering illness and death of her eldest son. In her grief she may have reproached herself, imagining that she had neglected him during the years when she lavished her interest and love upon the composer. These possibilities alone do not suffice to explain her cruel act, which she of all people knew would strike the hypersensitive man with terrible force. The answer seems rather to be a mental derangement.

Tchaikovsky did not realize at once the finality of her action, but as the months went by without word or explanation he slipped slowly into an abyss of depression. The next spring he was persuaded to undertake a concert tour of America. On the night of May 5, 1891, he was the guest of honor at the ceremonies which marked the formal opening of Carnegie Hall, in New York City. The composer conducted one of his own works and received an ovation. In that same hall in the course of the next three quarters of a century his music would receive the adulation of countless thousands of American music lovers.

He went on to Philadelphia, Baltimore, Washington, and Niagara Falls. America fascinated and frightened him. He was amazed by the overwhelming hospitality, by the fact that he was more famous here than in Russia; he was impressed by the bathtubs, the thirteen-story buildings, the kindness of the Negro porters on the trains, the uninhibited expansiveness of Mr. Carnegie. Through it all homesickness and melancholia hung like a dead weight upon his mind. He would sit alone in his hotel room and weep.

Back in Russia, he settled down during the summer of 1891 to work on an opera and a ballet which had been commissioned by the Imperial Opera in St. Petersburg. The opera was *Iolanthe*, his last, and a failure. The ballet was one of his most treasured scores, the incomparable *Nutcracker*. The suite drawn from this score has been deluged with performances for many years, so enormous has been its popularity.

Tchaikovsky had already written two ballets, *The Swan Lake* and *The Sleeping Beauty*, both melodious and charming scores. Tchaikovsky revealed here a lightness of touch, a feeling for decoration and a sense of humor that would hardly be suspected of the writer of the big, gloom-ridden symphonies. Let no one imagine that because music is "light" it is also easy. There is more melodic invention, more orchestral craftsmanship in these dainty miniatures than in many a symphonic movement. They are as charming and often as subtle as exquisitely made toys.

Like many other artists of greatness, Tchaikovsky never fully estimated his own prowess; or perhaps it would be nearer the truth to say that in his insistence upon expressing himself in the grand manner he underrated the simpler side of his art. There his genius flourished, without the inequalities, the conscious struggling that marred so much of his effort in the larger forms. There his delightful melodic ideas with their lush harmonies and their splendid orchestral investiture were ideally suited to their medium. The composer seldom saw it that way. It would probably have amazed him to know that he left whole operas and tone poems which the world today would eagerly trade for another little piece as charming as the *Waltz of the Flowers*.

### VIII

The last two years of Tchaikovsky's life were an odyssey of utter despair. He went wandering around Europe much of the time, subjecting himself to public appearances, receiving as a kind of desperate diversion the honors that were heaped upon him. He wrote home of melancholia so deep that he wondered why he did not go mad. Without Mme. von Meck to confide in the composer now wrote to a nephew, Bob Davydov, a young man for whom the description "weakling" would be charitable. He ended up years later a drug addict and a suicide in Tchaikovsky's house at Klin.

In the autumn of 1892, the composer began work on a new symphony. Before it was finished, he lost interest, decided that it was empty of inspiration, and destroyed the whole thing. Then late in the year on the way to Paris he began thinking about another symphony. "This time," he wrote, "a symphony with a program, but a program that will remain an enigma to all. Let them guess for themselves. . . . Often, while composing it in my mind during the journey, I shed tears." This was the genesis of Tchaikovsky's Sixth Symphony, in B minor, the composer's masterpiece, and one of the most celebrated works in symphonic literature. In February 1893, when he sat down to writing it, the notes flew from his pen. "In less than four days the first movement was done and all the rest clearly outlined in my head." He was buoyed up by the thought that his creative powers were still strong. There were interruptions later in the spring while he took time off to accommodate a publisher with some potboilers for the piano, and then to go to England to receive an honorary degree at Cambridge. By the end of August, after strenuous labor, the symphony was finished. There were no misgivings this time; Tchaikovsky knew what he had wrought. "I consider it the best of all my works to date. . . . I love it as I never loved any of my musical children."

He was destined never to know, however, just what the world thought of the work. When the Sixth Symphony was played for the first time, on October 28, 1893, at St. Petersburg, it was a failure. Only his own appearance as conductor saved the occasion from being a frost, and the critics were almost unanimous in declaring the Sixth inferior to his other symphonies. Ten days later, before he could hear another performance, Tchaikovsky was dead.

He had drunk a glass of unboiled water; his brother Modest observed what he had done—too late. "Petia—what crazy folly! It's November and you're in Petersburg!" Within a few hours the composer was in the agonies of cholera. He died on November 6, 1893.

Instantly the rumor spread that he had committed suicide. In all probability it was not true, but to those who knew his mental states, the incredibly careless episode of the drinking water seemed to have no other meaning. And then when the Sixth Symphony—sorrow-drenched and terrible—became known to the world, the evidence seemed overwhelming that Tchaikovsky not only had killed himself but also that he had deliberately written his own requiem.

The true circumstances were far less romantic. The doctors who attended him were certain that the suspected water had little to do with his death and that he had been carrying the germs of cholera in his system for some time. The ugly rumor had at least one salutary effect. It focused attention upon the composer's last work, with the result that its initial failure was quickly forgotten in the wave of interest which awaited its performances all over the world. In a short time it became the most famous and frequently played symphony since Beethoven's Fifth.

To this day no one knows what enigmatic program lies hidden under the notes of this score. Tchaikovsky had thought at first of calling it simply A Program Symphony, but on the morning after the first performance he seized the suggestion of Modest and called it Pathetic. Beyond that now famous title we know nothing.

In form the work is totally unorthodox. The first movement is almost as long as two full movements, the second is cast in an unusual waltzlike 5/4 rhythm, the third is a scherzo that winds up like a finale, while the slow movement is placed at the end of the work. Schumann's remark about Chopin's B flat minor Sonata might well apply here: the composer "bound together four of his maddest children." Similarly, what holds the four movements together is not a matter of technical device, or even of musical style; rather, it is a prevailing mood. The Pathetic

Symphony is what its name indicates—an essay in pathos. Even the barbaric clamors of the third movement are an exultation that hides but does not obliterate a substratum of morbidity; it is a wild and desperate irony in the face of terrible grief.

If a prerequisite to great art is the artist's ability to mirror the spirit of his time and his surroundings, then Tchaikovsky at last fulfilled the requirements in his closing work. Heretofore his grieving and his sobbing had been all too personal; now at last he achieved a nobility of utterance which made his music the voice of a nation and the emotion of a whole people. The stupendous tragedy of old Russia is written down in these notes for all to read.

The first movement of the *Pathetic* Symphony has been called a "convulsion of the soul." It does not matter that the composer came not much closer than usual to the structure and the organic growth of true sonata form. He makes up for lack of strict form with emotional force. The development section, with its long pedal point of the tympani on a low F sharp, the tortured writhing of the strings above and the relentless downward tread of the trombones, is like a descent into the inferno—and one of the most gripping pages in romantic music. Tchaikovsky gave himself a huge span to fill in this long movement, but his melodic ideas have the breadth and the dignity to encompass it.

The second movement was long a novelty because of its unusual 5/4 rhythm. The graciousness, the felicity of the chief theme do not prevail. It is joined to a second theme poignant with repressed sorrow. The third movement, Allegro molto vivace, begins like a conventional scherzo, but before long the racing, swirling figures have developed into headlong flight, likened to the sweep of Tartar hordes across the steppes. The furious energy, the Slavic violence of this music was hardly paralleled before Tchaikovsky's time.

The stunning climax at the end of the third movement would have meant the end of any conventional symphony; but Tchaikovsky, displaying the artistic growth that is one of the attributes of genius, had come to understand the emptiness of that kind of ending for a symphony which began as this one did. When Wagner as an old man had thought of writing a symphony he remarked that "the finales are the awkward things; I will steer clear of them; I will keep to one-movement symphonies." Tchaikovsky had learned his lesson with the Fifth Symphony. He did not repeat his mistake in the Sixth. He rounded off this work with an Adagio lamentoso, an elegy that belongs with the noblest expressions of human grief. Huneker, who knew all of the composer's failings, spoke of "this astounding torso, which Michael Angelo would have understood and Dante wept over"; and of "a page torn from Ecclesiastes."

That the composer was contemplating death in this closing effort of his life is almost certain. He found it intolerable; he protested and struggled against it with all the creative strength he could summon. Bruised and tormented by life, he was yet terrified and revolted by this iniquitous end of all man's striving. It is "death alone that can suddenly make man to know himself," said Raleigh. Tchaikovsky proved those words in his poignant Adagio. He came suddenly to know himself—a great artist whose powers had come at last to their flood. He had time for this single effort in which, for once, his reach did not exceed his grasp. After that, there was left only the indisputable truth of Raleigh's words:

"O eloquent, just, and mightie Death! . . . Thou hast drawne together all the farre stretchèd greatnesse, all the pride, crueltie, and ambition of man, and covered it all over with these two narrow words, *Hic jacet!*"

# Debussy
## 1862—1918

### I

The hiatus in French music after Hector Berlioz is a phenomenon difficult to explain. Berlioz himself was a dynamo of original ideas and impulses; his work was of a type that would ordinarily vitalize hordes of imitators and produce schools and cults to follow the leads that he plainly pointed out. His influence among German and Russian composers was in fact enormous. Yet in France he was generally misunderstood and ignored. He had not a single contemporary worthy of standing beside him. For more than forty years after he wrote the *Fantastic* Symphony the most enduring contributions to French music were his own. After his best productive period had ended, years passed before a talent as powerful as Bizet's appeared upon the scene. *Carmen* was finished in 1875—a masterpiece of musico-dramatics, melodic interest, color, and style; but Bizet died three months after its first performance, at the age of thirty-seven. César Franck's classic essays, which really signaled the regeneration of French music, began with the Quintet in 1879, at the end of a long career. Meanwhile the men who held the stage—Auber, Halévy, Thomas, Gounod, Delibes—were a mixture of competence and mediocrity.

It may be true that France as a social and political organism has been on the decline since the Napoleonic wars, but it would be dangerous reasoning to attribute to that national hemorrhage a period of sterility in the art of music. Wars produce strange and unpredictable effects upon the nations that lose them. The economy and the social life may be paralyzed or destroyed, or it may be stimulated. The half century in France after 1815 was certainly one of political instability, but as far as the arts were concerned the country was nothing less than a hive of productivity. The French contribution to romantic literature was an accomplishment unsurpassed in any other country in Europe. No one has ever explained why, at this same period, French music had gone into a serious decline.

At the high noon of the Second Empire the most popular composer in France was Jacques Offenbach, not a Frenchman but a Rhinelander. At least Offenbach's aims were as honest as his talent was prodigious. In the course of twenty-five years he wrote ninety works for the French lyric stage. He did not concern himself with the pretensions of grand opera; nearly all of his pieces were light operas or operettas. At least one was an enduring masterpiece—*Les Contes d'Hoffmann* [*Tales of Hoffmann*]. The rest were glittering, clever, and frivolous, the musical epitaph of the gaudy Second Empire as it lurched toward its doom at Sedan.

There is no mystery about the aftereffects of the Franco-Prussian War of 1870. Following that humiliating defeat, the entire French nation underwent a catharsis. Revolt against the existing order was nowhere more strongly motivated than in the arts. In literature the lead passed to the realists, headed by Zola, Maupassant, and Daudet. Zola's theme was a gigantic scourging of the degenerate society whose diseased roots, trailing back to the Second Empire, had ruined France. From his naturalism grew a new literature all over Europe and America. In painting there arose the most famous art movement in modern times—impressionism. It was founded by Manet, Pissarro, Monet, Renoir, Sisley, Guillaumin, and Cézanne; and it indirectly sired Degas, Toulouse-Lautrec, Van Gogh, Gauguin, and Seurat. The movement began with Manet's struggles against the reactionary Salon painters, as early as 1859; but the First Impressionist Exhibition, which crystallized the idea, dated from 1874. In the next twenty-five years these men and their followers produced an art that is one of the permanent assets of French culture.

The first indication that new life was also flowing in the veins of French music came in the 1880s, with the belated discovery of the work of an obscure organist at the Church of Sainte Clothilde in Paris. This man was César Franck, a Belgian by birth, who had spent a lifetime in Paris as organist and teacher, eking out a few hours each day at composition. He was fifty-five before he began the works that were his masterpieces—the Quintet for Piano and Strings; the Symphonic Variations; the Violin Sonata; the Prelude, Chorale, and Fugue for piano; the String Quartet; and the Symphony in D minor.

Franck was the French Brahms. He was a romantic whose real predilection was the classic forms. The romantic side of his music is its outward style, which is rich and colorful, flooded with prismatic harmonies (chromatic modulation is his hallmark) and endowed with a deep expressiveness. Beneath this romantic exterior is a foundation of classicism. When Franck turned in the closing years of his life to forms like the sonata, the symphony, the string quartet, he had found at last the bridge between his two natures. His formal ancestor was Beethoven; his roots were the polyphony of Bach. Liszt once went to Sainte-Clothilde to hear him in one of his celebrated feats of improvising, and the Abbé went away "evoking the name of J. S. Bach in inevitable comparison."

Franck left a group of pupils and disciples who were to carry on the work of regenerating French music—D'Indy, Duparc, Chausson, Lekeu, Pierné. The discovery by these young men of their master's superbly modern classicism gave them a new feeling of pride in their country's music and the belief that after all they would not be doomed to continual imitations of Gounod's *Faust*.

One of the most gifted of this new generation was Gabriel Fauré (1845–1924), whose beautifully wrought music combined the lyrical and the neoclassic. But the

real genius and the movement he was to produce had yet
to come. In the year 1887, when Franck was at work on his
Symphony in D minor, a young music student who had
won the Prix de Rome returned to Paris, disgruntled and
disillusioned, after several years at the Villa Medici. He
was Claude Achille Debussy. In the next twenty years he
would become the greatest composer that France has yet
produced.

II

Debussy's achievement was twofold—first as a musician
of France, and second as a force of enormous potency in
the history of music from the end of the nineteenth century down to the present time. Debussy freed his country
from the influence of German music, and right at the
time when the weight of Wagnerism lay heaviest upon
every creative source. He gave France a music that was
singularly its own—French in style, in mannerism, in spirit.
For music in general he created singlehanded the school
of impressionism; he gave it also a style, a technique, a
spirit, and he endowed it with its finest works. Following
the lead of Wagner, he made discoveries in the field of
harmony that place him on a par with Wagner as inventor,
explorer, and dauntless revolutionary. He was one of the
supreme stylists in music, as he was one of the most original thinkers ever to practice this art.

Debussy's personal life was one of only moderate interest. It was largely circumscribed by the city of Paris.
He was born (August 22, 1862) in Saint-Germain-en-Laye,
half an hour from Paris, and he spent the greater part of
his life in the city itself. He was the typical Parisian of
those years when she was at her most magnificent; he had
little interest in any other place, or in any country other
than France.

Debussy's father was the owner of a small china shop.
The "De" in their name was not an indication of noble
ancestry; the family had come from a long line of laborers,
farmers, and small merchants. There is no record of any
of them being notably gifted in the arts, musical or other-

wise. Debussy had no formal schooling. The family were poor, and during his childhood he was taught by his mother and an aunt.

There seems to have been something exceptional about him even as a child. He had a way of attracting older people who discerned in him evidence of talent and intellect. They invariably wanted to help him. When he was seven years old his aunt persuaded a banker to pay for his first music lessons. A year later Mme. Mauté de Fleurville, the mother-in-law of the poet Verlaine, became interested in him. This woman had been a pupil of Chopin years before. She taught Debussy the piano for three years, and through her he was able to enter the Paris Conservatory in 1873, when he was eleven. Some years later, when he was nineteen, Debussy was taken up by a wealthy family named Vasnier. Mme. Vasnier was young, beautiful, and a singer of talent. Her husband, much older than she, was an architect. The Vasniers did for Debussy what the Breunings did for Beethoven. They took him into their home, guided him to an appreciation of literature and art, introduced him to the refinements of a cultured life his own parents had never been able to give him. Debussy wrote some of his earliest music in their home, and he dedicated several of his songs to Mme. Vasnier.

Just before he met the Vasniers, he had been helped by still another person of wealth. By a curious twist of fate it happened to be Mme. von Meck, the friend and patron of Tchaikovsky. On one of her trips abroad, she had asked the authorities of the Paris Conservatory to suggest someone who could give music lessons to her children and play duets with her. The person chosen was eighteen-year-old Debussy. He joined the Mecks in Switzerland and traveled with them through Italy and Austria. Mme. von Meck liked the young Frenchman so well that she employed him again. He went to Moscow and lived in her house during the summers of 1881 and 1882. In her correspondence with Tchaikovsky, Mme. von Meck made several references to her "little Bussy," to his charming manner, his talent, and the pleasure he gave her when they played duets of Tchaikovsky's music. The end of the second visit came abruptly. Debussy had the misfortune to fall in love with one of Mme. von Meck's lovely daughters. When he proposed marriage, the girl's mother rejected him, tactfully but with firmness. He was taken weeping to the train for Paris, and out of the lives of the Mecks forever.

The Russian interludes in Debussy's life became important in an indirect way. Years later his mature musical style showed certain influences that stemmed from the Russians, chiefly Mussorgsky. Precisely how much of this can be traced to the summers in Moscow is a matter that has long puzzled musicologists.

Debussy spent eleven years at the Conservatory. He was a perplexing student. His teachers admitted that he had unusual talent, but he seemed perversely bent on misusing it; some thought him lazy and careless. He quarreled with his teachers about the orthodox rules of composition. He was particularly resentful of the old-fashioned laws of harmony. After his classes he would sit at a piano and amuse his fellow students with a display of strange chords and chordal progressions—bizarre effects that would have horrified his professors. Even as a youngster he was more interested in chords and all their various forms and usages than any other branch of musical technique.

When he was twenty-two, Debussy won the highest scholarship award that the Conservatory had to offer—the Prix de Rome. The composition that he had submitted in the competition was a cantata, *L'Enfant prodigue* [*The Prodigal Son*]. The award consisted of a three-year period of study at the Villa Medici in Rome, with expenses paid by the government. This honor (and it was an important one in the music life of France) left Debussy completely cold. At the time he was deep in his attachment for the Vasniers, and he left Paris with reluctance.

He was miserable all through his stay in Rome. Already a stubborn individualist, he hated even the mild restraints of life at the Villa. He was bored by his fellow students and he found Rome dull. Instead of working at the new compositions that he was expected to send back to Paris at regular intervals, he spent much of his time reading, or studying the operas of Wagner. He played *Tristan und Isolde* at the piano for hours at a time. Years later he wrote that he had been "a Wagnerian to the point of forgetting the most elementary principles of politeness."

It must have been evident to any discerning judge of character that this perverse and strong-willed young man was headed for one of two things in life: either he would be a dilettante who would dabble in music for a while and then give it up for something easier, or he would cut out for himself a career of surpassing interest and accomplishment. At any rate, he never finished the sojourn at Rome. He quit after the second year and returned to Paris.

III

Debussy was slow in reaching artistic maturity. Because of the nature of the style at which he finally arrived, its originality, and its tenuous connections with the music of the past, he had to go through a long and difficult struggle. For five years after he left Italy and settled down to a career in Paris he created much that was interesting, but not a great deal that was first-rate. During that time, however, forces were at work, outside his purely musical interests, which were molding his ideas and contributing to the shape and character of the mature artistry that finally emerged.

Paris itself contributed much. The city resembled the Paris of Chopin's time—a roosting place for many brilliant birds of the arts. In the early 1880s the life that had formerly centered in the Latin Quarter moved to Montmartre. In that section arose a new pleasure ground of cafés, bars, cabarets, and restaurants. For brilliance, gaiety, and variety, for all the ramifications of amusement that began with intellectual stimulation of the most serious sort and ended with every conceivable kind of vice, Montmartre has probably never been duplicated in the history of Paris. The historian of that epoch was not a writer but a painter—Toulouse-Lautrec, a hideously ugly little man with the legs of a dwarf and the face of a monster. Descendant of one of the oldest and most aristocratic families of France, Lautrec spent fifteen years in Montmartre, turning out with furious energy a torrent of drawings, paintings, lithographs, and posters that recorded everything he saw—everything from the art of great entertainers like Aristide Bruant and Yvette Guilbert to intimate scenes in the lowest brothels—until he died at thirty-seven, burned up by alcohol and sexual excess.

Debussy, a true Parisian, loved the stimulation of the Montmartre night life. In the eighties and nineties he frequented various cafés and brasseries, among them the Café Weber, a favorite haunt of Lautrec, of Marcel Proust, and Oscar Wilde. In such places he met the artists, writers, painters, and musicians who were interested as he was in new ideas in the arts. In 1891 he met Erik Satie, who was then working as a pianist in a Montmartre café. They remained close friends for many years, and the association had an important bearing on Debussy's music. Satie, who did not begin serious study of composition until he was forty, was for a long time dismissed as an archdilettante, a poseur, and even a clown, largely because he dared to apply to music a sense of humor.

In the 1880s two major movements were agitating the French intellectuals—impressionism in painting and symbolism in poetry. Both were throwing up clouds of controversial dust. The impressionist movement was by far the more important of the two, and by that time the painters had actually won their great victory. Debussy was powerfully drawn to the theories of these men, their experiments in color, their attempts to record less of photographic representation and more of atmosphere and evocation; above all he admired their courageous fight against reaction. However, even though Debussy's own work later took on the name "impressionism," it was actually from the symbolists that he derived most of the technical ideas which he applied to music.

Two great French poets had paved the way for symbolism. The first was Baudelaire, who was a passionate admirer of Poe, and who introduced to French literature the American's ideas of romantic grotesqueness, of horror, and morbid introspection. The second was Verlaine. This man, one of the prime enigmas of human character, lived in filth, saturated with absinthe and debauched by sexual indulgence; but he left some of the most exquisite, subtly formed and tenderly expressed verses ever written. Verlaine died in 1896, after having bequeathed a new style to French poetry, one which broke down the rigid laws of meter and imitated instead the cadences of music. From this starting point the symbolists went on to a style that also tried to destroy the tyranny of the direct statement; they sought instead to evoke thought and description, to suggest, to hint, to symbolize, and thus build up an impression of a thing rather than describe the thing itself.

The acknowledged leader of the symbolists was Stéphane Mallarmé, whose verses were called "the most unintelligible ever written in French." Debussy met Mallarmé in 1887, and he began attending the "Tuesdays" at which the symbolist poets and their followers foregathered. Among those whom he met were Henri de Régnier, André Gide, and Pierre Louÿs. The author of *Aphrodite* (called the "high priest of nudity . . . in art, literature, and the stage") became one of Debussy's closest friends. He was a lover of music and painting, and a gifted amateur photographer. He knew much more about art and literature than the composer did, and the latter seems to have learned much from him.

The kind of a man Debussy was and the outlines of his character begin to emerge from accounts of him at this time. He was drawn to art that was rare and exotic; he loved fine engravings and beautifully made books; Japanese prints were a source of special delight. As might be expected, he was a gourmet. His appetite for caviar was notorious. From personal descriptions the picture of an individualist is marked. When he appeared in the cafés he was usually wearing a cape and his favorite hat—the broad-brimmed Stetson of the American "Wild West." But there was nothing Western about his features. His black eyes and hair, pale face, and pointed beard reminded a contemporary writer of a nobleman painted by Titian. In England it was noted that he resembled Dante Gabriel Rossetti. His most salient feature was an enormous forehead, bulging, it was said, like the prow of a ship. Henri de Régnier wrote: "I can still see that flabby, indolent figure, the dull pallor of his face, the keen, black, heavy-lidded eyes, the huge forehead with its curious bumps, over which he wore a long wisp of fuzzy hair; there was something feline and at the same time gypsylike about him, something passionate, yet self-centered."

Debussy was indeed self-centered to a high degree. It was the keynote of his whole character. It made him appear sensitive, unsociable, even timid, but flashes of irony in his speech and at times a calculated sarcasm showed the real man beneath. He went through life and through art choosing exactly whom and what he wanted. The rest he thrust away. Many of the men to whom he was drawn and whose art he admired—Verlaine, Huysmans, Louÿs, Satie—were abnormal in one way or another; some were definitely decadent. With the taste of an eclectic, Debussy extracted from them only what he needed. That is the reason for the remarkable health of his own music. It is never morbid, never overpessimistic. Its vague outlines, its impalpability, its marvelous evocation of misty, dream-like states were never the product of a febrile, uncertain, or decadent mind. Rather, it was a mind of unfailing sharpness and certitude, which was capable of grappling with some of the most difficult problems in art and of solving many of them.

The way he handled the Wagner problem is an indication of the clarity of his perceptions and his mental strength. In the 1880s half the intellectuals of France were intoxicated and overwhelmed by Wagner's music. A generation of composers let their enthusiasm run away with them, ruining their own talents in fruitless imitation. Some of them even made public fools of themselves by weeping and fainting conspicuously at the Bayreuth festivals. The writers were even more extreme, especially the symbolists, who wrote verses in praise of Wagner and tried to link up their aesthetic theories with his. In 1888, when he was twenty-six years old, Debussy went to Bayreuth and heard performances of *Parsifal* and *Die Meistersinger*; the next year he went again and heard *Tristan und Isolde*.

When he came back from the second pilgrimage he had changed from one of the wildest of Wagnerian zealots to a skeptic and a dissenter.

It was not so much that Debussy was disillusioned about Wagner's music, for he always thereafter admitted much of its greatness. What he perceived was its destructive force upon new talent like his own. Thereafter he set his teeth against "old Klingsor." He took what he wanted of Wagner's discoveries and innovations and then deliberately set out upon a course of action totally at variance with the German's. For a man not yet thirty to attempt thus to swim against such a tide required courage of a high order.

### IV

In 1892, Debussy read Maeterlinck's drama, *Pelléas et Mélisande*. He was so impressed that he decided to make it into an opera. The idea and its execution occupied him for the next ten years, until 1902, when the work was finally finished and produced in Paris.

*Pelléas* is like a great pivot in the career of Debussy. It was his largest and most important work. It was also a laboratory and a testing ground for many of his impressionistic ideas in music. He made several versions of the opera, constantly revising and improving it. At the same time he was composing other important works—his String Quartet, the *Prélude à L'Après-midi d'un faune,* and the Nocturnes for orchestra, and a group of notable songs and piano pieces. Public performances of these works revealed to the world the new art of Debussy, a style far in advance of his earlier pieces, and they prepared the way for *Pelléas et Mélisande* itself.

The opera was first performed at the Opéra-Comique on April 30, 1902, with Mary Garden, then comparatively unknown, in the role of Mélisande. The result was a long and heated public argument. The story of the work and its musical style were so diametrically opposed to the trend of romantic opera and in particular to the grandiose conceptions of Wagner that it was bound to impress many on first hearing as fragmentary and thin. Fortunately, for every critic who imagined that the composer was playing some gigantic hoax, there were others who discerned in the score a fabric of unparalleled richness and originality.

Debussy himself remained aloof. He had definitely arrived as a composer, but as the public interest in him and his works grew in leaps and bounds, he became more of a recluse than ever. Debussy had a horror of self-revelation. His French biographers have also been reticent about exposing details of his life while many persons who might be affected are still alive. As a result there are years in which very little is known about him—for example, the five years after the Prix de Rome episode, when he had abandoned the Vasniers and was beginning to take up with the symbolists. It is known that he made a living chiefly by giving music lessons and by doing hack work for music publishers, but there are hints that friends like Pierre Louÿs occasionally had to come to his financial rescue.

During those early uncertain years he had a mistress, in the usual manner of the Montmartre habitués. She was named Gaby, and she had green eyes. They lived together during most of the ten-year task of *Pelléas et Mélisande*. Then Gaby with the green eyes was discarded (apparently after hurtful scenes) for a young dressmaker, Rosalie (or Lily) Texier. In 1899 the composer and Lily were married. From the meager accounts of their relationship it appears that Lily was a simple, unaffected person, with very little to stimulate the composer mentally after his early infatuation had worn away. The end of their marriage was a near tragedy. Debussy became enamored of Mme. Emma Bardac, the wife of a wealthy banker. In 1904, after a long struggle with his conscience, the composer deserted his wife for Mme. Bardac. Lily tried to kill herself. She was taken to a hospital with a bullet wound near her heart.

The scandal that followed created a crisis in Debussy's career. He was widely denounced for what appeared to be the most callous behavior. It seemed that Mme. Bardac was everything that Lily was not—a woman of unusual personal charm and a talented singer; she enjoyed a background of culture and social grace. Most damning of all, it appeared that she was wealthy. For a time the composer was ostracized by many of his friends, who believed that he had deliberately sold himself through marriage for the security and luxury he had always craved. In 1905, after a double divorce, Debussy married Mme. Bardac. A daughter, called Chou-Chou, was born. She was the composer's only child, and his devotion to her was fanatical.

At this time Debussy was in his early forties, and his art had reached maturity in a magnificent and prolonged flowering. During the decade after *Pelléas et Mélisande* he produced a long series of works that climaxed the entire impressionistic style which he had invented. Among them were the two orchestral canvases, *La Mer* and *Ibéria*; and for the piano, *Estampes*, *L'Ile joyeuse*, two series of Images, the *Children's Corner* and two groups of Preludes.

Practically all of these works were controversial. In France the center of opposition to Debussy clustered around Vincent d'Indy, the disciple of César Franck, who like his master was a romantic with a reverence for the classic forms. For once, however, it was not the opponents but the protagonists of the revolutionary artist who made the most noise. The Debussyites were so voluble and often so wrongheaded in propounding theories in favor of their idol that the composer himself more than once prayed for deliverance from his friends.

Shortly before his fiftieth year there appeared the first traces of the disease that was to ruin Debussy's art and finally end his life. He became afflicted with a cancer. For nine years he struggled against it, trying to hide it from his friends and suffering its agonies in silence. His work not only thinned out in volume but also finally underwent a decline. To the disease was added worry about his financial security. Contrary to general belief, his wife did not have unlimited wealth, and at various times the composer had to raise money by writing critical articles for the French press. He undertook several tours of England, Italy, Germany, and Russia, during which he appeared as conductor of his own works.

The catastrophe of August 1914 almost killed Debussy, but he hung onto life, confident of the ultimate triumph of France. He did not live to see the deceptive dawn of November 1918. On a day in the previous spring, the twenty-fifth of March, this man who had devoted his life to the creation of exquisite sound had to die while the shells of the German long-range gun were making their hideous din, tearing through the vitals of Paris.

He was buried in the cemetery at Passy.

v

Even the most cursory examination of Debussy's music reveals the clue to the main ideas that ruled his thinking and his purposes. He was in revolt against bigness. Specifically he was trying to get away from the overwhelming amplitude which German music had achieved in the late nineteenth century and which, it is now evident, had been one of the chief causes of its decline. The heroic spirit, the impressiveness of sheer size of the Beethoven symphonies (especially the Ninth) were a legacy that became both the glory and the curse of German music. When Wagner followed with his gigantic music dramas there was no turning back. The attempt to outbuild Beethoven and to outblow Wagner became one of the chief preoccupations of Germany's composers in the late nineteenth and early twentieth centuries, and it stultified some of her best creative minds.

The nine symphonies of Anton Bruckner (1824–96), composed in the three decades after 1866, are among the earlier manifestations of this malady. Bruckner was a church organist, a fervently religious man, whose world outside the church was illuminated by his adoration for the music of Schubert, Beethoven, and above all, Wagner. With the naïve soul of an Austrian peasant, and blinded by visions of mystical grandeur, Bruckner tried to erect vast tonal cathedrals. But when he moved from the surer ground of his Masses to the symphonic epic he struggled with an incongruous mixture of musical ideas. We sense his veneration for Beethoven's brooding slow movements and bounding scherzos, for Schubert's lyricism, and Wagner's orchestral opulence; yet Bruckner's own works seldom congeal into coherent structures. Like so many organ improvisations his symphonies are windy with unfilled spaces, areas that the composer's limited inspiration simply could not fill. What they needed more than anything else was what Brahms would have given them had they been his—ruthless cutting and compression. Only in his Ninth Symphony, left without a final movement at the composer's death, does Bruckner's vision seem wholly and nobly realized.

What Claude Debussy undertook to do was something that most Germans of his time would have been disqualified by nature to attempt. Congenitally impressed by size and anything complex, they would not stop until they had brought German music to a dead end. Debussy, on the other hand, realized as a young man in his twenties what he had to accomplish to bring about his own salvation and that of all modern music. First he had to abandon the chase after the colossal and return to smaller things. He had to forego the Faustian soul struggles and the strivings after universality and instead limit himself to more intimate and subtle ideas. He had to scale down almost every phase of musical art and technique to more reasonable proportions. Fortunately he was a Frenchman who could inherit those characteristics of French genius that were needed most—the urge toward simplification, reason, and restraint.

Debussy also had many technical ideas that ran counter to the prevailing fashion. He was tired of the formulas that the Germans and the Italians had been using for centuries for their basic designs. He wanted to change the old methods of creating and developing themes from their very embryos. Wagner and Liszt had broken down many of the old restrictions, but Debussy wanted to go much further.

He also had an unusual interest in rhythm. Here was another case where the influence of Wagner had been pernicious. The huge, slow-moving music dramas, with long stretches almost devoid of rhythmic pulse, were like mastodons with slow heartbeats. Due to the demands of his dramatic material and his facility as a harmonist, Wagner had neglected the rhythmic aspect of his music. Many of the Germans followed him slavishly, ignoring the splendid rhythmic inventions of Schumann and Brahms. Debussy sensed that rhythm could be revivified and developed just as harmony had been, until it attained once again its rightful place in the general musical scheme.

The most revolutionary of all Debussy's ideas had to do with harmony. Even as a boy at the Conservatory he had begun thinking of chords as entities in themselves, with the same fundamental importance as melodies. Long before he was able to use them in his music, he had mentally catalogued an enormous vocabulary of chords of every description. Some of them he derived from Wagner, some had long been in use but were regarded by composers merely as by-products. When Debussy began using this chordal vocabulary in his mature works it was not according to the old rules and formulas. He devised an entirely new way of handling chords and of creating musical fabrics in which the center of interest would be focused upon them.

VI

Debussy's work divides itself into three fairly definite periods. The first is the music of his student years and the time before he started work on *Pelléas et Mélisande*; the second begins with his start on the opera in his thirtieth year, and extends for almost two decades; the third is the last half-dozen years of his life, when his inspiration slowly expired.

Except for a remarkable group of songs, the compositions of the first period do not yield a very rich harvest. The largest works are the two cantatas—*L'Enfant prodigue*, which won Debussy the Prix de Rome, and *La Demoiselle élue* [*The Blessed Damosel*], which indicated the young composer's interest in the Pre-Raphaelite movement. The piano works include the two *Arabesques*, *Reverie* (made into an American popular song), *Ballade*, *Danse*, and

*Valse Romantique.* Most of this music can be described as lyrical, gracefully delicate and well made, but lacking the impress of real genius. The cantatas are good considering their composer's youth, but they would hardly live today had he not later achieved greatness. Debussy's musical ideas at this time were a mixture of Wagner and Massenet. The composer of *Thaïs* and *Manon* had fallen heir to the throne of French opera by producing a series of the most successful works in its recent history. He was also a professor of advanced composition at the Conservatory. Inevitably, a student like Debussy could not escape the idiosyncrasies of his style—its lyric sweetness and sentimentality, liberally flavored with sensuousness.

The songs must be segregated from criticisms of Debussy's early work. This was the one department in which he displayed his genius practically in adolescence. He became the most individual and the most widely imitated of all writers of French songs, by creating a style that was uniquely fitted to the spirit of French verse. Some of his finest songs date from the uncertain period just after his failure at the Villa Medici; a few even belong to the years with the Vasniers. His early song style is delicate, restrained, fastidious. With unerring instinct he went to poets like Verlaine, Paul Bourget, and Baudelaire, whose verses gave him rare word pictures, or new variations on the old themes of love and nature. The modernity of Debussy's style even in the earliest songs is astonishing. He was already avoiding many of the old clichés of the song forms—the rounded phrases and the stock repetitions—and was hearkening instead to the words. Moreover, he had already begun his most characteristic procedure of compressing his ideas down to a few essential notes, leaving sometimes only a half phrase, a fragment of melody, an isolated harmonic progression, a distinctive rhythmic effect that is the inspirational core. This core might be repeated many times and with subtle alterations, but the listener is left free each time to fill in with his own imagination the unspoken musical thought.

Debussy's new harmonic language, which later became his trademark, is more than hinted at in these songs. There are bold juxtapositions of keys, complex chord formations, extensive use of dissonance, and often a complete overshadowing of the melodic material by the chordal pattern. The accompaniments are models both of richness and restraint, often delicately suggestive of orchestral tints. Even the endings of many of the songs indicate the boldness of the young composer's ideas. The task of rounding off a musical work is a difficult one, and before Chopin (who produced a fund of new ideas to close his works) this was one of the most neglected of all phases of music. It was only natural that Debussy, with his hatred of the hackneyed and the stenciled, should start early in his career experimenting with cadences in an attempt to relieve their monotony.

In 1893, Debussy wrote a String Quartet, a work that is unique for a number of reasons. It is his first large-scale masterpiece, and one of the best pieces of chamber music after Brahms. It is in the usual four movements, and it is bound together by a cyclic plan, i.e., most of the melodic material is drawn from a single theme. Otherwise it has little in common with the conventional quartet style in either orthodox construction or thematic development. Instead it appears as a series of cleverly contrived studies in string tone. The four instruments produce a wide variety of effects, many of which had never before been heard in quartet works.

The first and last movements are full of splendid energy and rhythmic vitality, at times suggesting the broad-gauge power of the full string choir. The harmonies are often unusual, but without being daringly "modern." The second movement is one of the most charming scherzos in quartet literature. It is a faery piece, filled with the tiny gleamings and sparklings of pizzicatos, the rush of dainty little rhythmic and melodic figures. The third movement is a kind of nocturne. The tonal landscape is pale with silver moonlight; there are soft murmurings of muted strings, and a melody that is "like a whispered promise of mysterious delight."

The *Prélude à L'Après-midi d'un faune* [*The Afternoon of a Faun*] remains the most famous of all Debussy's works, as it is certainly one of the most perfect impressionistic works ever written for orchestra. It was composed between the years 1892 and 1894, at a time when the composer's admiration for the symbolist poets was at its height. The eclogue that forms its background was written by Mallarmé in 1876 and had become the outstanding example of symbolist vagueness and obscurity—a "famous miracle of unintelligibility." Various translations of the piece have been attempted and most of them have failed, for the reason that Mallarmé's style defies exact translation. Only Edmund Gosse seems to have been able to convey a full measure of Mallarmé's dream picture, in a paraphrase that is both a matchless piece of English prose and an indispensable companion to Debussy's music:

A faun—a simple, sensuous, passionate being—wakens in the forest at daybreak and tries to recall his experience of the previous afternoon. Was he the fortunate recipient of an actual visit from nymphs, white and golden goddesses, divinely tender and indulgent? Or is the memory he seems to retain nothing but the shadow of a vision, no more substantial than the "arid rain" of notes from his own flute? He cannot tell. Yet surely there was, surely there is, an animal whiteness among the brown reeds of the lake that shines out yonder. Were they, are they, swans? No! But Naiads plunging? Perhaps! Vaguer and vaguer grows the impression of this delicious experience. He would resign his woodland godship to retain it. A garden of lilies, golden-headed, white-stalked, behind the trellis of red roses? Ah! the effort is too great for his poor brain. Perhaps if he selects one lily from the garth of lilies, one benign and beneficent yielder of her cup to thirsty lips, the memory, the ever-receding memory, may be forced back. So when he has glutted upon a bunch of grapes, he is wont to toss the empty skins into the air and blow them out in a visionary greediness. But no, the delicious hour grows vaguer; experience or dream, he will never know which it was. The sun is warm, the grasses yielding; and he curls himself up again after worshiping the efficacious star of wine, that he may pursue the dubious ecstasy into the more hopeful boskages of sleep.

Debussy's music begins with the voice of a solo flute, "singing" (wrote Lawrence Gilman) "a drowsily voluptuous phrase that falls and rises indolently between C sharp and G natural, as if undecided whether to stay in the key of E or wander into C major." With that melody —exotic and unforgettable—the first notes of a new impressionism are sounded, and music has bridged a gap to a wholly new territory of the imagination. In all the history of this art nothing quite like it had been heard before.

First to be noted about this piece is its essentially non-Germanic style. By a bold departure from convention in all three departments—melody, harmony, and rhythm— Debussy creates a new style that henceforth will be one sign of a typically Gallic art. The tissue of this music is the antithesis of German solidity and forthrightness. It turns instead to vagueness and impalpability, to softness and to understatement; to subtle delicacies of sonority and the beauty of tone coloring for its own sake. An indeterminate key feeling in the opening measures continues throughout the work. It is hard to predict the exact tonality at any given moment; some chords move from one to another with very little formal preparation; what used to be called unrelated chords follow each other at will. Liberal use of the whole-tone scale helps to break up the bounds of tonality; dissonance is frequent, as is (in Léon Vallas' phrase) "the enveloping of the real notes of a chord in notes alien to it."

With this new harmonic freedom, melody is correspondingly unfettered. The chief theme of the flute, with its chromaticism and its strong suggestion of the interval of an augmented fourth, is typical of the new type of melody that Debussy has invented. The innumerable changes of time signature also indicate a new phase—a fluctuation of rhythm almost at will.

Except for two antique cymbals (which add "gleams of silver light" at the close) the instrumentation is remarkable for its modesty—a fair-sized woodwind choir, four horns, two harps, and strings. Solo flute, oboe, clarinet, horn, and violin are given some of the rarest melodic flights in modern music, while the harp is used with a new understanding of its exotic tonal coloring. These ingredients, with a polyphonic structure that is Wagnerian in its density and richness, bring about an entirely new color series to the orchestral palette.

After more than half a century *L'Après-midi d'un faune* retains its essential beauty. It has been imitated times without number, but never equaled. Debussy himself never returned to this particular phase of his art; hating repetition, he passed on to still further refinements and excursions. The "Faun" stands alone, unmatched in music for sheer voluptuousness of sound.

## VII

Debussy's next major work took the form of three Nocturnes for orchestra, completed in 1899. These were titled *Nuages* [*Clouds*], *Fêtes* [*Festivals*], and *Sirènes* [*Sirens*]. The third Nocturne requires a small chorus of women's voices in addition to the orchestra. The composer's original plan was to write a triptych for solo violin and orchestra, and he had in mind the famous Belgian violinist, Eugène Ysaÿe, as his first interpreter. Over a period of several years the general scheme of these pieces underwent various changes, until the solo violin idea was abandoned altogether. Soon after their publication the first two Nocturnes became standard works in symphonic repertoires all over the world.

On the occasion of their first performance Debussy provided short descriptions of his pieces in which he said that "the title *Nocturnes* is to be understood in a wider sense than that usually given it, and should be regarded as conveying a decorative meaning." For *Nuages* he had in mind "the unchanging aspect of the sky, with the slow melancholy passage of clouds dissolving in a gray vagueness tinged with white." There have been many successful landscapes in tone, many evocations of nature; but this small orchestral canvas remains unique. It is the quintessence of Debussy's mature style and technique. A model of economy and restraint, it never speaks boldly; rather it insinuates, in a vague dreaminess and with infinite subtlety. The technical process is one of distillation.

The mood and style are announced in the opening measures by two clarinets and two bassoons, in a progression of parallel fifths and thirds that must have convinced the Hanslicks of the time that a madman was at work. (This figure, by the way, may indicate one of Debussy's debts to Mussorgsky, for in the latter's song "*Retrospect*," in the "*Sunless*" cycle, there appears a similar figure in the accompaniment.) A moment later the English horn sings a phrase of singular mournfulness. It never develops; instead it reappears at various times, delicately poised against a shifting background. There is little of orthodox development of themes; this is replaced by repetition of a few basic ideas. The pace is unvaryingly slow, like the grave convolutions of clouds themselves; their drifting formlessness is indicated by bold progressions of unrelated ninth chords ("gliding chords," one musicologist has called this Debussy invention). The pentatonic scale lends its exotic melancholia; there are many suggestions of the open tritone, for its empty, keyless effect, its "vague grayness."

Far from lacking emotion, *Nuages* is one of the most affecting pieces Debussy ever wrote. It evokes those nameless, unspoken thoughts that clouds themselves evoke. There are many touches of emotional significance—brought about by a sudden change of a chord from minor to major, an alteration of some expected harmony, or a line of counterpoint (like that of the viola at the reappearance of the first theme) which accentuates the prevailing sadness.

In *Fêtes* the composer imagined "the restless, dancing rhythms of the atmosphere, interspersed with abrupt scintillations. There is also an incidental procession—a wholly visionary pageant—passing through and blending with the argent revelry; but the background of uninterrupted festival persists; luminous dust particles in the universal rhythm." In his descriptive notes as well as in his music, it might be observed, Debussy was using something of the symbolist-impressionist technique.

*Fêtes* is a crowded, phantasmagoric canvas of brilliant effect; at the same time it is light as air, impalpable and visionary as the dream stuff of the mind. An exotic rhythmic structure, complex and wayward, animates the entire work. The melodies fly past like themes blown along the wind; at the close they are like tunes heard at a distance in the hot languor of the summer night—vague, unfinished, vanishing into air at the touch. The pageant that interrupts this "argent revelry" is a breathless moment of sheer effect which has no equal in impressionistic music: distant trumpets and throbbing harps announce the coming of some new cavalcade of maskers; within the space of a few measures the orchestral scene is suddenly ablaze with magic light and color—and then in an instant they have all vanished, their themes calling back from afar as the scene fades away.

For a long time the third Nocturne was a neglected member of the group, largely because it demands a choir of women's voices able to cope with difficult problems of intonation. Debussy wrote that "*Sirènes* depicts the sea and its countless rhythms, and presently, amongst the waves silvered by the moonlight, is heard the mysterious song of the Sirens as they laugh and pass on." The voice parts of the mythical creatures are wordless; their melodic lines are lyric fragments that float upon the air—laughing, calling, full of enticement and mystery. Around them the orchestra depicts the sea with its endlessly undulating swell. Here Debussy creates a series of subtly formed, vividly evocative figures that presage his great seascape, *La Mer*, which would come a few years later.

It is easy to understand how the term "impressionism," which was in the forefront of controversy in the art world at that time, came to be applied to the new music of Debussy. Works like these Nocturnes are perfect examples of the power of suggestion which is the basis of the impressionistic idea. There is no attempt at graphic representation, no direct imitation of the sights or sounds of nature. There are only vague hints, purposeful elisions and dislocations, a studied diffuseness, which, given merely the word of the title to start the imagination, evoke in the listener's mind a train of images. In many of Debussy's finest impressionistic works, such as these, the listener often brings as much to his aesthetic enjoyment as he receives.

VIII

Debussy was fortunate in hitting upon Maeterlinck's drama, *Pelléas et Mélisande,* as the subject for an opera. The composer had an acute sense of theatrical values, but in the selection of a story he was limited by the peculiarities of his own musical style. His difficulties are indicated in the fact that *Pelléas et Mélisande* is his single completed opera. He tried hard to find other subjects. There were at least five different story ideas (including Shakespeare's *As You Like It,* and Poe's *The Fall of the House of Usher*) which he entertained at various stages of his career, but which were abandoned before any real progress was made.

There was no question about *Pelléas et Mélisande.* Debussy seems to have realized at once that it would be an ideal vehicle for his own ideas, and when he set about building his libretto he had to make comparatively few changes in Maeterlinck's original drama. The story itself is a variant of the Paolo and Francesca theme. Golaud and Pelléas are half brothers, grandsons of Arkel, the old King of Allemonde. Golaud, middle-aged and stern (a counterpart of the modern Soames Forsyte), finds Mélisande lost and weeping beside a spring in a strange forest. Her golden crown has fallen into the spring. She is a princess, but she will tell Golaud nothing of whence she came or why. Months later Golaud returns to the ancient castle of his grandfather, bringing Mélisande with him as his wife. There she meets Pelléas. The main part of the drama is concerned with the growing love between Pelléas and Mélisande and the torturing jealousy suffered by Golaud. The older brother finally kills Pelléas when he finds Mélisande in his arms. In the closing scene Mélisande herself is dying, after having given birth to a child. In an agony of remorse and doubt Golaud questions her about Pelléas. She admits that she loved him, but innocently.

Debussy was attracted to this story for its unusual emotional quality and also because Maeterlinck clothed it in an atmosphere of vague, elusive beauty. There is a spell of medieval mystery over the old castle, with its ancient towers and trees that shut out the sunlight, its caves and grottoes, its vistas of the near-by sea. In this setting the drama that unfolds is part real, part imaginary. The characters live in half shadows, their thoughts and actions repressed and indeterminate. Mélisande herself is a child of mystery, the embodiment of a fragile and disturbing beauty. The love between her and Pelléas remains unspoken throughout the drama until the very moment of his death. The old king, Arkel, is a compassionate witness to this human suffering, which he is powerless to prevent or assuage. The tragedy ends with an unresolved doubt in the tortured mind of Golaud.

The opera that Debussy fashioned from this story is a perfect example of the union of drama and music for which opera revolutionists from Gluck to Wagner had been striving. Debussy's debt to Wagner in this score is great. *Pelléas et Mélisande* could never have come into existence had not Wagner already freed opera from the dynasty that had made everything subservient to the voice —freed it by stripping it of aria, recitative, ensemble singing, and every other purely vocal advantage. Wagner ended up by centering the interest in his work not in the drama, as was his intention, but in the orchestra, where he created veritable symphonies. Debussy shifted the center of gravity back toward the drama, so that in *Pelléas et Mélisande* the music and the dialogue are in perfect harmony. There are no arias or recitatives to hold up the dramatic action, nor is there any thematic development in the orchestra to impede the dialogue. The vocal parts in general follow the inflections of the speaking voice. Under this the orchestra lays a tapestry of sound—restrained, delicate, incomparably rich—accentuating and assisting the drama, but never overwhelming it except in a few moments of emotional climax.

Debussy was also indebted to Wagner for an elaborate system of leading motives, but here again the Frenchman used the German's idea with refinements of his own. The Wagnerian motives are usually the chief thematic material wherever they appear, either in the vocal lines or in the orchestra, so that their purpose and importance can never be missed. In his critical diatribes against Wagner, Debussy always ridiculed this usage of leading motives, likening it to a person presenting his calling card every time he appears on the stage. The motives in *Pelléas et Mélisande* are often so concealed that many of them are not clearly identified even after repeated hearings, but can only be unearthed from a study of the score. This somewhat recondite procedure is in keeping with the substance of the drama itself.

That *Pelléas et Mélisande* should have been a puzzling and controversial work is not surprising. Even today it appeals to a limited sector of the operatic public. Here is an opera with not the slightest concession to display or effect; with singing parts that require not a note of vocal gymnastics, but instead a deep knowledge of the art of acting; with an orchestral part that has the delicacy of chamber music, and a story that progresses with little dramatic action in a world of shadow and impalpability. It required genius of a high order to infuse such material with vitality and enduring interest; it is obvious therefore why *Pelléas et Mélisande* remains an isolated work that Debussy himself was never able to duplicate.

Innumerable elements in this score indicate Debussy's gifts as a tonal dramatist. Every person in the story comes to life, portrayed first by the characteristics of his own vocal line and second by an orchestral commentary. The growing love between Pelléas and Mélisande, upon which the entire play revolves, is developed with a subtlety that only the French seem to understand. Through a series of scenes, that in other hands might well have become disjointed, the long curve of emotional interest rises steadily to the climax of Pelléas' death; it recedes with the death of Mélisande, a scene of pathos unsurpassed in the whole range of opera.

The score is strewn with remarkable tone pictures, all of them veiled in the same aura of misty illusion that clothes the drama. Those scenes dominated by Golaud are darkened by somber orchestral coloring; those between Pelléas and Mélisande are often bathed in brilliant instrumental light. Debussy's powers of evocation were never more compelling than in these references to the gloom and shadow of the ancient castle, to the forest and the fountain, and the magical vistas of the bordering sea.

The musical fabric of *Pelléas et Mélisande* is a synthesis of Debussy's mature style. One aspect in particular holds a clue to his artistic credo which was long misunderstood, i.e., his preoccupation with pure melodic beauty. Debussy's skill as a melodist was long overlooked because his melodies were not harmonized, developed, or featured according to age-old standards of practice. During his lifetime the criticism leveled against him had one recurring theme: that he was no melodist; indeed, that he was deliberately trying to destroy the importance of melody in the musical scheme. Against this idea Debussy himself protested vigorously. "My music," he said, "aims only at being melody. . . ." Now that the novelty is gone from its harmonic investiture, his melody appears in all its originality and charm—lines in which condensed, pregnantly expressed thematic germs and bold intervals alternate with delicate curves, with a feeling of the decorative always predominating. These melodies almost never extend or proliferate into the long-flowing contours of conventional development. Rather, they appear as sudden flashes of thematic light that float in the air for an instant and then are gone.

## IX

The sea held great fascination for Debussy, even though his life in Paris gave him comparatively few opportunities to view it at first hand. In *Pelléas et Mélisande* there are various allusions that clearly indicate its mysterious hold on his imagination. In 1904 these impulses bore fruit in

*La Mer* [*The Sea*], which he termed a set of three "symphonic sketches."

*La Mer* is the nearest that Debussy ever came to writing a symphony, that is to say, the nearest in point of spaciousness and general outline. Its three movements are entirely separate, but they are conjoined by a common style and a prevailing mood. The work is large, varied, and yet unified in the symphonic manner, even though it contains nothing of conventional symphonic construction or development.

*La Mer* is a complete refutation of the notion, often propagated, that Debussy's was necessarily a small-scaled art, that it was fragmentary, circumscribed, effeminate. That was an illusion too often created by the purposeful restraints that he imposed upon his style. In *La Mer* he gave scope to his music in accordance with the demands of the subject matter, and the result is a work of magnificent amplitude. It is Debussy's masterpiece in the field of orchestral writing, and one of the enduring monuments of musical impressionism.

The three parts of *La Mer* are titled: I. "*De l'aube à midi sur la mer* [*From Dawn till Noon on the Ocean*]"; II. "*Jeux de vagues* [*Sport of the Waves*]"; III. "*Dialogue du vent et de la mer* [*Dialogue of the Wind and Sea*]." Otherwise there is no record of any programmatic idea in the mind of the composer. Nothing more is needed, for his mastery of musical color, atmosphere, and evocation is so complete that the work becomes a procession of vivid canvases, each representing one of the endlessly changing aspects of the sea. The means by which these images are formed are never obvious. They spring from all sorts of subtle and devious uses of melody, harmony, rhythm, and orchestral coloring—an immense technical apparatus concentrated upon the central problem. The opening measures indicate the composer's method. A few notes are heard in the very low and high strings, the sound of tympani and harps, a woodwind, a muted trumpet—and instantly the feeling is projected of profound depth, with a surface of glassy calm. Thereafter that illusion of the sea is never for a moment lost, through three extended and varied movements. The mystery of a great body of water, its impenetrable and weighty depths, its surface that is either rippling with delicate spray or a tumult of enormous waves —even the sky that can be sullen with rain clouds or ablaze with the noonday sun—all this is contained in Debussy's music, for those who are willing to follow him with their own imaginations.

*La Mer* is heavy with unnamed and unexplained emotion, the emotion engendered by the sea itself in the heart of the beholder. This music is never static. It moves through a wide dramatic range, with climaxes of a magnitude and splendor seldom indulged in by this composer. At one moment the sky may be leaden, the sea green or deepest blue. In the next instant the whole scene is pierced by light; there is a gorgeous climax, startling as a seascape by Turner, in which the orchestral canvas is one suffusion of golden vaporous mist.

After *La Mer* Debussy spent some half-dozen years upon another orchestral task, one which caused him some of his hardest creative labors, but which yielded one final masterpiece. The work was a triptych titled *Images*, the separate pieces being called *"Gigues," "Ibéria,"* and *"Rondes de printemps."* It was the central panel—a dazzlingly exotic impression of Spain—which was the work of enduring quality.

Debussy knew almost nothing of Spain from personal experience. His biographers believe that aside from a few hours of a single day that he spent watching a bullfight in the town of San Sebastián, he had never actually set foot inside the country. He did know some Spanish music, in particular certain piano works of Albéniz, which captivated him. Out of this fragmentary experience he wove a vivid musical fabric, one whose authenticity was vouched for by Spain's greatest composer, Manuel de Falla. Falla could find nothing but praise for this "intensely expressive and richly varied music."

The three parts of *Ibéria* are titled: I. *"Par les rues et par les chemins* [*In the Streets and Byways*]"; II. *"Les parfums de la nuit* [*The Fragrance of the Night*]"; III. *"Le Matin d'un jour de fête* [*The Morning of a Festival*

Day]." It was said that Turgenev, in the process of creating a novel, usually wrote his story at great length; then he compressed it ruthlessly, until the finished product contained not a single phrase or word that did not contribute the maximum of strength to his story. Debussy did not actually work in this fashion (unless he did it subconsciously), but the effect of music like *Ibéria* is that of an even more extreme distillation. The composer extracts from the Spanish melodic idiom only the few essential notes, the characteristic contours; he animates them with rhythms that are the backbone of the Spanish style; and finally he tinctures his orchestration with the sound of castanets, tambourines, bells, and guitarlike strummings in the strings. Again, Debussy's method is still that of suggestion, of insinuation; his pictures shift and change and dissolve as in a vivid dream. One of his most exquisite pages is the second part, a nocturne that recalled for Falla "the intoxicating spell of Andalusian nights." The closing section, on the other hand, is Debussy's most brilliant movement, in which a riot of color and life, under the sun-drenched skies of Spain, is flashed across the musical screen.

x

In the period immediately before and after the composition of *La Mer*, Debussy's interest in the piano brought forth a series of remarkable works. The piano was singularly his own instrument; he loved it, and it was the only one of which he had any technical mastery as a performer. The creation of an impressionistic piano style, however, was one of the most difficult tasks that he attempted. This was owing both to the technical limitations of the instrument and to the type of piano writing which had been in vogue from the invention of the piano down to his own time.

Most of the important piano composers of the nineteenth century—Beethoven, Chopin, Schumann, Liszt—still based their music primarily on the idioms and figures that best accommodated the human hand and fingers.

True, they had not by any means bound themselves by these limitations to the extent that the eighteenth-century composers had; Chopin especially had made wide exploitations of the field of pure sonority. Nevertheless, it was the consideration of the fingers and their dexterity which still governed much of their thinking.

Debussy's advances in piano music are largely developments of new sonorities and tonal effects, for which he had to discard much of the conventional technical apparatus—the scales and arpeggios, the octaves and the orthodox chordal formations which had come to be "handy" to the pianist. For these he substituted his own highly individual chords and chord progressions, arpeggios full of alien notes, wholly new and different melody and accompaniment material, copious use of dissonance-creating chords, and a continual reliance upon tone color for its own sake.

The whole of Debussy's piano output is made up of short pieces. The early works bear chiefly abstract titles, but in his maturity pieces based on pictures or descriptive ideas predominate. The range of subjects is wide, as if the artist were chiefly concerned with letting his imagination range over as varied a field as possible. Some of these pieces are scenes from nature—*Clair de lune* [Moonlight], *Jardins sous la pluie* [Gardens in the Rain], *Reflets dans l'eau* [Reflections in the Water], *Poissons d'or* [Goldfish]. Others like *Pagodes* or *Soirée dans Grenade* recall a certain locality; a few are modern, sophisticated transformations of some old musical style or form—*Sarabande, Toccata, Hommage à Rameau*. Even in his two books of Preludes (which according to tradition are abstract in form) Debussy appended to each piece a short phrase that gives a descriptive clue, e.g., "*La Cathédrale engloutie* [The Engulfed Cathedral]," "*La Fille aux cheveux de lin* [The Girl with the Flaxen Hair]," "*Des Pas sur la neige* [Footprints in the Snow]," "*Feux d'artifice* [Fireworks]."

A work like *Reflets dans l'eau* may be quoted as typical of Debussy's piano style at its best, and an indication of his methods and his skill. The picture it calls to mind is that of a quiet pool, deep and secluded. For a brief moment the surface is disturbed by gusts of wind which set the water to rippling, the shadows to moving; then these vagrant reflections return slowly to repose. The piece has only the barest suggestion of melodic lines. It is all chords, glassy and dissonant, and arpeggios that swoop and glisten and undulate the length of the piano keyboard. The suggestion of wavering, distorted reflection is gained by dissonant chord formations and free modulations; there is in fact but one purely tonic chord in the entire piece—a magnificently contrived arpeggio on E flat, set with superb effect at the climax of the piece.

There is an intimate, personal quality about all Debussy's piano music. Like the composer himself, it is moody rather than sentimental. With its pictorial substance there is always a strong feeling of the decorative, and a craftsmanship that is always fastidious. It is also concise. The composer goes straight to the heart of whatever idea or picture he is projecting, no matter how subtle.

XI

The decline in Debussy's creative powers was a great misfortune to modern music. *Ibéria* was his last undisputed masterpiece; thereafter his output became uneven and at times dull. Undoubtedly his worsening illness contributed to a loss of creative vigor that left him falling back upon his own formulas and mannerisms.

In 1911 Debussy composed incidental music to *The Martyrdom of Saint Sebastian*, a miracle play by Gabriele d'Annunzio. At its production that year in Paris, Ida Rubinstein impersonated the Saint, and Leon Bakst designed the scenery and costumes. Debussy tried to evoke the mystical ecstasy of the youthful Roman martyr whose body was transfixed by the arrows of his fellow archers. To gain an archaic effect the composer made use of the Gregorian modes, successions of simple diatonic chords without sevenths, as well as some hints of organum. He tried to combine (as does the play) the ecstatic purity, the thin clear flame of the early Christian faith, with the empurpled sumptuousness of its Roman background. Debussy's score has been highly praised, and some have even called it a French *Parsifal*; but that estimate can hardly be sustained. Much of the time the composer was only imitating himself.

A more original work was *Jeux*, a ballet composed in 1912 and produced two years later by Serge Diaghilev, with choreography by Nijinsky. This is a singular score whose subtle and often fascinating details are still not wholly communicative to the music public. Its unusual construction followed a plan that Debussy had originated in *La Mer*—short musical phrases or melodic fragments that are pressed together to form a mosaiclike design, without obvious sequences or repetitions. The various elements are related, but in an obscure rather than an obvious way. In later years this method would be utilized by many contemporary composers, notably Igor Stravinsky.

Debussy's last works include two sets of Etudes for piano and a group of sonatas for various instruments. They indicate the composer's turn toward a kind of neoclassicism. For a time they were underrated and neglected, but in recent decades they have grown in critical esteem. With the suite *En blanc et noir*, for two pianos, they point the way toward a new phase in Debussy's art which was left only partially explored at his death.

The outbreak of World War I depressed Debussy terribly; following that there were surgical operations and continual worry over his financial affairs. Yet he tried to go on, exhausting himself with projects that were now beyond his strength. "There are mornings," he wrote, "when the effort of dressing seems like one of the twelve labors of Hercules."

Debussy bequeathed a very great legacy to music. His impressionism was clearly a part of the main romantic movement, but it was a new and revivifying influence at a time when romanticism was heading for decay. Moreover, Debussy's impressionism was far more than merely a personal style. It also included an immense new technical apparatus that gave the composers who came after him an entirely new set of tools with which to work. His uses of neglected scales like the whole-tone and pentatonic scales, his revival of the medieval modes and organum, his bold use of totally unrelated chords, his reliance upon chords of the seventh, ninth, eleventh, and thirteenth—above all his treatment of the chord as an element of beauty apart from melody—all these ideas can now be found in the music of every country, in popular media like music for sound films, and even in the commonest dance-band arrangements. They are part of the new language of music.

The power to attract imitators is by no means the criterion of greatness; Debussy had much more than that. It is clear now that for all its wraithlike incorporeality, its evocation of the dream within a dream, his music has nevertheless the peculiar vitality of all art that endures.

XII

It does an injustice to the music of Maurice Ravel when it is treated, even unintentionally, as an appendage to that of Debussy. Born in the French-Basque town of Ciboure in 1875, Ravel was thirteen years younger than the great impressionist, but their careers impinged constantly in Paris in the early years of the century. Their works were compared and contrasted, usually to the detriment of the younger man, who was even accused of plagiarism.

Ravel was no plagiarist. His affinity with Debussy's music was the result of a bond of admiration and of the fact that the two composers spoke a similar language—but each in his own way. That language was a new kind of harmony, originally devised by Debussy, but elaborated in richness and beauty by Ravel. It was to Ravel's credit that he did not simply imitate Debussy. The misty, wavering outlines of impressionism, its sacrifice of form for poetical suggestion—these were not to the liking of the younger man. Even though Ravel's music is often vividly pictorial and always decorative, his urge was toward a kind of neoclassicism, with clearly defined melodies, rhythms, and formal structure, e.g. in his *Sonatine* and *Le Tombeau de Couperin* for piano, his String Quartet, and the two piano concertos.

Stravinsky called Ravel a "Swiss watchmaker," which

was a left-handed way of describing one of the most scrupulous craftsmen of his age. Ravel himself wrote: "I never put down a work until I have made absolutely certain that there is nothing about it that I could improve." That is why his catalogue contains mostly single examples of a form. It also accounts for the high level of his accomplishment. From *Pavane pour une infante défunte* (1899) to the Concerto in G for piano (1931) he had few failures, few works that the music public does not continue to give its high esteem.

Evocation, the summoning not alone of exotic pictures and places but also of the mannerisms of other composers, delighted Ravel. Possible because of his partly-Basque ancestry he never tired of recalling Spain—in his piano piece *Alborado del Gracioso*, in his delightful opera *L'Heure espagnole* [*The Spanish Hour*], in the *Rhapsodie Espagnole* and *Bolero* for orchestra. *Le Tombeau de Couperin* is a modern tribute to the great seventeenth-century clavecinist; *La Valse* evokes the Strauss waltz in its glittering Viennese setting; *Tzigane*, for violin and piano, paraphrases Liszt's Hungarian essays; while in the Piano Concerto for the Left Hand there are touches of American jazz.

Ravel's piano music ranges from the tender sentiment and delicate sonorities of *Ma Mère l'Oye* [*Mother Goose*], to the super-brilliance of *Miroirs* and *Gaspard de la Nuit*, pieces that are Lisztian in their display of transcendant virtuosity. For these the pianist must conquer fiendish technical difficulties; he must command a huge palette of shifting, coruscating colors and moods that range from the whimsical to the mordant.

Ravel's other instrument was the orchestra, and here he was a master among masters. With the *Rhapsodie Espagnole*, *La Valse*, *Bolero*, the transcription of Mussorgsky's *Pictures at an Exhibition*, and above all in his finest work, the ballet *Daphnis and Chloë*, the composer brought to its climax the art of instrumentation that had begun with Berlioz.

As a man Ravel was small of stature and retiring and shy by nature. Like his art, his life was perfectly ordered, fastidious. He never married, had few intimate friends, but was admired for his dry wit and aristocratic manners. After World War I he lived almost the life of a recluse in his home at Montfort l'Amaury, near Paris. With his death in 1937, at the age of sixty-two, France lost one of her most brilliant and fascinating artists of this century.

# Strauss
## 1864—1949

### I

When Goethe was an old man, he revisited a chalet in the Thuringian hills, and on the walls of the bedroom he found the words he had written there on a night thirty-three years before. The inspiration of his young manhood was *Ein Gleiches* ("*Über allen Gipfeln ist Ruh'*"), one of the most famous, and surely one of the loveliest poems in the German language. As the old poet-philosopher retraced the faded writing of his lost youth, he wept.

It is not recorded that Richard Strauss in his later years ever acknowledged any such show of emotion as he turned the pages of his own youthful masterpieces (say, the closing measures of *Don Juan*, with its stabbingly poignant episode of the libertine's death); but if he did, he had more to lament than vanished youth. He would have had to weep, too, over the far more grievous decline of his genius. For more than thirty years—that is, after he produced *Der Rosenkavalier* in 1911—he went right on composing one score after another, turning the wheels of a technical machine that is one of the marvels of his time, but only occasionally tapping the waters of inspiration that had once poured from his pen.

As an old man he had the melancholy experience of sitting by and watching the slow disintegration of what was once the outstanding reputation in modern music. At the turn of the century he was the *Übermensch* of the art of music. His tone poems were a nine-days' wonder; later, two of his operas were the most provocative works yet set upon the lyric stage. Unfortunately for him, Strauss lived into a new day, and time scaled down almost everything he created. This is not to say that all his music is a dead issue; on the contrary, at least six of his orchestral works maintain their popularity in symphonic repertoires, and his *Rosenkavalier* is still one of the finest comedies the opera house has to offer. But no one is awed any longer by Strauss's music, or disturbed by it, or even puzzled. It is quite evidently the end of an epoch in the romantic movement in German music, not the beginning of anything radically new.

Strauss began life as a boy prodigy like Mozart; in adolescence he became a Brahmsian classicist; in early manhood he gave promise of becoming so great a revolutionist that some dared to compare him with Beethoven; finally he emerged as a super-Liszt, an electrifying romantic. Like Liszt's, his music has not been able to retain the prestige that an adulating world once pressed upon it.

Strauss was born in Munich on June 11, 1864. It seemed that the gods had given him all the gifts that a musical genius might require. There was a strong strain of music in his ancestry. His father, the first horn player of the Munich Opera, was a musician of distinction. There was also wealth in the family. His mother was one of the Pschorrs, brewers of a famous Munich beer. Richard Strauss began to indicate an unusual talent for music when he was only five years old, and at six he was composing pieces for the piano. After that he received every advantage of fine schooling and the best training in music. At the age of sixteen he had a large number of compositions to his credit, including a symphony. Two years later the symphony was performed in public, under the direction of Hermann Levi, who first conducted Wagner's *Parsifal*.

When Strauss was nineteen, another famous conductor, Hans von Bülow, took an interest in the young composer. Strauss became the assistant conductor of Bülow's orchestra at Meiningen, and that step produced two important effects in his life. First, he learned the art of conducting from one of the masters of orchestral craftsmanship. The method of the acid Bülow must have been both rigorous and harrowing. Strauss later recalled that the older man once made him compose a suite for wind instruments, and then made him stand before the orchestra and conduct it without a rehearsal. Strauss had great aptitude for what he was attempting. The orchestra was his personal instrument, and it became the medium around which much of his work revolved throughout his career.

The second important effect of young Strauss's stay at Meiningen was his friendship with a man named Alexander Ritter, who was a violinist in the orchestra. Ritter was an intellectual and a passionate admirer of the works of Wagner, Liszt, and Berlioz—the entire romantic movement that the younger Germans of the day called "the music of the future." Strauss admitted that Ritter's counsel and his enthusiasm had a great effect on him. Up to the Meiningen period (which began late in 1883) Strauss's works all bore the impress of classicism of the Brahms type; aside from certain songs, they were in the form of sonatas, serenades, concertos, symphonies, etc. In 1887, after he had left Meiningen and become an assistant Kapellmeister at the Munich Opera, he wrote *Macbeth*, which was a tone poem—and the tone poem, as everyone knows, was the invention of Franz Liszt. *Macbeth* was followed in 1888 by *Don Juan*, and in 1889 by *Tod und Verklärung* [*Death and Transfiguration*]. These last two works were enormously successful, and at the age of twenty-five they made the young conductor the most talked-of musician in Europe.

Strauss left Munich in 1889 to conduct at Weimar, where he held a post until 1894. Meanwhile, however, he had a physical breakdown from overwork which threatened his life. He spent a year touring Greece, Egypt, and Sicily, throwing off a dangerous ailment of the lungs. During his travels he worked on his first opera, *Guntram*, which was produced in 1894 at Weimar. Strauss later married the singer, Pauline de Ahna, who sang the leading role. *Guntram* is a gloomy tragedy of medieval Germany, with a libretto written by the composer himself. The opera was a failure, being a weak imitation of Wagner.

In the years that immediately followed, Strauss made many appearances as conductor in various important German cities, and in Moscow, London, Paris, Amsterdam, Zurich, and Madrid. His real work, during the four years between 1895 and 1899, was the composition of four more tone poems—*Till Eulenspiegel, Also sprach Zarathustra, Don Quixote,* and *Ein Heldenleben.* One of these appeared each year, for four years. When they were finished Strauss was thirty-five years old, and the most towering figure in modern music.

II

The tone poem (or symphonic poem) is one of the few inventions in form that we owe to the romantic movement in music, and, as we have seen, it was created practically singlehanded by Franz Liszt. The tone-poem idea was a distinct success. It was quickly taken up by other composers and resulted in some of the most picturesque music of the romantic era. It remained for Richard Strauss to develop the tone poem into a work of epic proportions. His early *Macbeth* and *Don Juan* are clearly in the style of Liszt—fairly short and easy to follow even without benefit of a guiding program note. The ensuing works become longer and more complex, until with *Ein Heldenleben* the form has grown into a gigantic structure of six sections, each almost as long as a single symphonic movement. For the full understanding of the work a detailed knowledge of the scenario is a necessity.

*Macbeth* must be classed as an immature work. *Don Juan,* however, is wholly remarkable, and as the work of a man twenty-four years old it must rank as one of the most extraordinary scores produced in the last decades of the nineteenth century. Strauss prefaced *Don Juan* with verses from a dramatic poem by the Hungarian poet, Nikolaus Lenau. The general theme, it appears, is something more than the libertine's search after women. "My 'Don Juan,'" explained the poet himself, "is no hot-blooded man eternally pursuing women. It is the longing in him to find a woman who is to him incarnate womanhood, and to enjoy, in the one, all women on earth, whom he cannot as individuals possess. Because he does not find her although he reels from one to another, at last disgust seizes hold of him, and this disgust is the devil that fetches him."

Strauss's portrait of this Don Juan is amazingly vivid, swiftly realized and, at the end, pathetic. It is a score of immense vitality and zest. In the very opening measures the music fairly rips itself from the instruments in its eagerness to be born. Thereafter it alternates between headlong impetuousness, even violence, and a sensuous lyricism. The scoring is brilliantly articulate throughout. Strauss at twenty-four is already a master of the orchestra, and every one of his effects is thrust home to the hilt. When Debussy once criticized his rival's music, he admitted its "cyclonic energy" and its composer's "amazing orchestral assurance." The terms were apt. With *Don Juan* a veritable cyclone was let loose in orchestral music, and it would be many years before the storm would begin to blow itself out.

*Death and Transfiguration* is a larger and more pretentious work than *Don Juan*, but it has not worn as well with the passage of years. It owes a heavy debt to Liszt, especially to *Les Préludes*. There is a striking similarity between the poetic ideas that shape the course of the two works. Strauss's scenario is set forth in a poem prefaced to the score. It was written by his friend Ritter after the music was finished. A man is lying upon his deathbed, exhausted by his struggle for life. In his delirium he relives the scenes of his childhood, of his youth, and the heroic aspirations of young manhood. At last death seizes him, but from the worn-out body the spirit ascends heavenward in a radiant apotheosis.

*Death and Transfiguration* is one of the most effective of Strauss's works. The long section at the close which represents the transfiguration is masterfully contrived—a prolonged crescendo that reaches one of the most overpowering climaxes in orchestral music. Strauss holds the orchestra in a giant grip, forcing from it the absolute maximum of sonority. For years this physical magnitude of *Death and Transfiguration* held listeners and composers alike spellbound. It was only after the German cult of vastness in music had collapsed in the years following World War I that the weaknesses of this score and the imitations it engendered became evident. It is the familiar story of thematic material that lacks the beauty and dignity necessary for the architectural frame it attempts to fill. There is a disturbing commonplace quality, even a cheapness, about some of the Strauss melodies which no amount of orchestral craftsmanship can efface.

*Till Eulenspiegel* followed five years after *Death and Transfiguration*. It is a piece of musical humor which many admirers of Strauss's work would not trade for anything else he has written. For cleverness and wit, for gusto and impudent high spirits, the piece has few rivals anywhere in music. The entire title of the piece gives some clue to its contents: *Till Eulenspiegel's Merry Pranks, Set in the Old-time Roguish Manner, in Rondo Form, for Full Orchestra*. Till Eulenspiegel is a comic hero and vagabond who appears in German literature as far back as 1515. (The name Eulenspiegel means literally "owl's mirror.") Till's escapades and pranks, many of them crude, elephantine, and even obscene, are part of the folklore of Germany.

Strauss supplied no written program for his rondo (he admitted that several of the episodes suggested "might even give rise to offense"), but the general idea has been pieced out. Till is followed through various scrapes—riding on a horse pell-mell through the market place and upsetting all the tinware; disguising himself as a priest, then as a cavalier boldly making love; and finally finding himself in the hands of the constabulary. The high court condemns the rogue to the gallows, and that indeed is his end—a final squeaking of woodwinds as he is strung up.

There can be little but praise for Strauss's sense of humor in this superb score. It is as vivid and colorful and essentially human as a Breughel canvas, and its coarseness would have been loved by young Mozart. The comic aptness of the themes and their charm, the expert handling of the orchestration, and above all the tremendous energizing speed and force of the piece have made it irresistible.

Strauss's creation of a tone poem based on Nietzsche's philosophical work, *Also sprach Zarathustra* [Thus Spake Zarathustra], was one of the most ambitious and difficult tasks he ever attempted for orchestra. He took for his model one of the most controversial books of modern times. The origins of *Also sprach Zarathustra* go back to the hero worship of Richard Wagner by the neurotic young philologist, Friedrich Nietzsche, during the composer's days at Triebschen. That friendship had ended in rupture, and then in bitterness and hatred. Later Nietzsche was so revolted by *Parsifal* that he poured vitriol over Wagner and all his works: "He flatters every kind of Christianity and every religious form and expression of decadence. . . . Wagner . . . a decrepit and desperate romantic. . . ." Meanwhile Nietzsche had had a dangerous mental breakdown and a broken love affair. He went to Italy and then high into the Alps where he brooded in solitude—frustration, egotism, and inspiration all boiling within him. In the spring of 1883, when Wagner was dying in Venice, Nietzsche began *Also sprach Zarathustra,* a flaming answer to the composer's theatrical Christianity, and his own masterpiece. This prose poem, this philosophical rhapsody was nothing less than a damnation of the entire idea of Christian morality, and a glorification instead of the pagan virtues of strength which should produce the Superman. When Richard Strauss composed his tone poem based on the work, a decade after it appeared, Nietzsche was long since hopelessly insane.

Nietzsche's Zarathustra is supposedly Zoroaster, the ancient Persian seer, who attempts to solve the riddle of the universe. His philosophical adventures form the basis of the book. Strauss specifically disclaimed any intention to "write philosophical music, or to portray in music Nietzsche's great work." He simply chose certain passages and episodes from the book, piecing them together to form a musical rather than a philosophical fabric.

In the introduction Zarathustra salutes the rising sun.

"Thou great star! What would be thy happiness, were it not for those for whom thou shinest?" Thereafter he begins his quest. He tries to find the answer to his questions in religion, in joys and passions, and in brooding upon death; but nothing satisfies him. He turns to science, and again is disillusioned; then to the dance and laughter and song. As night falls, he dreams of love, but his sleep is broken by the deep ringing of the midnight bell. The work ends in a veil of mystery, the music sounding in two keys at once, indicating that the enigma of the cosmos remains unsolved.

Even though he strictly limited the scope of his tone poem in relation to Nietzsche's original, Strauss nevertheless undertook an audacious task in welding a mass of amorphous material into a musical whole. His piece is in one gigantic movement, as long as an average modern symphony. There are some ten different sections, merging one into another; but they are varied in mood, giving the effect of a series of musical illustrations, each describing an episode in Nietzsche's book.

There has been wide disagreement about the ultimate value of this work. Some have called it Strauss's orchestral masterpiece; others find it his most uneven score, a failure that has served to point up the essential weaknesses of the composer's entire style. About the introductory section of the tone poem—Zarathustra's invocation to the rising sun—there has never been any disagreement. It is one of the great exordiums of music—enormous, portentous, a solemn declaration by the entire orchestra and organ in the blazing white key of C major. This is one effect that Strauss, the master of orchestral effect, never surpassed. If *Also sprach Zarathustra* could have maintained the inspirational level of these opening measures there would never be any question of its value; instead it is spotted throughout with unevenness and inequality. There is no denying the dramatic power of the work, the superb mixtures of contrapuntal sound, the enormous vigor, the breath-taking orchestral virtuosity. But vitiating its power are overmellifluous melodies and sugary harmonies that lack dignity and conviction.

## III

For his next tone poem Strauss turned from a modern literary masterpiece to a venerable classic, and from philosophy back to humor. His inspiration was Cervantes' *Don Quixote*. The piece was composed at Munich in 1897. Strauss gave it the subtitle: *Fantastic Variations on a Theme of Knightly Character*. Its form is roughly an introduction, theme and variations, and finale. The solo cello plays a part so important that the work is also in the nature of a modern concerto for that instrument.

As in the case of *Also sprach Zarathustra* the composer makes no attempt to digest the original work as a whole. His piece is simply a series of musical illustrations of some of the more famous episodes. In the introduction the old gentleman of La Mancha is portrayed as he "passed his time reading books of knight-errantry. . . . He would pore on until it was day, and a-days he would read on until it was night; and thus, by sleeping little and reading much, the moisture of his brain was exhausted to that degree, that at last he lost the use of his reason." The orchestra gradually becomes a fantastic confusion of sound as the would-be knight's reason finally cracks. Then the two-part theme is announced: Don Quixote is voiced by the solo cello; Sancho Panza is personified by a comical theme in the tenor tuba and bass clarinet (later taken by the solo viola). The ten variations that follow describe the various sallies of the pair in search of knightly adventure—the famous joust with the windmills; the attack on a flock of sheep which the Don imagines is a "prodigious army of divers and innumerable nations"; the Don's dissertations on the glories of chivalry; the attack on a band of pilgrims whom he mistakes for ruffians; his dreams of Dulcinea as the ideal woman; the meeting with three country wenches, one of whom he imagines is his beloved; the wild ride through the air and in a magic boat; his humiliating defeat and his resolve to become a shepherd—and so on until the melancholy end, when the knight, his wits restored, meets his death.

Out of this fanciful material Strauss constructed a huge, sprawling, baroque score—luxuriant, humorous, pathetic. It surpasses everything that he wrote for orchestra, with the exception of *Till Eulenspiegel*; it proves that humor was his great mood, and that as a humorist in music he has few peers since Mozart. Even more than *Also sprach Zarathustra* it leans upon an elaborate scenario, without which innumerable details become diffuse and unintelligible. But it far surpasses the earlier work in its lack of pretentiousness, its essential humanity, and above all in the fidelity with which the ideas, the scenes and the characters are painted in music.

Technically speaking, *Don Quixote* is a stunning piece of work. Such a large and exuberant score, filled as it is with all sorts of grotesque and incongruous details, was first of all a problem in organization. As his title indicates, Strauss built it upon the variation form, deliberately choosing for its appositeness to his story as old-fashioned a matrix as a composer has at his command. But there is nothing old-fashioned in the use he makes of it; on the contrary it is an amazing example of modernized classicism. From a few basic thematic seeds are developed a forest of melodic and accompaniment ideas.

The lasting greatness of *Don Quixote* depends upon something more than its mechanics. It will live because it is a segment of human life, portrayed not in words or in paint but in tone. Strauss is here the authentic creator of human character. Ernest Newman wrote that "Strauss's Sancho is very humorous, but your laughter at him is always softened with tears; while the portrait of Quixote has an added touch of pathos in that it invariably suggests the spare, worn frame of the poor, middle-aged knight." The composer is also the natural storyteller who can make a reader love a character enough to feel genuine grief at his end. Strauss had a peculiar affection for death scenes; he could not resist bringing his characters to the "quiet-colored end of evening." At the close of *Don Quixote* he achieved the most touching of all his descriptions of a dying man, and one that is likely to remain a classic in the art of music.

Like the swing of a pendulum, Strauss's next tone poem, *Ein Heldenleben* [A Hero's Life], took him away from humor and back again to the extremes of seriousness and sentimentality. This huge work was written in 1898 and was the last of the tone-poem series. It is based not upon any known literary work but upon a scenario that the composer evolved himself. It had grown to be Strauss's rather curious habit to deny the existence of a background story to his tone poems, and then later to give sanction to an "official description" by some friend or disciple. In the case of *Ein Heldenleben* he declared that he was not portraying any particular hero of fact or fiction, "but rather a more general and free ideal of great and manly heroism." Furthermore the hero's adventures were those of the spiritual rather than the material world.

The authentic guidebooks of *Ein Heldenleben* divide it into six main sections: I. *"The Hero"*; II. *"The Hero's Adversaries"*; III. *"The Hero's Courtship"*; IV. *"The Hero's Battlefield"*; V. *"The Hero's Works of Peace"*; VI. *"The Hero's Release from the World."*

The first section is a tremendous exposition of the man of valor, with bold themes—octaves wide—surging up through the orchestra and breaking into climaxes of overpowering height. Subsidiary themes indicate that the Hero is not only valorous; he is also noble, proud, sensitive, a paragon of virtue. His adversaries on the contrary are the meanest of the mean. The woodwinds utter "shrill and snarling phrases," music that is purposely repulsive and harsh. Two tubas proclaim a sinister phrase made up of open parallel fifths, which is Strauss's deliberate gibe at the reactionaries and the pedants of music. The Hero's beloved is portrayed by the solo violin in a series of elaborate cadenzalike figures. She is an elusive creature and definitely capricious; the Hero pursues her through a long and involved courtship that ends in a love scene of impassioned splendor.

The dream of love is interrupted by "grim-visaged war." There ensues the biggest of all musical battle scenes, and some of the loudest music yet written for orchestra. The Hero is triumphant, of course. He returns, his brow "bound with victorious wreaths," to take up his great works of peace. Oddly enough this portion of the music (and very beautiful music some of it is) appears to be made up of themes from Strauss's own previous works—the tone poems, the opera *Guntram*, and the song "*Traum durch die Dämmerung.*" After another short struggle with his adversaries, the Hero reaches the moment of his release from the world. His death is peaceful, made tender by thoughts of his beloved; but at the end the scene is a vast effulgence of orchestral radiance and light.

Strauss had hoped to create in this work a monumental study in valor. It is a miracle that he escaped producing instead a classic of pure sentimentality and fustian. The scenario is sophomoric in its conceptions of heroism, and the music never fully escapes that fact. It alternates between noble beauty and shoddy theatricality. This Hero has little of the blood of reality in him. Strauss did not realize what every great novelist has known—that characters who are all virtue are generally dull.

What saves *Ein Heldenleben* from ruin and makes it instead one of the composer's most popular works is his unfailing technical resource. Here (as in *Don Quixote*) he is working at the maximum of his powers, and for a combination of lush melodic invention, polyphonic resourcefulness, and orchestral virtuosity it would be hard to cap this work. Nevertheless *Ein Heldenleben* contains the unmistakable signs of disintegration that overtook both Strauss and the type of music he stood for. It was his last great success in purely orchestral writing, even though he had almost forty years of creative life ahead of him. He had pushed his style, his craftsmanship, and the tone-poem form itself to their very limits.

With the close of his tone-poem period Strauss entered, at thirty-five, the phase of his widest fame and prestige. In 1898 he had accepted the post of first conductor at the Berlin Imperial Opera, which was under the aegis of Kaiser Wilhelm II. That institution remained the center of his activities for more than twenty years, but at the same time he was a familiar figure in opera houses and on concert platforms all over Europe. His was a figure to command respect—well over six feet tall, lean and straight, with a splendid head crowned by a bulging brow. Before an orchestra and in the opera pit he seemed extraordinarily tall and dominating. His handling of the orchestra was individual, and expert.

With Richard Strauss the modern type of creative musician appears in full stature. This was a musician who was first of all a man of the world—cultured, sure of his social prestige, proud of his art. Moreover, he was wealthy, for the popularity of his works all over the world soon began to pay him liberal sums in royalties. The contrast between Strauss and many composers of the past is startling indeed. Bach, the poor church cantor, Haydn and Mozart, the social equals of servants and lackeys, Beethoven and Schubert living in their squalid Vienna lodgings, would have been amazed at the wealthy Strauss who was also the social equal of any aristocrat of his time. In the great days of prewar Europe he stood on a par with the most illustrious scientists and pedagogues, statesmen and militarists; and the entire German nation exhibited him with pride. The man of music had at long last come into his own.

Strauss's personal life was never one to excite unusual interest. It was circumscribed from first to last by the arduous and unceasing labor of creating and producing music. For years it was the composer's habit to spend his summers at some country retreat, where he would have the solitude and the atmosphere necessary for the tough task of composition. Here the chief creative work on his scores would be accomplished. Back in Berlin during the winter months came the less taxing business of instrumentation and the finishing touches, work that could be carried on between opera and concert engagements.

Strauss could never complain of a wife who failed to appreciate him. Frau Strauss, having been an opera singer herself, understood with peculiar intuition the demands of her artist husband. In the Strauss household, it is said, she presided as a combination of wife, major-domo, and manager, so that the man whose destinies she was helping to guide would always appear to the world in the most appropriate surroundings and still be screened from its too inquisitive gaze. She has been pictured as a somewhat dominating helpmate, who ruled with a firm hand a household in which beauty, quiet, and order were (with often insufferable thoroughness) maintained.

In 1923 Strauss composed an operatic comedy, *Intermezzo*, with a libretto supposedly by himself. The chief characters are a famous composer and his wife—that is, the Strausses themselves, disguised not even thinly. The plot is an actual episode in their early married life, when the composer's wife opened a letter sent him, through an error, by a strange lady. Frau Strauss, very jealous, almost started divorce proceedings before the mistake was cleared up. *Intermezzo* was a resounding failure. It was said that Frau Strauss herself had insisted that her husband make an opera out of the episode and that she was the real author of the libretto. The same has been said of Strauss's ballet, *Schlagobers* [*Whipped Cream*], which told the story of a small boy who ate too much pastry, with the results typical of childhood. This was another failure, and it was openly remarked that Strauss "gallantly took responsibility for the story," which was "tasteless and stupid."

The composer's own happiness in his home life during the early years of his career was published to the world in a unique way. In 1904 he made his first visit to America, bringing with him the score of a new work. It was first performed on March 21 of that year, in Carnegie Hall and under the composer's direction. The work was the *Symphonia Domestica*. It is in one extended movement with three subdivisions: Introduction and Scherzo, Adagio, Double Fugue and Finale. The composer announced at first that he wanted the work listened to as pure music, but later it appeared that the dedication of the score—"To My Dear Wife and Our Boy"—had a double significance. According to an official description published the next year the three main themes of the *Symphonia* portray the husband, the wife, and the child. One section is supposed to describe the noisy confusion of the baby's bath; another illustrates the ecstatic aunts saying that the child looks "just like his papa!" and "just like his mama!" There is also a lullaby as the child goes to sleep, and an awakening scene at seven in the morning.

The *Symphonia Domestica* is one of the most thoroughly lambasted of all Strauss's orchestral scores. It has been called dull, unhumorous, and downright embarrassing in its frank descriptions of the simple domesticities, and is often quoted as an example of the composer's unrestrained humor and his poor taste. It is true that many people do not appreciate the particular brand of humor that uses a huge orchestra, the biggest of musical forms, and the most complex and varied technical devices to portray the tenderest of all human relationships.

However, these criticisms seem beside the point. The real weakness of this *Symphonia* is the inequality of its musical ideas. It has its lovely moments, like the exquisite cradle song, and the deeply felt love scene in the Adagio; but surrounding these green patches are too many desert wastes. The melodic lines become dry and uninspired; no amount of polyphonic and instrumental legerdemain can hide their inherent sterility.

IV

As he approached his fortieth year, Strauss's widening reputation was based entirely upon his tone poems. His two operas, *Guntram* and *Feuersnot* (1901), were failures, usually regarded as proof that the composer's talent lay in the orchestra and definitely not in the lyric theater. Between 1905 and 1911, however, he produced three operas that created even greater excitement than any of the tone poems, and made him the most important contributor to German opera after Wagner. These were the two tragedies, *Salome* and *Elektra*, and the comic masterpiece, *Der Rosenkavalier*.

It would have been impossible to compose anything but a controversial opera on the subject of Salome. The original play was written by Oscar Wilde in French, and published in 1893. The next year it appeared in an English translation by Wilde's young friend, Lord Alfred Douglas, with the famous drawings by Aubrey Beardsley. Wilde had considerably embroidered the original legendary and scriptural story of the daughter of Herod's wife and her part in the death of John the Baptist. He contrived a drama in which Salome conceives an abnormal passion for the Evangelist, who rejects her with terrible anathemas. Herod is in turn enamored of his stepdaughter, and in a moment of drunken desire offers her half his kingdom if she will dance for him. Salome then performs the Dance of the Seven Veils. At its conclusion she demands her price—the head of John on a silver charger. Herod, almost insane with fear, tries to buy her off, but she is adamant. The severed head is finally brought to her and at last her desire is fulfilled: she kisses the mouth of John. Herod then orders his soldiers to crush Salome beneath their shields.

Wilde's original is a play to be read rather than performed. The bejeweled prose-poetry obfuscates the more revolting details of the plot, giving the work an air of unreality. Beardsley caught that quality in his drawings, which are superb in their fantastic decadence and grisly humor. The play was of course widely denounced as a work of corruption.

Strauss's opera follows the play faithfully, except that the dialogue is shortened somewhat. After the first performance in Dresden in 1905 it was an enormous success throughout Germany. In England it was banned, because of the law that forbade public portrayal of biblical characters. On the night of January 22, 1907, it was performed in New York, at the Metropolitan Opera House. The roar of public disapproval that arose forced the board of directors to withdraw the work after that single performance. *Salome* was not performed again at the Metropolitan for almost thirty years.

The critics of *Salome* in the early 1900s were all scandalized by what seemed to them a deliberate perversion of the art of music into something debased, if not positively diseased. They saw in it only the spectacle of a woman driven by a maniacal passion to sadism and necrophilia. Strauss's score was excoriated as a deliberate study in ugliness and morbidity, and as evidence of an alarming decay in the aesthetic of music itself.

*Elektra*, first performed in 1909, did little to allay the fears of the tender-minded. The central character, although chosen from one of the greatest classics of antiquity, was hardly less shocking than Wilde's daughter of Herodias. Nor was Strauss's treatment of his subject one whit less uncompromising.

The opera was based on a drama by the noted Austrian playwright, Hugo von Hofmannsthal, who had gone for his sources to the Greek drama. Agamemnon, the leader of the Greeks in the Trojan War, was murdered on his return by his wife Clytemnestra and her paramour Aegisthus. His death was finally avenged by his son Orestes and his daughter Electra. The story was a favorite theme of Greek legend and literature for several centuries. Aeschylus used it in his *Oresteia* trilogy, about the middle of the fifth century B.C. Later it was made the subject of dramas by both Euripides and Sophocles. The terrible story has had many ancient and modern counterparts, one of the most recent being Eugene O'Neill's trilogy, *Mourning Becomes Electra*.

Hofmannsthal's play follows the version of Sophocles. The action takes place in the courtyard of the palace of Agamemnon at Mycenae, near Athens. It is seven years after the close of the Trojan War. Elektra, wild with grief at the murder of her father, is living in a hovel in the servants' quarters, waiting only for the moment of revenge. When her brother Orestes secretly returns from exile she plots with him the death of their mother and Aegisthus. Orestes finally kills them, with the ax that had slain Agamemnon, and Elektra in wild exultation dances on her father's grave.

Hofmannsthal and Strauss intensified and made even more frightful the character of Elektra. Lawrence Gilman described her as "incarnate vengeance—a ragged, glaring, disheveled Maenad: a 'wildcat,' say the servants, who screeches and snarls in her execrations, and dwells among the dogs in the courtyard; while to her mother she is a 'puff adder.' . . . She is a great and terrible figure; never a paltry one."

*Elektra*, like *Salome*, at first made many enemies for

Strauss, and not a great many admirers. After the excitement of their early performances had died down, both operas began to suffer neglect, but today they are back in public favor. What stands in the way of even more frequent performance is no longer their subject matter (the music public today, it would seem, is corrupted less easily), but rather their enormous musical difficulty. Both works call for huge orchestras, which must conquer scores of great complexity. The leading roles are uncompromisingly cruel. They are exhausting enough in their sheer physical demands, merely as acting parts; added to that are vocal lines that struggle against rather than find support from a rampant orchestra. *Elektra* especially is a score of unparalleled violence. The classic story is told of a rehearsal for its *première*, at which Mme. Schumann-Heink as Klytemnestra was having difficulty in spite of her powerful voice. The composer finally stopped the rehearsal and complained about the orchestra to the conductor, "Louder! Louder! I can still hear the voice of Frau Heink!"

Recent revivals have proven that, given first-rate vocal and orchestral artists who have imagination, intelligence, and sheer physical strength, there is immense vitality and interest in these operas, despite wide inequalities. Strauss constructed them according to the Wagnerian formula. They are music dramas in which the music is controlled throughout by the dialogue and the stage situations. They also employ a system of leading motives, similar to Wagner's. Melodically and harmonically Strauss pushes ahead into a territory of modernism considerably beyond that of Wagner's later works. Melodic lines abound with daring, angular intervals; harmonies are harsh, astringent, with leaps from chord to chord and key to key almost at will. There is a whole new vocabulary of dissonance.

Both operas contain powerful examples of Strauss's gift for portraiture. In the first the character of the drunken, neurotic Herod is a masterpiece (as indeed it is in Wilde's play); in the second, Elektra herself, an embodied Fury, and her debauched and fear-ridden mother are completely convincing and at times shockingly real. The composer also succeeds in wrapping each work in an atmosphere that adds remarkably to its evocative power. The mood of horror and tragic suspense which broods over the grim, blood-soaked courtyard at Mycenae, and the morbid decadence that pervades *Salome* like a sickening perfume are both created with swiftness and originality.

His nature being what it was, Strauss could not long remain at work at the black caldrons of tragedy. Two years after *Elektra* he completed *Der Rosenkavalier* [*The Cavalier of the Rose*], one of the most brilliant and successful opera comedies since *Die Meistersinger*. Strauss's collaborator was again Hofmannsthal, who concocted a story of Vienna at the time of Maria Theresa. It was a splendid libretto, both for its own comedy value and for the opportunity it offered the composer to work in a mood that ideally suited his temperament and his technical equipment.

The opera is an agglomeration of several different musical styles and mannerisms which Strauss fused into a coherent whole. The general form of the piece could be called Mozartean. It is partly a modern music drama and partly an eighteenth-century baroque comedy, with solos, duets, trios, and finales. Woven into the score are a number of Viennese waltzes in the manner of Johann Strauss, a charming anachronism, because the waltz postdated the Vienna of Maria Theresa by half a century. Finally, the orchestral part is symphonically rich and complete in the manner of Wagner.

Hofmannsthal's story concerns the love affair between the handsome young Octavian and the Princess von Werdenberg (the Marshallin), a woman no longer in the bloom of youth. Surprised one morning in the princess's boudoir, Octavian puts on the dress of a lady's maid. Thus disguised, he attracts the fancy of the middle-aged, boorish Baron Ochs, who has come to ask the advice of the princess about the choice of a rose cavalier. He is engaged to the lovely young Sophie Faninal, and according to the custom of the Viennese nobility he must send his bride-to-be a messenger with a silver rose as a symbol of his love. After the baron has left, the princess broods upon her own fading youth, and finally she decides that Octavian shall be the baron's rose cavalier. Octavian delivers the rose, and instantly he and Sophie fall in love. The problem then is to get rid of the baron, who is only marrying Sophie for her father's money. Octavian, in his lady's-maid disguise, lures the baron to a country tavern, and in a riot of tomfoolery shows him up before Sophie's father. The princess arrives in time to dismiss the baron, and in a last gesture of renunciation she smiles upon the union of Octavian and Sophie.

The libretto of *Der Rosenkavalier* suited Strauss because it is a comedy of sentiment—of love and tenderness and affection, as extravagant as the silks and satins, the sachet-laden atmosphere of the luxurious period itself. Liberally mixed with that is pure slapstick nonsense. All through his career Strauss had been a sentimentalist with a flair for suave and, at times, saccharin melody. The tone poems are full of these lyric outbursts, from the love song in *Don Juan* to the closing section of *Ein Heldenleben*. This opera runs over with charming melody, bedecked like an eighteenth-century costume in the sheer luxury and gorgeousness of the composer's most opulent orchestration. The waltzes are now famous in their own right, and they deserve it, for they are the best of their kind after the waltzes of Strauss's namesake.

The composer had two vivid portraits left for *Der Rosenkavalier*. One is the boorish, pleasure-loving baron; the other, the princess. The close of Act I, in which this handsome, passionate, and deeply understanding woman realizes that she is no longer young, is one of the composer's finest pages. The princess knows that for all his avowals she cannot hold her young man for long; she must begin to face the tragedy of age. As she sends him away she knows that it is her own spring that has vanished with the rose.

v

The decline in the art of Richard Strauss, which began with the completion of *Der Rosenkavalier* in 1911, is a tragedy never explained. He did not by any means stop composing. He kept right on producing score after score, exactly as might be expected of a man only forty-seven years old and at the height of a great and vigorous career. For almost thirty years he went through the motions of composition, but most of what came out was now a mixture of gold and dross.

The first clear manifestation of Strauss's failing powers came in 1915 with the *Alpine* Symphony, his first work for orchestra alone since the *Symphonia Domestica* a dozen years before. Shortly after the outbreak of World War I the composer retired to his country place in the Bavarian Alps and there (in the space of one hundred days, so it was said) he produced this mammoth score. It is supposed to depict the composer's own adventures during a day of Alpine climbing. Considering its physical dimensions and the size of the orchestra employed, this work must be accounted one of the worst failures in symphonic literature, as it is surely one of the biggest bores.

Thereafter Strauss stuck closely to the lyric stage. In 1916 he finished a revision of his opera *Ariadne auf Naxos*; in 1919 appeared *Die Frau ohne Schatten*; followed by *Intermezzo* (1923); *Die Aegyptische Helena* (1928); and *Arabella* (1933), in the style of *Der Rosenkavalier*, his last collaboration with Hofmannsthal. After the latter's death Strauss wrote *Die schweigsame Frau* (1935), a comic opera after Ben Jonson, with a libretto by Stefan Zweig. By that time Adolf Hitler's Nazi Party had coiled itself around the German nation, and Strauss had to drop Zweig, who was a Jew. He took on one Joseph Gregor, and with him produced *Daphne* and *Der Friedenstag* (1938). In 1941 came *Capriccio*. The ballet *Schlagobers* had been composed in 1923.

The fate of this group of stage works was curious. It seemed at first that some of them had appeared only to be showered with the vegetables of criticism: "confected out of the dregs of genius," "Strauss gone to seed," "inept," "lifeless," "dull," "bloodless," "senile." No one believed that Strauss's technical mastery had ever deserted him; it was his inspiration that was supposed to have dried up completely. Today, however, the verdict is somewhat different. Several of these pieces, once considered hopeless failures, have turned with the passage of years into successes. *Ariadne auf Naxos, Arabella, Die Frau ohne Schatten,* and *Capriccio* are now widely performed, and are often classed among Strauss's finest works.

Meanwhile, the composer himself had continued to live the same industrious life, part of the year the hard-working creative artist in the seclusion of his lovely summer home in Bavaria, in the winter a figure of distinction and prestige in the art centers of Europe. After World War I he was lured by the Austrian Government to head the Vienna Opera and to conduct a number of performances there each season. In part remuneration he was given a splendid villa in which to live. The grounds were part of the park belonging to the imperial Belvedere Palace. In the 1920s the aging composer, very tall and lean, dressed always in solemn black, could be seen taking his daily walks among the magnificent trees and lakes that had once delighted Prince Eugene of Savoy.

Gradually Strauss's commanding reputation began to suffer a decline corresponding with a loss of respect for his creative powers. With world reconstruction after 1918 there arose a new generation of composers whose work began to make Strauss's seem old-fashioned. The nadir was reached perhaps in the early 1930s when Strauss associated himself with the Nazi order, returning to Germany to become president of the Reich Music Chamber and chairman of the League of German Composers. In 1935 his resignation was suddenly announced by Dr. Paul Joseph Goebbels, the reason given being the composer's advanced age. But the blanket of Nazi censorship did not quite smother the truth. Three weeks before, in Dresden, Strauss had produced his opera *Die schweigsame Frau,* with a libretto by the "non-Aryan" Stefan Zweig. Goebbels, fearing the lash of public opinion outside Germany if the opera was suppressed, permitted it to go on, but all the Nazi leaders absented themselves from the *première.* Strauss was supposed to have earned further disfavor because his son had married into a Jewish family, and because the composer himself had visited Jewish friends in Berlin.

During the next few years the silences closed in upon the composer as the "New Order" began to spread over the politics and culture of Europe. However, with the gradual revival of interest in romantic music and the revulsion against the excesses of postwar art, Strauss's music regained some of the prestige that it had lost outside of Germany.

On the eleventh of June 1939, a few months before the beginning of World War II, there appeared in the American newspapers a dispatch from Vienna: "Richard Strauss conducted the Vienna Philharmonic Orchestra today in celebration of his seventy-fifth birthday. He shared applause with another music lover, Adolf Hitler."

When World War II came to an end, Strauss had passed his eightieth year. It transpired that the once-affluent composer was now almost penniless. His personal fortune in Germany had been destroyed in the fiery tornado of Hitler's downfall, and his royalties abroad had been confiscated or impounded. But in the bitterness of poverty and old age there was still comfort to be found in the remnants of the art that he had practiced for so many years. He had composed a Second Concerto for Horn and Orchestra in 1943 (the first had dated from 1884). In 1945 followed *Metamorphoses* for String Orchestra, in 1946 a Concerto for Oboe and Orchestra, and in 1948 *Four Last Songs*. Astonishingly, there was no trace of senility in these scores, but rather the composer's mastery of technical resource, unfailing to the end, and even the warmth of a gently glowing inspiration.

Richard Strauss died on September 8, 1949, at Garmish.

VI

One other composer must be coupled with Strauss as a dominant figure in post-romantic German music. This was Gustav Mahler (1860–1911). Born in Bohemia, Mahler first achieved eminence as a conductor of great distinction. In 1907 he conducted at the Metropolitan Opera in New York, and for two seasons he directed the concerts of the New York Philharmonic Society. Mahler's own music, however, was slow in reaching a wide audience. For years after his death it remained a center of controversy, and to this day it is both widely criticized and ardently defended.

Mahler's nine symphonies and his unfinished Tenth Symphony represent the ultimate in German Titanism. As early as his Second Symphony (1894) he was already trying to outdo Beethoven's Ninth with a series of Promethean struggles, apocalyptic visions, funeral marches of epic proportions, and a final world resurrection—all projected by an enormous orchestra and a forest of voices. By the time he had reached his Eighth Symphony (called the "Symphony of One Thousand" because it requires that many performers), this form of megalomania had reached its outer limits.

Deeply sensitive as a man, and fanatically devoted to his musical ideals, Mahler was pursued through much of his life by an abiding sense of sadness. The woes of the world rested upon him, and his music, like Tchaikovsky's, is often drenched by personal melancholia. In part his pessimism may have come from the realization that he was struggling constantly toward an ideal that seemed to elude him. That ideal was universality in art, as achieved by a Beethoven or a Goethe.

"Symphony must be like the world," Mahler once said. "It must embrace everything . . ." Into his enormous symphonic frescoes he tried indeed to cram everything. Here are hymnic glorifications, Beethovian conflicts, heroic perorations, distant horn calls, heavenly fanfares, and the last trump sounding; here too are dark, brooding lamentations that may be relieved, naïvely, by gay folk tunes and peasant dances, military marches, serene nature-painting and the sound of bird calls, Viennese *chinoiserie*, and even moments of burlesque and parody.

Greater composers than Mahler would have failed at the task of welding such masses of amorphous material; Mahler's problem went even deeper. His real gift was for the song, not for the heroic symphony. Thus he was a lyric poet trying to be a prophet. It is significant that his masterpiece is *Das Lied von der Erde* [*The Song of the Earth*], which is scored for two voices and a modest orchestra, and pays no homage whatever to size or impressiveness. In this restrained and deeply felt work (as in the composer's individual songs) Mahler's essentially lyric genius is revealed.

The technical side of Mahler's music has inspired many composers of the present century. He was one of the most inventive of modern masters of the orchestra, and his handling of the individual instruments and choirs yielded new ranges of color and timbre. The texture of his later works was also a move toward the future, being oriented toward the linear and the polyphonic.

With Mahler's symphonies the heroic spirit in German music that had extended back to Beethoven comes virtually to an end. In a few more years the romantic age itself would be shattered by the impact of a gigantic war.

# Stravinsky

## 1882—

### I

When the future historians of the twentieth century, taking the long view of its happenings, decide upon its pivotal events and circumstances, they will find May 29, 1913, a date to be reckoned with. In the field of modern music it will hold a place as crucial as the political and military crisis that shook the world fourteen months later.

On that evening at the Théâtre des Champs-Elysées, in Paris, Sergei Diaghilev produced a new ballet, *Le Sacre du printemps* [*The Rite of Spring*]. The choreography, as performed by Diaghilev's famous Russian dancers, was by Nijinsky, with scenery and costumes by Nicholas Roerich. Igor Stravinsky had composed the music.

The Parisians who attended that *première* could not have come with the intention of creating a fiasco even more scandalous than the one provided half a century before by Wagner's *Tannhäuser*, but they succeeded nevertheless in doing just that. What enraged them and turned them into two warring factions, yelling, hissing, and stamping in defiance, was the music—a score of such cacophonous violence and emotional fury that it struck many listeners with the force of an explosion.

The sensation caused by *Le Sacre du printemps* only began with its *première*. A year later at a Paris performance of the concert version there was such an uproar that Debussy, who was in the audience, arose and pleaded with the noisemakers to let the music be heard. In London, too, the concert version outraged many listeners. One man in typically British fashion complained to the newspapers, saying that the score "stood for all the unnamable horrors of revolution, murder, and rapine." In New York, Philadelphia, and Boston there were no casualties, but public opinion was violently agitated. At first performances the partisans of the work did what they could to drum up enthusiasm, while members of the Old Guard exercised their ancient prerogative of walking out in droves. To the former *Le Sacre du printemps*, like a modern *Eroica* Symphony, was expected to fling open the doors to an entirely new era in music; to the latter it represented the "blasphemous destruction of music as an art."

Leaving for a moment the question of these doubts and opinions, one thing can be said with certainty about Stravinsky's score. It established Stravinsky himself as the most influential and potent force in modern music for a space of almost two decades. This composer became the storm center of a movement which swept through the concert halls of Europe and America and threatened for a time to blow away the last remnants of romanticism itself.

Stravinsky's style, as it appeared in *Le Sacre du printemps* and evolved further in later works, was a real threat to the old order. Debussy had wrought a broadening change in musical style and technique, but his impressionism was none the less part of the romantic movement. Stravinsky's creed was definitely anti-romantic. What he stood for is demonstrated in the change that came over the art of music in the decades following World War I, at the time when his influence was enormous. Young composers no longer copied the long-flowing melodies of Wagner and Strauss, the luscious harmonies, the tapestried instrumentation. Instead melodies became angular in the extreme—short, jolting phrases set in metallic orchestrations. Old-fashioned harmony disappeared, and dissonant counterpoint and polyharmony, bitter and astringent, took its place. Most radical of all was the new spirit that imbued much of this music—an attitude that disdained emotion for the coldness of tonal steel, and replaced the literary and pictorial aspects of romanticism with abstractions of the strictest and most impersonal sort.

To a certain extent the time itself was responsible for the change in the music art which Stravinsky's work typified. With the end of World War I, profound metamorphoses occurred in every phase of modern life and art. Europeans especially who had been through that conflict could no longer bear to look back upon a sentimental and romantic past. Literature, art, and music all reflected the strange and paradoxical obsessions of men who were striving to find reality and at the same time an escape from it. Cynicism replaced sentiment; the machine, man's modern slave, became a new instrument of inspiration in art. With so many ethical landmarks swept away by four years of wholesale killing it is no wonder that many artistic standards went with them, and that anything violently new—whether cubism or atonality—was likely to become the new religion of the moment, provided that it had no truck with the old romantic order.

*Le Sacre du printemps* was one of the original apples of discord in this revolution in music, and the man who produced it certainly fitted by temperament the movement that he helped inaugurate. Stravinsky is an avowed hater of sentiment in music, a man with one of the best-equipped and most sharply pointed minds in modern art, who prefers to avoid emotion whenever he can, and who works instead with the precision of a scientist and the logic of a *juris* doctor.

He was born in 1882 at Oranienbaum, near Leningrad. His father was a noted bass singer in the imperial opera in that city, but, like Schumann, young Stravinsky was at first slated for the study of the law. Although he received careful instruction in music from the age of nine and was reared in a household where music was of prime importance, he showed none of the signs of the musical prodigy.

According to his own *Autobiography*, Stravinsky hated school; he admits that he never found anyone during those years whom he liked. He was lonely, partly because no one seemed to appreciate his longing for music. His parents, too, were intent only upon educating him so that he could qualify for some post in the Russian governmental bureaucracy which would assure him enough to live on. For that reason he was sent to study law at the University of St. Petersburg.

Stravinsky disliked the law, and he finally persuaded his parents to let him take private lessons in harmony. This phase of musical science he found boring and dull, but later when he took up counterpoint he was thrilled immeasurably. When he was eighteen years old he was so interested in counterpoint that he began studying it by himself. By this means he developed his taste and judgment in music and laid the foundations of his mature technique as a composer.

The study of the law was not a total loss for Stravinsky. In fact it brought him one piece of very good fortune. One of his fellow students was the youngest son of Rimsky-Korsakov, and through him Stravinsky met the famous composer. Rimsky-Korsakov was at that time (1902) in the final phase of his career, and his fame and influence in Russia were great. When young Stravinsky approached him with his first attempts at composition, the old master's advice was disappointing—to continue the musical studies, but not to leave the university.

The young man persisted, however, and within a few years he was receiving instruction from Rimsky-Korsakov himself. His association with the older composer must have been an exhilarating experience. Rimsky-Korsakov was a superb teacher because he was able to impart his own prodigious knowledge of musical technique with lucidity and perfect sureness. When he began teaching Stravinsky form and orchestration, his method was to give his pupil the pages of a piano score of the opera on which he himself was working. These Stravinsky would orchestrate, after which Rimsky-Korsakov would show him how he had orchestrated the same passage. Stravinsky would be required to discover why his master had differed with him; if he could not, Rimsky-Korsakov would explain.

These studies continued for about three years. Meanwhile Stravinsky had completed his law course and had married. He also found time to write his first symphony, which he describes frankly as an imitation of Alexander Glazunov's music, then much admired in Russia. In 1907 he wrote his *Scherzo fantastique*, a tone poem inspired by his study of the life of the bees. He was also working on an opera, *Le Chant du rossignol* [*The Song of the Nightingale*], based on Hans Christian Andersen's story of the mechanical nightingale that sang for the Emperor of China. This opera was not completed until 1914, after which the composer converted it into a ballet for production by Diaghilev. Still later he turned it into a symphonic poem.

In all these early works Stravinsky was strongly influenced by his master's love of the fantastic and the pictorial, his penchant for lavish orchestral color. The marks go even deeper than that. For all his love of the extravagantly opulent in music, Rimsky-Korsakov was one of the most reticent of men. An emotional warmth appeared always in the kindly Russian eyes, but as he grew older a patriarchal beard accentuated the facial mask of aloofness and reserve. Stravinsky relates that the older man could never permit himself to make any display of his feelings. This fact is borne out by his autobiography, *My Musical Life*. In that splendid chronicle, which is a mine of information about his own career and the entire Russian musical scene when it was dominated by the Five, Rimsky-Korsakov rigorously excluded details of his personal life which did not bear directly on his music. Only once does the author drop for an instant the mask of reticence—when he relates the lingering illness and death of a five-year-old daughter. "My poor little girl," a phrase several times repeated, is the only clue to his feelings; but it is more indicative of this kindly man's repressed sorrow than a dozen paragraphs.

It is interesting to note how deeply the older man's example affected the pupil. Many years after Rimsky-Korsakov died Stravinsky wrote his own *Autobiography*. It is terse, frank, acidly critical, and at the same time stimulating and provocative in its opinions; but the Rimsky-Korsakov pattern is clear in the background. No word of personal emotion enters its cold pages of purely musical reminiscence. Stravinsky's marriage is recorded as follows: "In the autumn I became engaged, and I was married in January 1906." He does not identify his wife; even her name is not given.

In the spring of 1908, Stravinsky wrote a short orchestral piece which he called *Fireworks*. One of Rimsky-Korsakov's daughters was being married, so Stravinsky sent the score to his master as a contribution to the occasion. Before it could be delivered, the old man had died. It is likely that had Rimsky-Korsakov lived to examine the few measures that comprise *Fireworks* he would have realized that his pupil had suddenly become a master in his own right. Stravinsky's little score is deft and clever and brilliant, with perfect stylistic assurance. The composer's imitation of whirling pinwheels, showering sparks, all the blazing color, the noise and gaiety of the scene are achieved with few of the more obvious devices. There is a startling vividness in this score, and also subtlety, in both the thematic material and the orchestration.

The loss of his master must have been a serious blow to young Stravinsky. He paid his tribute by composing a funeral march. This work is now lost, having disappeared with other of the composer's effects during the Russian Revolution of 1917. Whatever doubts Stravinsky might have had about his own career were soon dispelled, with the appearance of another remarkable man in his life. This was Sergei Diaghilev, a twentieth-century Lorenzo the Magnificent, himself on the threshold of a fabulous career.

II

No one has ever found the single word adequate to describe the genius of Sergei Diaghilev. Impresario, organizer, manager, entrepreneur—he was all of these, and yet much more. The world remembers him as the man who brought the Russian Ballet to western Europe and the Americas, and that was a fact of prime importance; but his enterprise had ramifications all through the various fields of modern music, art, ballet, and stage decoration.

He was born in 1872, the son of a general in the Russian army. The family was noble and wealthy. Diaghilev himself was an aristocrat to the core—proud, pleasure-loving, imperious in the gaining of his ends and desires. He came to St. Petersburg when a young man in his teens to study the law. Like Stravinsky's, his interests lay in music, but he had no success when he tried to compose. He became interested in art, and before he was thirty was the most talked-of young man in Russian intellectual circles. He founded the provocative art journal *Mir Isskustva;* he organized exhibitions of paintings; he brought shows of the French impressionists from Paris. These were so successful that in 1907 he turned about and took a large exhibition of Russian art to Paris. His interests in music being as keen as ever, the next step was a logical one. In 1908 he produced in Paris a series of concerts devoted to Russian music. This brought about the most daring enterprise of all. He decided to bring the Russian Ballet to France. There existed at the Imperial Theater in St. Petersburg a company of superlative mimes and dancers who were bursting with talent but were being held in the grooves of tradition by a reactionary management. Using this group as his nucleus, Diaghilev gave a season of ballet performances at the Théâtre du Châtelet in Paris in the year 1909. The success of the venture was unparalleled in the history of the modern theater.

Diaghilev's achievement was far more than the importation of a company of great Russian dancers to western Europe, far more than the exhibition of brilliant ballets. He actually created a new art work. He conceived the ballet as the fusion of three elements—dancing, music, and stage picture—and he demanded that each element in itself be a sound work of art contributing to the whole. In the course of the next twenty years Diaghilev produced more than fifty ballet productions, besides various operas. The superlative nature of this work as a whole can be indicated from the mere listing of the artists who were under his aegis at one time or another during those two decades. The dancers included (among many others) Nijinsky, Pavlova, Karsavina, Ida Rubinstein, Fokine and

Fokina, Bolm, Mordkin, Massine, Lifar, and Dolin. The artists of stage design and costume included Benois, Bakst, Roerich, Golovin, Serov, Anisfeld, Soudeikine, Sert, Picasso, Derain, Matisse, Braque, and Robert Edmund Jones. Among his choreographers were Fokine, Nijinsky, Bronislava Nijinska, Massine, and Balanchine. The modern composers who created new works for him included Stravinsky, Ravel, Debussy, Falla, Prokofiev, Tommasini, Poulenc, Auric, Milhaud, Lambert, and Lord Berners.

Diaghilev's own contributions to the productions that bore his name cannot be pointed out with certainty. He was not a creative artist himself; he was neither dancer, choreographer, composer, nor painter. Yet he was able to assert a powerful influence over the creative ideas of other men. He brought various talents together, matching those he believed would create the perfect vision. Usually he gave his associates a free rein in the developing of their own ideas, for he understood artists and he stimulated them to do their best—but over the whole enterprise he ruled with a despotic hand, sure of himself, his taste, and his final judgment.

His greatest gift was the ability to discover new talent. When he first met Michel Fokine, the great choreographer was a struggling young dancer in Russia, trying to assert his revolutionary ideas in the face of the most hidebound reaction of the old-fashioned ballet masters. Diaghilev took him to Paris and set him free. After the season of 1909, Fokine was world-famous. He repaid Diaghilev with creations that now, after fifty years, are the recognized classics of a new age of dancing—*Les Sylphides, Prince Igor, Scheherazade, Carnaval, Le Spectre de la rose,* and *Petrouchka*—while Fokine himself became the acknowledged master of the modern ballet. Igor Stravinsky, among the composers, was to an even greater extent a Diaghilev discovery, and his effect on modern music was correspondingly profound.

Diaghilev himself was thus a phenomenon as rare as his precise function in the art he sponsored was obscure. He had the organizing ability and the mental energy of an empire builder, and with it the sensitivity of the born aesthete. In some respects he was effeminate; but in appearance he was heavy and masculine—his frame was large, his head enormous, with wide eyes and a heavy mouth, his thick dark hair streaked with a single distinctive thatch of white. He loved fine clothes, and he dressed the part of the impresario even to fur coats and a monocle. He could be jealous and magnanimous at almost the same moment; he could be aloof, taciturn, arrogant, or charmingly affable as the spirit moved him. He created nothing tangible himself; yet he was such a perfectionist with the work of others that he would threaten to cancel an entire performance if the electricians failed to give him the precise color he wanted in a single spotlight. Throughout his career he gambled fortunes on his ability to please the public, yet he was a hypochondriac with an absurd fear of disease. He wouldn't go near anyone who was ill, and in the summer he would ride only in closed carriages for fear of getting glanders from the horses.

Some months after the death of Rimsky-Korsakov, Stravinsky's little piece *Fireworks* and his *Scherzo fantastique* were played at a concert in St. Petersburg. Diaghilev happened to hear them. At the time he was preparing *Les Sylphides* for the first Paris season of 1909, and he commissioned Stravinsky to orchestrate two of the Chopin pieces for that ballet—the opening *Nocturne* and the final *Valse Brillante*. Neither Diaghilev nor Stravinsky could possibly have imagined the far-reaching results of that small task of instrumentation, which was the beginning of twenty years of collaboration between them.

Stravinsky did not go to Paris for the historic 1909 season; he remained in Russia working on his opera, *Le Rossignol*. Later Diaghilev returned in triumph, full of plans for a new Paris season of 1910. He again sought out Stravinsky and proposed that the young man write the music for a new ballet, *L'Oiseau de feu* [*The Firebird*]. Stravinsky accepted, but with secret misgivings. He was then twenty-seven years old but he still felt himself an amateur at music, unaware, he says, of his own capabilities.

During the next winter he worked hard at his score, keeping in constant touch with Diaghilev and Fokine. The latter had devised the scenario of *The Firebird* from ancient Russian legends. The story concerns the young Prince Ivan, who finds a marvelous golden bird with flaming wings. He captures her as she is plucking golden apples from a silver tree. When he sets her free, she repays him by giving him one of her plumes. The prince wanders into a secret garden, to find thirteen lovely princesses dancing and playing with the golden apples. They warn him that he is in the realm of Kastchei, a frightful ogre who turns his victims into stone. The monster and his henchmen swarm out and attack the prince, but he is saved by the power of the Firebird's plume. The bird herself appears and reveals to the prince the secret of Kastchei's power. It is contained in an egg kept in a casket. The prince finds the casket and smashes the egg. Kastchei dies, his victims are set free, and the prince claims one of the princesses.

As Stravinsky finished the various sections of his music, he turned them over to Fokine, who immediately composed his choreography. The two men worked in closest contact, with constant supervision by Diaghilev. The finished product was actually the first of a new kind of ballet. Theretofore composers of ballet music had usually worked independently, leaving the choreographer to devise his dances as best he could from the finished score. Even Diaghilev's first ballet productions had been created to music already in existence; often he utilized scores not originally intended for ballet purposes at all. *The Firebird* was a collaboration of the most fortunate kind, with the music governed throughout its composition by the precise demands of the choreography, and even influenced by the stage decoration.

*The Firebird* was first produced by Diaghilev at the Paris Opéra, on June 25, 1910, with settings and costumes by Golovin and Bakst. The success of the piece was immediate, and Igor Stravinsky, before that an unknown composer of uncertain gifts, was on his way to international fame.

*The Firebird* is a brilliant score, even if it is not marked by the powerful originality that was to come later. Rimsky-

Korsakov's pupil shows how well he had learned the lesson of scintillating orchestration. The piece is full of instrumental effects that are both exquisite and bold. The style of this music is Russian, with a strong flavor throughout of Russian folk tune, even when the composer is inventing his own themes. The gorgeously fantastic picture is realized with splashes of splendid color and, at times, beautifully detailed decoration.

### III

With the success of *The Firebird*, Diaghilev was hot for another work by Stravinsky. At first they discussed an idea that had occurred to the composer as he was finishing *The Firebird*. It was a weird vision of pagan Russian elders watching a sacrificial dance of death by a young girl. Before he started on the work, however, Stravinsky amused himself by writing a short orchestral piece featuring the piano. He thought of a puppet brought to life and annoying the orchestra with its antics. The composer was staying in Switzerland at the time and Diaghilev went to visit him. When the latter heard the puppet piece, he was enthralled. He would not rest until Stravinsky agreed to expand the idea into an entire ballet. With Alexandre Benois, the costume and scene designer, they worked out a scenario for a ballet to be entitled *Petrouchka*. Again, Fokine devised the choreography.

The action of *Petrouchka* takes place at a Russian fair in a St. Petersburg square, about the year 1830. The street is swarming with people—nurses, children, policemen, gypsies, coachmen, organ grinders, dancers, drunkards. On one side of the street an old charlatan has set up his booth. He has three puppets—a dancing girl, a blackamoor, and Petrouchka, a clown. By playing on his flute he brings them to life, and they dance for the crowd. Scenes behind the charlatan's curtain reveal the cruel life of Petrouchka. He suffers because he is so ugly and grotesque; he is kicked and beaten by his master and laughed at by the dancing girl, who spurns his love for that of the blackamoor. Tortured by these human feelings that he cannot understand, Petrouchka gives way to frenzied despair. Outside, the merrymaking reaches a climax with the appearance of a man with a bear, and with dances by the nurses and coachmen. Suddenly Petrouchka rushes out. He is pursued by the blackamoor, who splits his head with a sword and kills him. The charlatan quiets the crowd by showing them that Petrouchka is merely a sawdust doll, but as the curtain falls the spirit of the dead clown rises above the booth to mock and terrify his master.

The *première* of *Petrouchka* took place in Paris on June 13, 1911, with Nijinsky as Petrouchka and Karsavina as the dancing girl. The history of ballet changed with that moment. A new conception of emotional depth, of dramatic power, of inspirational freedom entered the ballet dancer's realm. Music, too, had annexed to itself a new realm of creative form, that is, the ballet as a vehicle for serious musical expression on a large symphonic scale. Stravinsky in his *Autobiography* passes on most of the credit for this new form to Tchaikovsky, because of the beautiful music his predecessor had written for *The Swan Lake* and *The Sleeping Beauty* ballets. This seems like undue modesty. Neither composers nor the public had taken ballet music seriously enough. It was always considered a diverting rather than a moving form of art. Tchaikovsky's ballet music, lovely as much of it is, did not change that conception. To Stravinsky must go the real credit for establishing the modern symphonic ballet, as large-scale, intensely serious, and solidly wrought art.

The composer's urge toward originality led him out in many new directions in this score. The rhythmic pattern is complex, with the time signature often changing every few measures. The rhythms, moreover, are angular and furiously energetic. The melodies have the raw freshness of folk tunes, but they seldom follow standard methods of development. The composer often uses Debussy's method of ignoring old-fashioned phrase patterns and sequences, sometimes breaking off his melodies abruptly or leaving them unfinished.

There are also daring harmonic procedures in *Petrouchka*, notably the first extensive use of polytonality.

In the scene in Petrouchka's room (which was Stravinsky's original puppet piece) the piano has a series of wild arpeggios which superimpose the key of F sharp major over that of C major. Strauss had hinted at this procedure at the close of *Also sprach Zarathustra*, but Stravinsky's use is much more elaborate and bold. The score abounds in dissonance. Stravinsky also makes use of Debussy's practice of passing the same chord at will through various notes of the scale—except that where Debussy had used these "glided chords" with discreet softness, Stravinsky slashes them out with immense gusto and emphasis.

The net result of these procedures is to give *Petrouchka* precisely the rawness, the crude colorfulness of the garish scene the composer is painting. The crowd that swarms through the street fair is careless and carefree, dulled by drink or dancing with violent energy, eager, gay, stupid, dirty, and human; the puppets are artificial as their paint-daubed faces, animated by passions, desires, and mean-nesses, by a pathetic struggle for happiness they cannot understand. Petrouchka himself is a "childlike soul crying in a withered hell." All this is painted by Stravinsky in his score—a living picture limned with incredible vividness and speed.

As ballet music *Petrouchka* exemplifies a basic prin-ciple: art once again revivifies itself by contact with life. The dead-hand conventions of the past are ignored; the Watteau-like refinements and artificialities that had ruled the ballet for generations are swept away by this gust of lusty, earthy freshness.

After the success of *Petrouchka*, Stravinsky returned to the idea of a ballet of pagan Russia. He went back to his family estate in Russia and called in Nicholas Roerich for consultation. Roerich was both a painter and a scholar, an authority on ancient Russian art. For Diaghilev he had designed the scenery and costumes for the *Prince Igor* dances. The ballet that he and Stravinsky finally evolved was *Le Sacre du printemps*, the most notorious and in many respects the greatest of this composer's works.

The full title of the piece is *The Rite of Spring: Pictures of Pagan Russia, in Two Parts*. It describes primitive man's worship of the earth and his ritualistic sacrifice for spring's consecration. Part I is called *"The Adoration of the Earth,"* and its various sections describe the Harbingers of Spring, Dances of Adolescent Girls and Boys, a Mock Abduction, Spring Rounds, Games of the Rival Tribes, a Procession of the Tribal Sage, and a Dance of the Earth. Part II is called *"The Sacrifice."* It begins with an introductory section, the Pagan Night, followed by Mysterious Circles of the Adolescents, Glorification of the Chosen One, the Evocation and Ritual of the Ancestors, and finally the Chosen One's Sacrificial Dance of Death.

The original choreography of *Le Sacre du printemps* was devised by Nijinsky. It did not please the composer, who shared the general opinion that Nijinsky, although a peerless dancer, had insufficient technical knowledge of music for the task of choreography. However, it was not the dancing that caused the near riot at the *première* of the work in Paris. It was the score—the nerve-assaulting fury of the music and its impact upon ears unaccustomed to this excursion into primitivism—which shocked and angered a large section of the public. Many were willing to admit the powerful originality of the work, but they were fearful that it might be turning the entire art of music in a new direction, away from the pure euphonies and melodic sweetness of the past toward some terrifying domain of sheer noise and violence. What gave the work an immediate historical importance was the fact that other composers all over the world made a feeding ground of its boldly fresh technical ideas and apparatus.

The orchestration, first of all, is masterly—a tour de force that has not been surpassed in half a century of orchestral writing. Stravinsky did not want mere brilliance in this score, and certainly not mellifluous beauty; his subject matter demanded something far different from that. His score is full of straining horns, trumpets, and trombones, shrill woodwinds, piccolos shrieking in the highest register, violent glissandos in the brass choir, percussion that shakes the very earth. Most of these effects were calculated to shock, but they were nevertheless powerfully evocative of the scene to be painted.

The score also contains some of Stravinsky's best melodic ideas. Most of his themes, although original, have the contours of crude folk tunes. They are often angular, pungent, purposely avoiding any hint of sensuous smoothness. All of them have the identity and the staying power that are the mysterious quality of all good melody. In the entire score there is hardly a measure of orthodox harmony. Dissonance and polytonality abound, with effects of deliberate harshness that set the teeth of the conservatives on edge. Moreover, there is no gliding over these dissonances by the use of soft strings. As often as not they are roared out with the full force of the brass.

The most extraordinary feature of *Le Sacre du printemps* remains Stravinsky's use of rhythm. He set a new standard of rhythmic complexity, with cadences sometimes so involved that the time signature changes with almost every measure—$\frac{3}{8}$, $\frac{2}{4}$, $\frac{3}{4}$, $\frac{4}{4}$, $\frac{5}{4}$, $\frac{6}{8}$, $\frac{7}{8}$, etc. The piece abounds in furious energy of a type usually associated with expressions of the primitive emotions, the wild stampings and threshings of zealots, medicine men, and dervishes. Rhythm rises to such paramount importance in this work that it could be said Stravinsky uses it as Debussy did the chord—as an entity in itself, overshadowing melody in importance in the general scheme.

Whatever its enemies once thought of this great work, its place in music is secure, if only for the reason that so much music that came after it has been affected by its presence. It provided composers with new techniques; it gave listeners new conceptions of musical beauty. It no longer terrifies. Above all it is superbly evocative. Its spring has nothing of the warm, sensuous, blossom-laden South; instead it is chill and steely, with bracing winds blowing through it from a land of melting ice. It reeks of the earth, of life that springs eternal from rotting death; of primitive man with his pathetic fears, his abounding energies, his fierce urge to stay alive in defiance of a malignant and unheeding nature.

## IV

Despite the scandals of its early performances, *Le Sacre du printemps* created an enormous reputation for Stravinsky. The work did not become widely known until the years immediately following World War I, and even then its performances were infrequent; but it remained in the music consciousness of its time like some potent and fearsome chemical force. Composers all over the world copied its outward style, until the postwar concert halls of Europe and America rang with a new and strange music —dissonant, complex, anti-romantic, and at times hideous. Few composers in history have occupied a place of such eminence and power as Stravinsky did during these years, when every note that he composed and every word he uttered was awaited by composers and the music public alike as a pronouncement from Delphi.

After *Le Sacre du printemps*, however, a gradual and deep-rooted metamorphosis began to affect the creative effort of Stravinsky himself. Far from carrying on where that shocking work had left off, he veered off in a direction totally unexpected. His work began to reflect a new attitude of mind and an adoption of styles and forms that seemed totally incongruous with everything for which he had stood. It created a state of confusion among his friends and enemies alike.

One phase of this evolution should have been understood by the public more readily than it was. It should have been realized that Stravinsky could not possibly maintain the furious pace of scores like *Petrouchka* and *Le Sacre du printemps*. They were the work of a comparatively young man, and in their vitality are typical of youthful genius. Other considerations also impelled Stravinsky toward more continent forms of expression. Like so many of his fellow artists, his personal life had been completely disrupted by the war. He was convinced that the golden age of great orchestras and elaborate ballet and operatic productions was over, and that the music art in order to survive would have to assume more modest shapes. For more than a decade he produced only small-scale works.

The first of these was *Les Noces* [*The Wedding*], composed chiefly in 1915–16, when Stravinsky was living in Switzerland. It was a time of economic difficulty and emotional turmoil for the composer. He had a wife and children to house and support, and creating a new home for them in a strange land was no easy matter. Finding a suitable workroom for himself doubled his problems, for he could not compose if anyone was within hearing distance of his piano. Part of *Les Noces* was composed in an unheated lumber room that looked out on a chicken run. The composer had only an upright piano, badly out of tune; he was so cold that for a few days he sat in an overcoat, fur cap, and boots, his knees covered by a rug.

*Les Noces* is a description of a Russian peasant wedding. The composer originally intended it for large orchestra and chorus; but he scaled it down to a medium remarkable for modesty and ingenuity—a group of four solo voices and a mixed chorus of twenty-four, four pianos, and about a dozen percussion instruments. The work is in four scenes, describing in detail the events of the peasant marriage ceremony in all its boisterous, good-natured humor. The music is exceedingly noisy, with vigorously sung or shouted vocal parts, insistent rhythms and pounding accents delivered with much gusto by the battery of percussion and the pianos. The uncouthness of these peasants, their rank healthiness and vigor, the reek of the soil around them, are etched with garish brilliance and originality.

While he was composing *Les Noces*, Stravinsky was also at work on *Renard*, a burlesque piece based on animal fables. This was scored for four solo voices and a small chamber orchestra of eighteen instruments. Even more spare in its medium was *L'Histoire du soldat* [*The Tale of the Soldier*], which required only a clarinet, bassoon, cornet, trombone, violin, double bass, and a percussion player with half a dozen instruments. This work had its origin in the year 1917, when the Russian Revolution put a stop to the income that had come intermittently to Stravinsky from his properties in Russia. He was more desperately hard up than ever. With the assistance of two friends in the same straits he conceived the idea of a small traveling theater that could be transported cheaply and taken on extended tours all over Europe. Searching Russian folklore, they chose the tale of a soldier who deserts his regiment and tries to bargain with the devil. The little show that they evolved called for a tiny orchestra seated on one side of the stage, on the other a reader who recited the narrative poem, with the actors in the center.

The score of *L'Histoire du soldat* is pungent, witty, and ironic in mood. In style it is a distillation of Stravinsky's ultramodern craftsmanship. It abounds in dissonant counterpoint, polyharmony, and new polyrhythmic effects obtained by mixing several conflicting rhythms in the same measure. The melodic material consists of scrappy, satirical uses of cheap marches, dances, music-hall melodies, and folk tunes—all distorted by a sophisticated and mordant stylization.

Stravinsky had become keenly interested in American jazz during the composition of this work, and one of its tiny dances is called *Ragtime*. Later he wrote two more essays in this style—*Ragtime* for eleven solo instruments (1918), and *Piano Rag Music* (1919). In 1922, Stravinsky wrote a short opera, *Mavra*, based on a story by Pushkin and composed in the style of Glinka and Tchaikovsky. It is a slight work, but it happens to mark a dividing line in the development of the composer's style. Up to this time his work had been strongly emotional and pictorial; after *Mavra* he sought to develop a new mode of expression which would be as abstract as the pure formalism of the eighteenth century. This style, he said, reflected his desire to become "a classicist, an objectivist, a constructive artist." His preoccupation with this idea resulted in a long series of works in a neoclassic style. *Pulcinella*, a one-act "ballet with song," was based on airs of Pergolesi, the Italian composer of the early eighteenth century. It was produced by Diaghilev in 1920, with designs by Picasso. For this work Stravinsky did not merely transcribe the original Pergolesi melodies; he restyled them into a thoroughly modern texture. The same year brought forth the *Symphonies of Wind Instruments*, a short work composed in memory of

Debussy and scored for some twenty instruments of the wind choir. A similar experiment in wind sonorities appeared as the Octet, in 1923. Then came two piano works —the Sonata in 1922, and the Piano Concerto, finished in 1924. In the latter piece the orchestra was made up of woodwinds and brass, but no strings. The composer referred to this ensemble as the "harmonic orchestra," as something entirely different from the "symphonic orchestra." He announced that "strings and piano, a sound scraped and a sound struck, do not sound well together; piano and wind, sounds struck and blown, do." Early in 1925, when Stravinsky made his first appearance in America, conducting concerts of his own works, he also played the solo part in this piece.

Almost without exception these works in the neoclassic style were received at first by the general public with bewilderment and complete disappointment. Their dryness and objectivity, their preoccupation with odd sonorities, their thin, abstruse unemotionalism—it seemed as though every drop of sentiment had been wrung from them— left audiences coldly hostile. Stravinsky himself announced with vehemence his disdain of the old order. He inveighed against excess of emotionalism, against "sentimental twaddle," too opulent orchestration, the injection of personality, individuality, and temperament into music—in short, the entire apparatus of romanticism, bag and baggage. Instead, he had embraced the pure abstractions of eighteenth-century music, with its simplicity, lucidity, and impersonal restraint. The man who had created the supreme modern Dionysian orgy in music, Le Sacre du printemps, announced that he was in truth an Apollonian.

"I dislike cajoling the public!" he exclaimed. "It inconveniences me. The crowd expects the artist to tear out his entrails and exhibit them."

It should be profitable at this point to seek some closer contact with Stravinsky the man, and to learn from the shell of his personality more of what the inner nature of the artist might be.

V

Even in the early days of the Diaghilev association it appears that Stravinsky never impressed anyone with shyness or lack of personal distinction. He is a small man, slightly built, and with the quick, vital mannerisms that indicate excess of nervous energy. Few composers since Wagner have been more opinionated. Janet Flanner described his "cyclonic temperament" and called him an "inventive, contradictory, complicated man, bent on comprehending everything immediately and from the ground up." This writer also found that he has "the drawing-room charm of the verbal virtuoso," that he could be witty in German and French as well as Russian, and that like all great talkers he hates to be alone.

A composer's opinion of the works of other men is often one of the most valuable clues to his own artistic purposes. Stravinsky has been candid with his own views, and in one case at least he runs true to expectations: he loathes Wagner and everything that archemotionalist stands for. Once Stravinsky went with Diaghilev to a performance of *Parsifal* at Bayreuth and came away feeling that he had been in a crematorium. Beethoven he admires for his instrumental and formal mastery, and in spite of the general "sentimental attitude" toward his works. Schubert and Brahms leave him cold, but to Donizetti and Bellini he has given the highest praise. He believes that the world has yet to realize the intrinsic greatness of the opera *Norma*. He has also praised Carl Maria von Weber, Gounod, Czerny, and, of course, Mozart.

Stravinsky may be opinionated, but he has a right to be, for he has informed himself on many subjects that appeal to the modern intellectual. He has studied the composers of the past and present with a thoroughness that would shame many a pedagogue, and he appreciates art and literature. He is a profoundly religious man, who goes regularly to the Russian Church and prays daily before an icon in his study. He is also beset by superstitions, and like Diaghilev he is a hypochondriac who flies from disease.

Stravinsky's personal life is carefully ordered. For years he composed with the regularity of an office worker and at a desk that is a model of neatness. His manuscripts are like Wagner's—almost as perfect as engraving itself. At one time he wrote them in several different colored inks. He loves fine clothes, dresses with care, and indulges in occasional odd affectations. For years he has subjected himself to a daily regimen of exercise.

Shortly after World War I, Stravinsky established a home in Paris with his wife and four children. He lived there for almost twenty years, becoming a French citizen in 1934. French culture in all its aspects impressed him. The neoclassic aesthetic that he finally embraced has many characteristics of Gallic restraint, symmetry, and elegance —an art based more on the intellect than the emotions.

Stravinsky's musical style in this period turned definitely toward the linear and the contrapuntal. In certain works the themes sound like busy, burbling imitations of Bach or Handel, with many of the old clichés of baroque figuration, and of course a stern avoidance of anything suggesting nineteenth-century lyricism; rhythms became less violent, but they are combined, or broken up, or even jazzed to avoid any hint of regularity; orchestrations are dry, crackling, and percussive, with somber neutral colors predominating, and no hint of richness for its own sake.

One of the statements most commonly made about Stravinsky is that his brilliant early works—*The Firebird, Petrouchka, Le Sacre du printemps, The Wedding*—were examples of his Russian talents working in their natural surroundings; but that after the opera *Mavra* he turned his back forever on nationalism and tried to erase every trace of his Russian heritage. This is actually a half-truth that overlooks a salient point about Russian artists in general.

It is true that the Russians are such keen nationalists that their best artists can usually contrive to give a strong native flavor to everything they touch. However, it is equally true (although generally overlooked) that they are also by nature eclectics. Russian music shows these two hemispheres very clearly. Glinka's music, for example, is not only characteristically Russian; it is also a colorful grab bag of a dozen other musical styles and idioms—Italian, German, French, Spanish, Near Eastern, Oriental—that attracted the composer in the course of his studies and travels. Glinka's musical descendants (with the exception of Mussorgsky) have all inherited these nationalist-eclectic traits. Thus Stravinsky has never really ceased being a Russian artist. With him the nationalist phase came first in his career, and as soon as nationalism began to pall he turned to the other phase and became a complete eclectic.

As an eclectic Stravinsky developed a method of procedure that at first caused much confusion among the unwary. This is his stylistic evocation, by which he recreates the technical mannerisms and the spirit of other composers and other ages. Stravinsky's procedure is never obvious. Rather he recalls the subject of his discourse by vague hints and suggestions, by characteristic rhythmic patterns, typical harmonic progressions, dabs of melody, pinpoints of instrumental color—all subtlety stylized, and sometimes parodied, by an ultramodern treatment that is uniquely Stravinsky's own.

Among the first examples of this procedure were his *Ragtime* and *Piano Rag Music*, based on American popular music; then followed *Pulcinella* in the style of Pergolesi, *Mavra* in the nineteenth-century Russian opera style, and the Piano Concerto, which resurrected the keyboard figurations of the baroque era. Many more examples were to come.

"The history of music," says Virgil Thomson, "became his chief theme."

In the midst of his early neoclassic period Stravinsky began to feel again the call of the stage and its big enterprises. *Oedipus Rex* (1927) is scored for large orchestra, chorus, six solo voices, and a narrator. This "opera-oratorio," as the composer called it, follows the tragedy of Sophocles. The text was prepared by Jean Cocteau in French; but the composer had it translated into an ancient tongue, rejecting Greek for Latin. "The choice," he said, "had the great advantage of giving me a medium not dead, but turned to stone and so monumentalized as to have become immune from all risk of vulgarization." The narrator, however, explains the action in French or another modern language. For the framework of his piece the composer used the old oratorio style of Handel—recitativelike declamations and solos in the florid eighteenth-century style, contrasted with solidly built choral numbers. The composer strives for the grand style, and in the main he achieves it. The work is grim and gray as ancient masonry, but its archaism is achieved by all the devices known to modern techniques. The melodic lines are severe, granitic, supported frequently by forbidding polytonal harmony. Of lyric sweetness, harmonic or instrumental velvet, there is no trace. *Oedipus Rex* has moments of great power, when its evocation of the ancient tragedy is convincingly revealed.

The same year (1927) brought forth the ballet *Apollo Musagetes* [*Apollo Leader of the Muses*], scored for strings only. This work was commissioned by Elizabeth Sprague Coolidge for one of her music festivals at the Library of Congress in Washington, D.C., and was first performed there in 1928. A few months later it was produced in Paris, this time with choreography by George Balanchine. This event was noteworthy, for it marked the beginning of the historic Stravinsky-Balanchine collaboration and a brilliant new era of classicism in the modern ballet theater.

In depicting the legend of Apollo inspiring three of the Muses—Calliope, Polyhymnia, and Terpsichore—Stravinsky declared that he aimed for a "white ballet" of the classical school which would be "wonderfully fresh" but devoid of excessive color or passion. A serene calm suffuses the work as the major mode prevails, with delicate melodies supported by Stravinsky's bittersweet diatonic harmonies. Balanchine's choreography has been praised for its blend of sensuous loveliness and classic grandeur, while the ballet as a whole has been termed "a work of capital importance in the arts of the twentieth century."

When Stravinsky announced that his ballet *The Fairy's Kiss* (1928), based on Hans Christian Andersen's tale of the Ice Maiden, was intended as a tribute to Tchaikovsky, confusion reigned for a time in the small world of music. But Stravinsky's violent antipathy to the works of over-emotional romantic composers happily excluded most of Tchaikovsky's music, which he proceeded to paraphrase with loving care. The piece failed on its first performance, but was later revived successfully by Balanchine.

Stravinsky's neoclassic style, meanwhile, continued to earn more enemies than friends among the music public; however, in 1929 he suddenly refuted the claims of his critics that he had lost his musical virility by composing the dashing showpiece, *Capriccio*, a three-movement concertolike work for piano and orchestra. Here he evoked the *Konzertstück* style of Carl Maria von Weber, whom he admired as a "prince of music."

Wholly contrasting was the *Symphony of Psalms*, composed in 1930 to commemorate the fiftieth anniversary of the Boston Symphony Orchestra. This three-movement work is based on verses from the Psalms in the Latin text of the Vulgate. The orchestra employed indicates the composer's search for new instrumental sonorities. It includes large woodwind and brass sections, with two pianos and a harp, but no clarinets; the strings consist of cellos and basses, but no violins or violas.

The *Symphony of Psalms* bears no resemblance to those choral symphonies of epic size which stem from Beethoven's Ninth. It is severe and somberly archaic, evoking visions of early Christian art that was both primitive and mystically ascetic. The moods vary from a wild, almost savage jubilation to a subdued exultation—chanting that might have echoed across the centuries from the churches of Byzantium, Antioch, or Alexandria. At times the workmanship is complex, as in the double fugue of the second movement, which is dense with modern dissonant polyphony. The total effect is one of grandeur.

VI

In 1933 Stravinsky returned to the Greek mythology with *Persephone*, a setting of a poem by André Gide that was based on the Homeric Hymn of Demeter. Scored for orchestra, chorus, a tenor soloist, and a speaker, the work embraces music, singing, spoken recitation, miming, and dancing. The three parts depict The Abduction of Persephone, Persephone in the Underworld, and the Rebirth of Persephone.

*Persephone* has been one of the least performed of Stravinsky's larger works—unfortunately, in the opinion of critics who know it best and place it among this composer's masterpieces. The legend of Persephone's descent into the underworld and her joyous return to earth is described in music of coolly beautiful, springlike freshness. Both the orchestral and vocal forces are delicately handled and generally subdued; there is little dramatic passion and nothing remotely resembling theatrical excess. One remembers with something like shock that the subject matter, spring, is the same as that of the composer's great work of twenty years before, *Le Sacre du printemps*. The difference in treatment is profound, underscoring the change in aesthetic outlook of the artist himself. Dionysus had indeed become Apollo.

From ancient mythology Stravinsky turned to—of all things—a modern game of cards. His whimsical ballet, *A Card Game* (1937), was composed for the American Ballet in New York, with choreography by Balanchine. The scene is a card table during a game of poker, and the action describes three deals. The music is gay and satirical, and through its bright texture flit melodic mannerisms of Rossini, Delibes, Tchaikovsky, Johann Strauss, Ravel, and perhaps others.

Meanwhile, during the years 1931–32, Stravinsky again had been pondering the classic abstractions. Exploring the possibilities of the violin, he composed his Violin Concerto in D and the Duo Concertante for violin and piano. The Concerto, which is said to show a relationship to Bach's unaccompanied sonatas, has so far attracted little interest from either virtuoso violinists or the music public. It was used successfully, however, by Balanchine in his classical ballet *Balustrade*. The five-movement Duo Concertante is believed to reflect the spirit of the bucolic airs and dances of Lully.

Stravinsky obviously found himself greatly stimulated by working in the classic forms, and in the course of the next fifteen years he demonstrated, as Brahms had done a century ago, that the old matrices can be rejuvenated when treated with fresh ideas. The Concerto for Two Pianos (1936) summons the keyboard idioms of Beethoven, Chopin, and Liszt, under the guise of Stravinsky's own dynamic modernism. The *Dumbarton Oaks Concerto*, in E flat (1938), is a chamber orchestra evocation of Bach's Brandenburg Concertos. The Symphony in C (1940) recalls the Viennese symphony of the late eighteenth century, while the Symphony in Three Movements (1946) recalls not the work of any other composer, but of Stravinsky himself. Its trip-hammer rhythms, short jolting phrases in irregular rhythms, machinelike rotation of small melodic figures, snarling brasses and shrieking woodwinds, punctuated by thunderous outbursts from the entire band, all startlingly recall *Le Sacre du printemps*. The symphony was composed in the midst of World War II, and some commentators suggested possible parallels with Picasso's *Guernica*. Stravinsky denied having intended any direct program or illustration, but hinted that the war might have left marks upon the work. It happened that when the war broke out he was lecturing at Harvard University. His personal life had been uprooted for the second time, when, in the course of one year his wife, his mother, and one of his daughters died. He gave up residence in Paris and established in Hollywood, California, what was to become his permanent home. In 1940 he remarried, and five years later he became an American citizen.

During the war years Stravinsky was busy with a group of works commissioned by various American producers, both in the symphonic and entertainment fields. *Dances concertantes* (1942), composed for the Janssen Symphony

Orchestra of Los Angeles, is a five-movement chamber work that was later produced with superb choreography by Balanchine; the *Circus Polka* (1942) was scored for the band of the Ringling Brothers and Barnum and Bailey Circus, to accompany a ballet of elephants devised by Balanchine; *Four Norwegian Moods* (1942), orchestral essays in the style of Grieg, was originally intended for a Broadway revue; *Scherzo à la russe* (1944) was composed for Paul Whiteman's Band; *Ballet Scenes* (1944) was commissioned by Billy Rose for his revue, *The Seven Lively Arts*. The *Ebony Concerto* (1945), composed for Woody Herman's Band, is a brief, four-movement suite in jazz idiom.

Excepting the *Ebony Concerto*, these pieces showed little influence of the new country upon the composer's art. Rather they seemed like transitory efforts while Stravinsky adjusted himself to his new surroundings. After the Symphony in Three Movements, however, there began to appear a long series of significant works that were to represent the ripest mastery of the composer's later years.

## VII

In 1947 the Greek mythology once more bore fruit for Stravinsky when he and Balanchine collaborated on their ballet masterpiece, *Orpheus*, a work that might be said to epitomize the composer's mature neoclassic style. All is disciplined, restrained, obedient to classic grace and understatement, with no hint of passion or sensuality to mar the mood of grave melancholy. This is music that hovers in a pale nether world between life and death, light and darkness.

Stravinsky's Mass, composed in 1948 for the Roman Catholic ritual, was more than a reflection of the composer's deeply religious nature. It was a forecast of a new phase in his own technical evolution, in which polyphony in its most ancient and most modern forms would blend. Stravinsky's travels through music's past had brought him to the great contrapuntists of the fourteenth and fifteenth centuries—Machaut, Dufay, Isaak, et al—and now his work began to be guided by the principles of this almost-forgotten art. The Mass employs a small chorus of men's and boys' voices, and ten wind instruments. It contrasts utterly with those baroque Masses that fill vast naves with the sound of angelic choiring, and vie with the gorgeousness of gleaming altars, gold embroidered vestments, and stained glass windows. Rather it is as bare of ornament as a Trappist's cell. Much of it evokes the style of the Flemish contrapuntists; but there are also hints of organum and plain song, and even echoes of ancient Gregorian and Byzantine chant.

What might be termed an interruption in Stravinsky's explorations in polyphony came in 1951 with his opera, *The Rake's Progress*. The English libretto, written by W. H. Auden and Chester Kallman, was based on the famous series of engravings by William Hogarth. Various episodes from eighteenth century English life are recreated, with certain embellishments, becoming a kind of morality play. Following his subject matter, Stravinsky went to the eighteenth century for his operatic formula: arias, concerted numbers, ensembles, and recitatives both accompanied and secco. Strongly evoked is the tragicomedy of Mozart's *Don Giovanni*. Melodies are based on a variety of old sources—Handel, Mozart, Bellini, Gounod, Tchaikovsky—but the accompanying harmonies are acidly dissonant, sharpening rather than smoothing the melodic lines.

So far *The Rake's Progress* has enjoyed mild success. Hostile critics have insisted on weaknesses they expect would prove fatal—a lack of human interest in the characters, a complexity of musical style that impedes rather than enhances the element of vocal beauty which is the soul of opera, and above all the suspicion that in his search after melodic novelty the composer had been working a dry well.

In 1951–52, when Stravinsky composed a secular Cantata, scored for small vocal and instrumental groups, and based on anonymous English lyrics of the fourteenth and fifteenth centuries, it was not at first apparent that the composer had reached another turning point of immense significance in his career. This avid explorer of musical techniques was now experimenting in a new field, one that he had sworn he would never enter. This was the twelve-tone, or dodecaphonic, system of composition elaborated in the early 1920s by Arnold Schoenberg. Although he had publicly acknowledged the mastery of Schoenberg himself and of Schoenberg's disciple Anton Webern, Stravinsky had also declared that there were too many twelve-tone "swindlers" at work, who really "do not know what they are writing."

Stravinsky had now reached his seventieth year; nevertheless, he took up and mastered the new technique. His works of the next decade can hardly be more than mentioned here, and only with the comment that they are astonishing in both the range of their subject matter and the modernity of their musical style. Following the secular Canata came a Septet (1953) for a chamber group; *Three Songs after William Shakespeare* (1953); *Dirge Canons and Song*, "In Memoriam Dylan Thomas," composed in 1954 after the tragic death of the poet, with whom Stravinsky had planned to write an opera; *Canticum Sacrum* (1957), a short cantata based on passages from the Bible; *Agon* (1954–57), a ballet with arresting choreography by Balanchine; *Threni: Lamentations of the Prophet Jeremiah* (1958), a superbly moving work for vocal soloists, double chorus, and orchestra; and most recently (1958–60) four short works—*Movements for Piano and Orchestra*; *Double Canon*, for string quartet, in memory of Raoul Dufy, the painter; *Epitaphium*; and *Monumentum pro Gesualdo*, an instrumental reworking of madrigals by the sixteenth-century master. This last became another Stravinsky-Balanchine ballet.

After composing the secular Cantata in 1952, Stravinsky had pointed out that his model had been Heinrich Isaak, the fourteenth-century contrapuntist: "He is my hobby, my daily bread. I love him. I study him constantly, and between his musical thinking and writing and my own there is a very close connection." In the Cantata and in the later works Stravinsky manipulated the old devices of fugue, canon, inverted canon, canon cancrizans, and all the rest, solving their intricate problems with a master mathematician's skill. Thus the music of this latest phase of his long evolution is like a tonal web that has been woven on patterns taken from the old Flemish contrapuntists, from Bach's *Art of the Fugue*, and from the ultradissonant serial procedures of Anton Webern. The sheer technical virtuosity here displayed is likely to be a source of study by music specialists for many years to come.

## VIII

Because at the present writing Stravinsky is still composing with little sign of flagging skill, although he is approaching his eightieth year, there can as yet be no summing up of his astonishing career. We can only point out those qualities which appear to us in mid-century to give his music its distinction, its power, and at the same time its limitations.

The outstanding characteristic of Stravinsky's music is the continuing modernity of its sound over a space of half a century. Modernity, of course, is not a constant; it shifts with every generation. But as Stravinsky has moved from Debussyan impressionism through an intense Russian nationalism to neoclassicism, and finally to serialism, his music has always held its place in the vanguard. The latest serial works seem to have penetrated farther than ever into interstellar space.

The other notable characteristic of Stravinsky's music is, paradoxically, its reactionary spirit. With clear vision and unshakable resolve this composer has reversed the art cycle, turning music from its romantic orientation back to the classic. Many were the means by which he brought about this reactionary process—by reviving the classic mood of restraint and understatement; by scaling down the size of the big romantic orchestra and bringing back into vogue the small chamber orchestra with winds dominating; by reviving interest in the old classic forms and giving polyphony precedence over harmony; by deliberately evoking the mannerisms of composers of the past.

All these phases of his art are manifestations of Stravinsky's great powers of origination. Although he has been an eclectic who borrows from a hundred sources, he is also an innovator beholden to none. His rhythmic inventions have given a new depth to that musical dimension. He has created a new range of tonal colors by his ingenious and wonderfully varied instrumentation. As a theater composer he has experimented continually with new forms, and by his work in the ballet he has raised to a high art what was once merely a diverting entertainment.

Stravinsky's influence upon other composers of our time has been profound. At the same time the public, while giving its highest accolades of popularity to his earlier pieces, still remains comparatively cold to the neoclassic works. Stravinsky is acknowledged by everyone to be a technician of enormous skill and a scholar of impressive learning; but in these talents the public has, rightly, only a passing interest. What matters is not an artist's technical skill but what he communicates by means of it.

Perhaps a clue to the public's attitude may be found in Stravinsky's scores for the theater, where, it is widely believed, he has been most successful. It is precisely here that he exhibits the one-sidedness of his nature. His preoccupation with ballet rather than opera, his constant use of mythology and ancient ritual, his penchant for subjects frozen by antiquity, all indicate his refusal to face the central and absorbing problem of the theater: human emotion. Rather he evades it. Thus much of his neoclassicism has seemed to this century to be needlessly emaciated, heartless, cold. He would not have it otherwise. His avowed purpose is to strip his art of the trappings of unnecessary story, picture, philosophy, heartthrob. Once music could rightly be termed "an order of mystic, sensuous mathematics;" but in many of Stravinsky's later works only the pure mathematics remains.

The public, of course, has an obligation to remember that a high emotional content is no more a necessity for great art today than it was in Haydn's time. If Stravinsky's sphere seems austere and narrow; if, to some, his tirades against romantic music seem as blind as Hanslick's, his view should nevertheless be understandable. We should sympathize with the rage of any composer of the past hundred years who has had to get away from the shadow of *Tristan und Isolde* and *Die Meistersinger*. That very rage has been Stravinsky's salvation because it drove him to find new avenues of expression, while the Wagner idolators remained impotent imitators.

# Other Modern Composers

The twentieth century has been an era of art in ferment, not to say torment. It has been a time of both wildly daring experimentation and aimless, futile drifting. Reflecting as it must the surroundings of a world in a state of vast turmoil, the art of this epoch has often seemed destructive rather than evocative of beauty and reason. Painting and sculpture have distorted and finally fragmented themselves into abstraction. Poetry has withdrawn behind a veil of obscurity. The drama and the novel ransack psychiatry and sex.

Music, too, is passing through a metamorphosis as profound as that of the other arts, but until recently the causes have not been the result of pressures from the external world. They are chiefly internal. The most startling development in the music of our century is the decline (one might almost say the death) of harmonic invention. This fatal weakening of one of music's three main components has presented composers with an almost insuperable obstacle. Every composer after Debussy has struggled with it. Stravinsky has said that the period of harmonic discovery is over, and that harmony is no longer open to exploration and exploitation. In his own words: "Harmonic novelty is at an end. Therefore, the contemporary ear (and brain) requires a completely different approach to music."

One of the first to recognize this impasse was a young Viennese composer, Arnold Schoenberg, who, in the last decades of the nineteenth century found that in his imitations of Wagnerian chromaticism he had reached a dead end. Schoenberg was born in Vienna in 1874. Except for instruction in counterpoint, he was practically self-taught in music theory. In the first phase of his career he struggled to make a living as a violinist and by orchestrating popular operettas by other composers. His own early works were drenched in romantic sentiment and Wagnerian chromaticism, e.g., his sextet for strings, *Verklärte Nacht* [*Transfigured Night*], composed in 1899. This work was Schoenberg's first, and only, "popular" success, becoming widely known years later when the English choreographer, Anthony Tudor, used it for his ballet, *Pillar of Fire*.

For ten years Schoenberg worked on the gargantuan song cycle, *Gurrelieder*, scored for five soloists, a speaker, several choruses, and a mammoth orchestra. Essentially a throwback to *Tristan und Isolde* in its ultrachromatic style, this piece was stale before it was even finished. However, in his symphonic poem, *Pelleas und Melisande* (1902–3), Schoenberg had already moved in a new direction, one that was taking him into a jungle of dense polyphony. With his first two string quartets and his Chamber Symphony (Op. 9) the center of interest had become a web of counterpoint so complex and so dissonant that the old landmarks of tonality began to recede and even disappear. Finally, in 1909, with his Three Piano Pieces (Op. 11), Schoenberg had arrived at the point of his "complete break with the past." His music would seldom return to the old territory.

What Schoenberg attempted was an assault upon tradition as fundamental as Einstein's undermining of Newtonian astronomy. He tried to destroy the tonal center. Music, as we have known it for more than three centuries, has been based on the twelve tones of the chromatic scale, with each of the tones producing two keys, major and minor, making twenty-four in all. Briefly stated, Schoenberg tried to compose music in which there would be no gravitational pull at any moment toward any single tone.

To express the idea of music composed *without tonality* the new words "atonal" and "atonality" were coined. (Schoenberg himself disliked these words, and preferred to say that he had "renounced a tonal center.") In order to give the ear of the listener no hint of any key center, Schoenberg had first to sweep away the entire system of traditional chords that cluster around the various keys. Instead, he used highly complex chords, including those based on intervals of the fourth instead of thirds; he used whole-tone scales and chords, and the long-banished tri-tone (e.g., F–B) both in melody and harmony. Thus, ato-nality really boiled down to continuous dissonance.

Schoenberg's melodies, too, began to break out of the old formulas. Avoiding scale lines, they became wide, zig-zag leaps of every possible interval. At one stage the com-poser tried to abolish all development or repetition of his themes; they would appear briefly and then be dropped. Later he went to an opposite extreme. He had always commanded an immense facility in contrapuntal writing; now his music became matted masses of polyphony based on the old traditional forms—fugue, inversion, retrograde inversion, canons of various kinds, including canon can-crizans—some of which had lain neglected since the death of Bach. Rhythms also became so complex that at times the music seemed totally free of meter and became a kind of musical prose, with tempos fluctuating incessantly.

Schoenberg also invented a revolutionary vocal device called *Sprechstimme* (speaking voice), which means a vocal line partly sung and partly spoken. This was first employed in *Pierrot Lunaire* (1912), a song cycle for chamber orchestra with reciter, and two stage pieces—*Ewartung* (1909), and *Die Glückliche Hand* (1912). The literary works upon which these pieces were based were examples of early expressionism—explorations of the inner recesses of the mind and character that were heavy with symbolism, and often reached the extremes of neuroticism and morbid subjectivity. Schoenberg's music, suiting the subject matter, generated immense tension and inner stress; its moods seemed to hover constantly on the borders of hysteria. Inevitably, the word "decadent" began to be applied to it, and invariably its performances created scandalous scenes and bitterly hostile audiences.

Schoenberg began to suffer a kind of martyrdom to his art which persisted throughout his career. But nothing daunted him. His next step was to organize his atonalism by means of a new technical invention that he called *Tonreihe*, or "tone rows." A tone row consists of all twelve tones of the chromatic scale arranged by the composer to suit his fancy, but with no tone repeated until all eleven others have been heard. The row is repeated in variation fashion, and becomes the chief structural basis of the work. Schoenberg began using this method of composition about 1923, and he is believed to have worked out its principles in collaboration with his two most famous pupils, Alban Berg and Anton Webern. The ramifications of the twelve-tone technique (also called the dodecaphonic or serial technique) finally became as complex as so many problems in mathematics. It became the chief generating force for Schoenberg's art, and was passed on through him and his pupils into the main stream of European and American music.

Schoenberg was an inspiring teacher. In the early decades of the century he held various teaching posts in Berlin and Vienna, where he instructed a number of the most gifted young composers of his time. With the Nazi conquest of Germany, however, he was forced to give up his professorship at the Prussian Academy of Art, in Berlin, moving first to Paris and then to the United States. He took up residence in southern California, and in 1936 was appointed professor of music at the University of California at Los Angeles, where he remained until his retirement in 1944. He became an American citizen in 1941, and died in his Los Angeles home in 1951. Schoenberg's American years produced a number of major works, but none that seem to bear any significant relation to his new environment. He left many works unfinished at his death, including the powerful opera, *Moses und Aron*.

Schoenberg's music presents immense problems both of appreciation and of appraisal. When his early atonal scores first made their appearance, the composer's penchant for clashing, screaming dissonance was widely considered preposterous if not actually mad. As the years went on, however, the force of his ideas spread from Vienna in an ever-widening circle of influence. Today the practitioners of the twelve-tone technique are a dominant faction in the music of every important country of Europe (except Russia) and in America. And yet, the music of Schoenberg himself continues to remain in a kind of limbo. Toward it the general music public still maintains an icy reserve. They respect it, they admit its vast technical ingenuity, they know its historical significance, but they have yet to love it.

One of the chief reasons for this lack of communication lies in the field of harmony. In all three of music's chief components—melody, rhythm, and harmony—a sense of motion is usually present. With the use of extreme dissonance, however, every chord begins to sound like every other chord, which means that although melody and rhythm still yield a sense of motion, harmony seems to stand still. Dissonance neutralizes its movement as though it were on a treadmill. Or, expressed in another way, what Schoenberg had done was to invent in effect a twenty-fifth key. By remaining rigorously atonal, music can become just as colorless and monotonous as if it had remained continously in any one of the regular keys.

Roger Sessions writes: "Our harmonic sense is essentially the awareness of one of the dimensions of music; having acquired that awareness, we cannot do away with it, and it would be ridiculous folly to try to do so. If art is to develop, awareness of every aspect of the art must increase rather than diminish. But harmonic effect as such has clearly ceased to be a major interest of composers . . ."

This, then, is the crisis in modern music created by the work of Schoenberg and his followers. The music public clings to its interest in harmony and refuses to give it up as one of music's major delights; while the composers, having exhausted its presently known possibilities, have turned their interests elsewhere.

"Rhythm, rhythmic polyphony, melodic or intervallic

construction," Stravinsky says, "are the elements of musical building to be explored today."

## II

Alban Berg was born in Vienna in 1885, and at the age of nineteen he became a pupil of Arnold Schoenberg, whose theories and ideals influenced him profoundly. Berg's early songs show his deeply romantic bent and his love for the German romantics: Schumann, Wagner, Brahms, Bruckner, and Mahler. His Piano Sonata, Op. 1, composed in 1908, blends Wagnerian chromaticism with Schoenberg's dissonant practices; but in the String Quartet, Op. 3 (1910), Five Orchestral Songs, Op. 4 (1912), Four Pieces for Clarinet and Piano, Op. 5 (1913), and Three Orchestral Pieces, Op. 6 (1914), Berg's own powerful personality began to emerge. He had quickly developed an interest in structures based on the traditional forms, and in exotic tonal coloring; already he was inventing new instrumental sounds of great beauty and originality. With these and a dissonant polyphonic style went a taut, explosive emotionalism. At a performance in 1913 of two of the Five Orchestral Songs the audience was incited almost to rioting. Clearly, Berg was following in the footsteps of his master.

In the spring of 1914, in a theater in Vienna, Berg witnessed a performance of scenes from Georg Büchner's drama, Woyzeck. Büchner was born in Darmstadt in 1813, and was brilliantly gifted in science, mathematics, poetry, philosophy, and the drama. When his political writings got him into trouble, he fled to Switzerland, where he died in 1837 at the age of twenty-four. It was not until 1879 that his unfinished play, Woyzeck, was found and published, after having been lost for more than forty years.

Berg was deeply moved by the Büchner drama, and he saw its possibilities as an opera. His work was interrupted by service in the Austrian army in World War I, but by 1921 he was able to complete the score. The first performance, at the Berlin State Opera, in 1925, was an immense success. Performances followed all over Europe, and in 1931 the work was also acclaimed in Philadelphia and New York.

The story of Wozzeck (as Berg titled his opera) is that of a poor, downtrodden army private in a small German town. Wozzeck's life is one of utter misery. An army doctor uses him to perform medical experiments; his mistress, Marie, by whom he has a child, is unfaithful to him, and her new lover, a handsome drum major, beats Wozzeck. The desperate man finally stabs Marie to death and then drowns himself in a lake.

Berg's Wozzeck at first received world-wide publicity as the first "atonal" opera. Much ink was also shed over the fact that the composer of this revolutionary work had based its fifteen scenes on some of the oldest of the traditional forms, e.g., the first act is based on a suite that contains a rhapsody, a military march, a lullaby, a passacaglia, and a rondo. The composer himself disclaimed any importance for these purely technical details, but insisted that his work must rise or fall on its power of communication to an audience.

Wozzeck was indeed a radically new species of opera, but its point of departure actually began with its story rather than its music. Büchner's drama has been called "a curious mingling of fantastic imaginings, stark realism, intense tenderness, and murderous brutality." The old apparatus of romantic or classic opera would have broken down under the shock of such a story, and Berg wisely used a new apparatus of his own, and Schoenberg's, devising. Wozzeck contains very little "ornamental" singing and almost no recitatives. Instead the singers half-sing and half-speak a "rhythmic declamation" that may sound either pleasant or tortured, depending upon the text. As in the Wagnerian music dramas, the true center of gravity lies in the orchestra. The color of the music is overwhelmingly dissonant, but with moments of startlingly effective tonality.

Of the greatness of Wozzeck there can be little question. Berg had dynamic powers of musical invention, and he knew instinctively the secrets for the creation of dramatic tension and contrast, character delineation, and the evocation of mood and atmosphere. In *Wozzeck* he convinces us that for the subject matter of the drama his is the perfect musical style.

After the completion of *Wozzeck*, Berg composed two important instrumental works: the Chamber Concerto, for piano, violin, and thirteen wind instruments, and the Lyric Suite for String Quartet. He had meanwhile begun to make use of Schoenberg's serial technique. He became absorbed in its polyphonic complications, to which he added his own special penchant for musical anagrams and hidden allusions to the works of other composers, so that his music often becomes a study in technical puzzles. But always, underlying its mathematical ingenuity, lies a strain of emotionalism that is deeply felt and highly communicative.

In 1928 Berg began work on a second opera, *Lulu*, which was based on two plays by the German dramatist, Frank Wedekind. The subject matter of these plays—a miasma of murder, suicide, sexual perversion, nymphomania, and prostitution—had caused their temporary banishment from the stage at the turn of the century. Berg worked for seven years on his opera, but had not quite finished it when he died in 1935. *Lulu* has since been performed, revealing that the composer had ripened and enriched his art immeasurably, and that his premature death was a great loss to twentieth-century music.

Berg's last completed work was his Violin Concerto, which he composed in a space of a few months during the last year of his life. Although worn down by illness, and deeply depressed by the death of the seventeen-year-old daughter of a friend, Berg was able to summon all his creative strength for this last effort. His Concerto is an elegy of great poignancy and beauty.

During the years when *Wozzeck* was scoring its first resounding successes and Schoenberg's music was receiving sensational publicity but few performances, little was heard of the work of Anton Webern, the third member of the atonal triumvirate. Webern was born in Vienna in 1883. After taking his Ph.D. at the Vienna University in 1906, he became Schoenberg's first pupil, and later one of the leading spirits in the development of the twelve-tone school. His life was devoted to composition, conducting, and teaching. His death, one of the senseless tragedies of World War II, occurred in 1945, when he was mistakenly shot to death outside his home by a soldier of the army of occupation.

Like Schoenberg and Berg, Webern was at heart a romantic with a reverence for the Viennese composers from Schubert to Mahler. He deplored the disintegration of formal structures that had come with impressionism, and the chaos that chromaticism had caused in harmony. But above all he rebelled against the giantism that had brought late nineteenth-century German music to its bloated end. From these extremes Webern took refuge in a microcosm—a tiny, tiny world unlike anything any composer had yet devised.

Notes were cheap in the spendthrift era of the *Symphony of One Thousand*. With Webern the note became infinitely precious. It was something to hear singly, to ponder over, to endow with hidden subtleties and meanings. In pursuing this ideal Webern had to subject his music to a merciless process of condensation. His themes and forms became minute entities, his instrumental forces mere skeletons. Thus, a Webern string quartet movement may be contained in only thirteen measures; the entire work may last but eight minutes. A concerto may last only ten minutes, a cantata but four and one half minutes, an entire symphony but ten minutes. Webern's entire life work has been recorded on four long-playing records of hardly more than four hours duration.

There is nothing dwarfish or misshapen about this composer's music; rather it impresses by the classic purity of its design, the precision of its thought. Webern's musical means have been described as "the minimum that will function." "No motive is developed," the composer himself said in describing his method. "Once stated, the theme expresses all it has to say."

Its tiny dimensions are not, of course, the sole distinguishing feature of Webern's art. His work is basically polyphonic, and it abounds in canonic devices, especially mirror canons. These he combined with serial techniques of great complexity. Another characteristic is the use of *Klangfarbenmelodie*. This formidable word means simply that the notes of a theme are distributed through the orchestra not in groups but singly, a single instrument taking one note at a time. Thus the orchestration becomes a series of small flashes of tonality which light up like fireflies among the instruments. In his vocal works Webern leads the vocalist through appallingly difficult intervals that leap in zigzags even more jagged than Schoenberg's.

Although he was the last of the atonal triumvirate to achieve recognition, Webern is now revered by the *avant garde* in music. That most frigid of critics, Igor Stravinsky, warmly acknowledges his mastery, and praises "his not yet canonized art."

### III

High on any list of composers of the present century whose work is believed most likely to endure, one would surely find the name of the Hungarian, Béla Bartók (1881–1945). Bartók was the rare case of a scholar and teacher who was also profoundly creative. As a young man he studied the piano and composition at the Budapest Conservatory, where he was later to teach for many years. He became a brilliant pianist, who might have followed the career of a virtuoso. Early in the present century, Bartók began his exhaustive studies of Hungarian folk song. He collected and systematically examined literally thousands of specimens, not alone from Hungary, but also from Romania, Central Europe, Turkey, the Near East, and North Africa. Many of these he published, with illuminating comments. Ultimately they became the central core of his own art.

Bartók's music represents the most complex and the most intellectually developed of all transformations of folk-into-art music. His method was imaginative and varied, but also uncompromising. The folk tunes of Hungary (not the gypsy tunes used by Liszt and Brahms, but the truer, Magyar songs and dances) have been described as "full of barbaric brutality, as becomes a race which has lived sword in hand, surrounded by superstition." Bartók made no attempt to soften their contours; rather he gave full play to their violently passionate moods, relentless rhythms, headlong tempos, and crudely dissonant harmonies. He greatly admired the music of Debussy, and he followed the French master in developing a harmonic style of enormous range and complexity, but with raw, dissonant sounds predominating. Thus his music at first repelled many listeners, who found it powerful but harsh, cerebral, difficult to hear and to grasp.

Donald Jay Grout has written that "Bartók's ideal was to express, in twentieth-century terms, Bach's texture of contrapuntal fullness, Beethoven's art of thematic development, and Debussy's discovery of the sonorous (as distinct from the functional) value of chords." To these components he added his own skill in developing new instrumental sounds and sonorities. His music glows with fascinating flashes of instrumental color.

Bartók was personally a proud, defiant, and difficult man. Because he tried to help the cause of the persecuted Jews of conquered Europe and deliberately antagonized the Nazis, he put his own life in danger. Friends finally persuaded him to emigrate to America, but he was not happy in this country. He was ill much of the time and almost penniless, but he refused to call attention to himself or his music. Ironically, wide public interest in his work did not begin until after his death.

Among Bartók's finest works are the *Cantata profana*, for soloists, double chorus, and orchestra; his Second and Third Piano Concertos; his Violin Concerto; the Concerto for Orchestra; *Music for Strings, Percussion, and Celesta*; and *Mikrokosmos*, a series of graded piano pieces for teaching. Crowning his life work are Bartók's six string quartets, which are by general acclaim among the finest works in their medium composed in the present century.

If any modern composer could be said to typify the German artist, that man would surely be Paul Hindemith (1895– ). It is not only that he is Germany's leading neoclassic composer, who has demonstrated enormous proficiency in almost every branch of theory and technique; he is also one of the most practical of musicians, with an expert's skill as violinist, violist, ensemble player, and conductor. Thus he is a true descendant of eighteenth-century masters like Bach, Handel, Haydn, and Mozart, whose art was always part of a practical way of life. Few composers today can match Hindemith in the range of his catalogue, the solidity of his workmanship, or the clarity with which he has taught and written about the art of music. He is one of the great professionals of our time.

In the 1920s, when Hindemith's career began, romanticism was already in *rigor mortis*; thus, many of his early works followed the new vogue, being comical, ironic, nonsensical, savagely satirical. But this exponent of practicality and common sense rejected the growing complexities of the new atonalism, with its opaque expressionism and its appalling technical difficulties, which were driving a wedge between composers and the music public. For Hindemith, music, like every other art, exists in order to communicate. He turned to *Gebrauchsmusik* (roughly, utility music), whose first virtue was its playability and singability. (To this day Hindemith finds that the immense labors necessary to mastering performances of much twelve-tone music to be all out of proportion to the results.)

*Gebrauchsmusik* was a passing phase, and the more mature Hindemith style soon emerged—essentially linear and contrapuntal, often highly dissonant but never wholly relinquishing a distant sense of tonality, a distinctive but subdued instrumental coloring. In nineteenth-century terms Hindemith would be a Brahmsian rather than a Wagnerian. Inevitably his music would be affected by his Germanic love for instruction and pure theory, e.g., his long series of sonatas for all sorts of solo instruments, many of them long neglected; and various teaching pieces, including *Ludus tonalis* [*Game of Tonalities*] for piano, a series of twelve fugues which has been termed analogous to the *Well-tempered Clavier*.

Many of Hindemith's scores are now fixtures in the modern repertoire—the superb symphony based on the composer's opera, *Mathis der Maler* [*Matthias the Painter*], the Symphony in E flat, the Concert Music for Strings and Brass, the Symphonic Dances, the *Marienleben* song cycle, the Third String Quartet, the ballet *Nobilissima Visione*, the *Symphonic Metamorphoses* on themes by Weber, and various concertos and sonatas. Hindemith's music is a rich mine that performers will doubtless be working for many years.

III

Erik Satie, that oddly gifted though willfully eccentric French composer, knew that there can be nothing more devastating than laughter. To him the state of music just prior to World War I was intolerable—romanticism grown absurdly pompous and monstrously inflated. To attack this horrid image there could be but one counterweapon—satire—the more stinging the better. Satie's own talents were limited, and minor; but he was a personality capable of acting as a catalyst upon other personalities around him, especially upon a coterie of young French composers who were eager to do new things in a new way.

In 1916, when the young poet and aesthete, Jean Cocteau, published a small tract called *Le Coq et l'arlequin*, a new movement suddenly congealed. Cocteau deplored the deadly seriousness of romantic music ("the kind one listens to with one's face in one's hands"); he praised Satie's music and Stravinsky's; he called for a new spirit in French music counter to Debussy's misty impressionism. And then, quite by accident, the young composers who were to answer Cocteau's call were thrust together and given a group name. A French music critic happened to write an article about "The French Six," comparing them with the famous Russian Five. Their names were Georges Auric, Louis Durey, Arthur Honegger, Darius Milhaud, Francis Poulenc, and Germaine Tailleferre. Years later Milhaud wrote that the critic had chosen the names arbitrarily, "merely because we knew one another, were good friends, and had figured on the same programs, quite irrespective of our different temperaments and wholly dissimilar characters." Nevertheless, the name, the Six, flew around the world, a terse journalistic symbol of a new force in modern music.

At first the Six carried on their anti-romantic jests with immense gusto. Milhaud wrote *Machines agricoles*, a suite for voice and chamber orchestra with words taken from a catalogue of farm machinery, and *Catalogue des fleurs*, based on a seed catalogue. Poulenc wrote songs based on Parisian street ditties. Honegger proved that romantic scene-painting was defunct. The new vogue would be the descriptive realism of his *Pacific 231*, an orchestral glorification of a giant locomotive that chugged its way, briefly, through concert halls everywhere. He later composed *Rugby*, a tonal football game. Satie himself, the mascot of the group, began a new era in the imaginative uses of percussion when he demanded in the score of his ballet, *Parade*, a typewriter, a roulette wheel, and a siren. Less successful was his attempt to compose background music that should *not* be listened to (*musique d'ameublement*).

Performances of the early music of the Six brought delightfully scandalous scenes to the Paris concert halls—demonstrations and counterdemonstrations, hisses, shouts, animal noises, people slapping other people's faces, tumult, battle, and final quelling by the police, who once went to the extreme of throwing a music critic out bodily.

A sense of humor can be a dangerous thing. It helped to ruin the career of Satie, whose originality and underlying seriousness of purpose the public at first could not fathom. Fortunately, the members of the Six refused to remain musical buffoons. Humor was in fact only one of their devices aimed to rescue music from the swamps of romanticism. They demanded simplicity, clarity, lightness of spirit, charm. ("Down with Wagner!" cried Milhaud.) Melodies became naïvely simple, often directly quoting folk songs, café songs, or nursery tunes; but their treatment could be deceptively sophisticated, with traditional harmonies suddenly splashed by the acid of dissonance, and clear tonalities moving in and out of polytonality. Rhythms might imitate folk dances, the jazz of the period, or the complexities of *Le Sacre du printemps*. Thus a new classicism was born.

Although their music had repercussions all over the music world, the comradeship of the Six was actually short-lived. Like the Russian Five they were widely disparate in aims and abilities, and they soon went their separate ways. Quickest to drop from international notice were Tailleferre (1892– ), the woman member of the group, and Durey (1888– ). Auric (1899– ) is remembered chiefly as the composer of several mildly successful ballets produced in the 1920s by Diaghilev, and of various film scores.

Darius Milhaud (1892– ) became one of the most prodigiously fertile composers of modern times. His catalogue is encyclopedic—symphonies large and small, concertos, floods of chamber works, piano pieces, songs, film scores, and stage works. The last range from vaudevilles to ballets, and from "minute" operas of ten-minute length to mammoth music dramas. The opera stories themselves run the gamut from Paul Claudel's historical *Christophe Colomb*, to the classic Greek drama, parodies of ancient legends, and news stories dredged up from the daily record of crime.

All through the 1920s and later, after Ravel's death, Milhaud and Honegger dominated the music scene of Paris. But when the Nazis occupied France, Milhaud was forced to flee to America, where he took up a teaching career at Mills College, in Oakland, California. In the ensuing years, and despite recurring illnesses, he still poured forth torrents of music.

All the techniques of music, old and new, are at Milhaud's command, but he has refused to let any one system bind him. He takes his materials wherever he finds them: for him a melody can be good whether it comes from an opera or a honky-tonk. He was one of the first serious composers to exploit American jazz, and he has processed French, Brazilian, Portuguese, and Mexican folk songs. His music can be cleanly lyrical or dense with the harshest polytonality. He assumes styles and idioms in endless variety.

About the quality of this composer's music there has been the widest critical disagreement. "The whole stream of Milhaud's production," writes Ernst Křenek, "carries at times some gravel and dead wood—no wonder, such enormous quantities of music are set in motion." But others have spoken of "the tragedy of a composer with a huge surplus of energy that he is unable to direct."

Arthur Honegger (1892–1955) was a Swiss, born in Le Havre of Swiss parents; but his life, the major part of his education, and his interests identified him with the music of France. He did not stay long with the gaieties of the Satie-Six group. After *Pacific 231* he began to show his true stature—an artist of intense seriousness of purpose, a prodigious worker and a fine craftsman who deserved to be one of the most admired of his group. Honegger was never an inventor in the forging of the new techniques of modernism; rather he assimilated, perfected, established. Like Milhaud he could move at will from the humorous simplicities of folk song and jazz to a severely classical contrapuntal style, replete with dissonance and alive with jagged rhythms and raw color. He rejected impressionism, but his music can be deeply emotional and moving, and essentially romantic.

Much of Honegger's finest work is contained in his five symphonies, although several stage works have enjoyed more popular successes. His early *Le Roi David*, a "symphonic psalm" for chorus, orchestra, and soloists, evokes scenes from the life of the psalmist-king. It is uneven, but its choral splendors, its flaming orchestral colors, and its moods of wild, barbaric exultation project something of Old Testament passion and grandeur. More likely to endure is the dramatic oratorio, *Jeanne d'Arc au bûcher* [*Joan of Arc at the Stake*], based on a play by Paul Claudel. Described as something between an opera and a mystery play with incidental music, it projects, again, great theatrical power. The best of Honegger's operas is *Antigone*, with text by Cocteau after Sophocles.

It was Francis Poulenc (1899– ) whose gift of humor fitted him best for the early satirical experiments of the Six. He was born in Paris, studied the piano, but was largely self-taught as a composer. He has been called a musical clown of the first order and a clever eclectic who has fashioned a personal style out of various odd pieces of cloth. Although his sense of humor is often a delight, Poulenc has other strings to his bow. His handling of words is expert, and he has built up an impressive reputation in the field of vocal music, both for songs in great variety and for several fine religious choral works. As a stage composer, Poulenc's best work is probably his *opera buffa, Les Mamelles de Tirésias* [*The Breasts of Tiresias*], in which he parodies the styles of Massenet, Offenbach, Richard Strauss, Ravel, and several others. His recent serious opera, *Dialogues des Carmélites* [*Dialogues of the Carmelites*] has been widely performed both in Europe and America.

With the passage of almost half a century since their early notorious successes, it becomes possible to assess with reasonable accuracy the accomplishment of the Six. The result is a sense of disappointment. No one of them has risen anywhere near the stature of Debussy or Ravel. Collectively their movement seemed quickly to disintegrate before it could bequeath any truly lasting legacy to French music, a marked contrast to the enormous collective accomplishment and influence of the Russian Five. Meanwhile, the future of French music may lie in the hands of a composer (and influential teacher) who can be but mentioned here—Olivier Messiaen (1906– ), a neoromantic and neoimpressionist, in whose deeply emotional music is found a rebirth of Catholic mysticism. Messiaen, it should also be noted, is the teacher of Pierre Boulez (1925– ), the front-runner of a new group of ultraradical composers whose methods stem in part from Webern.

## IV

At the turn of the century there appeared on the Russian scene two young composers of unusual talent and promise—Alexander Scriabin (1872–1915), and Serge Rachmaninoff (1873–1943). Both were products of the Moscow Conservatory, but no two artists could have differed more sharply in their personalities, their lives, their artistic aims, and the ultimate fate of their music. Scriabin practically ignored his Russian heritage, deriving a piano style chiefly from Chopin and an orchestral apparatus from Wagner. But Scriabin was driven by a daemon—a strange, mystical theosophy that filled him with ecstatic, megalomaniac visions. His orchestral scores—*The Divine Poem*, *The Poem of Ecstasy*, and *Prometheus*—were attempts to symbolize these visions in tone; but with the passing years their substance proved to be far cooler than their composer's white-hot inspiration. Nevertheless, Scriabin was a courageous innovator (especially in his ten piano sonatas) who startled the world of music in his time with bold technical adventures, e.g., his use of chords built upon fourths instead of thirds, his experiments with dissonance, his use of whole-tone scales and chords, and a device that he called the "Mystic Chord." Scriabin's music had a brief period of sensational success, but outside Russia his star fell as rapidly as it had risen.

By contrast, Rachmaninoff was a thorough-going conservative who virtually ignored the currents of modern music as they swirled past him. As a young man in Moscow he succeeded brilliantly as composer, conductor, and pianist; but underlying his immense talent was a curious lack of self-confidence that weighed upon him all his life. Innovation and change were thus alien to his nature. In his piano and orchestral works and in his songs he remained firmly in the nineteenth-century Russian nationalist tradition, with Tchaikovsky's melancholy lyricism his abiding model.

Rachmaninoff was one of the thousands of Russian artists whose lives were disrupted or ruined in the chaos that followed the revolution of 1917. He and his family escaped from Soviet Russia in 1918 and finally reached America, where he made his home for the rest of his life. He never returned to his native land. There is little doubt that this caused a psychological breach that affected him profoundly. He gave up conducting almost completely and composed only a handful of scores, but became one of the great pianists of his time.

During the hectic years that followed World War I, when the new anti-romantic, furiously dissonant music ruled the concert halls, few believed that Rachmaninoff's sweetly sad, incurably sentimental scores would long survive their melancholy creator. We know now that they had an inner vitality that was lasting. Rachmaninoff's finer works—his piano Preludes and Etudes-Tableaux, his Second Symphony, his Second and Third Piano Concertos, the little-known Vesper Mass, and the Variations on a Theme of Paganini—are likely to hold their own as long as there is breath in the old romantic movement itself.

Serge Prokofiev was born in the Ukraine in 1891. He was a musical child prodigy, had first-rate teaching at the St. Petersburg Conservatory, and became the *enfant terrible* of Russian music circles when hardly more than twenty years old. With the coming of the Revolution, Prokofiev tried to get away from the new dictatorship of the proletariat, and in the spring of 1918 was permitted to leave the country. He spent the next fifteen years in America and Western Europe, where he became a familiar figure as a brilliant pianist and the composer of some of the most provocative music of his time. Ultimately a nostalgia for his native land drew him back to Russia. There he remained, except for infrequent visits to the West, until his death in 1953.

Like so many Russian composers, Prokofiev was an eclectic who admired the resources of Western art, music, literature, and the drama; and he utilized them freely in fashioning his own art. He was a composer of immense natural gifts, a facile but scrupulous craftsman with a fund of pungently original ideas. Witty, urbane, sardonic, he personified the new anti-romantic age. He tried to rescue Russian music from its worked-out formulas of romantic melancholy based on folk song, creating instead a new musical language to suit the modern age. One of his trademarks was the sharp, mechanistic scherzo or toccata that raced with the speed and clatter of an engine; another was graceful but wholly unsentimental melody supported by bittersweet harmonies. In the early stages of his career he reveled in dissonance as shocking as shattering glass, but as he matured his art grew more mellow.

Prokofiev was a master of many forms. His dainty Classical Symphony forecast the neoclassic age, while his Fifth Symphony is a masterpiece of large-scale tonal architecture. His Third Piano Concerto has been called the finest piano concerto of our century. His *Love for Three Oranges* is a hilarious wedding of opera and sheer farce, while *Peter and the Wolf*, for orchestra and reciter, has the charm of an authentic fairy tale. His piano sonatas gave that instrument a new percussive dimension, and his ballet, *The Prodigal Son*, gave George Balanchine a vehicle for the creation of a stage masterpiece.

With Dmitri Shostakovich we come to the first important Russian composer whose art has been shaped in large measure by the new force of governmental control. Born in St. Petersburg in 1906, he was a child of eleven when, in his own words, he "met the revolution in the street," being an eyewitness to the rioting and killing. His family were cultured intellectuals who suffered cruel privations in the post-Revolution years so that their musically gifted son could attend the St. Petersburg Conservatory. He was only nineteen years old when he completed, as his final student work, his First Symphony (Op. 10). It made him famous not alone in Russia, but all over Europe and America.

Although obviously in debt to Tchaikovsky and the Five, Shostakovich was not merely a facile imitator. His music had astonishing assurance, and a stylistic imprint that was his alone. Once out of the Conservatory, he quickly developed an interest in the *avant garde* music of the West. He wrote symphonies, ballets, film scores, and much incidental music for stage plays, utilizing the techniques of Schoenberg, Berg, Stravinsky, and Hindemith. In 1936, however, Shostakovich's burgeoning career reached a sudden and totally unforeseen crisis. His opera, *Lady Macbeth of Mzensk*, had been playing to packed houses when, without warning, the official newspaper, *Pravda*, issued a blast that damned the piece on all counts. The story was called vulgar and decadent; the music was deplored as "formalistic," neurotic, perverted, and ugly. *Lady Macbeth of*

*Mzensk* was driven from the stage and Shostakovich was publicly disgraced.

*Pravda's* action was believed to have been personally ordered by Joseph Stalin, after he had witnessed a performance of the opera. The results were drastic, not alone for Shostakovich, but for all Russian composers. The policy of the Soviet government toward all the arts soon became plain: Artists were supported by the state and they must contribute their share toward the glorification of the state. Moreover, *avant garde* art in all its forms was taboo. It was undoubtedly Stalin's belief that such art was incomprehensible to the masses (as it was to him), and was therefore unsuited to the purposes of effective propaganda.

Shostakovich at first met the crisis by surrender. His Fifth Symphony, first performed in 1937, is essentially an old-fashioned throwback to Tchaikovsky. With the ensuing years Shostakovich made many contributions to the Soviet-glorification literature, with works like his Seventh and Eighth Symphonies—huge tonal editorials that blended the giantism of Mahler (whose music Shostakovich adored) with the clichés of the nineteenth-century nationalists. Shostakovich gradually reached a compromise. A few of his expertly written works take a bold stand in the heart of modernist territory, but for the most part the daring has gone out of his art.

The situation that faces all the serious composers of Soviet Russia can be understood only when the throttling nature of the dictatorship around them is made plain. Directly or indirectly the government controls all musical performances, in concert halls, opera houses, on the radio, on television. It decides, through various committees, what music shall be played and by whom. It sets the amount of performance fees. It operates and controls all music-publishing establishments and dictates the amount of royalties. Similarly, it controls the recording industry, and, of course, the entire Soviet press, including the journals devoted to serious music. Obviously, under such a system no artist who hopes to remain alive can do other than operate according to strict governmental fiat.

Thus the somber truth is that Russia, which once blazed

with musical talent of the first order, has in the past thirty years produced little of enduring interest to the rest of the world. Instead there is a depressing sameness of style and purpose, and an almost total lack of daring and enterprise. As a result, only a few Soviet composers have risen to widespread prominence since the revolution. Some of them are of an older generation, for example, Nicolas Miaskovsky (1881–1950), who was a contemporary and close friend of Prokofiev. Miaskovsky is famous as the most prolific symphonist since the eighteenth century; but except for his Twenty-First Symphony, a work of unusual beauty, little of his output is known in the West. Once an avid explorer of advanced Western techniques, he gave up modernism and often wasted a precious talent on propaganda pieces of various sorts, some based on folk songs, factory songs, and workers' marches.

A measure of world fame has been won by Aram Khachaturyan (1904– ). This composer was born in Tiflis, and his work is saturated with the folk tunes of his native Armenia and of other southwestern Soviet republics. Pieces like his Piano Concerto and the ballet *Gayane* rely chiefly on exotic melody and garishly colored harmonies and instrumentation for their popular success. Also well known in the West is some of the work of Dmitri Kabalevsky (1904– ), a graceful lyricist and expert craftsman.

v

Jean Sibelius (1865–1957) lived to such an advanced age and was silent as a composer for so many years before his death, that in the world between the two wars he seemed like an anachronism. He was in fact a contemporary of Debussy, Mahler, and Richard Strauss who lived on into the era of the magnetic-tape composers. When he was a young man, the sparks from the brilliant Russian blaze had begun to light the fires of nationalism all over Europe—in Bohemia with Smetana and Dvořák, in Norway with Grieg. Those fires would burn for many years, and down to our own time—in Spain with Falla, in Denmark with Nielsen, in Hungary with Kodaly and Bartók, in

Moravia with Janáček, in Romania with Enesco, in England with Vaughan Williams, in Mexico with Chávez, in a re-created ancient Hebraism with Ernest Bloch, and with many more.

In this galaxy Sibelius was for many years typed as an exponent of Finnish nationalism, and in part he was. After receiving his advanced musical training in Berlin and Vienna, he returned to Finland in the early 1890s strongly impelled to paint both the sagas of ancient Finnish mythology and the magnificent panorama of nature that surrounded him. A favorite source became the *Kalevala*, the Finnish national epic. One of its runes inspired *Pohjola's Daughter*, a tonal painting of the mythical maiden who sits upon the rainbow, spinning. Another is set in *The Origin of Fire*, for baritone solo, male chorus, and orchestra. In this work Ukko, the Northern counterpart of Zeus, dispels the darkness of the world by restoring sunlight and warmth. *Luonnotar*, for soprano and orchestra, is the *Kalevala* version of the Creation. *The Song of Väino*, *The Return of Lemminkäinen*, and *The Swan of Tuonela* are based on runes from the same epic. *The Oceanides* is an impressionistic tone picture of the sea, while *Tapiola* derives its name from Tapio, the Finnish god of the forest.

For the painting of these spacious musical frescoes Sibelius developed a style that was distinctly his own—masculine, full-blooded, sinewy, with little of the soft lyricism of German post-romanticism. Athough he never used actual folk tunes, many of the Sibelius melodies have a strong folk flavor. His harmonies extend from somber richness to harsh dissonance. His instrumentation runs to the dark colors.

It was not until the 1920s that Sibelius's seven symphonies came into prominence in England and America, and now they are generally regarded as his most enduring works. The First and Second Symphonies date from the turn of the century; they are a romantic blend of the lyrical and the dramatic, but they are also aggressively strong in general style and orchestration and often highly individual in detail. With his Fourth Symphony, completed in 1911, Sibelius had reached a turning point of great interest. At this early date he saw the handwriting on the wall, presaging the end of romantic opulence and giantism. This symphony waited for years for an appreciative public, for it is a study in repression and attenuation. Its form is skeletal, its themes are reduced to spare, laconic utterances that are put together with a minimum of padded development and no hint of instrumental luxury. Within this slender framework the composer generates, nevertheless, an underlying emotionalism of great power and suggestion, a brooding sadness that gives way to defeat and despair.

Sibelius's Fifth Symphony has been a more popular work than the Fourth, for its moods are for the most part serene, and its final movement develops a climax of brilliance and power. The crown of the Sibelius symphonies is undoubtedly the Seventh, a single movement that is at once lyrical and dramatic, closely knit and spaciously laid out. In a sense it sums up Sibelius's progress as an artist— a nineteenth-century romantic nationalist coming at last to the classicism of a new age. Here, as in his Violin Concerto, one of the best works of its kind in our time, the composer showed that he was a Brahmsian who could breathe new life into an old form.

VI

There is far more than a merely frivolous reason for tracing the beginning of the renascence of English music to that happy day in 1870 when Arthur Sullivan first met William Schwenck Gilbert. Of their comic operas it need only be said at this late date that what the English-speaking world has hailed so long and joyously as masterpieces of their kind should also be acknowledged, frankly, as works of art likely to endure. When, at the turn of the century, Edward Elgar (1857–1934) also appeared on the scene with his magnificent *Enigma Variations* and his oratorio, *The Dream of Gerontius*, the signs and portents could not be mistaken. England's two-hundred-year musical drought had come to an end.

Although the British public praised him with nationalistic fervor, Elgar was an eclectic who derived his style chiefly from Wagner, Liszt, and Brahms. German music, in fact, still ruled England as despotically as Italian music had ruled it in the eighteenth century. But change was in the air. England's young composers were trying to escape the suffocating dullness of generations of windy oratorios. Some of them had their eyes on the Russians and were thinking about nationalism. The new generations, it transpired, were to contain great names and lesser ones—Holst, Vaughan Williams, Bax, Delius, Lord Berners, Bliss, Lambert, Warlock, Butterworth, Walton, Britten. Collectively they raised English music once again to a resplendent eminence.

Gustav Holst (1874–1934) had a mystical and venturesome mind that brought to his music a variety as curious as it was refreshing—operas and other works that reflected his absorption in the Hindu epics; his grandiose *Hymn of Jesus*, a choral and orchestral setting from the apocryphal Acts of St. John; his picturesque delineation of astrology in his orchestral suite, *The Planets*; his irreverent spoof of *Parsifal* in his comic opera, *The Perfect Fool*; a Japanese suite for orchestra; works based on texts as diverse as Walt Whitman, Euripides and Sanskrit verse; and, most significant for the future, his exquisite arrangements of English folk songs.

Holst was drawn to English folk song at a time when the noted folklorist and scholar, Cecil Sharpe, was doing his pioneer work in collecting and publishing these almost-forgotten native tunes. Another young composer and friend of Holst's, Ralph Vaughan Williams, realized the richness of this lyric vein and also that of the historical treasure that lay untouched in England's church music and her madrigals of the fifteenth and sixteenth centuries. Vaughan Williams was born in Down Ampney, Gloucestershire, in 1872, the son of a clergyman. He studied music at Cambridge, at the Royal College of Music, and later on the continent with Max Bruch and Maurice Ravel. Early in the century he began collecting folk songs in Norfolk, and soon they began to leave their marks upon his own works.

This man who was to become the most national of modern English composers once proclaimed his creed: "The greatest artist belongs inevitably to his country as much as the humblest singer in a remote village . . ." In point of fact he was an eclectic as well as a nationalist, and into his mill went grist from Debussy's impressionism, Mussorgsky's realism, and even Schoenberg's atonalism; withal, Vaughan Williams remained singularly of his own country. Most of his works are to be appreciated (in the words of Eric Blom) "only on condition that there is some understanding of the English world of music in the hearer, a world rather apart that he must try to see from the point of view of art and life. The early *Fantasia on a Theme by Thomas Tallis* (1909) is not to be appraised without some recognition of the great Tudor polyphonists, nor the Mass in G minor (1920) without some acquaintance with the traditions of Anglican church music (though the text is Roman). The sombrely splendid *Job* ballet (1930) needs some taste for the seventeenth-century English masque and the nonconforming genius of William Blake; the *Sancta Civitas* oratorio (1926) calls for some realization of the magnificence of Biblical English; something of the English musical festival spirit must enter into a hearing of short but impressive choral works like the *Magnificat*, *Benedicite*, and *Dona nobis pacem*. The quiet enchantment of the most secluded rural England must be known to those who wish to find all there is in the *Pastoral Symphony* (1922) and in *The Lark Ascending* for violin and orchestra (1914); and only the Londoner, perhaps, can enter quite lovingly enough, as distinct from just admiringly, into the spirit of the *London Symphony* (1914)."

Vaughan Williams once cautioned young composers against "making the mistake of imagining that they can be universal without at first having been local." He himself showed how the transition could be made, in the realm of the symphony. His nine works in this form were at first locally evocative, in the *London Symphony* and the *Pastoral Symphony*; but in the bitter, violently rebellious Fourth Symphony, in F minor, he had passed on to a greater cosmos. Thereafter he spoke a universal language, even though his characteristically English accent remained with him. Each succeeding work, however, probed to some new frontier of form and content. When Vaughan Williams died in 1958 he was one of the master spirits of the English art of our time.

Frederick Delius (1862–1934) was born in England of German parents. In early manhood he left home to escape a career in his wealthy father's woolen business, trying instead to be an orange grower on a plantation in Florida. He soon abandoned the fruit industry and took up the study of music with an organist in Jacksonville. Later he gave music lessons in Virginia and played the organ in New York. On the basis of these vagrant beginnings, Delius determined to be a composer, and in 1886 he went to Leipzig to study at the Conservatory. Two years later he settled in France, where he made his home for the rest of his life. Delius's later life was tragic. When he was in his fiftieth year paralysis overtook him, and within a few years he was totally blind and helpless. Undaunted, he continued to compose with the aid of a devoted secretary.

Critics of Delius's music have said that he was hardly an English composer at all because his impressionistic style and his luscious harmonies derived from Debussy. It is also true that his music is uneven, tragically so in such large-scale works as his opera *A Village Romeo and Juliet* and the choral symphony *A Mass of Life*; but at his best Delius could bring to life vivid landscapes and seascapes, suffusing them with his own poetical and deeply felt moods, e.g., in *Over the Hills and Far Away, In a Summer Garden, On Hearing the First Cuckoo in Spring, The Walk to the Paradise Garden* (from *A Village Romeo and Juliet*), *Brigg Fair, Summer Night on the River, Eventyr,* and the remarkable choral and orchestral *Sea Drift*, after Walt Whitman.

Although a prolific composer, Arnold Bax (1883–1953) came into his own rather late in Britain, and is still little known in America. He has been called an English Sibelius, in that his work is divided between formal abstractions—

symphonies, sonatas, and chamber works—and picturesque evocations of nature. Noteworthy are his sympathetic settings of verse by Irish poets—Yeats, Synge, and Padraic Colum.

With the end of World War I and the rise of the new antiromantic generation headed in France by the Six, it was inevitable that some of the younger English composers should veer off toward satire. The sometimes witty pieces of Lord Berners (1883–1950) and Constant Lambert (1905–1951) proved ephemeral; but the hilarious *Façade* by William Walton (1902–  ), a setting of poems by Edith Sitwell, set audiences everywhere to laughing. Walton soon developed into one of the most serious and assured of English composers. His Viola Concerto is a solid work, and actually of finer stuff than the dazzling oratorio *Belshazzar's Feast*, which brought Walton wide fame. This Old Testament evocation, for baritone, organ, brass bands, and huge orchestra is a tour de force of volcanic energy, rich in Biblical splendor, but essentially as melodramatic as a Gustav Doré illustration. In his later large works—a violin concerto, two symphonies, a cello concerto, the opera *Troilus and Cressida*—Walton's style has remained largely eclectic, with little conscious attempt to claim an English ancestry. It can be romantic and lyrical or full of harsh polytonality and angular melody, with derivations as widely separated as Stravinsky and Sibelius.

With Benjamin Britten (1913–  ) we come to the present in English music, and to a talent that gives every promise of continued growth and enrichment. Britten is above all a natural composer. He uses instruments with perfect surety, he has a genuine lyric gift, and he translates English words into melody superbly. These and an instinct for the theater have brought him unusual success in the opera house. His *Peter Grimes*, *The Turn of the Screw*, and *A Midsummer Night's Dream* are outstanding in a poverty-stricken operatic age.

## VII

The most common criticism applied to modern American music in its serious forms is that it lacks character, a sharply defined profile, and is instead merely another faceless imitation of great European models. Americans themselves never cease to wonder why their popular music, as summed up in the phenomenon of jazz, should be so teeming with ingenuity, originality, vigor, and healthy vulgarity while their serious music is generally considered pallid, timid, imitative, or simply dull. The immense world-wide influence of jazz on every musical level is one of the astonishing developments of our time, but few American composers, oddly enough, have made really significant use of it on an intellectual level. The truth is that America's serious composers would probably be better off if jazz had never been invented, because even though they are now among the best-equipped musicians in the world, they are treated as stepchildren less gifted than their rowdy half brothers.

Most Europeans make the mistake of searching in American serious music for something characteristic, something nationally distinctive like the jazz idiom in popular music. No such characteristic exists. Instead, the distinctive thing about this music is its variety. We may mention here the work of only a few American composers of the past few decades, and only in meagerest detail; even so, the point should become clear that hardly any two of these men are alike, that they have been exploring in all directions, and that their products are as diverse as the multifarious nationalities that have made up America herself.

For example, Aaron Copland (1900–  ), who studied in Paris with the celebrated teacher, Nadia Boulanger, has gone through various phases of influence and growth—including a period of heavy debt to the rhythmic and harmonic practices of Stravinsky, a polyrhythmic jazz period, a phase of austere and complex neoclassicism, a return to simplicity, and to portraits of the American scene based on uses of the folk idiom.

Virgil Thomson (1896– ) is another Boulanger pupil, who lived for a number of years in Paris and returned home with an abiding admiration for French culture and a loathing of heavy German romanticism. Essentially a miniaturist and a dealer in vignettes, Thomson developed a style that is disarmingly uncomplex. Its naïveté, however, is that of the complete sophisticate, springing from a mind that is urbane and highly cultured. (Thomson's critical writings about music are brilliantly witty and discerning.) His *Four Saints in Three Acts* is an operatic hors d'oeuvre as clever as it is original.

A third Boulanger pupil is Roy Harris (1898– ), whose work has been split by his admiration for the classic forms and procedures and a wholly romantic interest in the life and color of the American scene. Thus his Fourth, or Folk Song Symphony, is based on native American tunes, and his Sixth Symphony evokes Lincoln's Gettysburg Address; but Harris's Third Symphony, his best work, is a tragic abstraction.

Another exploiter of the American scene is William Schuman (1910– ), whose range of interest covers the circus, baseball, Walt Whitman, and the tunes of the pioneer American composer, William Billings. At the other end of the spectrum Schuman has composed symphonies, concertos, chamber works, and ballet scores that are harshly modern in style—full of dynamic energy, bitter polytonality, and angular rhythms.

Nationalism, American or otherwise, holds no interest for Roger Sessions (1896– ), who studied at the Yale Music School and later with Ernest Bloch. Sessions is an inspiring teacher, whose writings about music are unfailingly lucid and revealing. No hint of the pedantic enters his vigorous and often highly emotional music, which is marked by aggressively dissonant sounds, complex textures, and immense technical difficulties.

An academician in the best sense is Walter Piston (1894– ), also a Boulanger pupil, whose career has centered around Harvard University, first as student and then for many years as professor of music. Piston is America's leading neoclassicist; on his art there is little or no native imprint. Aaron Copland has written that Piston's music "sets a level of craftsmanship that is absolutely first-rate in itself and provides a standard of reference by which every other American's work may be judged."

Deems Taylor (1885– ) and Howard Hanson (1896– ) are romantic composers whose view is usually that of the late nineteenth century; while Samuel Barber (1910– ) is a neoromantic with one of the best melodic gifts among American composers. Gian-Carlo Menotti (1911– ), born in Italy but partly trained in America, is one of the most successful opera composers of our time. Menotti has inherited both an Italian sense of theatrical values (he is his own librettist), and a flair for writing vocal melody. His music is romantic, eclectic, and uncomplex. Many musicians today call Elliott Carter (1908– ) the most gifted of living American composers. Leonard Bernstein (1918– ) writes with success on two levels— ambitious, large-scale works for the concert hall, and popular pieces for the Broadway stage.

Wallingford Riegger (1885–1961) was one of the leading exponents in America of the twelve-tone system; Carl Ruggles (1876– ) has been an uncompromising modernist for many years; while Henry Cowell (1897– ) is best known for his invention of "tone clusters," an attempt to create new pianistic sonorities by striking the keyboard with the fists, elbows, and forearms. Audaciously experimental and bold is the work of John Cage (1912– ), a pupil of Cowell and Schoenberg. Cage's field has been percussion and, lately, the new electronic medium. It deals, in Cowell's phrase, "in shades of refinement of noise." Because the word music must be strained to contain efforts of this kind, Cage's work easily invites the appellation "ludicrous" from the congenital enemies of progress in either art or science.

An extraordinary man and artist was Charles Ives (1874–1954), who studied music with his father and later at Yale University, and then pursued a long and successful career in the insurance business. But Ives also led a kind of secret life, not wholly revealed until after his death. For years he composed—songs, symphonies, sonatas, and chamber and choral works in great numbers, many of them saturated with Americana. Ives seemed not to care that little of his work was published or even heard during his lifetime. Most incredible of all was his technical daring. He began using extreme dissonance and even polytonality before Stravinsky and Schoenberg; in fact, Ives exploited independently most of the apparatus of modernism—polyrhythms, tone clusters, complex jazz rhythms, experiments in fractional tones, chordal structures based on seconds, angular melodic lines, and many more. Much of his work remains a fascinating mystery still to be explored.

Finally there was George Gershwin (1898–1937), the one composer who has so far merged with outstanding success the popular and serious sides of American music. Significantly, perhaps, Gershwin's is the only American music widely known abroad. After four decades there is still no loss of freshness and charm in his *Rhapsody in Blue*, *An American in Paris*, and his Concerto in F; while his *Porgy and Bess* is one of the most original and moving operas of our time.

## VIII

We come now to the present in the art of music, and to the end of this chronicle. We have traced the music of the past three hundred years, a period during which most of this art was dominated by the marvelous productivity of the Germans. But now the Germans no longer dominate. The stream of music has spread out into a broad delta, fed by streams from many nations and colored by many cultures and individualities. More than ever music is becoming a universal art.

The work of the younger composers of today cannot concern us here. It is still in an unfinished stage, and to comment upon it would mean passing from history to speculation. A few remarks should be made, however, about certain new directions in which music is now moving; and at least mention can be made of a few men who

may be the Monteverdis of the future. We have noted
that until recently music had not been struck by the vast
turmoil of outward events that have shaken the other arts
profoundly, driving them to the extremes of sheer audacity. Now, however, music is undergoing such a change.
The machines are at last reaching out into the tonal art.
We do not mean the phonograph, which is a means of
preserving and reproducing musical performance. The
new science of electronics, and specifically the magnetic
tape recorder, is now offering the composer an entirely new
means of *creating* music.

The invention of the magnetic tape recording process
some years ago brought to the attention of both recording
technicians and musicians the fact that it is now possible
to tamper with the basic materials of sound, musical or
otherwise. For example, the note of an instrument or a
human voice, when recorded on magnetic tape and then
replayed, can be slowed down and its pitch lowered, or
speeded up and its pitch made higher; it can be plucked
out of a sequence of sounds; it can be played backward,
or repeated indefinitely. As single examples, a flute note
played at slow speed on a tape recording machine can be
made to sound as deep as an organ bourdon; while a note
struck on a piano and then played backward becomes a
long crescendo, beginning with a pianissimo and ending in
a fortissimo cut off as abruptly as a pistol shot. Any sound
can be treated to thousands of ingenious uses, including
fragmentation and reassembly in endless variety. Most
significant of all, heretofore unrelated collections of
sounds can now be brought together into a single montage
of sound.

One of the pioneers of these manipulations of sound
was Pierre Schaeffer, an amateur French musician whose
experiments were broadcast on radio programs as early as
1948. For these Schaeffer proposed the name *musique
concrète*. Independent experiments were carried out in
New York by two professors of music at Columbia University, Vladimir Ussachevsky and Otto Luening, who began
collaborating in 1951. Two "schools" quickly developed
among the pioneers of the new art. One group limits the

materials to sounds of musical instruments and the human voice; the second group uses sounds from nature: machines, birds, railroad trains, ocean waves, insect buzzing, footsteps, handclaps, coughs, cries, laughter, etc. A third school, which sprang up in Germany, works only with sounds produced by electronic machines themselves—the whistles, howls, squeals, growls, and roars familiar to electronic technicians. The barriers between the schools soon became fluid.

The outstanding practitioner of the electronic school is Karlheinz Stockhausen, who was born in Mödrath, near Cologne, in 1928, studied music in Paris with Messiaen, and was heavily influenced by the music of Webern. Stockhausen composes for the West German Radio, in Cologne, where he uses specially constructed oscillators to produce his tones, which he then records on magnetic tape. Weirdly exotic are some of his works, for example, *Song of the Young Boys in the Furnace*, which adds to the electronic sounds others taken from a human voice after the vowel and consonant sounds have been fragmented and reassembled.

In America John Cage carries on tape composing along with his work in the percussion field; and so does Edgard Varèse (1885–    ), the remarkable dean of the percussionists, whose early pieces—*Ionization, Hyperprism*, and *Amériques*—stunned audiences as long ago as the 1920s.

All phases of this new music deal with the organization of noise, and in its creation science and mathematics make new and tremendous demands upon the composer. The notation systems alone are a complex of graphs, charts, and mathematical symbols that make the old notes and staves seem as simple as a child's drawings. At the same time, much of this music is quite free, offering a high degree of improvisation and far more of the element of chance and the accidental than ever was permitted before.

There is no doubt that the new machine music is due for exploitation beyond anything we may now conceive and that a new generation of composers will deal with it avidly. As for the older generations, they will simply have to brace themselves for the shock. We cannot expect musicians to go on composing, as they have, with the same instruments that Berlioz used more than a century ago. Moreover, the hostility that has existed for the past three decades between composers of contemporary music and listening audiences can hardly be interpreted as a sign of health. We must expect that a new generation will try with all its might to break the monopoly of the older music. Art has the attributes of living organisms; it lives, grows, and dies. Deaths must be expected in art as in life.

In these dark satanic times prediction is a hazardous business, but as the rule of war is now the rule of life, it may be that the best advice can come from a man of battle —from General Lee, who found himself sustained by these words:

> The truth is this: the march of Providence is so slow, and our desires so impatient, the work of progress is so immense, and our means of aiding it so feeble, the life of humanity is so long, and that of the individual so brief, that we often see only the ebb of the advancing wave and are thus discouraged. It is history that teaches us to hope.

# BIBLIOGRAPHY AND ACKNOWLEDGMENTS

The literature of music is enormous. Inevitably, there is much duplication. There is also a considerable mortality among books once believed to be indispensable, but now outmoded in style and opinion. Therefore, rather than print the standard type of bibliography that aims to acknowledge every source consulted, I am giving only a selected list, which I believe will be of more value to the average reader. These books were all helpful in the preparation of the present volume. Many of them were sources of special profit and enjoyment. I am happy to acknowledge my indebtedness to their authors and to recommend them to anyone wishing to gain a broad grounding in the subject of music.

Abraham, Gerald, *A Hundred Years of Music*. Alfred A. Knopf, New York, 1938

—— *The Music of Tchaikovsky*. W. W. Norton & Co., New York, 1946

Anderson, Emily, editor, *The Letters of Mozart and His Family*. 3 vols. The Macmillan Company, New York, 1938

Bauer, Marion, *Twentieth Century Music*. G. P. Putnam's Sons, New York, 1933

Berlioz, Hector, *Memoirs of Hector Berlioz 1803 to 1865*, edited by Ernest Newman. Alfred A. Knopf, New York, 1947

Blom, Eric, *Mozart*. E. P. Dutton & Co., New York, 1935

Bowen, Catherine Drinker, and Meck, Barbara von, *Beloved Friend*. Random House, New York, 1937

Brenet, Michel, *Haydn*. Oxford University Press, London, 1926

Burk, John N., *Clara Schumann*. Random House, New York, 1940

Calvocoressi, M. D., *Mussorgsky*. J. M. Dent & Sons, Ltd., London, 1946

—— and Abraham, Gerald, *Masters of Russian Music*. Tudor Publishing Company, New York, 1944

Capell, Richard, *Schubert's Songs*. E. P. Dutton & Co., New York, 1928

Dent, Edward J., *Mozart's Operas*. Chatto & Windus, London, 1913

Einstein, Alfred, *Mozart: His Character, His Work*. Oxford University Press, New York, 1945

Flower, Newman, *Handel*. Charles Scribner's Sons, New York, 1948

Grace, Harvey, *The Organ Works of Bach*. Novello & Co., Ltd., London, 1922

—— *Beethoven*. Harper & Bros., New York, 1927

Hartog, Howard, editor, *European Music in the Twentieth Century*. Frederick A. Praeger, Inc., New York, 1957

Huneker, James, *Chopin: The Man and His Music*. Charles Scribner's Sons, New York, 1900

Láng, Paul Henry, *Music in Western Civilization*. W. W. Norton & Co., New York, 1941

Mason, Daniel Gregory, *The Chamber Music of Brahms*. The Macmillan Company, New York, 1933

Murdoch, William, *Brahms*. Rich & Cowan, London, 1933

—— *Chopin: His Life*. The Macmillan Company, New York, 1935

Nestyev, Israel V., *Sergei Prokofiev*. Alfred A. Knopf, New York, 1946

Newman, Ernest, *The Life of Richard Wagner*. 4 vols. Alfred A. Knopf, New York, 1933–1946

—— *Fact and Fiction About Wagner.* Alfred A. Knopf, New York, 1931

—— *Wagner as Man and Artist.* Garden City Publishing Co., Garden City, N.Y., 1937

Parry, C. Hubert H., *Johann Sebastian Bach.* G. P. Putnam's Sons, New York, 1934

Riesemann, Oskar von, *Moussorgsky.* Alfred A. Knopf, New York, 1929

Rimsky-Korsakov, N. A., *My Musical Life.* Alfred A. Knopf, New York, 1942

Rolland, Romain, *Beethoven the Creator.* Harper & Bros., New York, 1929

Rosenfeld, Paul, *Discoveries of a Music Critic.* Harcourt, Brace & Co., New York, 1936

Schweitzer, Albert, *J. S. Bach.* A. & C. Black, Ltd., London, 1938

Seroff, Victor I., *Dmitri Shostakovich.* Alfred A. Knopf, New York, 1943

—— *Rachmaninoff.* Simon & Schuster, New York, 1950

Stravinsky, Igor, *Stravinsky: An Autobiography.* Simon & Schuster, New York, 1936

—— *Poetics of Music.* Harvard University Press, Cambridge, Mass., 1947

Sullivan, J. W. N., *Beethoven: His Spiritual Development.* Alfred A. Knopf, New York, 1927

Terry, Charles Sanford, *Bach, A Biography.* Oxford University Press, London, 1940

—— *The Music of Bach.* Oxford University Press, London, 1933

Thomson, Oscar, *Debussy: Man and Artist.* Dodd, Mead & Co., New York, 1937

Vallas, Léon, *Claude Debussy, His Life and Works.* Oxford University Press, London, 1933

Weinstock, Herbert, *Handel.* Alfred A. Knopf, New York, 1959

In a few cases I have availed myself of extended quotations from certain books. They are made with the kind permission of the publishers: Oxford University Press, publishers of *The Music of Bach*, by Charles Sanford Terry, and *Haydn*, by Michel Brenet; Charles Scribner's Sons, publishers of *Mezzotints in Modern Music* by James Huneker, and *Mozart*, by Marcia Davenport; The Macmillan Company, publishers of *Chopin: His Life*, by William Murdoch; W. W. Norton & Company, Inc., publishers of *Music in Western Civilization*, by Paul Henry Láng; Alfred A. Knopf, Inc., publishers of *The Book of Modern Composers*, edited by David Ewen; and Henry Holt & Co., publishers of *Polonaise*, by Guy de Pourtalès.

R. A. L.

# INDEX